THE TALENT OF SHU

蜀才

SUNY SERIES IN CHINESE PHILOSOPHY AND CULTURE

Roger T. Ames, editor

J. Michael Farmer

THE TALENT OF SHU

蜀才

QIAO ZHOU AND THE INTELLECTUAL WORLD OF EARLY MEDIEVAL SICHUAN

State University of New York Press

Published by

STATE UNIVERSITY OF NEW YORK PRESS

ALBANY

Printed in the United States of america

For information, contact
State University of New York Press Albany, NY
www.sunypress.edu

Production and book design, Laurie Searl
Marketing, Michael Campochiaro

Library of Congress Cataloging-in-Publication Data

Farmer, J. Michael, 1965-
The talent of Shu: Qiao Zhou and the intellectual world of early medieval Sichuan / J. Michael Farmer.
p. cm — (SUNY Series in Chinese philosophy and culture)
Includes bibliographical references and index.
ISBN-13: 978-0-7914-7163-0 (alk paper)
ISBN-13: 978-0-7914-7164-7 (pbk. : alk.paper)
1. Intellectuals — China — Sichuan Sheng. 2. Sichuan Sheng (China) — History. 3. China — History — Han Dynasty, 202 B.C.–220 A.D. I. Title

10 9 8 7 6 5 4 3 2 1

to my teachers

Jeannette L. Faurot (1943–2005)

and

Robert Joe Cutter

好古述儒

He loved antiquity and transmitted classical scholarship.

"Encomium for Qiao Zhou"

Li Tong 李通

late third century CE

Contents

List of Illustrations

MAPS

FIGURES

Preface

The Talent of Shu (Shu *cai* 蜀才), in the strictest historical sense, was a man from Sichuan who compiled commentaries on two early mystic texts: the *Yijing* 易經 (*Canon of Changes*; a.k.a. *Zhou Yi* 周易/*Zhou Changes*) and the *Laozi* 老子 (a.k.a. *Daode jing* 道德經/*Canon of the Way and Its Potency*) during the early medieval period. These texts are both lost, as is the identity of The Talent of Shu. By the sixth century CE, efforts to link the pseudonym to a historical individual had resulted in at least two scholars concluding that the mysterious commentator was none other than Qiao Zhou, the featured figure of this study. There is no surviving evidence to confirm this identification, nor was there likely any during the sixth century, but that is really not the issue. Whoever the early medieval commentator was, he most likely wished for his identity to remain concealed—hence the use of the pseudonym. It is the mystery and ambiguity of the name The Talent of Shu that led me to employ it here as the title of this book. It may well refer to Qiao Zhou, but, then again, it may not. But, from a broader perspective, it can represent the collective "Talent of Shu": all the intellectuals of the Sichuan region who have been largely overlooked by the eyes of later historians, until now.

Acknowledgments

Nearly a decade has passed since I first stumbled into the world of early medieval Sichuan. During that time I have been the beneficiary of numerous acts of kindness and support—intellectual, institutional, and personal. While it is impossible to acknowledge all of the assistance I have received in this limited space, I do wish to recognize the contributions of several important individuals and institutions for their support.

My debts to many scholars are acknowledged in the notes of this book. Moreover, I am especially grateful to my teachers for introducing me to the intellectual tradition of Sinology. As an undergraduate at the University of Texas at Austin, Professors Jeannette L. Faurot and Edward J.M. Rhoads nurtured my interests in Chinese Studies and encouraged me to pursue these interests in graduate school. At the University of Wisconsin–Madison I was trained in Chinese history by Professor Maurice Meisner, and mentored in Sinology by Professors Robert Joe Cutter and William H. Nienhauser Jr. I have also benefited greatly from the opportunities to study with Li Zehou, Julia K. Murray, and Mark Csikszentmihalyi in Madison. The intellectual and moral support of my friend and classmate Scott Galer was, and remains, invaluable. I also wish to recognize and thank several friends and colleagues for their comments and suggestions on this manuscript: Michael Murdock, Rodney Bohac, and Paul Kerry, all of the History Department at Brigham Young University. Each read and critiqued earlier drafts of this study. This book is better for their efforts.

In addition to the support of these individuals, I have also received assistance from various institutions. The dissertation on which this book is based was completed with financial help from the Department of East Asian Languages and Literature and Center for East Asian Studies at the University of Wisconsin, as well as a Fulbright-Hayes Doctoral Dissertation Fellowship. I am grateful for the assistance of several individuals and institutions in Sichuan, where I conducted research in 1998, 2000, and 2001. In particular, I would like to acknowledge the support of Professor Fang Beichen and Mr. Miao Yuanlang of Sichuan University, and Professor Long Xianzhao of Sichuan Normal University in Nanchong. The conversion of my dissertation to a book was facillitated by support from the Department of History and College of Family, Home, and Social Sciences at Brigham Young University. I express my appreciation to Mr. Benjamin Sykes of the BYU Mapping Services Center for preparing the maps for this volume, and to Cynthia Chennault for granting permission to reprint much of Chapter 6, which was previously published as "Qiao Zhou and the Historiography of Early Medieval Sichuan," *Early Medieval China* 7 (2001): 31–69.

Special thanks to my old friend and wordsmith extraordinaire, Gerrie McCall, and to Nancy Ellegate and Laurie Searl of the State University of New York Press for shepherding my manuscript through the process of becoming a book.

Finally, I wish to thank my family for their tireless support of my studies and professional activities. My parents and grandparents encouraged me to pursue my scholarly goals and offered their financial and moral support from afar. My wife, Maren, provided even greater assistance at home, wherever that may have been. She and my children, Rose and Brooks, have cheerfully followed me from Houston to Austin to Madison to Chengdu to Boulder to Provo as I have conducted research and taught. They, along with the Jade Dog of Supreme Mystery and Coltrane, bring joy to my life and put my scholarly endeavors into their proper perspective.

Terms and Conventions

The pinyin system of romanization is used throughout this study, except when an alternate system appears in the title of a published work. In cases where I have adopted another scholar's translation that uses a different romanization system, I have converted that usage to the pinyin system.

Geographic terminology presents a special challenge. While this study focuses on the region roughly analogous to present-day Sichuan 四川 Province, the names attached to the specific locales changed over the two-hundred-year period under review. Moreover, even the historical sources were often anachronistic in their uses of place names. To minimize confusion, I have adopted the following usage of geographic terms. The area equivalent to Sichuan Province was known during the Han and Three States period as Yi Province (Yizhou 益州). I use this term to reference the specific administrative unit during the period. Yi Province was further subdivided into commanderies and prefectures. These smaller administrative units are referenced by their individual names (i.e., "Shu" 蜀 refers to Shu commandery). More general references to the region without regard for political administration use either the modern name "Sichuan,"[1] or the geographic designation "Chengdu Plain" (Chengdu *pingyuan* 成都平原), taking into account the mountainous areas that surround the plain itself. The term "Chengdu" 成都 is used to refer to the city of Chengdu, which functioned as the seat of Shu commandery, Yi Province, as well as the capital of the state of Shu-Han. While Chen Shou's *Records of the Three States* referenced this state as "Shu," I employ the later term "Shu-Han" 蜀漢 to distinguish the state from its constituent commandery. Present-day locations of historical sites are offered in the notes. These identifications are generally based on the historical atlases compiled by Tan Qixiang 譚其驤.[2]

Traditional Chinese naming conventions are often troubling to Western readers. Individuals typically possessed, in addition to their surnames, a given name and one or more appellatives (*zi* 字; rendered elsewhere as "style name") or nicknames. In this study, names of individuals are presented in the form of surname–given name, with appellatives, and Chinese graphs provided at the initial reference to the person.

The issue of dates is generally complicated, and sometimes unresolvable, especially in regard to founding and terminus dates for dynastic periods, the birth and death dates of individuals, composition of texts, and other chronological questions. In this study, dates are sometimes presented in terms of the traditional year-title (*nianhao* 年號; often mistranslated for the early medieval period as "reign period"), followed by a conversion to the Western calendar date. In matters of date conversion, I have followed the general dynastic chronologies outlined by Tung Tso-pin in his *Chronological Tables of Chinese History*, and Fang Shiming 方詩銘 and Fang Xiaofen's 方小芬 *Zhongguoshi liri he Zhong-Xi liri duizhao biao* 中國史曆日和中西曆日對照表 [*Chinese Historical Calendar Days and a Calendrical Concordance of Chinese and Western Days*].[3] For the dates of individuals, I have utilized Jiang Liangfu's 姜亮夫 *Lidai renwu nianli beizhuan zongbiao* 歷代人物年里碑傳綜表 [*Table of Dates and Places of Birth, Dates of Death, with Epitaphs and Biographical Sketches Referenced of Historical Personages*].[4] For persons of the Three States period, I have also consulted the *Sanguo zhi cidian* 三國志辭典 [*Records of the Three States Dictionary*], compiled by Zhang Shunhui 張舜徽.[5] The term "early medieval" refers to the general period from the last half of the second century CE through the early seventh century CE.

For official titles, I have generally followed the translations in Hans Bielenstein's *The Bureaucracy of Han Times*, even for titles of the Jin 晉 period.[6] Descriptions of official duties are drawn from Bielenstein's work, as well as from Charles Hucker's *A Dictionary of Official Titles in Imperial China* and Sun Fengji's 孫逢吉 *Zhiguan fenji* 職官分紀 [*Official Positions Arranged Chronologically*].[7]

Titles of books and other written works are given first in romanized form, followed by Chinese graphs and a translation. Subsequent references to titles of written works are generally rendered in English translation. Citations of the standard (or dynastic) histories reference the Zhonghua shuju 中華書局 editions, unless otherwise noted. Citations of canonical texts reference the *Shisan jing zhushu* 十三經注疏 [*Thirteen Canonical Texts with Commentary and Sub-commentary*] edition, and follow the standard Sinological practice for those texts (i.e., *Lunyu*, 3/14; *Yijing*, hexagram *qian* 乾, line 2).

Map 1. Three States Period China

Introduction

The Three States period (Sanguo 三國; ca. 220–280 CE)[1] stands as one of the most recognized but misunderstood eras in the history of traditional China. Weakened by continual conflicts at the imperial court between emperor, palace women, imperial in-laws, eunuchs, and scholar-bureaucrats, the Han dynasty 漢 (206 BCE–220 CE) was in terminal decline by the last half of the second-century CE.[2] Following a failed rebellion by a millenarian Daoist sect in 184 CE, various warlords only nominally loyal to the Han court carved out their own territorial power bases and fought for control of the dying empire. Four excruciating decades later, the Han emperor formally abdicated, leaving the three rival states of Wei 魏, Wu 吳, and Shu-Han[3] 蜀漢 to battle for control of the shattered remains of the Han empire.[4] In popular memory, the Three States period is viewed as an age of political turmoil and martial heroes, and the colorful generals and crafty statesmen who stood at the center of the upheaval and warfare have become iconic figures of the age.

These views have been significantly shaped and propagated by the immensely popular literary account of the age, *Sanguo (zhi) yanyi* 三國志演義, commonly translated as "*Romance of the Three Kingdoms*," but more accurately rendered as "*Extended Meanings of the Records of the Three States*,"[5] and its myriad derivative accounts, including comic books, television shows, and computerized video games.[6] The *Three Kingdoms* and its modern multimedia progeny vividly depict the chaos of the age and clearly privilege military heroes over intellectual figures. At the center of the novel stand the warlord-dynast Liu Bei 劉備 (161–223 CE),[7] his sworn brother-generals Guan Yu 關羽 (d. 219 CE) and Zhang Fei 張飛 (168–221 CE),[8] and his magical strategist Zhuge Liang 諸葛亮 (d. 234 CE).[9] These heroes are opposed by other men of similar military heritage: Cao Cao 曹操 (155–220 CE)[10] and Sun Quan 孫權 (182–252 CE),[11] as well as their own generals and strategist-advisors. The heroic martial exploits of this cast of characters are only briefly interrupted for matters of culture or scholarship, and most references to noted intellectuals of the age present them only in their public roles as officers of state, with no mention of their scholastic or literary accomplishments. Elsewhere, the novel's treatment of scholars reveals a more open disdain for intellectual pursuits in general. In this regard, some scholars are presented as eccentric and disrespectful (i.e., Mi Heng 彌衡),[12] or talented but useless (i.e., Yang Xiu 楊修).[13] Rather, military strategy is privileged as the highest form of intellect, with figures such as Zhuge Liang and Zhou Yu 周瑜 (175–210 CE)[14] receiving historically unwarranted praise for their respective genius. Because of their accessibility and popularity, *Three Kingdoms* and other derivative accounts have largely supplanted the surviving early historical documents as the primary sources of information on the era, resulting in a strong degree of familiarity with the events and personages of the Three States period, complicated by views fraught with value-laden distortions.[15]

The period was not solely one of warfare; there were numerous advancements in the realms of thought and culture. In this regard, the era witnessed the emergence of lyric poetry, the establishment of the Daoist religion,[16] the spread and growth of Buddhism, the cultivation of a profound sense of self in Chinese thought and literature, and the creation of new modes of critical scholarship.

While a comprehensive history of Three States period thought and culture has yet to be written, most studies of these trends have focused on the northern state of Wei and its intellectual achievements, such as the ethical metaphysics of He Yan 何晏 (190–249 CE) and Wang Bi 王弼 (226–249 CE),[17] the literary and philosophical consciousness of the "Seven Masters of the Jian'an Era" (Jian'an qizi 建安七子),[18] and the eccentric individualism of the "Seven Sages of the Bamboo Grove" (Zhulin qixian 竹林七賢).[19] Etienne Balazs's article "Nihilistic Revolt or Mystical Escapism: Currents of Thought in China During the Third Century A.D." (originally published in 1948, and which in many respects remains the standard overview of the intellectual history of third-century China) deals almost exclusively with the activities around the Cao's Wei dynasty court.[20] These northern intellectual and cultural developments have been termed the "Wei-Jin 魏晉 renaissance," standing in contrast to what has been deemed the "ossified" nature of traditional (i.e., late Han) scholasticism.[21] This view ignores the continued vitality of canonical exegesis and other forms of scholarship. Moreover, the notion of a "Wei-Jin renaissance" belies a deep-seated geographic bias. While the term "Wei-Jin" is generally employed as a convenient shorthand for the period roughly equivalent to the third and fourth centuries and has it roots in the question of which of the states succeeding the Han were politically legitimate, its omission of other contemporary states (i.e., Wu and Shu-Han) subtly draws attention away from developments in thought and culture in these other (southern) states. The emphasis in recent scholarship on the thought and culture of Wei mirrors and perpetuates traditional biases against southern culture and results in a distorted and incomplete picture of intellectual life in early medieval China.[22] While a few recent studies have examined intellectual activity in the Yangzi River basin, the intellectual history of Shu-Han in the southwest has been largely ignored.[23]

This general neglect of the Chengdu Plain results in the enduring popular view of the region as one devoid of any serious scholarly activity, and of Zhuge Liang as the state's only intellectual. In the matter of Zhuge Liang, despite the widespread assertion of his intellectual genius, the surviving historical materials offer no evidence to support such claims. The contents of a twenty-four fascicle collected works compiled by Chen Shou 陳壽 (233–297 CE) and cited in his *Records of the Three States* biography of Zhuge Liang lists writings on the topics of civil administration, military campaigns and strategy, law, epistles, and "miscellaneous quotations."[24] This list, along with the biography itself, portrays Zhuge Liang as a recluse-turned-statesman and emphasizes his role in managing the civil and military affairs of Shu-Han after the death of its founding ruler. No evidence remains to indicate that Zhuge Liang actively engaged in any sort of scholarly activity. Thus, Zhuge Liang might be more accurately viewed as a patron of scholars rather than as one himself.[25] Nevertheless, most casual observers and even many serious scholars of the period would be hard-pressed to name another intellectual from the region during the Three States period. Sadly, these popular assessments widely miss the mark. My study seeks to counter these conceptions of Sichuan as an intellectual backwater with an analytical narrative history of the significant intellectual and scholarly activity in the region during the late Han and Three States period.

The focal point of this study is a noted mantic artist (*fangshi* 方士),[26] classicist, historian, and statesman of Shu-Han named Qiao Zhou 譙周 (ca. 200–270 CE) [pronounced something like "Chow Joe"].[27] Qiao Zhou stands as an apt figure to represent the intellectual world of third-century Sichuan. In the world of public scholarship, Qiao was an heir to, and perhaps the final major practitioner of a distinct regional scholarly tradition that combined celestial observation and interpretation of coded speech to predict future political events. These skills earned Qiao a lifetime of official appointments in the Shu-Han administration. Through his activities as a scholar in the service of the state we gain valuable insights into the relationship between the academic and political worlds of early medieval Sichuan. In the world of private scholarship, Qiao was trained in traditional canonical studies and excelled as both a canonical and historical critic and a local historian. His scholarly writings demonstrate a devotion to the canon as historical documentation of China's antiquity, as well as a drive to "correct errors" in the canon and its interpretations that clouded that golden age from contemporary view. Qiao's academic works were both grounded, perhaps even mired, in the late Han scholastic traditions, and groundbreaking as they introduced a new element of criticism to the study of the canon and history. In this regard, Qiao

Zhou embodies the intellectual transitions of the age. His activities in the mantic arts and canonical studies are decidedly "old school," while Qiao's studies in historiography herald significant innovations in the field. In this study, I seek to explore the rich intellectual traditions of the Chengdu Plain through a critical biography of Qiao Zhou that involves detailed analysis of the scholarly writings of Qiao and contextualization of his activity into the broader intellectual and political worlds of third-century Sichuan and China at large.

OUTLINE OF THIS STUDY

This book is divided into six chapters. Chapter 1 introduces the intellectual background from which Qiao Zhou emerged. From the early Han through the third century CE, distinct forms of intellectual activity developed on the Chengdu Plain. In the early years of the Han dynasty, local intellectuals gained attention at the imperial court for their literary accomplishments. By mid-dynasty, a syncretic blend of classicist and esoteric scholarship emerged, as did a preference for a life of contemplative reclusion over one of public service. These mid-Han developments, while never becoming dominant modes of intellectual activity on the Chengdu Plain, spread eastward and northward, and eventually blossomed into Mystery Learning (*xuanxue* 玄學), one of the hallmark intellectual trends of early medieval China. In the Later Han, the paths of politics and thought intersected with the rise of political prophesy. In particular, a regional family tradition in the mantic arts developed on the Chengdu Plain, with its prophetic methods transmitted within the region for two centuries. These skills were eagerly sought (and simultaneously feared) by rulers who demanded signs supporting their dynastic ambitions. The chapter concludes with a snapshot of scholarly activity at the Shu-Han court during the third century where the earlier local academic traditions collided with those from outside the region.

Chapter 2 provides a brief biography of Qiao Zhou that situates him within the intellectual traditions of the region. The Qiao family had been influential on the Chengdu Plain and beyond since the early Han, with several members of the family holding posts at the imperial and provincial levels. Moreover, the Qiaos had an established reputation as "cultured gentlemen" (*shi* 士). At the time of Qiao Zhou's birth in the early third century, the family appears to have suffered an economic downturn, but their dedication to intellectual pursuits continued. The second part of the chapter focuses on the education of Qiao Zhou. Qiao's father, a noted scholar of the canonical histories, died while Qiao Zhou was still young, leaving him to seek training with some of the region's most esteemed scholars. Qiao was tutored in the local mantic traditions of political prophesy by Du Qiong 杜瓊. Additionally, Qiao was trained in history and criticism by Qin Min 秦密. The skills learned from Du Qiong and Qin Mi connected Qiao to the region's intellecual traditions and shaped both the public and private scholarly activities of Qiao Zhou for the remainder of his life.

Chapter 3 examines the manner in which Qiao Zhou's academic training was employed in the service of the state. Appointed to office at the age of twenty-one or twenty-two on the basis of his skills in interpreting astronomical signs and prophetic wordplay, Qiao served Shu-Han from its inception in 221 CE until its demise in 263 CE. His first three decades of service were in the field of education, first as a teacher, later as director of the imperial academy, and finally as a tutor to the heir apparent. Later in his life, Qiao reached higher levels of governmental service, providing him access to the emperor and leading to his participation in several important policy debates. Drawing on his training in the mantic arts and history, Qiao Zhou influenced the decision to surrender the state to the approaching armies of Wei, and consequently has been widely regarded as a traitor, leading later moralizing historians to ignore his significant scholarly works.

The next three chapters seek to reintroduce the long-overlooked private scholarship of Qiao Zhou by examining his surviving writings in the fields of classical or canonical studies, historical criticism, and local historiography, and the relationship between these texts and earlier, contemporary, and later scholarly trends. These chapters illustrate not only Qiao Zhou's own intellectual activity, but also the similarities and differences between the regional traditions of the Chengdu Plain and those of the Central Plains.[28] The clear dichotomy between the biographically oriented chapters 1–3 and the textually-oriented chapters 4–6 reflects the public-private distinction in the scholarly activities of Qiao Zhou, and is indicative of the nature of the surviving source materials.

Chapter 4 presents the state of classical studies in early medieval China through an examination of Qiao Zhou's work in the field of canonical exegesis and, in particular, the subject of ritual. From the surviving texts, Qiao appears to have been largely in harmony with the late Han exegetical traditions, and the interpretations of Zheng Xuan 鄭玄 (127–200 CE),[29] whose views would later be taken as orthodox. However, during the third century, the views of Zheng and Qiao were out of fashion, displaced by the metaphysical interpretations of the canon as presented by various scholars of the emerging Mystery Learning movement in the north. In this regard, Qiao Zhou may be seen as a conservative classicist who held to traditional views of the canon in the face of new popular interpretations, though his critical view of the canon places his exegesis beyond the typical late Han fixation on textual glosses. More broadly speaking, in this chapter the Chengdu Plain emerges as a bastion of traditional canonical studies.

If Qiao Zhou appears intellectually conservative in the field of canonical studies, in chapter 5 he emerges as an important innovator in the field of historical criticism. His major work, *Gushi kao* 古史考 [*Investigations of Ancient History*] has long been regarded as the first major commentary on Sima Qian's

Shiji 史記 [*The Grand Scribe's Records*]. However, this chapter seeks to expand this view, presenting *Investigations of Ancient History* as a larger critique of several efforts to write the history of early China. In particular, the work illustrates Qiao's view of the canon as history and his almost obsessive drive to correct perceived errors in earlier histories. Comparing Qiao's historical exegesis with other such works from the early medieval period reveals Qiao to be a misunderstood innovator, with his *Investigations of Ancient History* standing as the earliest work of critical exegesis on a historical text. Most later scholars recognized his work as commentary, utilizing the work as a source of information, but overlooking his critical methodology. Only two later scholars, Sima Zhen 司馬貞 (*fl.* 745 CE) in the Tang and Liang Yusheng 梁玉繩 (1745–1819) in the Qing appear to have recognized the significance of Qiao's critical and skeptical approach to ancient history.

Chapter 6 presents Qiao Zhou as an innovator in the field of local history. He compiled four distinct histories of the Chengdu Plain, demonstrating a mastery of earlier forms of local historiography and adding a significant new approach of his own. Qiao's inclusion of "locality stories," which linked local sites with imperial activities, functioned as a statement of local and regional pride and was widely imitated by later local historians.

Through the examination of the scholarly writings of Qiao Zhou, particularly those in the field of history, I shall present evidence to support the claims of two early medieval historians, one who accorded Qiao Zhou a place among the greatest minds of the age, and the other who judged Qiao Zhou to be the only "good historian" (*liangshi* 良史) of the late Han period,[30] as well as argue the vitality of the scholarly and intellectual world of Sichuan during the third century.

CHAPTER 1

The Intellectual World of Early Sichuan

The region occupied by present-day Sichuan Province in southwest China has long been viewed with a certain degree of ambivalence by traditional Chinese historians, with most writing from the perspective of the north. Ban Gu's 班固 (32–92 CE) "Geographic Treatise" in his *Han shu* 漢書 [*Han History*] presents the earliest synoptic view of the region. Drawing descriptions from the canon, he writes:

> Previously, the Yellow Thearch (Huangdi 黄帝) made boats and carriages, but because of the rushing waters [people] could not pass. So he set out in all directions throughout the subcelestial realm, organizing the myriad districts, drawing boundaries and separating provinces, resulting in one-hundred *li* states and myriad districts. This is what the *Changes* refers to as "The Former King established the myriad states and gave them to his kinsmen to be their various sovereigns."[1] The *Documents* says, "He harmonized the myriad states."[2] This refers to [the Yellow Thearch's actions]. Yao 堯 encountered a great flood which encircled mountains and drove against the cliffs. The subcelestial realm was cut off and divided into twelve provinces. [Yao] sent Yu 禹 to control [the flood]. The waters and the earth were leveled and he organized nine provinces and arranged five domains, piled earth and made a sacrifice. Thus it is said, "Yu disposed the lands. Going along the mountains, he cut down the trees. He determined the high mountains and great rivers."[3]

Here, Ban Gu offers a Genesis-like account of the origins of Chinese administrative geography, crediting the legendary sage-kings of high antiquity with the division of the subcelestial realm (*tianxia* 天下; literally, "all under heaven") into districts, domains, and provinces. Among the administrative territories said to have been organized by the sage-king Yao was Liang 梁 Province, located south of Mount Hua (Hua shan 華山) in the upper reaches of the Yangzi River basin.[4] Physically cut off from the Chinese heartland of the Yellow River basin by mountain ranges and rivers, the region developed early civilizations distant from those of the Central Plains, and, even after coming under the control of later northern polities, maintained a high level of independent regional identity.

The heart of ancient Liang Province consists of the Chengdu Plain, a high-elevation basin ringed by rugged mountains and well watered by numerous rivers. This simple fact of geography plays an important part in the history of the region, isolating it from the traditional centers of imperial power and providing would-be rebels with a secure base. From the vantage point of the Central Plains looking to the southwest, one must traverse the Qinling 秦嶺 mountains in southern Shaanxi, cross the Han River 漢水 valley, then pass through the narrow Jian'ge 劍閣 ("Sword-gallery") Pass in the Daba 大巴 mountains further to the south to enter into the flat and fertile Chengdu Plain. This plain is bounded by the Daxue 大雪 mountain range to the west, and several lesser parallel ranges running north of the Yangzi River basin from southwest to northeast, and finally the larger Dalei 大纇 mountains south of the Yangzi. A multitude of waterways flow into the basin from the north and west, most conjoining with the Yangzi. The Yangzi runs eastward, passing through a series of tight gorges as it leaves the basin at Mount Wu (Wu shan 巫山) and enters the moist lands of the former state of Chu 楚 (present-day Hubei Province). The climate in the basin is mild and the area enjoys a long growing season.

The produce of the Chengdu Plain is frequently noted in the early sources. The *Shang shu* 尚書 [*Hallowed Documents*] describes the region's soil as "bluish black" and of third (or lowest) class quality, and notes its revenues also of the third (or lowest) class. Continuing, the *Documents* enumerates tribute items conveyed to King Yu's capital in the Central Plains by the region's "felt-wearing" (i.e., non-Sinicized or barbarian) inhabitants as "gold, iron, silver, steel, arrow-head stones, musical stones, black bears, brown and white bears, foxes and wild cats."[5] This account survives as the earliest description of the Chengdu Plain, with its general characterization of the region as having an abundance of natural resources. By the third century CE, the region's agricultural bounty led to its designation as "Heaven's Storehouse" (*tianfu zhi guo* 天府之國), a Chinese "land of milk and honey."[6] Later, Chang Qu's 常璩 (ca. 291–ca. 361 CE) *Huayang guo zhi* 華陽國志 [*Records of the States South of Mount Hua*] provided detailed descriptions of each commandery and district within the region, including their agricultural products and output, climate, and dispositions of the local population. From these gazetteer entries, the impression of a rich and bountiful land emerged,[7] yet, despite this favorable characterization, an equally negative view of the region as "uncivilized" remained in force for centuries to come.[8]

Though the Chengdu Plain played an important role in the political affairs of the early empire,[9] it was largely viewed as a provincial backwater by scholars and officials from the north. Ban Gu's assessment of the region in his "Geographic Treatise" is particularly harsh. It reads:

> Ba 巴, Shu, and Guanghan 廣漢 commanderies were originally [populated by] the Southern Yi 南夷 [barbarian tribes]. After [these areas] were annexed by Qin, they were made commanderies. The land is fertile and beautiful, possessing rivers to water the wilds and a bounty of mountain forests, bamboo and trees, vegetables, and edible fruit. To the south they purchase young slaves of Dian 滇 and Bo 僰; to the west it is near the horses and yaks of Qiong 邛 and Zuo 莋. The people eat rice and fish, and have no worry about famine years. Since the common folk do not suffer hardships, they are easygoing and profligate, weak and mean.[10]

The land's bountiful resources, according to Ban Gu, led to character flaws among its people, who while not specifically identified as local minority groups, are portrayed as uncivilized. While Ban Gu's prejudices against the south may be somewhat extreme, the fact remains that despite over three hundred years of Central Plains (Qin and Han) influence in the area, many outsiders were still unconvinced that the region was an equally cultured part of the empire.

"CIVILIZING" THE SOUTHWEST: INTELLECTUAL ACTIVITY IN THE FORMER HAN

Ban Gu's characterization of the early Chengdu Plain as intellectually backward serves as the backdrop for a tale of remarkable change in the intellectual climate of the region. The *Han History* biography of Wen Weng 文翁 (fl. c. 140 BCE) contained in the section devoted to the lives and actions of virtuous officials portrays the Central Plains native as a precocious young man sent to govern the backwater Shu commandery during the early years of the Han,[11] and lauds the transformation he effected on the area and its people.[12] Ban Gu describes Wen Weng as "kind and caring, and fond of transformation through learning," and "desiring to guide and advance" the backward population of his new domain. To this end, the tradition holds, Wen Weng selected ten or so talented low-level officers from the commandery and prefecture and sent them to the Han capital at Chang'an to receive training from the erudits at the national academy. The benevolence of this action is further emphasized by Ban Gu's assertion that Wen Weng personally purchased bolts of Shu brocade and book knives—each regarded as the finest in the empire—to cover the cost of educating these young men at the capital.[13] When their training was complete, the Shu scholars returned home where Wen Weng employed them in local offices. Additionally, Wen Weng established an academy in Chengdu for the purpose of training functionaries for positions at the commandery and prefecture levels. The more talented students at the academy were placed in local offices, while the less talented were granted honorary posts. Because of the status attached to studying at the academy, and perhaps also due to the waiver on corvée labor service granted to students, local families fought to place their sons in the Chengdu academy, often sending large sums of cash to beseech Wen Weng. Ban Gu's narrative offers the following positive evaluation of the results of these activities:

> From this great transformation, scholars from Shu at the [Han] capital were compared to those of Qi 齊 and Lu 魯.[14] During the time of Emperor Wu 武 (r. 140–86 BCE), an edict ordered all of the commanderies and states under heaven to establish academies. This was begun by Wen Weng. . . . To the present day, the people of Ba and Shu are fond of cultural refinement. This is a result of Wen Weng's transformation.[15]

In his "Geographic Treatise," however, Ban Gu's assessment of Wen Weng's results is rather different. Here Ban Gu writes, "[Wen Weng] taught the people how to recite texts, laws, and ordinances, but they were not yet able to believe truly in morality and used their fondness for writing to satirize and ridicule, though they honored and admired power and authority."[16] The net result of their education, Ban Gu argues, was cosmetic: the people of Shu had taken on the external trappings of scholarship, but had failed to internalize the moral teachings of their education. This particular judgment on the enterprise of Wen Weng sustains Ban's portrayal of the southwest as "uncivilized," while the glowing review found among the biographies of virtuous officials supports Wen Weng's inclusion among the ranks of Central Plains worthies.

The biography of Wen Weng contained in the *Records of the States South of Mount Hua* makes few claims as positive or negative as Ban Gu's accounts of Wen's life. Nevertheless, it does offer a few additional details on the career of this outsider who made his mark on the Chengdu Plain. Chang Qu notes Wen Weng's accomplishments in the area of water conservancy—the construction of a new irrigation channel that opened up some 25,000 new acres of farmland for cultivation. The account of Wen's activities in local scholarship echoes that of Ban Gu, noting Wen's sponsorship of students to Chang'an, along with the additional information that, on their return, some were given posts as teachers at the Chengdu academy.[17] The *Records of the States South of Mount Hua* also provides a brief history of Wen's academy through the Later Han period, noting specific buildings on the campus, its destruction and renovation, administrative history, and location.[18]

While certain basic elements of the tradition of Wen Weng are undoubtedly factual, the life of this young commandery administrator has clearly been embellished, transforming Wen into a culture hero, or, more literally, the bearer of Central Plains culture to the backward southwest.[19] The attributions of Wen's benevolent motives, the elevation of the region's scholarship from non-existent to rivaling the established seats of classical learning, and the subsequent devotion of the people of the area to their intellectual messiah are all tropes that further drive the tradition.

It is relatively easy, however, to debunk portions of the Wen Weng mythology. Recently, scholars have argued against several aspects of the tradition, including the belief that the famous Han writer Sima Xiangru 司馬相如 (179–117 BCE) was among those sent by Wen Weng to Chang'an for training,[20] the claim that Wen's academy led to an imperial edict ordering all commanderies and states to establish similar schools,[21] and the tradition that Wen Weng himself had illustrations of Confucius and his disciples placed on the walls of the academy.[22] By stripping away these layers of embellishment from the basic narrative, we are left with a simple tale of an administrator who established a mechanism for training local men to meet his needs in the commandery bureaucracy. Yet, it is the glow of the tradition of Wen Weng that continues to form the basis of the intellectual history of the Chengdu Plain.[23]

Even disregarding the claims that Wen Weng single-handedly transformed the Chengdu Plain from an intellectual backwater to a thriving center for classical studies, the region did produce several notable figures during the Former (or Western) Han period. From the activities of the region's most noted scholars we can see a microcosm of intellectual trends during the period, as well as observe the development of distinct regional academic styles. Among these intellectual trends were the composition of encyclopedic yet didactic rhapsodies (*fu* 賦), divination, and syncretic interpretations of canonical texts—both orthodox and otherwise.

During the Former Han, several Chengdu Plain intellectuals received imperial recognition, often for their literary accomplisments, but this recognition rarely came with any substantial rank or office. The earliest of these Chengdu intellectuals to appear on the national stage, Sima Xiangru, established himself first on the basis of his literary talents, and later was given charge over a military-diplomatic affair in the region.[24] Sima Xiangru was a native of Chengdu, and as a youth was said to have been fond of both reading and swordplay. Because of the high status of his family, he was appointed as a gentleman[25] under Emperor Jing 景 of Han (r. 156–141 BCE), and later made martial regular mounted attendant.[26] This post, however, was not to Sima's liking. Sima Qian's account attributes Sima Xiangru's dissatisfaction with his post to the fact that Emperor Jing was not fond of rhapsodies. While serving at the court of Emperor Jing, the Filial King of Liang (Liang Xiao wang 梁孝王) Liu Wu 劉武 visited the capital. Among his entourage were several noted rhapsodes and scholars. Claiming illness, Sima Xiangru resigned his post at the imperial court and attached himself to the court of Liu Wu where he quickly gained favor for his skills in composing rhapsodies. Upon Liu Wu's death in 144 BCE, Sima Xiangru returned to Shu where, though unemployed, he enjoyed the generous treatment bestowed on him by the local elites anxious to make the acquaintance of a local who had served at the imperial court. It was during this time that Sima Xiangru became involved with the young widowed daughter of the powerful Zhuo 卓 clan.[27] Later, when one of his rhapsodies was brought to the attention of Emperor Wu, Sima Xiangru was recalled to the imperial court where his literary skills again earned him the low-ranking post of gentleman.[28] During the reign of Emperor Wu, Sima Xiangru was also appointed general gentleman of the palace[29] and sent to lead troops into the western fringes of Yi Province as part of the Han effort to expand imperial control to the lands beyond the Chengdu Plain. In addition to leading military campaigns in the region, Sima Xiangru was later called upon by the court to negotiate an end to the costly marches in Yi Province. By appeasing the local elites and ensuring their cooperation in the peacemaking mission, Sima Xiangru contributed to the pacification of the southwest.[30] His mere presence at court earned Sima Xiangru the adulation of the regional elites, including the father-in-law who had previously disowned his daughter over her marriage to Sima, and allowed him to live a luxurious life in retirement.[31]

Sima Xiangru's summons to the imperial court on the basis of his literary abilities may have contributed to the inspiration of other Chengdu Plain intellectuals to compose rhapsodies.[32] But the case of Sima Xiangru's being recognized by the imperial court for his literary abilities without reaching high office reflects the hierarchy of intellectuals of the age, with rhapsodes being regarded as lowly jesters or entertainers.[33] Moreover, his experiences underscore Ban Gu's negative assessment of the intellectual scene on the Chengdu Plain during the Former Han: "[Wen Weng] taught the people how to recite texts, laws, and ordinances, but they were not yet able to believe truly in morality, and used their fondness for writing to satirize and ridicule, though they honored and admired power and authority."[34]

Near the end of the Former Han period, the intellectual trends on the Chengdu Plain shifted from the composition of rhapsodies toward a new type of syncretic classical scholarship, argued by some to have laid the foundation for the later Mystery Learning movement. Moreover, while the recognition of Sima Xiangru's literary abilities by the imperial court served to solidify his reputation as one of the most esteemed intellectuals of Former Han Sichuan, others established their fame closer to home.

Zhuang Zun 莊遵, appellative Junping 君平 (ca. late first century BCE), was a Chengdu native and regarded as a scholar of broad learning.[35] According to the *Han History*, Zhuang supported himself as a fortune-teller in the Chengdu market, and after earning enough money to meet his daily needs, he closed shop and taught the *Laozi* and *Zhuangzi* to his students. Zhuang Zun assessed his career as follows:

> Divining fortunes is my vocation, but it can also help people. When it is a matter of things evil or incorrect, then I say what would be profitable or harmful according to the tortoise or milfoil. I advise sons according to filiality, younger brothers according to deference, and subjects according to loyalty. According to their individual circumstances, I lead them toward good, and over half do as I say.[36]

Thus, the reclusive Zhuang was able to be a positive influence while avoiding the dangers of public political activity, repeatedly refusing to accept office at various levels of government.

Zhuang Zun's intellectual interests lie primarily in the mystic texts of the early Chinese tradition, particularly the *Changes*, the *Laozi*, and *Zhuangzi*. The *Records of the States South of Mount Hua* goes so far as to describe Zhuang as "a master of Daoist texts."[37] Despite his characterization as a "Daoist," Zhuang Zun appears to have possessed a phenomenal breadth of knowledge. Ban Gu notes, "He was broadly read and there was nothing he did not completely understand."[38] A late-second-century Chengdu Plain scholar, Li Quan 李權 (d. ca. 188–93 CE),[39] compared Zhuang to Confucius, saying: "Confucius and Junping gathered a multitude of books and thereby completed the *Spring and Autumn* and *Gist of the Veritable Classic of the Way and Its Potency*. Thus, as it is the merging of the rivers that makes the sea great, it is vast knowledge that makes the gentleman great."[40] A few additional details on Zhuang Zun's life and scholarship can be found in comments made by Zhuang's most noted pupil, Yang Xiong 揚雄 (53 BCE–18 CE), who in a letter to Liu Xin 劉歆 (53 BCE–23 CE) discussed his master's love for exegesis, mastery of various historical texts, and linguistic expertise.[41]

Zhuang Zun's wide-ranging interests and expertise appear to have been passed on to his student Yang Xiong, who was, without question, the most impressive intellectual to emerge from the Chengdu Plain during the Former Han. In Yang's works we can see the synthesis and expansion of the region's earlier intellectual traditions. According to the *Han History*, Yang was a native of Chengdu whose ancestors were related to the Zhou ruling house and had gradually moved up the Yangzi until reaching Mount Min (Min shan 岷山) northwest of Chengdu.[42] As a youth, Yang studied in Chengdu with Zhuang Zun, and later remained in Chengdu, away from the spotlight of national politics until his middle years, when his rhapsodies came to the attention of Emperor Cheng 成 (r. 33–7 BCE). Yang, as a youth, had admired the literary stylings of Sima Xiangru and made conscious efforts to imitate them. Though he later rejected the genre for its didactic failures, Yang Xiong is still regarded as one of the leading practitioners of the rhapsody in Chinese literary history.[43]

Yang Xiong's interests and talents, however, went well beyond a single literary genre. In fact, Yang's enduring fame is based in no small measure on the breadth of his knowledge in a variety of fields. Ban Gu notes that Yang "was broadly read and there was nothing that he had not seen."[44] This breadth is manifest in a statement in the *Records of the States South of Mount Hua* that reads:

> Because of the classics, none was greater than the *Changes*, [Yang Xiong] composed *Xuan* 玄 [*Mystery*]; of the teachings, none was greater than the *Analects*, so he composed *Fayan* 法言 [*Model Sayings*];[45] of the histories, none was better than *Cangjie* 蒼頡 [*Treasury of Explanations*], so he compiled *Xunzuan* 訓纂 [*Explanations on the Fascicles*]; of the admonishments, none was more beautiful than *Yu zhen* 虞箴 [*Admonitions of Yu*], so he

> composed *Zhouzhen* 州箴 [*Admonitions on the Provinces*]; of the rhapsodies, none was greater than "*Lisao*" 離騷 ["Encountering Sorrow"], so he refuted and expanded on Qu Yuan; of the canonical texts, none was as correct as *Erya* 爾雅 [*Approaching the Refined*], so he compiled *Fangyan* 方言 [*Regional Sayings*].[46]

In the realm of classical studies and philosophy, Yang Xiong's *Taixuan* 太玄 [*Supreme Mystery*] (often abbreviated as *Xuan* [*Mystery*]), stands as a complement to its model, the *Changes*, and as an expression of late Former Han syncretic thought.[47] The text "embodied in sensuous language and tightly articulated structure an ideal scheme of cyclic change in the realms of heaven, earth, and man."[48] As Nylan and Sivin point out, the source of the "sensuous language" and mystical images in the *Mystery* was generally the *Laozi*, while the canon of Confucianism provided Yang with cosmic and moral wisdom to accompany the images.[49] Thus, Yang combined the orthodoxy of the canon with the mystical images and language from the philosophy of Daoism and created a systemic text by which to support and explicate the *Changes*.[50]

The influence of Yang Xiong's *Mystery* and its syncretic classicism cannot be overstated. Later scholars such as Huan Tan 桓譚 (ca. 43 BCE–28 CE), Zhang Heng 張衡 (78–139 CE), Ma Rong 馬融 (79–166 CE), and Song Zhong 宋衷 (second–third century CE) each expanded on Yang's holistic interpretation of the canon and early mystic texts.[51] In particular, Song Zhong's academy at Jingzhou 荊州 trained a significant number of late Han and Three States period intellectuals in methods broader than the narrow classical orthodoxy of the day.[52] These thinkers, in turn, established Mystery Learning as the hallmark intellectual trend of early medieval China.

Thus, in addition to his talents in composing rhapsodies, Yang Xiong established himself as one of the great polymaths of the Former Han. In his works, one can see the fulfillment of the earlier intellectual traditions of the southwest: rhapsodies, classical studies, and mystical Daoist philosophy—all with a slightly syncretic bent.

It was on this basis that Ban Gu was led to conclude his overview of intellectual life in the Former Han Chengdu Plain with the following judgment:

> When Sima Xiangru made his foray into officialdom among the lords of the capital and became renowned to the age for his exquisite literary language, his fellow townsmen longed to follow in his footsteps. Later, there were the likes of Wang Bao, Yan Zun, and Yang Xiong, whose writings were the best in the subcelestial realm. This was from Wen Weng's guiding their instruction and [Sima] Xiangru's serving as a model.[53]

Moving from the Former Han to the Later Han, these Chengdu Plain intellectual traditions were largely retained, and as we will see below, developed a distinctly regional flavor.

OBSERVING THE STARS: INTELLECTUAL ACTIVITY IN THE LATER HAN

While literary ability opened doors to minor political office at the Former Han imperial court for several Sichuan intellectuals, new general intellectual and political trends led to changes in the intellectual traditions across the empire, including the southwest. Two interrelated trends merit mention: changing views of canonical studies and the rise of political prophesy.

Recent scholarship has greatly challenged long-standing views of the intellectual milieu of the Han. The traditional impressions of Han scholarship, propagated by literature on classical studies compiled by eminent nineteenth- and twentieth-century Chinese scholars, offer a portrait of an intellectual world formed around master–student lineages transmitting individual canonical texts. Academic debates during the Han, these traditional views hold, were centered around the authenticity of two sets of canonical texts, the so-called Old Texts (*guwen* 古文) and New Texts (*jinwen* 今文).[54] Re-examinations of the evidence, however, cast considerable doubts on these venerable views. First, the notion of "schools of thought" (*jia* 家) appears to be a later construction—established in Fan Ye's *Later Han History*, compiled in the fourth century.[55] Furthermore, evidence shows that while both Old and New texts existed during the Han, academic discourse centered around proper interpretation of the canon and official patronage rather than textual authenticity.[56] What was ultimately important to the state, which had established an imperial academy in 124 BCE, was the ability of classicists to provide "adornment to the rigors of the law with literary discourse."[57] In other words, utility of scholarship appears to have been more important than orthodoxy in the Han.

Another intellectual trend of the later Han period exemplified this notion of scholarship in the service of the state: the rise of prophetic-apocryphal (*chenwei* 讖緯) texts and the political prophesy associated with these writings.[58] Though technically two separate forms of discourse, *chen*—literally "subtle words"—and *wei* ("weft" texts) came to be viewed as a single type of political object, one that through the interpretation of various coded communications lent or denied legitimacy to early medieval dynastic enterprises.[59] The ability to interpret Heaven's signs as manifest in the prophetic-apocryphal texts and in other forms such as celestial observations was regarded as esoteric and secret, and the transmission of this knowledge and skill was common but regulated within tight master–student lineages. Moreover, the political implications of the mantic and prophetic arts were not lost on rulers or challengers to the throne. Individuals possessing the ability to read the will of Heaven were regularly summoned to court—invitations that were received with mixed degrees of enthusiasm. On the other hand, at least nine official bans on prophetic-apocryphal learning were issued from the third through seventh centuries.[60] The regular appointment of mantic artists and the prohibition of their works indicates the ambivalence of early medieval rulers who possessed both a need for and fear of the products of this intellectual activity.

The intersection of canonical studies and mantic arts played a significant role in the lives of intellectuals from Later Han Sichuan. With the establishment of the imperial academy and orthodox interpretative traditions of canonical texts in the early Han, demonstrating intellectual genealogies became critical in ensuring fame for the master and legitimacy for the student. Additionally, the state bestowed positions on members of authorized intellectual lineages, accompanied by positive reputations and financial benefits.[61] This situation is reflected in the treatment of intellectuals in the biographies contained in histories compiled during the late Han and throughout the early medieval period. In the cases of intellectuals from the Chengdu Plain, the *Records of the Three States*, *Records of the States South of Mount Hua*, and the *Later Han History* present individuals as members of scholarly lineages, noting the lineage founder and enumerating his disciples and their official successes. The case of the most prominent intellectual lineage of the Chengdu Plain illustrates both the range of scholarly activity, as well as the direct line of teachings inherited by Qiao Zhou.

The Yang 楊 clan of Guanghan 廣漢 commandery[62] and their disciples traced their intellectual roots to studies in the canon, but their reputation was based largely on their ability to predict political events on the basis of celestial observations and other forms of prophesy.[63] Biographical information from various historical texts enables the construction of an intellectual family tree spanning ten generations with thirty-six named scholars and mention of thousands of anonymous students (see Figure 1.1). Although the lineage began with what appear to be teachings transmitted solely within the Yang clan, outside teachers and students were soon introduced. Moreover, the teachings of this lineage quickly expanded beyond a single canonical text, eventually including materials far outside the bounds of orthodox scholarship. In keeping with the intellectual trend toward politically practical scholarship, the teachings of the Yang lineage centered on the prediction of political events, and, as such, members of the lineage regularly attracted the attention of powerful political figures.

Surviving information on the earliest members of the lineage illustrates this expansion of intellectual activity from canonical to esoteric, and from familial to communal. The purported founder of the intellectual lineage, Yang Zhongxu 仲續, was a native of Hedong 河東 commandery[64] and a specialist in the *Xiahou Tradition* on the *Hallowed Documents*.[65] He became fascinated with the customs and people of Yi Province and, as a result, moved his family to the town of Xindu 新都 in Guanghan commandery where he "cultivated canonical studies" and transmitted the *Xiahou Tradition* on the *Documents*.[66] Significantly, no further mention of this interpretative tradition of a canonical text is found in the accounts of the lives of subsequent members of

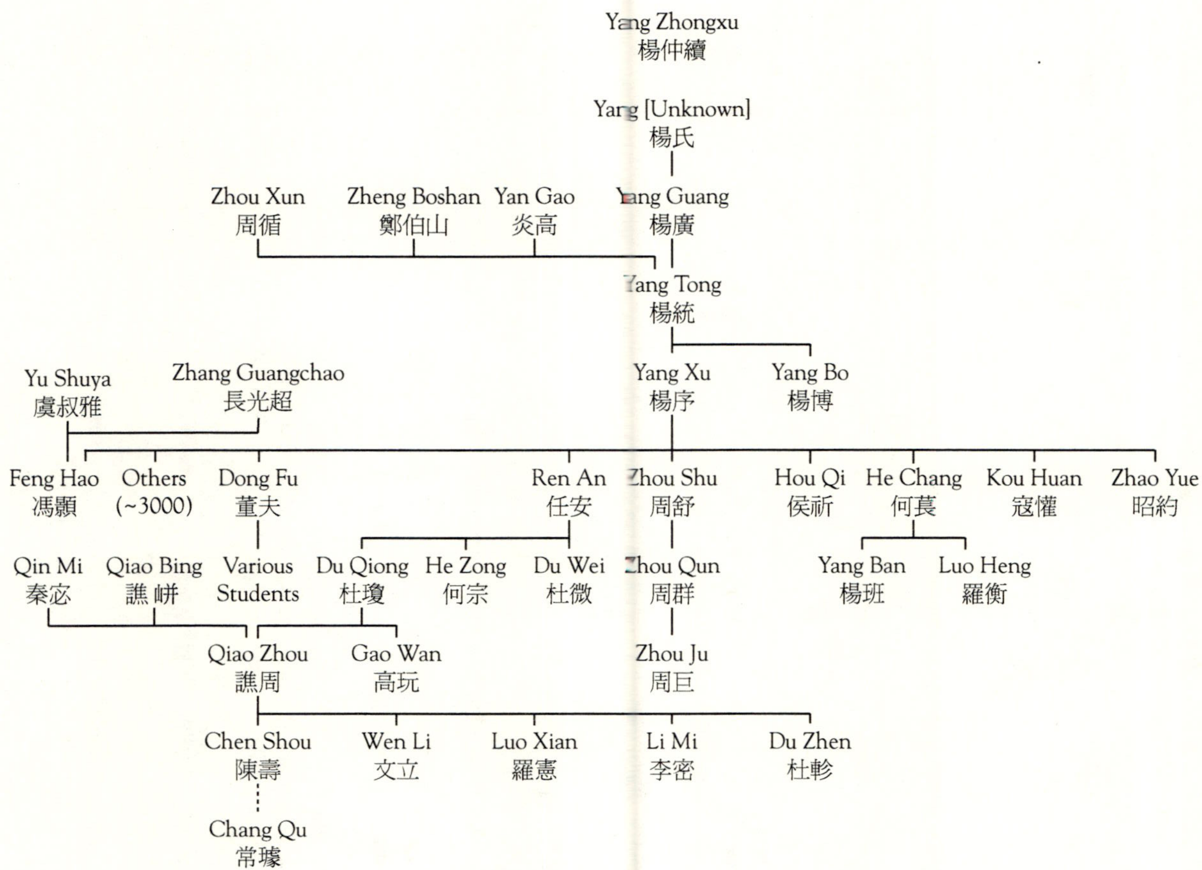

Figure 1.1 Intellectual Lineage of the Yang Family of Guanghan Commandery

this scholarly lineage. Rather, the content of the intellectual tradition turns toward the esoteric. For example, Yang Zhongxu's grandson, Yang Guang 廣, appellative Chunqing 春卿, was noted for his skills in charts and prophetic learning (*tuchen xue* 圖讖學). As a result, Yang Guang was pressed into the service of Gongsun Shu's 公孫述 (d. 36 CE)[67] regime in Chengdu, and when Han forces pacified the region, Yang Guang summoned his son Yang Tong 統 and gave him charge over the family's teachings, saying, "Inside my coarse bookbag are secret records passed down by our ancestors. They are of use to the House of Han. [I would that] you study them."[68] Yang Guang then killed himself. Yang Tong, reportedly moved by his father's dying admonition, and after observing the proper period of mourning, left his family to study with three local masters: Zhou Xun 周循 of Qianwei 犍為 commandery, Zheng Boshan 鄭伯山, and Yan Gao 炎高, also known as the Master of Hua District (Huali xiansheng 華里先生).[69] The *Later Han History* claims that Yang Tong studied the "methods of the ancestors" (*xianfa* 先法) with Zhou Xun and the *He tu* 河圖 [*River Charts*] and *Luo shu* 洛書 [*Luo Documents*][70] with Zheng Boshan, while the *Records of the States South of Mount Hua* notes Yan Gao's admonition to Yang Tong to master the [esoteric] charts and documents in order to serve the Han imperial family.[71] Though not explicitly stated in the history, we may presume that the materials passed to Yang Tong by his father and the curriculum studied with Zhou Xun, Zheng Boshan, and Yan Gao were all related to political prophesy and prognostication.[72]

The resumé of Yang Tong's political activity supports this assumption. Yang was appointed to office during the Yongping 永平 period (58–76 CE), during which time he compiled two volumes of commentary and explanations on the Yang family teachings and submitted them to the throne.[73] The practical application of the Yang intellectual traditions can be seen in an anecdote recorded in the *Later Han History*. It notes that during the Jianchu 建初 period (76–84 CE), the province experienced a serious drought. Yang Tong, serving as prefect of Pengcheng 彭城 district, was said to have divined the heavens and dispelled *yin* and *yang*, causing rain to fall on his district. When word of his feat reached the commandery administrator, Yang was summoned to relieve the drought in the commandery as well. The history testifies, "Thereupon, the rains fell."[74] Later, Yang Tong was frequently consulted regarding omens, portents, natural anomalies, and so on, presumably in his various official posts at the imperial court.[75]

Yang Tong's vocation was continued by his younger son Yang Xu 楊序[76]—knowledge that also led to political appointments. An anecdote in the *Later Han History* illustrates Yang Xu's mastery of the arts of divination at an early age. In Yongchu 3 (110 CE), Venus passed through the stars of the Dipper and the Han capital at Luoyang was inundated by floodwaters. Yang Tong was serving as a palace attendant at that time and was summoned by the court for consultation on these anomalies. Claiming that his eyes and ears were not clear due to age, Yang Tong recommended his son Yang Xu as one able to explain the portents. Hearing this, the Empress Dowager Deng 鄧太后 sent an attendant to question the younger Yang on the matter. Yang Xu explained, "Many of the princes are in the capital. Their appearance [there] is not normal. They should immediately leave and return to their own states." The empress dowager heeded Yang Xu's counsel and the planet disappeared from the Dipper and the waters at the capital receded as predicted. As a result, Yang Xu was appointed as palace attendant.[77] He was later summoned by the empress dowager to speak on charts and prophesies, but claiming a lack of skill in this area, retired to Qianwei. While living in retirement, he was repeatedly summoned by local and imperial officials to take up office, but all these summons were refused.

During the time of Emperor Shun 順 (r. 126–145 CE), Yang Xu again became somewhat active in court matters. In 128 CE, Yang traveled as far as Chang'an, but, because of illness, was unable to report to the court at Luoyang, though he submitted a memorial prophesying of numerous natural disasters and political problems. The *Records of the States South of Mount Hua* neatly summarizes these matters as follows:

> He submitted a memorial saying the western regions including Jing, Yang, and Jiao provinces would have military uprisings, the people would suffer from pestilence, Luoyang would have a great flood, the palace would burn, the [heads of the] bureaus would be dismissed, and close kinsmen would plot treason. All of these came to pass.[78]

The *Later Han History* adds, "Each time there was a calamity or anomaly, Yang Xu immediately submitted a method for dispelling [the trouble] and saving [them from the disaster]. But the eunuchs had taken over the government and his words were not trusted."[79] When the general-in-chief Liang Ji 梁冀 (d. 159 CE)[80] seized power as regent for the Emperors Chong 沖 (r. 145–146 CE), Zhi 質 (r. 146–147 CE), and Huan 桓 (r. 147–168 CE), Yang Xu resigned his post at the capital and returned to Yi Province. Here, Yang Xu was said to have cultivated the "arts of the Yellow Thearch and Laozi" and taught over three thousand students.[81] During these later years, Yang Xu ignored repeated summons from Empress Dowager Liang 梁太后, the sister of Liang Ji. Upon his death at the age of eighty-two, he was given the posthumous title of Father of Patterns (Wenfu 文父)[82] by Emperor Huan, and his students erected a shrine and offered biannual sacrifices.[83]

In many respects, Yang Xu exemplifies the early Yang family intellectual tradition. He was instructed in the esoteric family teachings by his father and he employed his knowledge in the service of the Han, as per the instuctions of his late grandfather. Yang Xu's ability to interpret the political meanings of omens and portents led to political appointments, but perhaps recognizing the danger that such knowledge also carried, he often chose to remain aloof from matters at the capital. The later years of his life were spent transmitting his family's teachings to others.

The students of Yang Xu were said to have numbered over three thousand, but of these masses, only the names of several have survived. The *Records of the States South of Mount Hua* notes:

> His disciples Zhao Yue 昭約, [appellative] Jiezai 節宰 of Luo 雒 [prefecture]; Kou Huan 寇懽, [appellative] Wenyi 文儀 of Mianzhu; He Chang 何萇, [appellative] Youzheng 幼正 of Shu; Hou Qi 侯祈, [appellative] Shengbo 升伯; Zhou Shu, [appellative] Shubo of Ba; and Ren An 任安 and Dong Fu 董扶 were all summoned and recommended for office, and their reputations spread throughout their generation.[84]

The final three names on this list, Zhou Shu, Ren An, and Dong Fu, were widely regarded as the most brilliant of Yang Xu's pupils, and each occupied important positions as heads of major branches of the Yang family intellectual lineage.

The branch headed by Zhou Shu 周舒 of Langzhong 閬中 in Baxi commandery, though shorter than those headed by Ren An and Dong Fu, played a significant role in the political affairs of the Chengdu Plain during the late Han and Three States period. Little is known of Zhou Shu's life other than a brief introduction in the *Records of the Three States* biography of his son, Zhou Qun 群,[85] which confirms Zhou's study with Yang Xu and places Zhou with Dong Fu and Ren An as the most regarded of Yang's students. An ardent recluse, Zhou Shu was frequently appointed to official posts, but rejected all of these summons. His reputation stems from his interpretation of a famous prophesy from the *Chunqiu chen* 春秋讖 [*Prophesies of the Spring and Autumn*][86] that said, "That which succeeds Han is lofty and faces the path" (*dai Han zhe, dang tu gao* 代漢者當塗高). Zhou Shu explained this riddle as meaning that Wei would follow the Han—an interpretation of the prophesy that was widely disseminated and accepted.[87]

The lives of Yang Xu's two most revered students, Dong Fu and Ren An, are closely linked, and their influence on later generations of Sichuan scholars perpetuated the Yang family traditions through the chaos surrounding the fall of the Han and the establishment of the state of Shu-Han in Chengdu during the early third century. Both men were natives of Mianzhu prefecture in Guanghan commandery and each was repeatedly recommended by the local bureau of merit, resulting in their traveling to Luoyang where they studied the canon at the imperial academy. As per the tendency toward broad learning, both Dong Fu and Ren An were said to have studied several canonical texts, but each specialized in one interpretative tradition: Dong Fu mastered the Ouyang tradition on the *Hallowed Documents* and Ren An was trained in the Meng tradition on the *Changes*.[88] The biographies of Dong Fu and Ren An also mention their study of "charts and prophesies" from Yang Xu in Guanghan, and that these traditions were passed on to their own students.[89] As a result of their training, both orthodox and esoteric, Dong Fu and Ren An were highly sought after by both local and imperial-level political powers.

Both men repeatedly shunned these appointments to office, each expressing a preference for remaining in Guanghan and teaching private students.

Dong Fu, however, appears to have been enticed to become an active participant in the imperial bureaucracy at some point. Moreover, his training in the mantic arts resulted in his resignation of the post and a significant shift in the power structure in the province. According to the *Later Han History,* while serving as a palace attendent under Emperor Ling 靈 (r. 168–190 CE), Dong Fu perceived the coming fall of the Han dynasty and reported his prophesy to the then-grand master of ceremony Liu Yan 劉焉 (d. 194 CE), saying, "The capital will soon be in disorder. In the astral sectors corresponding to Yi Province, there is the pneuma (*qi* 氣) of a Son of Heaven."[90] Liu Yan believed Dong Fu's prophesy and immediately requested a transfer to serve as shepherd of Yi Province, secretly hoping to make good on the prediction himself. Dong Fu likewise requested a transfer out of the capital and back to the Chengdu Plain. The transfer requests were granted and both men headed to the southwest. When Emperor Ling died the following year (190 CE), Dong Fu resigned his post in Chengdu and retired for good, devoting his energies to teaching an unknown number of students. He died in Guanghan at the age of eighty-two. The *Later Han History* concludes its biography of Dong Fu with a statement asserting the validity of Dong Fu's famous prophesy, stating, "Later, Liu Bei claimed the title of Son of Heaven in Shu, just as [Dong] Fu had said."[91]

The biographical materials on Ren An, while scant on details, illustrate the scholar's reluctance to participate in political matters and testify to his intellectual reputation. The *Records of the States South of Mount Hua* notes that Ren An refused to report to any of the various political appointments offered by the local and imperial governments, even rejecting official carriages sent to fetch him to office.[92] Despite eschewing an official career, Ren An nevertheless established a reputation as a virtuous scholar. There are no extant records of his teachings and we have only the praises passed down by admirers to testify to Ren's accomplishments. Ren was regarded by many as the finest of Yang Xu's disciples and principal heir to Yang Xu's traditions. According to Fan Ye, the people of Ren's time said of him, "If you want to know [Yang Xu] Zhongheng, then ask Ren An."[93] Perhaps the greatest compliment to Ren's abilities is recorded in his biography in Huangfu Mi's 皇甫謐 (215–282 CE) *Gao shi zhuan* 高士傳 [*Biographies of High-Minded Gentlemen*] that proclaimed him as "Confucius Ren" (Ren Kongzi 任孔子).[94] Though lacking details about Ren An's intellectual activity, the sources note that his reputation led to "students overflowing from his gate."[95]

The intellectual lineage founded by the Yang clan of Guanghan embodied the world of the mind in late Han Sichuan, as well as played significant roles in the political history of the region. In intellectual terms, the lineage developed from a family enterprise with a curriculum of a canonical text as well as a body of esoteric teachings, to one dominated by the skills of prophesy based on celestial observation by a larger community of intellectuals bound by a common knowledge of the relationship between the cosmos and the political world. Although some traditional and modern scholars have sought to emphasize the lineage's links to a Former Han model of canonical scholarship (i.e., one canonical text transmitted by one master to a student or students),[96] the Yang traditon demonstrates the late Han trend toward broad learning. In the biographies of members of the Yang lineage, we see individuals seeking multiple teachers for the transmission of various categories of knowledge (i.e., charts [*tu* 圖], prophesies [*chen* 讖], celestial patterns [*tianwen* 天文], secret records [*miji* 秘記], methods of the ancestors [*xianfa* 先法], and arts [*shu* 術]). In this regard, the Yang family tradition is consistant with Later Han intellectual trends. But the heart of the tradition, the ability to observe the heavens and interpret these meanings on the basis of secret teachings, though not unique to Sichuan, formed the core of this regional tradition to the significant exclusion of more orthodox classical studies.[97]

In political terms, the activities of members of the Yang intellectual lineage were closely related to the growing belief in and reliance on prophesies during the Han. These scholars were regularly called on by the state to interpret natural anomalies, and they ably and accurately interpreted the signs and offered solutions to the crises. This fact illustrates the practical nature of the Yang scholarly tradition, as well as the demand by the state for individuals possessing such skills. However, these skills also posed risks to those holding them, resulting in a number of these scholars choosing lives of reclusion and political detatchment. The reclusive tendencies seen in some scholars trained in the Yang tradition also reflect the rise of the rhetoric of reclusion in the late Han and period of disunion that followed.[98] This search for seclusion from the turbid world led several of the Yang lineage scholars to the texts and practices of the Way of the Yellow Thearch and Laozi, noted in their biographies by the shorthand "Huang-Lao" 黃老.[99] Yet for many of these Chengdu Plain intellectuals, we find evidence of their observation of and commentary on the political world and its link to their world of the mind of the late Han. The traditions of these gentlemen continued into the Three States period.

A THREE STATES "FOREST OF CLASSICISTS": INTELLECTUAL ACTIVITY IN SHU-HAN

In the face of a long-standing popular perception of Shu-Han as a state lacking in scholarship, Chen Shou offers a divergent view of scholarly activity on the Chengdu Plain during the third century. The forty-second fascicle of his *Records of the Three States*, though not explicitly labeled as such, appears to be modeled on the *The Grand Scribe's Records* and *Han History*'s "Biographies of the Forest of Classicists" (*rulin zhuan* 儒林傳)[100] fascicles in its presentation of Shu-Han scholars, with notation of both intellectual activity and political involvement. Chen Shou presents dedicated biographies of ten intellectuals, plus brief notes on several lesser figures, organizing the chapter around three groups of interrelated figures. These subgroupings of biographies within the chapter serve to illustrate several important themes of Chen's account of Shu-Han intellectual life: the continuation of the Yang family intellectual traditions, the tensions between local and outside intellectual traditions, and the relationship between scholars and the state. Notably missing are accounts of Zhuge Liang and Qin Mi, popularly believed to have been Shu-Han's most brilliant (or, in some views, only) scholars, whose political activities are treated elsewhere in the *Records of the Three States*.[101]

Chen Shou's "Forest of Classicists" fascicle opens with the lives of three latter-day members of the Yang intellectual lineage and their activities under the state of Shu-Han. These three biographies illustrate the continuation of the Yang traditions of celestial observation, prophesy, and political ambivalence into the Shu-Han period.

The first individual treated by Chen Shou, Du Wei 杜微, appellative Guofu 國甫, of Fu 涪 prefecture was a student of Ren An. Although Chen Shou makes no mention of Du Wei's intellectual activity, he notes that Du followed his teacher's example of political disengagement by repeatedly refusing to accept appointments proffered by Zhuge Liang. When the chancellor Zhuge Liang personally visited Du's home to persuade him to take office, Du claimed to be deaf, and the entire "conversation" was conducted in writing. In the end, it appears that Du Wei accepted a post, then later resigned on grounds of illness and age.[102]

Next, Chen Shou presents an account of Zhou Qun, the son of Zhou Shu, offering considerably more detail in regards to Zhou Qun's intellectual activity and its political implications. Zhou Qun, while following in his father's vocation, deviated from Zhou Shu's reclusive path by playing an active role in regional politics. His biography notes, "When Zhou Qun was young, he received instruction from [Zhou] Shu, focusing his mind on the enterprise of predicting."[103] To this brief statement, Chen Shou adds significant detail, illuminating the methods of the Yang tradition. Zhou Qun was said to have constructed an observational platform in the courtyard of the family estate. Here, he posted servants day and night to watch the heavens for anomalies. When a pneuma was spotted, a report was immediately sent to Zhou Qun, who would then personally mount the tower to observe the phenomenon for himself. According to Chen Shou, "Whenever there were pneumatic omens, he saw them all. For this reason, many of his predictions were accurate."[104]

Several other early historical sources corroborate Chen Shou's assertion. Pei Songzhi 裴松之 (372–451 CE), citing Sima Biao's 司馬彪 (240–315 CE) *Xu Han shu* 續漢書 [*Continued Han History*], notes the fulfillment of Zhou Qun's political prophesies. The first natural anomaly, noted in Jian'an 7 (203 CE), involved the case of a man who changed into a woman in Yuexi 越巂 commandery.[105] Zhou Qun's explanation of this event was that it was an omen of the changing of the dynasty. As predicted, Emperor Xian of Han abdicated to

Wei in Jian'an 25 (221 CE).[106] In the second case, a shooting star was observed leaving the Quail Tail (*chunwei* 鶉尾) in the astral sector corresponding to Jing province in 207 CE.[107] Zhou's interpretation of this astronomical event was that the shepherd of Jing Province, Liu Biao 劉表 (144–208 CE), would soon die and the territory of Jing would be lost. Liu Biao died the following year (208 CE), and Cao Cao's troops claimed the province. In 212 CE, another shooting star was observed, this time in the constellation known as the Five Marquises (*wu zhuhou* 五諸侯).[108] This anomaly was read to mean that those who held territory in the west would soon lose their holdings. As predicted, in 214 CE Liu Zhang 劉璋 (d. 219 CE) lost Yi Province, Han Sui 韓遂 lost Liang Province, and Song Jian 宋建 lost Baohan 枹罕, while in 215 CE, Zhang Lu 張魯 (d. early third century CE) lost Hanzhong.[109]

Because of his skill, Zhou Qun was appointed to various official posts under Liu Zhang and, later, Liu Bei.[110] In this capacity, Zhou Qun was consulted by Liu Bei regarding a plan to attack Cao Cao at Hanzhong.[111] Zhou's reply to Liu Bei's query was, "You will obtain the territory, but not the people. If you send out the lieutenant generals, you will certainly not prevail. You must guard with caution!"[112] Chen Shou follows this brief note with the account of Zhang Yu 張裕, whose skills in prognostication were said to be greater than those of Zhou Qun.[113] Zhang Yu also advised Liu Bei against a campaign in Hanzhong. Liu Bei ignored both Zhou Qun and Zhang Yu and sent his troops to Hanzhong, where he was successful in obtaining the land, but his military commanders were all killed in this battle, just as Zhou Qun had predicted.[114] The texts are silent as to why Zhou Qun and Zhang Yu were consulted on this matter of military strategy, but presumably celestial signs were involved.[115]

Following this presentation of Zhou Qun's life, Chen Shou offers a similarly detailed account of another of Ren An's students, Du Qiong, appellative Boyu 伯瑜 of Chengdu. Chen Shou claims that Du Qiong "thoroughly mastered Ren An's art,"[116] while the *Records of the States South of Mount Hua* notes that Du excelled in the study of canonical texts, apocryphal texts, and the [mantic] arts.[117] Du Qiong was politically active in the region, holding office under the provincial administrations of both Liu Zhang and Liu Bei, and later serving in Liu Bei's state of Shu-Han in a variety of positions, some with direct access to the ruler.[118]

Chen Shou's biography of Du Qiong places great emphasis on Du's personality and character. Chen writes, "As a person, he was quiet and of few words, keeping himself behind closed doors and not concerning himself with the affairs of the world."[119] Echoing Chen Shou's evaluation, Chang Qu's encomium on Du reads, "The Grand Master of Ceremonies, pure and removed. Remote and distant, abstruse and deep."[120] Later, Chang also notes, "[Du] was quiet and valued his privacy, and was regarded as the purest of the students [of Ren An]."[121] From these statements, we may suppose that although Du Qiong accepted positions in the government, he was not considered an active participant in court politics. As a result of his reputation as a pure scholar, Du Qiong was highly esteemed by many of the most powerful figures in the state of Shu-Han, including the generals Jiang Wan 蔣琬 (d. 246 CE),[122] Fei Yi 費禕 (d. 253 CE),[123] and others.[124]

Following the notice of Du Qiong's death in 250 CE, Chen Shou appends the customary bibliography of this scholar's works, then comments that Du did not transmit his teachings to his sons, and "there was none to carry on his inner teachings (*neixue* 內學)."[125] This is an odd statement, for the *Records of the States South of Mount Hua* contains a brief biography of Gao Wan 高玩, appellative Bozhen 伯珍, of Jiangyuan who was said to have been a student of Du Qiong.[126] This account of Gao Wan notes, "As a youth, he received instruction from the grand master of ceremonies Du Qiong, and his [mastery of] the mantic arts was subtle and marvelous. He was broadly learned, yet plain and simple. While young, his reputation was comparable to that of [Li] Mi, and their official positions were equal."[127] Chen Shou and Li Mi were both students under Qiao Zhou, and Chen Shou would have certainly been aware of Gao and his study with Du Qiong. Since the *Records of the States South of Mount Hua* account specifically mentions Gao's mastery of the "arts" of Du Qiong—presumably the arts of prophesy and divination—Chen Shou's statement is baffling. Ignoring Gao Wan, Chen Shou devotes the remainder of the biography to illustrating the influence of Du Qiong's teachings on Qiao Zhou.[128]

By opening his "Forest of Classicist" fascicle with this group of intellectuals, Chen Shou demonstrates the continuity of the Yang family traditions into the Shu-Han era, as well as illustrates the continued political interest in these skills. Moreover, Chen Shou subtly asserts the primacy of this, his own, intellectual tradition through the contrasting account of outsiders and outside scholarship in Shu-Han that follows.

The second cluster of biographies in Chen Shou's "Forest of Classicists" fascicle relates the activities of six scholars who introduced outside scholarship to Chengdu and illustrates the general intellectual milieu of the Shu-Han capital. Four of the figures treated in this section were Central Plains intellectuals who, for various reasons, found themselves in Chengdu. The remaining two individuals were natives of the Chengdu Plain who were trained in the intellectual traditions of Jing Province. Chen Shou's presentation of the activities of these men in Chengdu, while often humorous, depicts a rather low state of intellectual affairs in the early years of the state. He notes:

> After the Former Sovereign [Liu Bei] stabilized Shu, the region had been in chaos for dozens of years and scholarly activity was in decline. [The Former Sovereign] thus ordered canonical texts be collected and the academies be put back in good order. [Xu] Ci 許慈 and [Hu] Qian 胡潛 were named as erudits, and along with Meng Guang 孟光, Lai Min 來敏, and others, collated old texts. Because things were at an early stage of development, there were many divergent ideas.[129]

Chen's depictions of these scholars support his overall characterization of the age.

Introducing Xu Ci, appellative Rendu 仁篤, Chen Shou offers a basic resumé of Xu's background and intellectual aptitude. Originally from Nanyang 南陽,[130] Xu Ci studied under Liu Xi 劉熙[131] and excelled in the scholarship of Master Zheng [Xuan], mastering the *Changes*, the *Hallowed Documents*, the *Three Ritual Texts*, the Mao *Odes*, and the *Analects*. Chen Shou notes that Xu Ci entered the Chengdu Plain with Xu Jing 許靖 (150–222 CE)[132] during the Jian'an period via Jiaozhou.[133] A vague resumé is provided for Xu Ci's counterpart, Hu Qian. Hu was a native of Wei commandery, and Chen Shou frankly states, "We do not know what he was doing in Yi Province."[134] Chen Shou describes Hu Qian's scholarship as "not especially deep," but notes his strong memory in matters of sacrificial and mourning ritual.[135]

Following this matter-of-fact introduction to these two outside scholars, Chen Shou presents an anecdote illustrating their character and contributions to the intellectual world of Shu-Han. According to Chen Shou, both men were conceited and bickered constantly. In their official duties as collators of texts, they were said to have withheld documents from one another and even came to physical blows. Liu Bei was reported to have been so disturbed by their petty behavior that he ordered actors to mock the two scholars at a large court gathering. Chen Shou's account of this event is both amusing and telling. It reads, "At first, [the actors] disputed the meanings of words, but by the end [of the skit] they were thrusting at each other with swords and spears."[136] In this manner, Chen Shou illustrates both the pettiness of some scholars at the Shu-Han court and Liu Bei's concern over the current poor state of academic affairs. Pei Songzhi's *Commentary* includes a brief comment by the Jin historian Sun Sheng 孫盛 (ca. 302–375 CE),[137] who endorses Chen Shou's appraisal of the two men and the general intellectual atmosphere at the Shu-Han capital, saying, "Shu lacked cultured gentleman, and for that reason [Xu] Ci, [Hu] Qian, and the others were employed."[138]

In Chen Shou's presentation of the cases of two other outside scholars at the Shu-Han court, he continues to focus on personality and character over intellectual contributions. First, Chen introduces Meng Guang, a native of Luoyang who fled to the Chengdu Plain around the time Dong Zhuo 董卓 (d. 192 CE) moved the capital to Chang'an (ca. 190 CE). Meng Guang was said to have been widely read, to have possessed expertise in historical texts, with a special fondness for the Gongyang interpretation of the *Spring and Autumn* annals and a strong disdain for the interpretation of Zuo Qiuming 左丘明. Meng received numerous low-level appointments in Liu Bei's provincial administration, as well as under the Shu-Han imperial venture, but reportedly grew increasingly frustrated over the court's refusal to act on his suggestions, strengthening his perception that the Liu clan was not particularly interested in scholarship. As a result, he often openly criticized his superiors, leading to his dismissal from office. He died at the age of ninety-one, reportedly a bitter man.

In similar fashion, Chen Shou presents the case of Lai Min, appellative Jingda 敬達, a native of Yiyang 義陽 in Xinye 新野 prefecture.[139] Lai Min was related to Liu Zhang by marriage, and entered the Chengdu Plain with his sister and her husband (a kinsman of Liu Zhang) during Liu Zhang's tenure as inspector of Yi Province. An avid collector of books, Lai Min was fond of Zuo Qiuming's interpretation of the *Spring and Autumn* and skilled in archaic graphs. Following Liu Bei's takeover of the province, Lai Min was named as colonel for direction of education and put in charge of provincial education matters. Chen Shou notes that Lai Min's outspoken nature resulted in frequent dismissals from his posts. One anecdote quotes Lai Min questioning a group of high-ranking officials, saying, "What merit do you new people have that warrant you taking my glory? Everyone hates me! Why?!" Chen Shou then comments, "Lai Min was old and crazy, and thus he made such utterances."[140] Perhaps not surprisingly, Meng Guang took a liking to Lai Min, and "considered him to be somewhat better" than the other scholars at court. Chen Shou's account of Meng Guang and Lai Min depicts these scholars as bright but arrogant, and adds to his already somewhat negative view of outside scholars in Chengdu.

The final two scholars treated in this grouping of biographies within the "Forest of Classicists" fascicle were both natives of the Chengdu Plain who were educated in the canonical studies tradition concentrated at Liu Biao's academy at Jingzhou. The eldest of these two figures, Yin Mo 尹默, appellative Siqian 思潛, was a native of Fu prefecture in Zitong commandery. According to Chen Shou's account, Yin Mo felt that the scholars of Yi Province "were not broadly learned," and hence journeyed to Jingzhou to study "ancient learning" (*gu xue* 古學).[141] In Jingzhou, he studied various canonical texts and their associated "chapter and verse" commentaries, as well as historical texts with Sima Decao 司馬德操 and Song Zhong.[142] It appears that Yin Mo may have been acquainted with Liu Bei during his time in Jing, for shortly after Liu Bei took control of Yi Province in 211 CE, he named Yin as attendant for encouragement of education. Later, in the fifth month of Zhangwu 章武 1 (221 CE), Liu Bei named his son Liu Shan as heir and appointed Yin Mo as coachman of the heir's household, in which capacity Yin Mo tutored Liu Shan in *Master Zuo's Traditions*. Yin Mo later served in a variety of low-ranking consulting posts within the palace.

Like Yin Mo, Li Zhuan 李譔 (d. ca. 258–263 CE), appellative Qinzhong 欽仲, was a native of Fu prefecture and educated in the academic traditions of the Jing academy. In this case, however, Li Zhuan's training in the Jing traditions came secondhand, by way of his father, Li Ren 李仁, who had been a classmate of Yin Mo's at the Jing academy, and through Yin Mo. Chen Shou describes Li Zhuan as well-read and broadly learned, with expertise in not only the classical learning of Jing, but also in art, prognostication, divination, medicinal herbs, archery, and engineering. On the basis of these skills, Li Zhuan was given posts in the imperial academy and in the office of the masters of writing. Like his teacher Yin Mo, Li Zhuan was appointed as a coachman and palace attendant in the service of the heir apparent, in this instance, Liu Xuan 劉璿 (224–264 CE).[143] Although the heir apparent was fond of Li Zhuan, Chen Shou reports that Li's frail physique and his "love of jokes" made him unsuitable for important positions.[144] In terms of his intellectual activity, Li Zhuan wrote commentaries in several Old Text canonical works, including the *Changes*, *Documents*, Mao *Odes*, *Three Ritual Texts*, and *Master Zuo's Traditions*. Significantly, Li also prepared a commentary on Yang Xiong's *Supreme Mystery*, a Chengdu Plain text that was highly esteemed at the Jing provincial academy. The biographies of these nine intellectual figures of Shu-Han, constituting the opening third of Chen Shou's "Forest of Classisicts" fascicle, illustrate the two distinct camps of intellectual activity in Shu-Han and offer a glimpse of the differing relationships these groups of scholars had with the state.

Following these accounts, Chen Shou offers a lengthy biography of his mentor Qiao Zhou. Since Qiao Zhou's life and works will be discussed in greater detail later, here I will simply outline Chen Shou's treatment of Qiao in the context of the "Forest of Classicists" fascicle. Having already introduced Qiao Zhou as a student of Du Qiong and thus an heir to the Yang family intellectual traditions earlier in the fascicle, here Chen Shou focuses his attention on Qiao's political activity. Qiao Zhou is presented as a teacher, a low-ranking courtier, and, later in life, as a critic of state policy. These political roles are all illustrated with lengthy citations of Qiao's political writings. These include his memorial to Liu Shan opposing the ruler's frivolous excursions, an embellished account of a debate at court over military policy, and two memorials advocating the surrender of Shu-Han. Despite Qiao's position as a member of the Yang intellectual tradition, Chen Shou only offers one small piece of evidence to illustrate his teacher's aptitude in prophesy—a prediction of Qiao's own coming death. A brief notice of Qiao Zhou's sons and a short listing of Qiao's major works conclude the biography.

The final figure treated in the fascicle, Xi Zheng 郤正, appellative Lingxian 令先, was the grandson of the late Han inspector of Yi Province, Xi Jian 儉, who was killed during the uprising of the "Yellow Turban" bandit Ma Xiang 馬相.[145] Following the death of Xi Jian, the family remained in Yi Province where Xi Zheng was born. Xi Zheng's father surrendered to Wei and his mother remarried while Zheng was a youth. As a result, Xi Zheng was independent at an early age. Chen Shou notes his scholarly aptitude and willingness to endure poverty for the sake of learning. In particular, Xi Zheng was fond of the rhapsodies of early Han Sichuan intellectuals like Sima Xiangru and Yang Xiong, as well as other literary works by people of Yi Province. On the basis of his literary talents, Xi Zheng served in various posts under Shu-Han, including office of imperial library clerk, chief clerk, gentleman, and finally as prefect. However, Xi Zheng never advanced beyond these minor posts. Chen Shou attributes this to Xi Zheng's relationship with the eunuch

Huang Hao 黃皓[146] who "neither loved nor despised" Xi. Thus, "[Xi Zheng's] official rank never exceeded that of six-hundred bushels, but he avoided misfortune."[147] In an expression of his frustration at not being promoted, Xi Zheng composed a hypothetical discourse (*shelun* 設論) entitled "Shi ji" 釋譏 ["Dispelling Ridicule"].[148] The lengthy essay, reproduced in full by Chen Shou, features Xi Zheng's "reply" to an anonymous interlocutor who mocks Xi Zheng for his low official position. In it, Xi Zheng states that his failure to advance "after nine evaluations" is a necessity of the times (i.e., the ruler's need to allocate resources for the benefit of the common people rather than to enrich court officials), and that those who have advanced in rank are truly superior in ability. The statement, of course, should not be taken at face value. The humble self-deprecating tone is clearly a critique of the corruption and favoritism at the Huang Hao-dominated court.

Following the lengthy quotation of Xi Zheng's "Dispelling Ridicule," Chen Shou notes Xi Zheng's role in the surrender of Liu Shan and Shu-Han. After accepting the recommendation to surrender, Liu Shan ordered Xi Zheng to compose the document. After the surrender, Liu Shan and his family were relocated to Luoyang, and only Xi Zheng and one other official accompanied the deposed ruler. According to Chen Shou's account, Xi Zheng abandoned his wife and sons to follow the Later Sovereign to his new benefice. While in Luoyang, Liu Shan frequently relied on Xi Zheng's advice in matters of ritual and propriety. As Xi Zheng neared death, he was honored with an edict appointing him to a post in Yi Province. The edict reads, "[Xi] Zheng was previously in Chengdu. When [Shu-Han] fell, he held to propriety and did not abandon loyalty. He has been employed and exhausted his heart in service. He has obtained the results of ordered principles. Let [Xi] Zheng be made grand administrator of Baxi."[149] He died shortly thereafter in 278 CE. Chen Shou's inclusion of the edict proclaiming Xi Zheng's loyalty echoes his treatment of Qiao Zhou, arguing that loyalty to the person of the ruler was of higher virtue than loyalty to the political entity of Shu-Han.

Chen Shou's final appraisal of the individuals treated in the fascicle echoes the themes illustrated in the biographies. It reads:

> Du Wei cultivated his body in reclusive solitude and did not throw himself into affairs of the world, approaching the ideals set by [Bo] Yi and the Hoary-heads. Zhou Qun divined the minutia of the heavens; Du Qiong delved deeply into the esoteric. Both lived sincerely. Xu [Ci], Meng [Guang], Lai [Min], and Li [Zhuan] possessed broad experience and were well-known. Yin Mo's essence was in the *Zuo Tradition*; although his potent vocation was not well-known. Truly, all were learned gentlemen of the age. Qiao Zhou's words and principles were deep and penetrating. He was a great scholar of his generation, possessing the principle of Dong [Zhongshu] and Yang [Xiong]. Xi Zheng's writings were brilliant, possessing the air of Zhang [Heng] and Cai [Yong]. Add to this his actions and here you have a Gentleman. These two

> masters' affairs in the Jin dynasty were few, while their affairs in Shu were many. For this reason, I have included them in this chapter.[150]

In the life of Du Wei, the virtue of reclusion is extolled, while the link between moral character and the intellectual traditions of prophesy are honored in the treatment of Zhou Qun and Du Qiong. Chen Shou's remarks on the outsider-scholars in Chengdu (Xu Ci, Meng Guang, Lai Min, and Li Zhuan) are vague and reflect his lesser opinion of these individuals, though he does call them, along with Yi Mo, "learned gentlemen of the age." Chen Shou's greatest praise is reserved for Qiao Zhou and Xi Zheng who illustrate the principle of scholarship in the service of the state (i.e., loyalty).

As a whole, the forty-second fascicle of the *Records of the Three States* stands as a vivid snapshot of the intellectual world at the court of Shu-Han. In it, Chen Shou recounts his own intellectual tradition (i.e., the Yang clan of Guanghan) through Qiao Zhou, and illustrates the condition of intellectual affairs at court, especially Liu Bei's efforts to restore academic institutions. In fact, the overarching theme of the fascicle is that of the relationship between scholars and the state. Local scholar-prophets served the state through their interpretations of Heaven's will manifest through omens, portents, and human speech, while outside academics filled the bureaucratic offices of Liu Bei's imperial enterprise. Chen Shou's contrasting accounts of these two groups of intellectuals is striking. The local scholars openly expressed reservations about serving the state, preferring reclusion over public office. The outsiders, on the other hand, bickered over their status. In the lives of Qiao Zhou and Xi Zheng, Chen Shou presents his vision of an ideal intellectual: talented, engaged, and loyal. In particular, the political and moral aspects of these two scholars' lives take the fore in Chen's biographies, while their specific academic achievements are mentioned only briefly. In this fascicle, Chen Shou illustrates the triumph of scholars like Qiao Zhou and Xi Zheng in a general climate of intellectual decline.

CHAPTER 2

The Early Life of Qiao Zhou

THE QIAO FAMILY IN BA

Qiao Zhou, appellative Yunnan 允南, was born in Xichongguo 西充國 prefecture,[1] Baxi 巴西 commandery, in the eastern half of Yi Province, around the year 200 CE.[2] His official biography in the *Records of the Three States* notes the passing of his father, Qiao Bing 譙峅[3] while Qiao Zhou was still young, and that he was raised by his mother and an elder brother.[4] The family, though impoverished, clung to a higher self-image: that of the *shi*, or "cultured gentleman."[5]

The historical records affirm the past glory of the Qiao clan. According to the *Records of the States South of Mount Hua*, the Qiaos ranked among the great families of Xichongguo prefecture, having held offices at the local and national levels as early as the second century BCE.[6] While the early historical records offer no direct evidence as to the manner of the Qiaos' rise to power, it seems likely that the clan possessed landholdings in the resource-rich region, and that proceeds from agricultural, commercial, or industrial activity allowed males in the clan to pursue educational interests.

The *Records of the States South of Mount Hua* discusses the economic activity of the commandery, noting its level plains, abundant water, and flourishing horse, cattle, mulberry, and silk industries.[7] Following this listing of material products, Chang Qu enumerates the commandery's human resources, specifically mentioning Qiao Rongshi 譙榮始 [Bing] as one who "learned how to simultaneously master the three powers"[8] and Marquis Qiao [Zhou] as having "cultivated letters at the beginning of the Jin dynasty."[9] Chang Qu's list of prominent individuals of the commandery progresses along a continuum of literacy, placing local scholars first, followed by literate locals, and concludes with individuals who were illiterate but distinguished themselves through their actions. Qiao Rongshi appears second in this list of some sixteen figures from the Han period, while Qiao Zhou appears at the head of the list of figures from the Jin era. The high placement of the Qiaos in this hierarchical ranking of Baxi commandery notables testifies to the esteem in which Chang Qu held Qiao Bing and Qiao Zhou as intellectuals, and to the family's characterization as cultured gentlemen. A brief examination of the biographies of important men of the Qiao clan illustrates a long history of scholarship and official service, key elements of the ethos of the cultured gentleman (see Figure 2.1).

Few details on the life of the earliest member of the Qiao clan mentioned in the historical records, Qiao Long 譙隆, are available. The fragments at hand document Qiao Long's involvement in matters at the Former Han imperial court, with two extant references to a passage purportedly from the *Records of the States South of Mount Hua* presenting Qiao Long as a low-ranking officer fulfilling his moral obligation to censure the emperor. At the time, Qiao Long served as the prefect of the Park of the Supreme Forest, a post overseeing the maintenance of wildlife in the imperial hunting reserve.[10] In Jianyuan 建元 3 (138 BCE), Wuqiu Shouwang 吾丘壽王 urged Emperor Wu to annex local farmland and expand the park. Qiao Long remonstrated, saying, "Yao and Shun magnified their rule by expanding virtue. Do not concern yourself with the forest park."[11] While this brief notice does not record whether the emperor followed Qiao Long's advice, it does note that Qiao was promoted to the office of palace attendant. Qiao Long was not alone in his objections to the expansion of the park. Accounts in Sima Qian's *The Grand Scribe's Records* and Ban Gu's *Han History* note the protests of Sima Xiangru and Dongfang Shuo 東方朔, as well as the emperor's reaction to their opposition: the expansion of the hunting park as planned, and the promotion of the protesters to higher posts in the imperial bureaucracy.[12] Owing to Qiao Long's newly advanced position at the court of Emperor Wu, Chang Qu eulogized him as follows: "Loyal and upright, the palace attendant Qiao Long, appellative Bosi 伯司, was a man of Langzhong."[13] There are no further details available on the life of Qiao Long, but his service at the imperial court, and in particular his remonstrance to the emperor, set a standard for public service that would be reflected in the lives and activities of later men of the Qiao clan.

The next member of the Qiao clan to appear in the historical records, Qiao Xuan 譙玄, appellative Junhuang 君黃, distinguished himself at the national level during the disorder at the end of the Former Han. Fan Ye's *Later Han History* follows the standard biographical trope in introducing Qiao Xuan, noting his fondness for study as a youth and his talent in reciting canonical texts, specifically the *Changes* and *Spring and Autumn*.[14] Qiao Xuan held some unidentified posts at the commandery and provincial levels prior to being recommended for imperial office and his subsequent appointment as gentleman consultant in 14 BCE.[15] During this time, Emperor Cheng was reportedly inattentive to governmental matters, spending his energy on excursions and the newly established Empress Zhao Feiyan 趙飛燕.[16] According to Fan

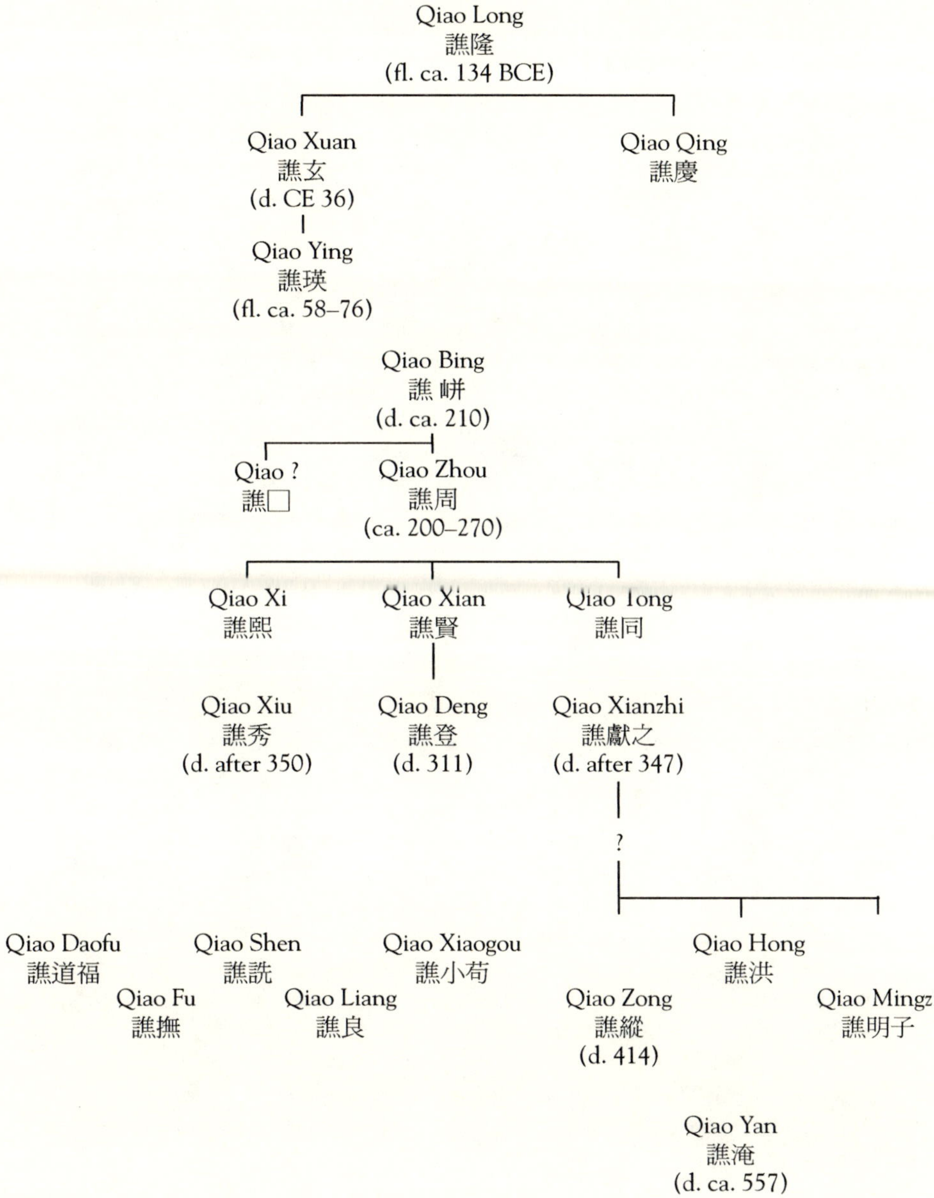

Figure 2.1. Lineage of the Qiao Family of Baxi Commandery

Ye, "The empress monopolized [the emperor's] affections and was extremely jealous. Many of the princes inexplicably died young."[17] Qiao Xuan memorialized on this matter, urging the emperor to curtail his pleasure outings and his interactions with the empress. Lamenting the lack of an imperial heir, Qiao said, "I have heard that in the rear quarters princes have been born but not raised. When your servant heard of this, I was distressed, my heart pained and wounded. I brood over the sorrows of the state and do not forget them [the dead princes] for even a moment."[18] Warning of the threat to the empire from minority and bandit uprisings resulting from his lack of attention to the matters of state, Qiao Xuan concluded his memorial with an exhortation that read: "Your majesty must remember the supreme importance of the subcelestial realm, cherish the golden and jade body, equally interact with many women, preserve your inexhaustible blessing, then the joy of the subcelestial realm will be great."[19] Even in the face of rebellion within the empire, Qiao Xuan's greater worry was over the lack of an heir to the throne.

Interestingly, the evidence to support Qiao Xuan's concerns was presented in the form of natural disasters and celestial anomalies.[20] According to the *Later Han History*, Qiao Xuan interpreted these portents for the court, but his warnings were ignored. As a result, Qiao Xuan languished in the gentlemen's office before being transferred to serve as assistant grand master of ceremonies.[21] While Qiao Xuan's biography makes no mention of his receiving training in the mantic arts, from his interpretation of the natural signs demonstrated in this anecdote, it appears clear that Qiao was versed in the prophetic traditions of the Chengdu Plain.

Later, when Wang Mang 王莽 (45 BCE–23 CE) took the throne in 9 CE,[22] Qiao Xuan "changed his name and secretly returned to his home and hid."[23] Qiao Xuan's later fame and reputation stems largely from this action and his subsequent reclusion. While Qiao Xuan managed to avoid entering the service of Wang Mang, when Gongsun Shu proclaimed himself emperor in Chengdu, Qiao Xuan was summoned to office. Qiao did not report. Gongshu Shu, angered by this rejection, sent the grand administrator[24] to personally appoint Qiao in 36 CE. In addition to the "imperial appointment," the envoy also carried a measure of poisoned liquor, purportedly only to frighten Qiao Xuan into accepting the post.[25] The *Later Han History* account includes a dialogue between the grand administrator and Qiao Xuan. It reads:

> [Grand Administrator:] "You are a man of high purity and the court bestows its favor. If you do not accept this appointment, you will certainly bring harm upon yourself."
>
> Qiao Xuan looked toward the heavens and sighed, saying, "Tang Yao 唐堯 was a great sage, yet Xu You 許由 was ashamed to serve.[26] King Wu of Zhou attained virtue, but Bo Yi 伯夷 preserved his hunger.[27] What kind of men were these? What kind of man am I? I preserve my lofty ambitions and die with regret!"

Qiao Xuan drank the poisoned liquor and died in the presence of his son, Qiao Ying 譙瑛.[28] Distressed and concerned over the impact of his father's action, Qiao Ying immediately offered eight million in cash to the grand administrator and asked him to convey the sum to Gongsun Shu to obtain forgiveness for Qiao Xuan's suicide.[29] He then secretly buried his father in the wilderness. Later, after the Han court regained control of the region, Qiao Xuan's younger brother, Qiao Qing 譙慶, submitted a complaint to the newly enthroned Emperor Guangwu 光武 (r. 25–57 CE) over the treatment of his family at the hands of Gongsun Shu. The emperor was moved and ordered the local commandery administration to present animals for sacrifice and return the Qiao family's cash.[30]

For his refusal to serve the regimes of Wang Mang and Gongsun Shu, Qiao Xuan was remembered as a man of purity and integrity, qualities immortalized in a verse composed by an anonymous poet from the capital. It read:

Stern, stern the pure official,	肅肅清節士
Holding to virtue, he was truly firm in doing what was right.	執德寔固貞
Avoiding the crude and offering his own life,	違餓以授命
We shall never forget his honorable reputation.[31]	沒世遺令聲

In addition to this praise for Qiao Xuan's moral character, Qiao Xuan was also regarded as a unique intellectual of his time. Fan Yan wrote, "At that time, fighting had gone on for years and none were able to cultivate the scholarly vocation. Only Qiao Xuan was able to search the various thinkers and study the classics."[32] Unfortunately, there are no details on Qiao Xuan's scholarly activities. The intellectual and public service aspects of Qiao Xuan's life were carried on by his son, Qiao Ying, who held several imperial-level governmental posts, and was regarded as an expert in the *Changes*, later tutoring Emperor Ming 明 (r. 58–76 CE) in the text.[33]

The tradition of scholarship and political acuity followed by Qiao men since the early Han continued into the early third century with the life of Qiao Zhou's father, Qiao Bing. Though there is little information on Qiao Bing other than a brief mention in the *Records of the Three States* biography of his son and a fragmented encomium in the *Records of the States South of Mount Hua*, these sparse accounts note his intellectual and political orientations. In the *Records of the Three States*, Qiao Bing was described as a master of the *Hallowed Documents*, as well as comprehending various canonical texts, charts, and apocryphal texts, indicating some skill in the mantic traditions of the Chengdu Plain. Qiao Bing rejected numerous appointments offered by the province and commandery, and was ultimately named preceptor-companion attendant—a consulting post with no set duties.[34] This brief biographical notice is supplemented by two short mentions in Chang Qu's *Record of the States South of Mount Hua*. There, Qiao Bing received high praise, with Chang Qu including Qiao Bing in a list of the leading scholars of the age.[35]

Additionally, Chang Qu composed an encomium for Qiao Bing. Unfortunately, this encomium has not survived intact and is missing its first two graphs—the laudatory adjectives. The extant piece reads, "**, the summoned scholar Qiao Bing, appellative Rongshi, was a man of Xichongguo and the father of Qiao Zhou."[36] From this limited amount of source material, Qiao Bing's reputation as a broad scholar and recluse can hardly be confirmed, yet his greatest claim to fame was his son, Qiao Zhou.

From these brief accounts of Qiao family members, several generalizations about the family can be made. First, the Qiaos had been residents of Ba since at least the early Han period. While it remains unclear when the clan had migrated to the Chengdu Plain, it does not appear likely that they were natives of the region. We may gently speculate that the clan was resettled during the great Qin social experiment of the third century BCE.[37] Moreover, the Qiaos were clearly in possession of considerable financial resources. The anecdote in which Qiao Ying presented a huge sum of cash to the commandery administrator on the suicide of his father is evidence of the family's wealth. While the historical records do not afford us a glimpse at the sources of the Qiaos' fortune, their location in a fertile portion of eastern Sichuan would seem to indicate that some combination of agricultural, commercial, and industrial pursuits contributed in part to the family's income.[38] Regardless of their origins or economic activities, it is obvious that, during the Han period, members of the family used their economic situation to develop themselves as an educated and cultured *shi* clan. In particular, the scholarly reputations of Qiao Xuan, Qiao Ying, and Qiao Bing were lauded by later historians who noted individual Qiaos' mastery of various canonical texts and the local traditions in the mantic arts.

For the Qiao men, education also translated into governmental service. Records indicate that Qiaos had been selected for governmental service at various levels and had been active in their offices, including posts at the Han imperial court. While the information at hand is too vague to support a statement such as 'the Qiao clan held influence at the Han court,' Qiaos appear to have had access to the throne and were not timid about speaking their minds. Qiao Long, Qiao Xuan, and Qiao Ying each demonstrated a willingness to remonstrate to their sovereigns, and none appears to have suffered serious consequences from these actions. In addition to their outspokenness, members of the family also appeared willing to leave office to preserve a higher moral standard. The case of Qiao Xuan's retirement to avoid serving Wang Mang and his suicide over a summons by Gongsun Shu were the foundation of his reputation. Thus, the characterization of the Qiaos as a wealthy, educated, and politically active clan is well-founded, and to conclude, as did Chang Qu, that the Qiao family was among the leading families of the commandery is unavoidable. Finally, the Qiaos' ability to maintain their position in society and in government for roughly three centuries marks the clan as one of the great ones of not only the commandery, but certainly of the province, and perhaps even the Han empire.

YOUTH AND EDUCATION

The principle source of information on the life of Qiao Zhou comes from a biography written by his student Chen Shou, contained in the forty-second fascicle of the *Records of the Three States*.[39] While there are obvious biases to be negotiated in reading the life of a teacher as told by the student, Chen's account provides a solid outline of the life and career of Qiao Zhou, as well as preserves several specimens of Qiao's ouevre. Specific problems of the biography will be discussed. However, at this point, Chen's work will serve as the basis for a brief report of the life and career of Qiao Zhou.[40]

Chen Shou's "Biography of Qiao Zhou" follows the usual format of the standard histories in its presentation of the life of Qiao Zhou. The account begins with the recitation of Qiao's name, appellative, and native place. Chen Shou makes no mention of the date of Qiao Zhou's birth, but, based on the recorded date of death (270 CE) and Qiao's prophesy regarding his age at the time of his impending death (past seventy but not yet seventy-two *sui*), we can extrapolate the date to be approximately 200 CE.[41] Chen Shou then offers a brief biography of Qiao Zhou's father, Qiao Bing (previously summarized). A description of Qiao Zhou's youth follows this pro forma introduction. Chen Shou notes that Qiao Bing died while Qiao Zhou was a child, and Zhou was raised by his mother and an older brother. Next, Qiao Zhou's scholarly interests are outlined, though in more detail than the typical standard history trope of "he was fond of learning in his youth." Here, Chen Shou notes Qiao Zhou's academic interests emerging as Qiao entered adulthood. Chen describes the breadth of Qiao Zhou's academic interests as ranging from the *Liujing* 六經 [*Six Canonical Texts*] to astronomy, but having little interest in the writings of the various philosophers. Adding a touch of personality to this narrative, Chen Shou notes, "When he read the canon, he happily laughed to himself and forgot about sleep and food."[42]

The biography describes Qiao's family as poor, though it is unclear whether the entire Qiao clan had suffered a reversal of fortune or if this statement simply refers to the nuclear family bereaved of Qiao Bing. At any rate, Qiao Zhou's economic situation appears to have differed greatly from his ancestors' during the preceding centuries. The enterprise of scholarship—the hallmark of a male from a *shi* clan—was not backed by vast financial resources in the early life of Qiao Zhou. Chen states, "His family was poor, and he never once asked about work."[43] Chen's portrayal of his teacher emphasizes the devotion of Qiao Zhou to the academic enterprise in general, and supports the Qiao family's self-image as cultured gentlemen. Particularly in times of economic hardship, Qiao's rejection of material comforts in order to pursue his studies would have served to maintain and even enhance the family's reputation as scholars.

Although Chen Shou's biography of Qiao Zhou makes no mention of where Qiao received his early training, information scattered throughout the biographies of other Sichuan intellectuals in the *Records of the Three States* sheds some light on this issue. First, we may suppose that Qiao Zhou received some instruction in the home from his father, Qiao Bing. As noted earlier, little information is available on Qiao Bing, other than the mention of his specialization in the *Hallowed Documents* and mastery of several other unnamed canonical texts, and the staples of prophetic-apocryphal studies—charts and apocryphal texts—in the *Records of the Three States* biography of his son, Qiao Zhou.[44] Particularly unfortunate is the lack of information on Qiao Bing's own academic training, for none of the extant records makes any mention of where or with whom he may have studied. Qiao Bing was a member of the same generation as the noted intellectuals Zhou Qun, Du Wei, He Zong, and Du Qiong, and, on the basis of his intellectual interests noted by Chen Shou, it seems plausible that Qiao Bing may have studied under one of the previous generation's masters of the Yang family traditions—that is, one of Yang Xu's disciples. If he had studied under one of Yang Xu's more noted pupils, such as Dong Fu or Ren An, one would presume that Chen Shou would have included this information. As it stands, the identity of Qiao Bing's teacher(s) remains a mystery. Regardless, Chang Qu notes Qiao Bing's reputation as one of the leading intellectuals of his generation.[45]

It is unclear what direct impact Qiao Bing may have had on the education of his son. The *Records of the Three States* notes that Qiao Bing died while Qiao Zhou was still a child (*you* 幼), and that Qiao Zhou's immersion in academic studies did not begin until he was grown (*chang* 長). The language denoting Qiao Zhou's ages at the time of his father's death and the beginning of his active pursuit of learning is vague, but since Qiao Zhou was appointed to his first official post around the age of twenty-three, his studies certainly began well before that time. Regardless, it appears that Qiao Zhou had but a brief opportunity to study with his father. Rather, two other important Sichuan intellectuals set Qiao Zhou on his scholarly path.

From the noted intellectual Du Qiong,[46] Qiao Zhou seems to have been instructed to some degree in the Yang family traditions of celestial observation and prophesy. The historical record presents Du Qiong as a reluctant teacher of this art. In the *Records of the Three States* biography of Du Qiong, Chen Shou notes Du's refusal to "observe the celestial patterns and discourse on them."[47] According to Chen, Qiao Zhou often questioned the older scholar on the reason behind this. Du Qiong's reply demonstrates both the regard in which the prophetic arts were held and the difficulty in obtaining a mastery of the skill. He said:

> If you wish to understand this art, it is very difficult. You must observe for yourself and become familiar with their [i.e., the celestial bodies] form and color. You cannot rely upon other people. Morning and night you must suffer and toil. And after this, you will know [the art]. Then you will worry about [their secrets] leaking out. It is better not to know them at all! For this reason, I do not look anymore.[48]

Chen Shou does not mention a time frame for this encounter between Qiao Zhou and Du Qiong, but given the elementary nature of the questions posed by Qiao, we might suppose that the meetings occured while Qiao Zhou was still rather young. It also seems likely that Qiao was attempting to supplement his knowledge of the canonical texts and their interpretative traditions with additional information from the secret teachings of the Yang family traditions.

This passage also reveals something of both Du Qiong's and Qiao Zhou's learning and dispositions. Du Qiong clearly possessed the skills necessary to interpret the celestial omens and portents, yet chose to remain aloof from the political affairs that this knowledge was intimately linked to. As for Qiao Zhou, it is unclear what background he may have had in the art of celestial observation and prophesy prior to his consultation with Du Qiong. Nevertheless, Qiao appears to have paid mixed attention to Du's admonition. Chen Shou notes, "[Qiao Zhou] had inclinations to understand the celestial patterns, but he did not allow them to keep his interest,"[49] but this statement may be more indicative of Chen Shou's own skepticism about the arts of prophesy than an accurate reflection of Qiao Zhou's interests. Later traditions, including the fictional *Three Kingdoms*, hold Qiao as an expert in the observational prophetic arts, and several later gazetteers include entries identifying sites said to be associated with Qiao Zhou's practice of the art. The nineteenth-century *Sichuan tongzhi* 四川同志 [*Comprehensive Gazetteer of Sichuan*] notes that five *li* north of the commandery seat in Nanchong was a structure known as "Qiao Zhou's Watching the Stars Terrace" (Qiao Zhou *guanxing tai* 譙周觀星臺), located at the site of Qiao's old home.[50] The *Nanchong xianzhi* 南充縣志 [*Gazetteer of Nanchong County*] records, "Next to Qiao Zhou's old residence there is a dirt hill two *zhang* in height [4.6 meters]. Its top is flat and three *zhang* across [6.9 meters]. Tradition has it that Qiao Zhou watched the stars there."[51] It is unclear whether this structure was built before or after Qiao's consultation with Du Qiong, or even if such a platform was built and used by Qiao Zhou. Given the prominent role that stargazing plays in the literary representation of Qiao Zhou in the *Three Kingdoms* and its later influence, the possibility also exists that these gazetteer accounts—all compiled after the composition of the novel—are simply linking a local site to the figure of Qiao Zhou in accordance with a popular literary view rather than any historical evidence. Regardless, the tradition of Qiao's practice of the celestial observation prophesies remains strong. As we shall see, however, most of Qiao Zhou's surviving prophesies were not based on the observations of the celestial patterns, but rather on prophetic wordplay.

Du Qiong's influence on Qiao Zhou in this regard is also obvious. The *Records of the Three States* describes another conversation between Qiao and Du which reads:

> Qiao Zhou took advantage of the opportunity [to question Du Qiong] and asked, "Previously, Appointed Gentleman Zhou [Shu][52] considered 'That which faces the path' to be Wei.[53] How did he determine this?" Du Qiong

> replied, saying, "'Wei' is the name of a lookout tower above a gate. It faces the road and is lofty. The sagacious have only spoken of this [i.e., the fall of the Han dynasty] in terms of this metaphor." He went on and asked [Qiao] Zhou, "Could it be that there is something [in this explanation] that you still feel strangely about?" [Qiao] Zhou said, "I still do not understand." Du Qiong then said, "The ancients, in naming official positions did not call them bureaus (*cao* 曹). Beginning in the Han and down to the present, named officials are all called bureaus. [Military] personnel (*li* 吏) are spoken of as serving bureaus. This is probably the intent of Heaven."[54]

The entire prophesy turns on a homophonous pun. "Cao," the term for "bureau," was also the surname of the rulers of Wei who accepted the ritual abdication of the final Han emperor. To say that the officials belonged to the bureaus and the soldiers served the bureaus was also to say that the officials belonged to the Caos and the soldiers served the Caos and their state, Wei. The historical records give no indication of Qiao Zhou's response to this explanation, or to the degree in which Qiao accepted the prophesy.[55]

In the *Records of the Three States* biography of Du Qiong, Chen Shou notes the scholar's death and remarks, "There was none to carry on his inner teachings, so Qiao Zhou followed [Du] Qiong's words, thereupon analogizing them and expanding them."[56] The continued influence of Du Qiong's teachings on Qiao Zhou can be seen in repeated episodes throughout Qiao's later political career, and will be discussed in detail later. What is obvious at this point, however, is that Qiao Zhou was a regular visitor to the elder Du Qiong, and that Du's "inner teachings," again, likely the core of the Yang family traditions, were passed on to Qiao Zhou. Thus, one facet of Qiao Zhou's later reputation as one skilled in reading the celestial signs and interpreting prophetic wordplay can be firmly linked to his training with Du Qiong, and places Qiao squarely within the Yang family intellectual lineage.

The other significant portion of Qiao Zhou's intellectual reputation—as a critical scholar of the canon and historian—has its roots in his relationship with a recluse-turned-official from Guanghan named Qin Mi. Chen Shou's biography of Qin notes in stereotypical fashion that "as a youth, [Qin Mi] possessed a talent for scholarship."[57] Throughout the course of his biography of Qin Mi, Chen Shou quotes several passages from Qin's writings and purported dialogues from which we can compile a list of texts, canonical and otherwise, over which Qin appeared to possess some degree of mastery, resulting in an image of a broadly read scholar who appears to have been heavily trained in the canonical texts with substantial interests in history (ancient and local) and inclinations toward mystical Daoist thought.[58]

Additionally, we may also assume some relationship with his co-commanderymen, the Yang family and their intellectual traditions. The *Records of the Three States* contains a memorial submitted by Qin Mi to the shepherd of Yi Province, Liu Yan, recommending Ren An for a governmental post.[59]

While this is insufficient evidence to argue that Qin was a student of Ren An, the memorial does illustrate Qin's familiarity with Ren's reputation and connects, albeit superficially, Qin Mi to this important regional intellectual tradition. Efforts to locate indications of a mastery of the Yang family traditions of celestial observation and prophesy by Qin Mi in the surviving historical records, however, reveal little. From this evidence the image of a different sort of scholar emerges.

Chen Shou's biography of Qin Mi emphasizes two aspects of Qin's life and activity: his aversion to public service and desire to remain a recluse-scholar, and his critical view toward the received canon and accepted opinions of history. He frequently rejected the appeals of local officials to take office, citing various canonical texts to support his reclusive stance. In particular, he espoused the view that the wisdom and principles contained in the canon were suited as models for contemporary affairs. He also appears to have been especially critical of works outside the orthodox canon, though his conceptions of these bounds seems somewhat arbitrary at times. The *Record of the Three States* contains a lengthy discourse on the canon offered in response to Li Quan's[60] request to borrow Qin's copy of the *Stratagems of the Warring States*. When Li Quan explained his reason for wanting to read the text as part of his quest to become a great gentleman through broad learning after the manner of Confucius and Zhuang Zun, Qin Mi retorted:

> Except for the books that were historical records or Zhou dynasty charts, Confucius did not select from them. Except for the Way that was vacuous and natural, Yan Ping did not develop it. The sea in accepting silt, each year must agitate itself clean. [Though] a gentleman seeks broad knowledge, he does not look upon that which is improper.[61]

The *Stratagems*, according to Qin Mi, did not meet the criteria of the classical or Daoist canon, and were improper for study by a gentleman. Qin's response also included numerous allusions to the canonical *Zuo Tradition*, *Hallowed Documents*, and *Changes*, each supporting his argument for a moral and proper educational curriculum for a gentleman.

In addition to his devotion to the canon, Qin Mi also demonstrated a deep knowledge of the history of the Chengdu Plain. Two anecdotes in the *Records of the Three States* illustrate this aspect of Qin's scholarly interests. In the first, Qin Mi chastises Wang Shang 王商[62] for his desire to erect a shrine honoring two local worthies, Zhuang Zun and Li Hong 李弘,[63] noting that the only reason that people of his age knew of Zhuang and Li was because they were mentioned in the writings of Yang Xiong and Sima Xiangru. Because of this, Qin Mi argued, Wang Shang should instead erect shrines for Yang Xiong and Sima Xiangru.[64] With this view, Qin Mi demonstrates a veneration of the historian over the historical figure. The second anecdote displays the extension of Qin Mi's knowledge of local history beyond the historical personages of the recent past and illustrates something of the localist agenda that he, and later his student Qiao Zhou, would advocate. In this case, a group of Central Plains officers serving in Chengdu question Qin Mi on how the local worthies compared to those of the Chinese heartland. Qin's reply turns the question slightly and outlines a history of the region, linking the basin to the divine and legendary figures. Qin argues:

> Shu has Mount Minfu 汶阜 with the Jiang (i.e., Yangzi) flowing from its waist. The Celestial Lord used [this place] to gather felicity and the divinities used [this place] to establish blessings. For these reasons, [the Jiang] is able to water a thousand *li* of wilderness. The Jiang is the head of the Huai 淮, the Ji 濟, and all of the four rivers. This is my first point.[65]
>
> Yu was born at Shiniu 石牛, the site of present-day Minshan 汶山 commandery.[66] Previously, Yao encountered the floods and Gun was unable to control them. Yu dredged the Jiang and breached the He. [The flood] poured eastward to the sea, saving the people from harm. Of those who have labored for the people, none can surpass [Yu]. This is my second point.[67]
>
> The Celestial Lord practiced his government in the astral sectors of *fang* 房 and *xin* 心 and set policy in the astral sectors of *shen* 參 and *fa* 伐. *Shen* and *fa* are the astral sectors of Yi Province.[68] The Three August Ones rode their carriage out of Gukou 谷口. This is the site of present-day Xiegu 斜谷.[69] These are the paths that separate the provinces. The illustrious governor has used lofty ideas to discuss this. How does this compare to [other provinces] of the subcelestial realm?[70]

This overview of Sichuan history is both unorthodox and partisan. It presents the traditional sage-kings of the past in a context different from that of the standard accounts, situating their activities on the Chengdu Plain rather than the Yellow River basin. This response thus meets its intent to illustrate the long-standing importance of the region in the affairs of the Chinese empire by recounting local lore linking the region to the highest antiquity.

Chen Shou, in yet another passage on Qin Mi's intellectual activities, hints at this critical and unorthodox aspect of Qin's scholarship. He writes, "Previously, Qin Mi had seen a discourse on the genealogy of the thearchs which claimed the Five Thearchs were of the same lineage.[71] [Qin] Mi argued the reasons for why this was not true. He also discoursed on the tradition that the august thearchs and hegemons had raised dragons. [These arguments] were deeply principled."[72] Unfortunately, these writings were not preserved. Yet, despite the relatively limited amount of material available on the intellectual activities of Qin Mi, based on surviving sources and the appraisals of his contemporaries, he appears to have been a man of extraordinary intelligence and creativity, demonstrating a mastery of a wide range of canonical texts and a penetrating view of history. Both aspects of Qin's intellectual prowess influenced his pupil, Qiao Zhou.

The details of the relationship between Qin Mi and Qiao Zhou remain unclear, but several extant sources provide information on this intellectual pairing. Chen Shou writes, "Qiao Yunnan, as a youth, often went to inquire of [Qin Mi], and recorded [Qin's] words in his *Chunqiu ranfou lun* 春秋然否論 [*Discourse on Truths and Falsehoods in the Spring and Autumn*]."[73] Chang Qu's biography of Qin Mi concludes with the following statement: "[Qin] Mi possessed a deep and penetrating logic, and his disciple Qiao Zhou transmitted his vocation."[74] Even with these two statements, the precise nature of the relationship between Qin and Qiao remains somewhat vague. Chen Shou seems to imply that Qiao Zhou was a regular visitor of the older scholar, but not necessarily a formal student. Chang Qu's use of the term "disciple" (*dizi* 弟子) would imply otherwise. Nevertheless, both Chen and Chang note the role of Qiao Zhou in transmitting the teachings of Qin Mi. The *Records of the Three States* mentions the name of one particular text, *Discourse on the Truths and Falsehoods in the Spring and Autumn [Annals]* as containing the words of Qin Mi. It was presumably part of Qiao Zhou's longer work, *Discourses on the Truths and Falsehoods in the Five Canonical Texts*.[75] From Chen Shou's terse statement, however, it is unclear whether Qiao Zhou collected writings from the hand of Qin Mi and included them in his larger work, or if Qiao simply followed the ideas expressed to him during his visits with Qin and then wrote them himself. Regardless, comparing the characterization of Qin Mi's scholarship gleaned from his extant writings and descriptions offered by Chen Shou and Chang Qu with the extant works of Qiao Zhou, we can see striking similarities.

The preceding gleanings from the historical documents provide a general outline of Qiao Zhou's academic training, highlighting various aspects of Chengdu Plain scholarship and its connection with Qiao. While it is unknown what, if anything, Qiao Zhou may have studied with his father, Qiao Bing, the family's reputation as scholars and his father's individual esteem as a leading intellectual of the age certainly inspired or motivated the young Qiao Zhou toward intellectual activity. With his father's early passing, Qiao Zhou was forced to seek out additional instructors. While the formal nature of the tutorial relationships between Qiao Zhou and his two known teachers Du Qiong and Qin Mi remains unclear, in the descriptions of the lives and scholarship of these two men we see similarities to characteristics of Qiao Zhou's surviving scholarship and activity. From his consultations with Du Qiong, Qiao Zhou appears to have gained knowledge in the Yang family tradition of prophetic-apocryphal learning, while from his study with Qin Mi he developed a critical eye toward and a devotion to the canonical texts, as well as insights into new historiographical techniques. As we continue to examine the political and intellectual activity of Qiao Zhou in the following chapters, we will see further evidence of the influence of these two teachers.

CHAPTER 3

Scholarship and the State

Born in the eastern half of the Chengdu Plain during the turmoil of the late second century, Qiao Zhou came of age in an era of warlords competing for control of the moribund Han dynasty. Moreover, his training in the mantic arts, the canon, and history provided him with a set of skills in demand by local leaders and led to a lifetime of official appointments. Qiao was, like most early Chinese intellectuals, what would be termed today a "public intellectual." That is, he used his academic training in a public venue; in Qiao's case, as a government official. An examination of Qiao Zhou's public career illuminates the points of intersection between the worlds of scholarship and politics, and serves as a point of comparison for the more private aspects of Qiao's intellectual activity, to be discussed in the following chapters.

The Chengdu Plain had been occupied by overlords only nominally loyal to the Han since 189 CE when Liu Yan entered the region as shepherd[1] of Yi Province and fought local peasant rebels and local elites. Liu Yan's imperial ambitions were derailed by the rupture of an absess on his back which killed him in 194 CE.[2] His son, Liu Zhang inherited his father's administration in Chengdu and continued his father's feuds with various powerful locals, including the leader of the Daoist theocracy in Hanzhong, Zhang Lu.[3] In 211 CE, faced with widespread defection of his former allies, Liu Zhang invited Liu Bei to enter Yi Province and assist in his battle against Zhang Lu and put down popular unrest in the province.[4] But when Liu Bei entered Ba commandery, many of Liu Zhang's former supporters enthusiastically welcomed him and pledged their support and troops to Liu Bei. In Jian'an 19 (214 CE), Liu Bei turned on Liu Zhang in Chengdu, and after a brief siege of the city, Liu Zhang tearfully surrendered to Liu Bei, leaving Liu Bei with the title of shepherd of Yi Province and undisputed control of the region.[5] Liu Bei administered the province in the name of the Han emperor for six years (214–20 CE), continuing his military campaigns against other warlords.

WEI
Shu-Han
State Capital
Provincial Seat
Commandery Seat
Prefectural Seat
Town
Yellow River
Yangzi River
Yong
(Chang'an)
Qinling Mts.
Mianyang
Hanzhong
Han River
Yi Han (Jialing) River
Yinping
Shou River
Fu River
Daba Mts.
Jian'ge Pass
Zitong
Baxi
Fu
Xichongguo
Badong
Dangqu River
Guanghan
Anhan
CHENGDU
Yi Province
Shu Commandery
Yangzi River
Daxue Mts.
Qianwei
Luo River
Ba
(Jiangzhou)
Fuling
Dalei Mts.
SHU-HAN
WU
Yunnan
Yongchang
Kunming
Dianchi Lake
Dianchi
Mekong River
N
W
E
S
Gulf of Tonkin

Map 2. Shu-Han

Though Liu Bei seized power in Chengdu as a nominal subject of the Han imperial court, he quickly took on the trappings of a would-be dynast himself. According to his biography in the *Records of the Three States*, with his purported aristocratic lineage[6] and despite his immediate impoverished situation, Liu Bei harbored imperial ambitions. The biography describes Liu Bei as one who was not interested in study, but rather preferred dogs, horses, music, fine clothing, associating with rogues, and engaging in swordplay. He was charismatic and well-liked and quickly developed a following of martial comrades. His personality enabled him to float from patron to patron amid the turmoil of the age, and eventually allowed him to gather a cohort of loyal followers and establish his own dynastic enterprise on the Chengdu Plain.[7]

Following Liu Bei's conquest of Hanzhong in 218 CE, several of his leading military officers submitted a memorial to the Han court outlining Liu Bei's accomplishments and criticizing Cao Cao for usurping governmental power. They asked the emperor to appoint Liu Bei as "King of Hanzhong" (Hanzhong wang 漢中王) in recognition of his service to the court.[8] Undoubtedly the submitters of this document knew of Cao Cao's control over the emperor—Cao had taken Emperor Xian into a form of 'protective custody' in 196 CE—and the memorial was clearly meant for Cao Cao's eyes. Not waiting for the emperor's reply, Liu Bei was named King of Hanzhong at Mianyang 沔陽.[9] Liu Bei immediately submitted his own memorial to the emperor, affirming his loyalty to the Han court and denouncing Cao Cao's seizure of imperial power. Knowing that Cao Cao had control of the emperor, Liu Bei's memorial was more likely a challenge to Cao Cao than a sincere expression of loyalty to the emperor.[10] Liu Bei then moved his administrative headquarters to Chengdu and continued to oversee his military campaigns against both Cao Cao and Sun Quan.

Events of the following year brought Liu Bei's own imperial ambitions into the open. On the *guimao* 癸卯 day of the eleventh month of Jian'an 25 (11 December 220 CE), Cao Cao's son Cao Pi 曹丕 (187–226 CE) accepted the ritual abdication of Emperor Xian, formally marking the end of the Han dynasty.[11] Cao Pi's declaration of his founding of the Wei dynasty dramatically changed the political landscape of China. In Chengdu, a rumor circulated claiming Cao Pi had killed Emperor Xian, but, in fact, the emperor was not dead. After abdicating to Cao Pi, the deposed ruler was given benefice as the Duke of Shanyang 山陽, where he lived for another fourteen years.[12] Nevertheless, when Liu Bei heard the rumor of the emperor's death, he donned mourning attire and bestowed the "posthumous" title of Emperor Min the Filial (Xiao Min huangdi 孝愍皇帝) upon the deposed ruler. Shortly thereafter, on the *bingwu* 丙午 day of the fourth month of Jian'an 26 (221 CE),[13] Liu Bei proclaimed himself emperor of Han at Chengdu. The following year, Sun Quan made public his own dynastic ambitions and named himself emperor of Wu. In this fashion, the Han dynasty was laid to rest, three independent states were established, Chengdu became an "imperial" capital, and Qiao

Zhou began to use his intellectual skills of prophesy, the canon, and history in the service of the state.[14]

THE FOUNDING OF SHU-HAN

The historical records note Qiao Zhou's initial foray into the political arena as a young man of approximately twenty-one *sui* when he joined the group of officials urging Liu Bei to claim the Han throne for himself after news of Emperor Xian's "death" reached Chengdu.[15] According to the *Records of the Three States*, following Liu Bei's bestowal of posthumous titles on the last Han emperor, a steady stream of interpretations of prophesies and omens flooded into Chengdu. On the basis of these signs, twelve individuals, identified in the document by their offices, jointly submitted a memorial to Liu Bei in an effort to convince him to proclaim himself emperor.[16]

The memorial presents "evidence" in the form of prophetic wordplay and celestial observations, often linking the circumstances surrounding the founding of the Han by Liu Bang 劉邦 (256–195 BCE) with the contemporary situation of Liu Bei. Opening with a brief introductory testimony to the nature of political prophesy, the memorial begins, "Your subjects have heard that the *River Charts*, the *Luo Documents*, the prophesies of the five canonical texts, and that which Confucius has explicated [display] their intent from afar."[17] Thus testifying to the ability of these apocryphal-prophetic texts to foretell the future, the memorial then presents four passages from various texts, each relying upon vague language with tenuous connections to the events at hand to persuade Liu Bei to take the throne.

The first passage, taken from *Luo shu zhenyao du* 洛書甄曜度 [*Explications of the River Documents*], reads:

> 赤三日德昌，九世會備。合為帝際。
>
> Vermillion: the potency of three suns shines. Nine generations have gathered and completed, conjoining as an imperial lineage.[18]

While offering no written explanation, the passage is ripe with meaning. Vermillion, or red, was the color associated with the Han dynasty. The three suns refer to the three epochal founders: Liu Bang, Liu Xiu [Emperor Guangwu], and Liu Bei, while the nine generations point to the major emperors of the Later Han: Emperors Guangwu, Ming 明 (r. 58–76 CE), Zhang 章 (r. 76–89 CE), He 和 (r. 89–106 CE), An 安 (r. 107–26 CE), Shun, Huan 桓 (r. 147–68 CE), Ling, and Xian.[19] The term "completion" in this prophesy is key, for *bei* 備, or "completion," is the given name of Liu Bei. The prophesy's conclusion can then be construed as "nine generations [of Later Han rulers] have converged on [Liu] Bei, conjoining with this imperial lineage."

Other prophesies cited in the memorial employ similar rhetoric. A passage from *Luo shu lu yun qi* 洛書錄運期 [*River Documents' Record of the Movement of the Seasons*] says:

九侯七傑爭命民炊骸，道路籍籍履人頭，誰使主者玄且來。

Nine marquises and seven heroes battle for the Mandate, and the people eat gristle. On the roadways are scattered piles of human heads, trampled. Who will rule them? The Mystery thus comes.[20]

The opening lines of this prophesy offer a vivid description of the chaos of the last decades of the Han, including the human toll of the civil war between contending warlords. The answer to the question of "Who will rule them?" contains the key link to Liu Bei. "Mystery" (*xuan* 玄) is the first graph of Liu Bei's appellative, Xuande 玄德 (Mysterious Potency), again signifying divine or supernatural approval of Liu Bei's would-be imperial venture.[21]

Following this presentation of word prophesies linking Liu Bei to the imperial enterprise, the memorial then offers verification of another sort: celestial omens. The memorial notes the observation of "several yellow pneuma in the southwest," along with "auspicious clouds and favorable winds," and additional indications in the stars of the dipper constellation. Interpreting these signs from apocryphal-prophetic texts, the memorial argues, "There must be a Son of Heaven emerge from that place [i.e., the southwest]."[22] Citing more recent observations of the heavens, the memorial links the movements of the stars at the present time with those some four hundred years earlier at the time of the Han founding. The text reads:

加是年太白、熒惑、填星，常從歲星相追。近初興，五星從歲星謀；歲星主義，漢位在西，義之上方，故漢法常以歲星候人主。當有聖主起於此州，以致中興。

This year, Venus, Mars, and Saturn have followed Jupiter. [When they came] in close proximity, Han first arose. The five planets[23] follow the motion of Jupiter; thus, Jupiter is their leader. The position of Han is in the west; this is the position of the leader. Therefore, the methods of Han have always considered Jupiter as the principal forecaster. There will be a sagacious ruler arising from this province who will lead to the resurgence [of the Han].[24]

Summarizing and justifying these arguments, the memorial notes that while "the Emperor at Xu 許 (i.e., Emperor Xian whose court had been relocated to Xu by Cao Cao)[25] was still alive," officials did not dare to point out these heavenly omens foretelling of Liu Bei's rise to the imperial throne out of deference to the sitting ruler. Moreover, the memorial claims, the formal and taboo names of Liu Bei are frequently manifest in the prophesies, and the number of celestial signs is great. Quoting the *Changes*, the memorial urges Liu Bei to follow the will of Heaven:

聖王先天而天不違，後天而奉天時。

When the sagacious ruler precedes Heaven, Heaven is not contrary to him; when he follows Heaven, he obeys the timing of its movements.[26]

The memorial concludes with a plea for Liu Bei to

願大王應天順民，速即洪業，以寧海內

follow Heaven and the masses, and quickly complete this great enterprise in order to bring felicity to the land within the seas.[27]

A second memorial, submitted by six additional officials of the province was also submitted.[28] This document notes over eight hundred reports of omens and interpretations of prophesies, including the sighting of a yellow dragon mounting the clouds near the Han River. The second memorial urges Liu Bei to do likewise and mount the throne as emperor of Han, again noting the similarities between the cases of Liu Bang and Liu Bei. In the end, Liu Bei acquiesced and proclaimed himself emperor of Han with his capital in Chengdu.[29]

Although Qiao Zhou's name is listed in the final position of the list of signatories of the first memorial urging Liu Bei to take the throne—a position typically denoting the author of the document—there remains some controversy surrounding Qiao's participation in the event. Lu Bi's 盧弼 (1876–1967) *Collected Explanations of the Records of the Three States* presents several arguments against Qiao's inclusion among the signers and presentors of the memorial. These arguments can be classified into two general views: age and textual error. For example, Gu Yanwu 顧炎武 (1613–1682) calculated Qiao Zhou's age at the time of the submission of the memorial to be twenty-three *sui*, and thus not old enough to be included among the group of older supporters of Liu Bei.[30] Opposing the inclusion of Qiao Zhou among the list of signatories on other grounds, Zhao Yiqing 趙一清 (ca. 1710–ca. 1764), Shen Jiaben 沈家本 (1840–1913), and Qian Yiji 錢儀吉 all offered various theories of textual corruption in the *Records of the Three States* account, proposing various other individuals in the place of Qiao Zhou.[31] These arguments by Qing dynasty scholars have also been accepted by modern scholars, including Ren Naiqiang.[32]

These arguments against Qiao Zhou's participation based on age and claims of textual corruption should not be accepted unquestioningly. On the matter of Qiao's young age as a disqualifying factor, recent studies have shown that, during this period, the average age of appointment to political office was twenty-two *sui*.[33] Depending on one's interpretation of Qiao Zhou's deathbed prophesy, this could have been his precise age at the time. The various claims of corruption to the text of both the *Records of the Three States* and *Records of the States South of Mount Hua* defy logic. All extant editions of both texts list Qiao Zhou among the signers of the memorial. Additionally, both texts are generally regarded as relatively free of textual corruption.

Finally, although Qiao Zhou was unquestionably younger that the others, he is nevertheless linked to the group in a meaningful fashion. The content of the memorial—the interpretation of prophetic wordplay and celestial omens—fits closely with the academic training of Qiao Zhou. Both his study of celestial portents with Du Qiong (himself another signatory of the memorial) and numerous other surviving prophesies attributed to Qiao Zhou demonstrate that the young Qiao possessed the ability to read and discourse on these matters. Chen Shou's biography of Du Qiong emphasizes the influence of the elder scholar on Qiao Zhou's intellectual development, especially in the field of prophesy, noting Qiao's instruction in both the observation of celestial patterns and word prophesy.[34] Since several of the examples offered by Chen Shou to illustrate the influence of Du Qiong on Qiao Zhou relate not to the founding of Shu-Han, but rather its demise, they will be discussed later.

EDUCATING THE HEIR AND THE PROVINCE

After the establishment of Liu Bei's imperial court in Chengdu, Qiao Zhou formally entered the service of the Liu clan and Shu-Han. According to the *Records of the Three States*, after Zhuge Liang was named shepherd of Yi Province in 223 CE, he appointed Qiao Zhou to the position of attendant for the encouragement of education.[35] There is little information on the nature of this office; and in fact, the title appears only in the context of the state of Shu-Han, and was attached to only three individuals: Zhang Shuang, Yin Mo, and Qiao Zhou.[36] Yin Mo's biography notes that he received his appointment from Liu Bei while Liu was serving as shepherd of the province.[37] That Yin Mo and Qiao Zhou each received their appointments from the shepherd of the province would seem to indicate that the post was under provincial jurisdiction.[38] No specific duties were mentioned, though its link to the provincial education system is obvious. Qiao Zhou appears to have held this office for over ten years. In 234 CE, after the death of Zhuge Liang, Jiang Wan was appointed shepherd of Yi Province, and Jiang, in turn, appointed Qiao Zhou to the office of attendant for direction of education.[39] As with Qiao's previous post, while the office was clearly involved in education, no details are available, and the title is only mentioned in the case of Qiao Zhou.[40] Qiao held this office for four years, when he was appointed to serve in the household of the heir apparent, Liu Xuan.

Qiao Zhou served the heir apparent in a variety of offices for twenty years. His first post, accepted in 238 CE, was in the role of coachman. Though the office had originally included duties involving the heir's horses and carriages, during the Three States period the title of "coachman" was applied to various dignitaries assigned to the heir apparent's residence.[41] Later, Qiao was transferred to serve as prefect of the household of the heir apparent, another post in the service of Liu Xuan, though presumably with some supervisory responsibilities.[42] In 246 CE, Qiao Zhou was demoted to the office of palace attendant grandee,[43] still in the service of the heir apparent, for his criticism of the Later Sovereign's frequent excursions. Twelve years later, Qiao's tenure in the household of Liu Xuan came to an end when he was promoted to the post of imperial household grandee.[44]

Though the first thirty-five years of Qiao Zhou's official career were split between what appear to be two distinct spheres of activity—provincial education and service in the household of the heir apparent—these two sets of posts may not have been mutually exclusive. Even upon being transferred from the provincial academy to the residence of the heir apparent, Qiao Zhou was likely involved in the formal education of Liu Xuan. Biographical information on other individuals serving in the heir apparent's household supports this notion. For example, the *Records of the Three States* notes that on Liu Bei's establishment of Liu Shan as heir apparent, he named two prominent intellectuals to posts similar to those held by Qiao Zhou. Lai Min, formerly a student at Liu Biao's academy in Jing Province and an expert on several canonical texts, was appointed to the offices of colonel for the direction of education and prefect of the household of the heir apparent.[45] Another alumnus of the Jing academy, Yin Mo held the posts of attendant for the encouragement of education and coachman for the heir apparent, Liu Shan. In this latter capacity, Yin was said to have taught Liu Shan the *Zuo Tradition* on the *Spring and Autumn Annals*.[46] This tendency to appoint noted intellectuals to both educational posts and those serving the heir apparent continued during the reign of the Later Sovereign, Liu Shan. The *Records of the Three States* biography of Li Zhuan notes that Li served the heir apparent Liu Xuan in the posts of cadet and coachman.[47] Chen Shou emphasizes Li Zhuan's breadth of learning, listing his mastery of such topics as debate, the *Five Canonical Texts*, the writings of the various persuaders, as well as the diverse arts of numerology, divination, medicine, archery, and so on. Significantly, the *Records of the Three States* claims that the heir apparent Liu Xuan "loved him for his broad learning and took great delight in him."[48] Li Zhuan's biography also notes a transfer to the office of palace attendant grandee, still in the service of the heir apparent. Given the similarities in the career paths of Lai Min, Yin Mo, and Li Zhuan to that of Qiao Zhou, we may conclude that while the general descriptions of positions in the household of the heir apparent did not specifically mention tutoring the heir among the duties of the office, these men probably served as educators, perhaps augmenting the curriculum provided by the heir's official tutor. The fact that such generic household positions were repeatedly filled by some of the most talented scholars of the state points strongly toward this conclusion.

Furthermore, extant passages from a collection of Qiao Zhou's writings entitled *Faxun* 法訓 [*Model Teachings*] appear to be directed toward a would-be ruler of state and may provide clues about both the intended audience of the text and the content of his instructions to the heir apparent. The *Model Teachings*, originally in eight fascicles but now with fewer than thirty surviving fragments, resembles earlier collections of dialogues and aphorisms, especially Yang Xiong's *Model Sayings*.[49] Several extant passages begin with the phrase "Someone asked," followed by "Master Qiao said," or a simply stated question and the phrase "replied" (*da* 答). In the dialogues, the interlocutor remains anonymous, but, given the nature of some of the responses, we may surmise that some of the questions to Qiao Zhou were posed by the heir apparent.[50]

The art of rulership emerges as a major theme in the extant fragments of the *Model Teachings*. These passages addressed two significant points: concerns the ruler should have and models for the ruler to emulate. Regarding appropriate concerns for the ruler, Qiao Zhou writes, "One who governs the state should not concern himself over whether the scholars harm the farmers. He should concern himself over those who rule over the people but are not learned."[51] While no historical context is provided within the text itself, the *Records of the Three States* notes concerns over Liu Xuan's academic training expressed by an older scholar at the Shu-Han court, Meng Guang. In particular, Meng Guang was bothered by the heir's failure to consult with the various scholars attached to the court, including himself.[52] And while it is difficult to link Meng Guang's concerns directly to Qiao Zhou's admonition, there was a general worry over Liu Xuan and his education among the intellectuals at the Shu-Han court. Moreover, this push by Qiao Zhou for increased attention to education was consistent with his early career as the director of education in Yi Province, as well as his classicist persuasion.

Additional fragments of *Model Teachings* present a model for the ruler to follow. One, offered in question-and-answer format, reads, "A king resides in the central state. Why is this? [Qiao Zhou replied], Following the amiable [nature of] Heaven, he unites the lands of the four directions."[53] Here, the central position and radiating influence of Heaven is presented as a model for the sovereign. This aphorism is in tune with a similar saying from the *Analects* that reads, "The rule of virtue can be compared to the Pole Star which commands the homage of the multitude of stars without leaving its place."[54] Moreover, Qiao Zhou's model to the heir provides an idealistic solution to the problem of the fragmented empire: Through the ruler's moral example, based on the way of Heaven, the empire will gravitate toward the righteous leader, thus unifying the subcelestial realm.

As a professional educator for twenty-five years (223–238 CE), Qiao Zhou undoubtedly influenced the lives of hundreds of young men from Yi Province. Of the multitude of students who passed through the gates of the provincial academy in Chengdu, the historical sources recorded only the names of five of Qiao's most important pupils: Luo Xian 羅憲 (d. 270 CE),[55] Li Mi 李密 (224–287 CE),[56] Du Zhen 杜軫,[57] Wen Li 文立,[58] and Chen Shou.[59] An examination of when, where, and what these individuals studied with Qiao Zhou provides a small window into Qiao's career as a teacher.

The issue of chronology in the matter of when these individuals studied with Qiao Zhou is a difficult one. Of these five students, only the birth years of Li Mi and Chen Shou are certain. Li Mi, born in 224 CE, would have been fourteen *sui* at the time Qiao Zhou left the provincial academy to enter the service of the heir apparent, and thus it is possible that he studied with Qiao in his official capacity as attendant for direction of education. The same situation may also be true for Luo Xian, Du Zhen, and Wen Li. Each of these men was active in political matters during the middle of the third century, making them likely of the generation coming through the academy during Qiao's tenure there. Only Wen Li's biography makes the explicit claim that Wen studied under Qiao Zhou at "the Shu imperial academy" (i.e., after 220 CE).[60] The case of Chen Shou is more difficult. Chen would have been only five *sui* when Qiao Zhou left the academy, making it unlikely that the master–student relationship between Qiao Zhou and Chen Shou was cultivated at the Chengdu academy. Yet another option is possible. In his biography of Qiao Zhou, Chen mentions that in the years after 258 CE, "Young scholars often asked [Qiao Zhou] difficult questions."[61] At this time, Qiao was serving as imperial household grandee—a court post with no obvious educational duties. We might tentatively presume that the "young scholars" referenced by Chen Shou included himself, and that his relationship with Qiao was one of pupil to a private teacher.

In terms of curriculum, several specific texts and types of material are mentioned in the biographies of Qiao's students. For the older generation of students, references to the *Zuo Tradition* (Li Mi), the *Mao Tradition* on the *Odes* (Wen Li), the *Three Ritual Texts* (Wen Li), and the various interpretative traditions on the *Spring and Autumn* (Chen Shou) are all listed among the works studied. That the commentaries on various canonical historical texts and the ritual texts are included among topics taught by Qiao Zhou should not be surprising given his own intellectual interests. Only the *Odes* seems out of place in this curriculum list. It is possible, however, that the *Odes* was taught to Wen Li at the Chengdu academy by a scholar other than Qiao Zhou. The listing of texts studied by Chen Shou varies only slightly with its inclusion of the *Documents*, Sima Qian's *The Grand Scribe's Records*, and Ban Gu's *Han History*. These historical works clearly reflect Chen Shou's own academic interests, and for a budding historian there could have been no better teacher in Chengdu than Qiao Zhou. Unfortunately, excluding those by Chen Shou, extant writings by the students of Qiao Zhou are extremely limited, leaving us with little more than the brief enumerations of texts studied as evidence of their academic activities.[62]

Regardless of where and when these men studied with Qiao Zhou, their experiences with a common teacher created a strong sense of community among these intellectuals. This bond is illustrated in a curious detail included in the biographies of four of Qiao Zhou's students. The *Jin History* biographies of Luo Xian, Li Mi, Wen Li, and Chen Shou each mention nicknames attached to these men by their classmates. On Luo Xian, the *Jin History* notes, "Qiao Zhou's students called him 'Zigong' 子貢,"[63] after Duanmu Si 端沐賜, appellative Zigong (b. 520 BCE), a disciple of Confucius regarded as being "quick in speech and skilled in language."[64] While the *Jin History* makes no specific references to Luo Xian's abilities in speech or debate, the attachment of this nickname to Luo would seem to indicate the presence of these attributes in his person. Similarly, Li Mi's biography notes the nicknames of "You" 游 and "Xia" 夏,[65] referring to Yan Yan 言偃, appellative Ziyou 子游 (506–443 BCE), and Bu Shang 卜商, appellative Zixia 子夏 (507–425 BCE), both characterized as "cultured and learned."[66] The *Jin History* biography of Wen Li indicates that Wen was given the nickname of "Yan Hui" 顏回, the favorite disciple of Confucius noted for his virtuous conduct.[67] The biographical accounts of Wen Li also emphasize his personal virtue, but there is insufficient evidence to conclude that Wen Li was likewise Qiao Zhou's favorite student, though the account of his visit to his ailing teacher indicates that Wen Li remained close to Qiao Zhou throughout the years.[68] Finally, the *Jin History* mentions that Chen Shou was also regarded as "You" and "Xia."[69]

The context in which these nicknames were bestowed remains unknown, and we must be cautious in how much we read into them. Were they given to each other, by other unknown students, or by their teacher? They may be read as indications of a playful camaraderie, or perhaps of excessive egotism. Regardless, the characteristics of Confucius's disciples can in some regards be seen in the lives of Qiao Zhou's most talented students. Most important, in addition to illustrating the evaluations of their classmates' abilities, these nicknames may also indicate the manner in which Qiao Zhou's students viewed their master. With Qiao's students adopting the roles of Confucius's disciples, by extension, Qiao Zhou was placed in the role of Confucius. In this fashion, these nicknames functioned as an honorific for Qiao Zhou, and bonded master and students into a classically inspired community of cultured gentlemen.

In addition to its intellectual implications, the community of scholars built around Qiao Zhou also linked the master and his students in political activity. This esprit manifest itself in three different avenues. First, Qiao Zhou and his students often strove to secure suitable official positions for each other. Two of Qiao's students, Luo Xian and Li Mi, served in the household of the heir apparent Liu Xuan during the same period that Qiao oversaw the affairs of that office as prefect of the household of the heir apparent. The obvious inference is that, after his own appointment, Qiao then named his students as his subordinates. This favoritism may also be viewed as further evidence of the close nature of the intellectuals within the circle of Qiao Zhou.

Second, Qiao Zhou and his students were often united in political issues of the day. When the eunuch Huang Hao began to exert control at the Shu-Han court, Qiao Zhou frankly opposed his actions in open debate and the "Discourse on Enemy States." The biographical accounts of Luo Xian and Chen Shou also indicate their refusal to support Huang Hao and their subsequent political demotions.[70]

Finally, most of Qiao Zhou's major disciples held office under Shu-Han, and after the conquest by Wei, none of these men accepted positions offered by officers of Wei. Yet, after the establishment of Jin, all five of Qiao's main students accepted posts under Jin, as did Qiao himself.[71] Moreover, in an interesting display of loyalty, some of Qiao's disciples also demonstrated continued concern for the affairs of the former ruler of Shu-Han and the local population of the Chengdu Plain. Li Mi's appraisal of Liu Shan as "second to Duke Huan of Qi" is telling. Li evaluated his former ruler's strengths and weaknesses, clearly lamenting the Later Sovereign's shortcomings and the effects they had on the state.[72] Wen Li's memorial to Sima Yi urging that the descendants of former Shu-Han worthies be employed in the administrative offices in Yi Province in order to "comfort the hearts of the people of Ba and Shu" demonstrates a continuing concern for his former state and the citizens of the home region.[73] Interestingly, none of these actions was viewed by the Jin rulers as disloyal to their regime; rather Qiao's students were seen as trustworthy and their attentiveness to the affairs of their former state was viewed favorably.

While in the service of the heir apparent Liu Xuan, Qiao Zhou extended the sphere of his instructional activities and entered the high-stakes realm of court politics, offering a sharp and critical remonstration to his sovereign Liu Shan for the ruler's inattention to matters of state. In 223 CE at the age of sixteen, Liu Shan inherited his father's title of Emperor of Han. But even on his deathbed, Liu Bei had doubts about the abilities of his heir, instructing Zhuge Liang, "If my heir can be assisted, then assist him. If he has no talent, then take [the throne] yourself."[74] For the next nine years, the chancellor Zhuge Liang directed governmental affairs in addition to managing the war effort against Wei and Wu and several campaigns against non-Han groups in the south. With the death of Zhuge Liang in 234 CE and the deaths of his successors Jiang Wan and Dong Yun 董允[75] in 246 CE, Liu Bei's fears were confirmed as Liu Shan's ineptitude became apparent and his vulnerability to manipulation was exploited.

The Later Sovereign's weakness for pleasurable pursuits is presented in several passages in the *Records of the Three States*. Shortly after taking the throne, Liu Shan wished to increase the size of his harem. Dong Yun remonstrated against this, arguing that, in the past, the number of empresses and consorts had not exceeded a dozen, and reminding the young ruler that he already had a requisite number. Because of this remonstrance, Liu Shan's respect for Dong Yun was said to have increased.[76]

Another weakness of Liu Shan's was for taking excursions away from the palace. These habitual pleasure trips began immediately after the death of Zhuge Liang. In the summer of 236 CE, Liu Shan left Chengdu for an extended outing, apparently to enjoy the scenery in the mountains northwest of the capital, returning after ten days.[77] The Later Sovereign's pleasure outings appear to have continued for a period of ten years or more before a direct complaint was made by Qiao Zhou. The *Comprehensive Mirror for Aid in Governing* fixes the date of Qiao's remonstrance to 246 CE, giving the appearance of Qiao Zhou stepping up to fill the void in leadership at court after the deaths of Jiang Wan and Dong Yun. Chen Shou's biography of Qiao sets the historical context for the text of the memorial in simple and somewhat vague terms, noting, "At the time, the Later Sovereign was inclined toward excursions and sightseeing, and he increased the number of his [court] musicians. [Qiao] Zhou submitted a memorial criticizing this, saying . . ."[78] Following this historical preface, Chen Shou reproduces the entire text of the memorial.

In the remonstrance, Qiao Zhou utilized a simple historical allusion to criticize his sovereign's practice and to provide a model for Liu Shan to follow. The exemplar of choice was none other than Liu Xiu—Emperor Guangwu, the founder of the Later Han. Qiao Zhou introduces Guangwu as one of many contenders in a chaotic period devoid of a strong imperial leader. Worthies were attracted, Qiao argues, "not necessarily for the extent of [a leader's] influence, but only for the amount of his virtue."[79] Qiao presents a litany of Guangwu's virtuous actions, along with a list of notable figures who were attracted by this virtue. Gaining the support of righteous subjects and the hearts of the common people, Guangwu "was able to become strong from the weak," and "complete the work of becoming an emperor."[80] Continuing the account of Emperor Guangwu, Qiao Zhou narrates an incident directly related to the situation at hand:

> Upon reaching Luoyang, [Emperor Guangwu] once wished to go on an excursion. The carriages and horses were already prepared when Yao Qi 銚期[81] admonished him, saying, "The subcelestial realm is not yet pacified. I am truly unwilling for Your Majesty to put on the clothes of a commoner and go out on numerous excursions." Immediately, the carriages were returned [to the stables].[82]

Next, Qiao Zhou outlines the dangers to the state when "bandits" are aware of an emperor's inattention to affairs of state. Additional examples from the reign of Guangwu are cited, concluding with the emperor's successful suppression of the uprisings through a personally led campaign.

Following this simple retelling of Later Han history, Qiao Zhou directly addresses the matter at hand. First commenting on Liu Shan's reputation for his filiality, Qiao Zhou then lays bare his hopes for the young emperor. The memorial concludes with a frank, yet mild condemnation and exhortation:

> In offering sacrifices to the four seasons, sometimes you are not nearby, but sightseeing among your ponds and gardens. Sometimes you go out, and your servant, though ignorant, is not at peace. One who has worries and responsibility on his shoulders has no leisure time to exhaust himself in pleasures. Regarding the Former Emperor's ambitions, his hall is not raised nor his roof completed.[83] This surely is not a time to exhaust yourself in pleasures. I hope you will reduce the growing number of music officials and rear palaces. Cultivate the actions of the Former Emperor, and teach restraint and temperance to your sons and grandsons.[84]

Chen Shou appends what amounted to a historical postface to the text of the memorial, noting Qiao Zhou's transfer from prefect of the household of the heir apparent to palace attendant grandee, still serving the heir apparent.

This transfer was in fact a demotion. The office of prefect of the household of the heir apparent drew a salary of one thousand bushels, while the position of palace attendant grandee drew only six hundred bushels. The *Comprehensive Mirror for Aid in Governing* account adds, "The Han sovereign did not listen."[85]

DEBATES ON MILITARY POLICY

Following the rejection of Qiao Zhou's remonstrance opposing Liu Shan's excursions, a faction at court led by Liu Shan's childhood friend, the eunuch Huang Hao, began to consolidate power and manipulate the emperor. The flash point in the struggle for power and influence at court was the question of Shu-Han military policy. Between the years 253 CE and 257 CE, Jiang Wei 姜維 (202–264 CE)[86] led a series of campaigns against Wei in the north. In early 253 CE, Jiang sought to conscript additional men of the Qiang 羌 ethnicity to supplement his forces. The general Fei Yi blocked this plan, arguing against continued aggressive actions against Wei. Fei's objections are recorded in Xi Zuochi's 習鑿齒 (ca. 318–95 CE) *Han Jin chunqiu* 漢晉春秋 [*Spring and Autumn of the Han and Jin*], which says:

> Fei Yi spoke to Jiang Wei, saying, "We are not equal to the Chancellor [Zhuge Liang]; no, far from it. The Chancellor was unable to stabilize the Central Plains. How can we? Is it not better to protect the state and govern the people, revere and protect the altars of the soil and grain as his accomplishments for future generations? Do not become arrogant in the hope of defeating our enemy in one swoop. If things do not turn out as you desire, your regret will be too late."[87]

After Fei Yi's murder in the spring of 253 CE, Jiang Wei began to implement his plan.[88]

Fei Yi was not the only Shu-Han military leader to oppose Jiang Wei's ambitious campaigns. In the eighth month of 255 CE, the general who marches on the west, Zhang Ji 張翼 (d. 264 CE),[89] opposed Jiang Wei, arguing against additional military excursions on the grounds that "the state was small and the people [tired from] labor."[90] Jiang Wei ignored Zhang Ji's objections and promoted him to the office of general who presses the south and set forth to attack Didao 狄道.[91] At Didao, Jiang defeated the Wei inspector of You Province Wang Jing 王經 (d. 260 CE),[92] killing thousands of Wang's men at Tao River 洮水.[93] After this victory, Zhang Ji again urged Jiang Wei to end the offensive, arguing, "We should stop. It is not proper to advance again. If we advance, someone will destroy this great success."[94] Jiang was furious at Zhang Ji's opposition and, disregarding Zhang, laid siege to Wang Jing at Didao. Jiang was unable to overcome Wang's defenses, and was later forced to retreat when the Wei general Chen Tai 陳泰 (d. 260 CE) arrived and broke the siege.[95]

After a humiliating defeat at the hands of Deng Ai 鄧艾 (197–264 CE)[96] at Duangu 段谷[97] in the seventh month of 256 CE, Jiang Wei issued a letter of apology to the Shu-Han court. This defeat had been especially demoralizing to Shu-Han: Deng Ai had predicted Jiang Wei's every movement, and the loss of life was great among Jiang's troops.[98] The following year (257 CE), Jiang advanced on the Mang River 芒水,[99] intending to battle Deng Ai and Sima Wang 司馬望 (205–271 CE).[100] However, the Wei forces held their positions, refusing to engage.[101]

In 258 CE, Jiang Wei began to pursue a new strategy. Previously, Liu Bei had placed defensive troops at strategic locations to prevent an invasion of the Chengdu Plain. Jiang Wei considered these defensive garrisons to be a waste of troops and an obstacle to obtaining a great victory over Wei. Therefore he disbanded most of these defensive posts, hoping to lure the Wei forces into a trap on the plain.[102] Later historians have argued that Jiang's reduction of defensive posts directly led to the final defeat of Shu-Han. For example, in his appraisal of Jiang Wei, Chen Shou notes:

> Jiang Wei was unrefined in letters and strategy. His ambition was to establish his works and reputation, and he manipulated the masses and casually went forth [on campaigns]. Good judgment was not obtained, and in the end, it led to his downfall. The *Laozi* says, "Governing a large state is like cooking a small fish."[103] How could he be so petty in all aspects and cause so much chaos?[104]

The poor judgment that Chen refers to certainly includes Jiang's dismantling of Shu-Han's defenses. Additionally, Hu Sanxing 胡三省 (1230–1287) comments specifically on this strategy in his commentary to the *Comprehensive Mirror for Aid in Governing*. Hu writes, "Jiang Wei abandoned strategic positions in order to fix his crafty heart, which sought to enlarge the borders [of the state]. This was the primary reason for the defeat of Shu."[105]

Many in the Shu-Han military establishment did not support Jiang Wei's campaigns. In addition to the objections of Fei Yi and Zhang Ji previously noted, general of chariots and cavalry on the right Liao Hua 廖化 (d. 264 CE)[106] voiced his opposition and issued a warning to Jiang Wei in 262 CE. His warning is quoted in the *Spring and Autumn of Han and Jin*, and reads:

> In the fifth year of the Jingyao period (262 CE), Jiang Wei's troops left Didao. Liao Hua said, "If you do not put aside the troops, you will burn yourself."[107] This is a shortcoming of Boyue [Jiang Wei]. The wise do not come out against an enemy, but being of lesser strength, they lay in wait. Using troops without resting them, how can you succeed? The *Odes* says, "It was not before me, it was not after me."[108] These are the affairs of this day.[109]

While several objections to Jiang's campaigns were voiced from among the military, only Qiao Zhou opposed these military actions at court. Chen Shou introduces Qiao's protest with a terse background statement, again only hinting at the significance of Qiao's opponents. Chen writes, "Qiao Zhou and the prefect of the masters of writing, Chen Zhi 陳祗 (d. 258 CE), debated the merits and demerits [of these campaigns]. Returning to his home, he wrote this, calling it 'Discourse on Enemy States.'"[110] In his introduction to the treatise, Chen Shou simply notes the name and office of Qiao's opponent in this debate at court, leaving the reader to comb the history for details that bring the gravity of the situation into full view.

In an appendix to the biography of Dong Yun, Chen Shou provides a brief biographical account of Chen Zhi.[111] Chen Shou's rhetorical strategy is quite clear in his treatment of these lives. Dong Yun was a highly respected and loyal official, and during the later years of his life, his power and authority kept the Later Sovereign protected from would-be usurpers like Huang Hao. Regarding this, Chen Shou writes:

> As the Later Sovereign was growing up, he became fond of the eunuch Huang Hao. [Huang] Hao was [skilled at] fawning and flattering, and sought favor [with the Later Sovereign]. [Dong] Yun was proper [in his relations with] the ruler, and harsh [in his relations with Huang] Hao. [Huang] Hao feared [Dong] Yun, and dared not oppose him. At the end of [Dong] Yun's life, [Huang] Hao's office did not exceed Assistant of the Yellow Gates.[112]

Chen Shou notes that Chen Zhi "together with Huang Hao collaborated as Hao began to meddle in governmental affairs."[113] Following this terse statement, Chen Shou outlines Huang Hao's rise in office and power, noting that "all the people of Shu thought of Dong Yun."[114] Thus linking the careers of Huang Hao and Chen Zhi, Chen Shou proceeds to offer a standard biographical notice of Chen.

Chen Zhi was orphaned as a youth and raised in the household of his great-uncle Xu Jing, who had served Liu Bei as minister over the masses.[115] The young Chen Zhi developed a reputation for his various talents and was quickly appointed to serve the state. So impressed was Fei Yi with Chen's abilities that, he personally recommended him to take the office left vacant by Dong Yun's death. According to Chen Shou's account, "He was trusted and loved, and his authority was equal to [that of] Jiang Wei."[116] That Chen Zhi had endeared himself to his sovereign is without question. However, Chen Shou then points out the results of this favor:

> Because Chen Zhi had obtained his favor, the Later Sovereign became more and more angry toward [Dong] Yun, saying that [Dong] had disrespected him. Because of the flattering nature of [Chen] Zhi, [Huang] Hao was able to scheme an excuse to infiltrate [court].[117]

Thus, Qiao Zhou's opponent in the debate over Shu-Han military policy was no lightweight. Chen Zhi held both rank and influence. Additionally, he was allied with perhaps the most powerful individual at court, Huang Hao. By criticizing a policy supported by Huang Hao and Chen Zhi, Qiao Zhou faced a great personal risk. At the time, Qiao Zhou was fifty-eight *sui* and had been an official of Shu-Han almost since its inception. Though during his thirty-plus years of service to the Lius' state Qiao had gained some notice at court, Chen and Huang's power was dominant as Qiao presented his argument.

While Chen Shou offers no precise date for the debate between Qiao Zhou and Chen Zhi, the *Records of the States South of Mount Hua* provides one in the form of a year-title: Jingyao 景耀 1 (258 CE).[118] Chen Zhi died in this same year, but no specific date of his death is given. Sima Guang's *Comprehensive Mirror for Aid in Governing* offers an earlier date for the composition of the treatise, placing it at the end of Wei Ganlu 甘露 2 (257 CE).[119] Unfortunately, we cannot more accurately date the debate.

In addition to providing the year of the encounter between Qiao and Chen, the *Records of the States South of Mount Hua* offers further background information, supporting and enhancing Chen Shou's account. The *Records of the States South of Mount Hua* notes:

> In the first year of the Jingyao period, [Jiang] Wei was defeated by [Zhuge] Dan 諸葛誕 (d. 258 CE).[120] Retreating, [Jiang] returned to Chengdu, where he was again appointed as general-in-chief. The historian's office reported that an auspicious star had been seen. A general amnesty was issued and the year-title changed. The eunuch Huang Hao and the prefect of the masters of writing Chen Zhi collaborated and began to meddle in governmental affairs. [Huang] Hao advanced from assistant of the Yellow Gates to general of chariots and cavalry, and regular palace attendant. Though Jiang Wei had been transferred to [Chen] Zhi's right (i.e., a superior rank), his authority and duties were not equal [to Chen's]. All the people of Shu thought of Dong Yun. At that time, troops and chariots were long employed, and the people were tired from labor. The grand palace grandee Qiao Zhou wrote "Discourse on Enemy States," which said [Liu Shan] could do as King Wen, but it would be difficult to do as the Han founder. No one questioned this.[121]

From the historical narratives of Chen Shou and Chang Qu, one can sense various tensions at play. On the surface, we find the debate between Qiao Zhou and Chen Zhi over whether the state should pursue an aggressive military campaign against Wei. However, underlying this debate appears to be a deeper and more volatile conflict. Both Chen Shou and Chang Qu hint at latent hostility between Jiang Wei and the Huang Hao-Chen Zhi faction. While both camps shared a desire to engage in campaigns against Wei, these desires were driven by very different motives. As Chen Shou noted in his appraisal of Jiang Wei, Jiang was obsessed with establishing his reputation as a military leader. To defeat Wei would have elevated Jiang's fame above that of even Zhuge Liang, whose spectre seemed to haunt Jiang. For Huang Hao and Chen Zhi, having Jiang Wei away on military expeditions freed them from Jiang's control at court, allowing them to manipulate Liu Shan as they desired. Indeed, personal aggrandizement seems to be the unspoken theme of the *Records of the Three States* and *Records of the States South of Mount Hua* narratives. It is in contrast to this theme that Qiao Zhou's treatise appears so extraordinary.

The document that survives under the title "Chouguo lun" 仇國論 ["Discourse on Enemy States"] is a literary reworking of the debate between Qiao Zhou and Chen Zhi over Shu-Han military policy. In it, Qiao Zhou utilizes various rhetorical strategies to argue against aggressive campaigns versus Wei. Qiao's treatise opens with a restatement of the position of Shu-Han as the legitimate successor to the Han dynasty, calling the opposing states in his discourse the "Vestigial State" (*yinyu zhi guo* 因餘之國) and the "Newly-founded State" (*zhaojian zhi guo* 肇建之國), representing Shu-Han and Wei, respectively. Qiao presents himself and his opponent in the debate, Chen Zhi, in the form of allegorical interlocutors, with himself as the lowly "Mr. Falling-down Fool" (*fu yu zi* 伏愚子) and Chen as the haughty "Mr. Lofty-worthy Minister" (*gao xian qing* 高賢卿).[122] Qiao's use of the literary device of allegorial interlocutors, a common feature of the didactic and often satirical Han rhapsody, provides his suasive essay with a touch of literary flair and humor, as well as thinly disguises the actual participants. The discourse is arranged in question-and-answer format, with Mr. Lofty-worthy Minister (Chen Zhi) posing the question to Mr. Falling-down Fool (Qiao Zhou): "Now the affairs of state are unstable. From top to bottom, minds are troubled. In the past, the weak were able to overcome the strong. By what art was this accomplished?"[123] or, in other words, 'How can our small state defeat the larger and more powerful Wei?' Mr. Lofty-worthy Minister's initial question to Mr. Falling-down Fool begins with a statement of the present situation, and ostensibly seeks a solution from an historical parallel that can be successfully applied to the problem at hand. The Vestigial State [Shu-Han] is not only small, but also weak. Yet in the past, small weak states had succeeded in overcoming their larger, stronger opponents. Mr. Lofty-worthy Minister seeks the method, or art, by which this was done. But the query is more than an appeal to Qiao Zhou's command of history. It is an attempt to lure the older scholar into a trap—a ruse to trick Qiao into openly criticizing the court's support for Jiang Wei's aggressive military campaigns against Wei. The phrasing of the question itself implies as much. Mr. Lofty-worthy Minister himself is aware of the historical precedents, and the question is purely rhetorical. Stylistically, Mr. Lofty-worthy Minister's question is presented in the dialogue as straightforward and even simplistic. The question, as phrased in the "Discourse," contains no literary embellishments such as parallelism or rhyme, and could well have been exactly as posed in the historical debate. This appears in stark contrast to Qiao Zhou's response as Mr. Falling-down Fool.

Qiao's reply begins with the statement of a principle of action, followed by a historical example of the application of the principle. The principle is expressed as follows:

When a state is large and has no worries, it will frequently become very indolent.

When a state is small and has worries, it will frequently ponder ways to make things good.

Great indolence results in chaos.

Pondering ways to make things good results in order.

This is a constant principle.[124]

The significance of Qiao's idea is not difficult to grasp. Qiao Zhou argues that due to the small size and difficult circumstances faced by Shu-Han, those in government must constantly strive to improve the conditions of the state. This necessity is seen as a virtue, contrasted against the frequent fall into degradation seen in states who have relatively fewer concerns.

As examples supporting this principle, Qiao Zhou uses the cases of King Wen 文 of Zhou and Gou Jian 勾踐 of Wu. The meaning of these allusions to these classical figures would have been obvious. Each of these rulers nourished the people of their small states and bode their time until the proper opportunity presented itself for a successful campaign against their larger enemies. As a result of their concern for their subjects, a deep sense of loyalty toward the state was cultivated.[125]

Mr. Lofty-worthy Minister refutes Mr. Falling-down Fool's response to the initial question with a counterexample: the case of the Han founder, Liu Bang, who took advantage of an opponent's internal strife and conquered, despite the exhaustion of his own forces. It is not surprising to find Chen Zhi opposing Qiao Zhou's examples from classical history with appeals to Han history. First, since Liu Bei and Liu Shan claimed to rule over the third epoch of the Han dynasty, the precedents of the dynastic founder would be ideologically, if not situationally correct models. Second, Liu Bang had consolidated his power from the strategic location of Ba, Shu, and Hanzhong commanderies—the same territory held by Shu-Han. The implied message was clear: if Liu Bang could engage a larger and more powerful enemy outside of the borders of his state and succeed, so too could Liu Shan. With this ideologically correct counterexample on the table, Chen Zhi asks the question: "Why is it that we must follow the affairs of King Wen?"[126] Mr. Lofty-worthy Minister's question has the appearance of both a trap and a prop. On the one hand, compelled to respond, Mr. Falling-down Fool must take a stand on the successful strategy of the Han's Exalted Ancestor, Liu Bang. To criticize the dynastic founder would be dangerous. To imply that the Later Sovereign, Liu Shan, was not the equal of his imperial ancestor would be treasonous. On the other hand, the question provides Chen Zhi with the opportunity to express the motives for his stance on an aggressive Shu-Han military strategy. Mr. Lofty-worthy Minister expresses this justification as follows: "The Newly-founded State has trouble and sickness. Because of this fissure, I [want to] attack their frontier, hoping to add to their troubles and destroy them." Chen Zhi's reference to "troubles and fissures" refers to the power struggle within the state of Wei, in which the Sima 司馬 clan began asserting their control over a succession of young and weak Cao emperors.[127]

Qiao Zhou, in his response to Chen Zhi's question, rejects the historical parallel drawn by Chen and argues for a divergent strategy based on different historical models, emphasizing the importance of acting in accordance with the particular circumstances of the day. Drawing on an allusion to the Zhou conquest of Shang, Qiao argues that strategies that were effective under one set of historical circumstances may not necessarily be so under another. This is followed by a warning against overburdening the people of the state, supported by the case of the fall of Qin. Moving from historical examples to a direct comment on the present situation, Qiao argues that these times are not like those in the case posed by Chen Zhi, and the strategies of the Han founder are inappropriate for the day. Qiao's own suggestion on the direction of Shu-Han military policy is stated clearly: "Therefore, the wise man does not shift his objective for small profit or change his path for the illusory. When the time is right, he acts. When the many [factors] are in accord, then he reaches out. . . . If you follow the extreme and constantly march troops, the country will collapse."[128]

Following his quotation of Qiao Zhou's treatise, Chen Shou presents a brief historical conclusion. Unfortunately, Chen does not discuss the reaction of Chen Zhi, Huang Hao, or Liu Shan to the "Discourse on Enemy States." However, in a manner similar to the historical introduction to the treatise, Chen Shou provides enough information from which to draw some basic conclusions. First, Chen notes that, afterward, Qiao Zhou received a promotion to the office of imperial household grandee, "second only to the nine ministers in rank," and was frequently consulted by young scholars.[129] At the time of the debate, Qiao Zhou served as palace attendant grandee—a relatively minor post at court with a salary of six hundred bushels. The promotion to imperial household grandee included a significant salary increase—to the level of two thousand bushels. Additionally, the post marked him as "an intimate imperial aide and advisor."[130] Yet despite this advance in rank, Qiao Zhou does not appear to have engaged in everyday political matters. Chen Shou notes, "[Qiao] Zhou, even though he was not involved in governmental affairs, was highly esteemed because of his scholarly actions. He was often consulted on important matters, and he immediately relied upon canonical texts to respond."[131] From Chen Shou's conclusion, we can see that Qiao Zhou did not appear to suffer any consequences from his opposition to the military faction at court. However, it is important to note that Chen Zhi died during the same year as the debate. The opportunity to retaliate against Qiao Zhou may have been lost with Chen's death. On the other hand, Chen Zhi might have been convinced by Qiao's rhetoric and changed his own hawkish position. The historical records, unfortunately, do not provide these details.[132] We do see, however, that Qiao Zhou was promoted, esteemed, and consulted by both the emperor and admiring young students. Clearly, Qiao Zhou had spoken his mind on the matter against powerful opponents and suffered little as a result. While Chen Shou presents an image of Qiao Zhou remaining aloof from political matters despite his promotion to the inner palace, the fact remains that Qiao Zhou was involved in one more major political affair in Shu-Han.

THE FALL OF SHU-HAN

The overall state of decline at the court of Liu Shan coupled with a dramatic policy change in Wei placed Shu-Han in a grave situation by 263 CE.[133] Prior to this time, the consensus in Wei had been that the first objective was to defeat Wu, then turn their attention to the geographically secure Shu-Han. However, under the direction of Sima Zhao 司馬昭 (211–265 CE), defeating Shu-Han came to be seen as the stepping-stone to the conquest of Wu and the reunification of the empire. Several new generals were appointed by Sima Zhao, and in the fifth month of Jingyuan 景元 4 (263 CE), troops headed by Deng Ai, Zhong Hui, and Zhuge Xu 諸葛緒 set out from Luoyang. When word of the Wei troop movement reached Jiang Wei, he requested additional troops to reinforce his defensive positions in Hanzhong. These reinforcements were not enough, however, to allow Shu-Han to hold Hanzhong. Jiang Wei was forced to retreat to Yinping 陰平, and from there to Jian'ge pass. Here, the Shu-Han forces were able to keep Zhong Hui's army at bay. During this stalemate, Deng Ai marched his troops seven hundred *li* from Yinping through undefended territory, constructing plank roads along the way, until they reached Jiangyou 江油, under the protection of the Shu-Han generals Ma Miao 馬邈 and Zhuge Zhan 諸葛瞻 (227–263 CE). When Deng Ai's forces arrived in the eleventh month of 263 CE, Ma Miao immediately left his position and surrendered. Zhuge Zhan repelled Deng Ai's advances, blocking him at Fu 涪 prefecture. However, Deng's next offensive forced Zhuge to retreat to Mianzhu, where the Wei forces routed the Shu-Han army, killing Zhuge Zhan. Deng Ai's path to Chengdu was unimpeded.[134]

When word of the advancing Wei forces reached Chengdu, panic ensued. Chen Shou writes, "At first, [the leaders of] Shu said that the enemy would be unable to reach [the capital] quickly, and therefore did not make preparations to protect the city. When they heard that [Deng] Ai had already entered the inner plain, the people were agitated and scattered into the mountains and wilds and could not be restrained."[135] Liu Shan summoned his advisors to court to discuss the situation. Some argued that the court should seek refuge in Wu, while others suggested the court flee to the rugged territory in Nanzhong commandery to the south. Qiao Zhou, who was among the ministers at this council, proposed a third alternative. Qiao argued:

> From the past to the present, there has never been one who lodged in another state who ruled as Son of Heaven. Now if you enter Wu, you must become a subject of Wu. Moreover, if the governments of the two states are not different, then the larger will swallow up the smaller. This is natural. According to this, Wei is able to annex Wu, but Wu is unable to annex Wei. This is clear. Isn't it better to become a subject to a large state than a small state? Isn't it better to be disgraced only once? Moreover, if you desire to flee to the south, then you should have planned for this earlier, only then could [this plan] have reached fruition. Now a great enemy is approaching and disaster and defeat are imminent. Of the hearts of the people below, there is not a single one that can be relied upon. I fear that in the day that you leave, their vicissitude cannot be estimated. How could you ever reach the south?[136]

Qiao's plan was met with ardent objections from other ministers at court. Chen Shou notes:

> Of the various ministers, there were some who contended with [Qiao] Zhou, saying, "Now [Deng] Ai is not far away. We fear that he will not accept our surrender. Then what will we do?"
>
> [Qiao] Zhou replied, "Now, Wu in the east has not submitted. Under the circumstances, [Wei] cannot but accept our surrender. After accepting our surrender, they cannot not but treat us with propriety. If Your Majesty surrenders to Wei and Wei does not split its territory and give Your Majesty benefice, then I request to go personally to the capital [of Wei] and contend with them by means of ancient principles."[137]

The account concludes, "There was no one among the assembled ministers who was able to refute [Qiao] Zhou's opinion."[138] Despite Chen Shou's claim that no one was able to counter Qiao's plan, Liu Shan himself still harbored doubts and was inclined to flee to the south.

Sensing these doubts, Qiao Zhou submitted a memorial to the throne opposing this idea. Qiao began his persuasion with four main points. First, he argued that the ethnic minorities of the southern commanderies had only begrudgingly submitted to Shu-Han after being pressed by Zhuge Liang's southern campaigns. As such, the potential for uprisings in the area was great. Second, Qiao reminded the emperor that the objective of the Wei troops was not merely to capture the territory around Chengdu, but to secure the defeat of the state. These troops would certainly pursue the fleeing court to the south. Third, Qiao again expressed his concerns over the native population in the south, citing the need to increase the taxes on these people to provide the imperial court with its necessary supplies. Finally, Qiao noted the loyalty of those who had assisted Liu Shan and his father in Chengdu. To abandon them to the troops of Wei would completely undermine the support of the local population. Following these points, Qiao Zhou appealed to the canon for rhetorical impact. First, he paraphrased a passage from the *Changes*, saying, "The meaning of 'overbearing' is to know how to gain, but not how to lose; to know how to preserve but not how to decline; to know gain and loss, preservation and decline, and not lose what is proper. This person is a sage!"[139] In case the emperor did not understand the meaning of this passage, Qiao Zhou reiterated, "That is to say, a sage knows fate and does not forcefully persist."[140] The memorial concludes with two historical allusions. The first noted that the sages Yao and Shun bypassed their sons in transferring the mandate of heaven, and thus avoided the calamity that would have come from these unrighteous sons taking the throne. The second noted the surrender of the prince of Wei, younger brother of King Zhou 紂 of Yin to King Wu of Zhou.[141] Qiao asks the rhetorical question, "Was he pleased to do this? There was no alternative."[142]

The initial points made by Qiao Zhou are clear and logical. Qiao's concerns over the state of affairs between Shu-Han and the ethnic groups of Nanzhong were well founded. The area had never been brought fully under Chinese control. During the reign of Emperor Wu of Han the territory was organized into commanderies and prefectures, but this meant nominal control at best. When Liu Bei established his state at Chengdu, he sent officers to govern the Nanzhong commanderies. In particular, Li Hui 李恢 (d. 231 CE) was able to pacify the region. After Liu Bei's death, local uprisings were frequent and a major concern to Zhuge Liang. In 225 CE, a three-pronged force led by Ma Zhong 馬忠 (d. 234 CE), Li Hui, and Zhuge Liang left Chengdu for the south. In less than a year, the southern uprisings had been quelled, and administrative changes enacted. The Shu-Han policy toward Nanzhong, known as "pacification and appeasement," consisted of three main principles. First, the area was brought under Shu-Han control by harsh military actions. Second, the loyalty of the local populations was to be obtained by using local leadership to represent the Shu-Han government. Finally, the resources of the area were to be siphoned off to serve the interests of Shu-Han.[143] In particular, local men were conscripted for the Shu-Han armies and sent to fight against Wei in the north, and natural resources like livestock, precious metals, lacquer, and so on were extracted for use by the military and court. One aspect of the Shu-Han policy in Nanzhong was to not leave a large military presence in the area. Despite this policy of non-occupation, the historical records indicate that even after Zhuge Liang's southern campaign, local uprisings were still frequent occurrences, and the presentation of local produce [as tribute] to Chengdu was often neglected. This was the basis for Qiao Zhou's concerns over the plan for the Shu-Han court to flee to the south.[144]

The final phase of Qiao Zhou's persuasion is somewhat perplexing. The recitation of the passage from the *Changes* would appeal to Liu Shan's ego. To know the state was lost, but not to lose more—for example, his own life, or the lives of his subjects—could still mark Liu Shan as a sage of sorts. But the two historical examples offered by Qiao Zhou are somewhat difficult to comprehend. How was Liu Shan to have interpreted the matters of Yao and Shun abdicating to worthies not their sons? Was Liu Shan to envision himself as these sage-rulers? In this case, the allusion would be a criticism of the heir apparent, Liu Xuan, who Qiao Zhou had served for some twenty years. Or were the unfilial sons in the allusions meant to represent Liu Shan himself, with his father Liu Bei as the sage? This would have been a dangerous insinuation. The main point of the example was to argue that by transferring the mandate (i.e., the throne) to Wei, a disaster could be avoided. The second historical example presented in the memorial is also strange. Clearly, in urging Liu Shan to surrender, he is pushing the emperor to identify with the historical Prince of Wei in recognizing the illegitimate rule of his sovereign and submitting to the rightful successor. Is this a critique of the enterprise of both Liu Bei and Liu Shan?

The abtruseness of the allusions aside, Qiao Zhou's memorial convinced the emperor. Chen Shou's biography of Liu Shan states simply, "Following the advice of imperial household grandee Qiao Zhou, he surrendered to [Deng] Ai."[145] On hearing his father's decision to surrender, Liu Chen 劉諶 (d. 263 CE)[146] angrily denounced the plan. The *Spring and Autumn of the Han and Jin* records the outburst as follows:

> The Later Sovereign was going to follow Qiao Zhou's plan, and the King of Beidi, Liu Chen, angrily said, "If principle is exhausted, then let us strike with force. If defeat is imminent, then father and son, lord and subject should put their backs to the wall and fight one last battle, dying together with the altars of the soil and grain, in this manner we can join the former emperor."[147]

When Liu Shan rejected his son's proposal, Liu Chen wept at the ancestral temple of Liu Bei, killed his wife and children, then took his own life. The *Spring and Autumn of Han and Jin* notes, "Of those in attendance, there were none who did not weep."[148]

When Deng Ai's troops reached the north wall of Chengdu, they were met by a hearse bearing a coffin and the Later Sovereign, Liu Shan, who was bound and presented himself to Deng Ai as a captive. The document of surrender, along with the imperial seals and tassels, were presented to Deng Ai by three officials chosen as Liu Shan's personal representatives—the palace attendant Zhang Shao 張紹, Qiao Zhou, and chief commandant of attendant cavalry Deng Liang 鄧良.[149] Deng Ai immediately loosened the cords and invited Liu Shan for an audience, bestowing the office of general of agile cavalry on the Later Sovereign.[150] Following the surrender, Liu Shan and his family were relocated to Luoyang where he was given benefice as Duke of Anle District (Anle xian gong 安樂縣公).[151] At the time of his surrender, the Later Sovereign was fifty-eight *sui*, and had occupied the Shu-Han throne for forty-one years.[152]

Both major facets of Qiao Zhou's intellectual training can be seen in his public political discourse. In his remonstrance against Liu Shan's excursions and his account of the debate against aggressive military policy, Qiao displayed his knowledge of history, employing frequent references to both ancient and more recent history to make his case. Qiao's historical allusions and rhetoric have been criticized by some contemporary scholars for appearing overly simple. However, the intended audience for the various persuasions must be kept in mind. Liu Shan, by all accounts, was not a terribly bright or attentive ruler. As such, Qiao's arguments necessarily appealed to well-known (i.e., "simple") historical examples, with Qiao often following his allusions with explanations of what might appear to be obvious to a more educated audience. Qiao Zhou was not alone in adopting this approach or in receiving criticism for it. Zhuge Liang, popularly regarded as Shu-Han's most brilliant figure, was also denigrated for his simple language and rhetoric.[153] In this regard, both Zhuge Liang and Qiao Zhou, recognizing the limits of their audience, pitched their arguments at a level that could be comprehended by their sovereign. In the case of Qiao Zhou, the depth of his abilities in history are seen in his private scholarship rather than his public discourse.

The second major aspect of Qiao Zhou's intellectual training—the ability to discern the will of Heaven through celestial omens and human speech—was also manifest in his political activity. As mentioned earlier, Qiao Zhou was one of several Chengdu Plain intellectuals who urged Liu Bei to take the throne on the basis of their readings of various omens and prophesies. These same skills were also used later in Qiao Zhou's life as he prophesied regarding the decline of Shu-Han and its imminent fall. These prophesies are not recorded in the biography of Qiao Zhou, but rather included in Chen Shou's account of Du Qiong, and were presented to illustrate the influence of the elder Du on the younger Qiao. Following his account of Du Qiong's death (d. 250 CE), Chen noted that Qiao Zhou "followed Du Qiong's words, thereupon analogizing them and expanding them. . . ."[154] The two examples cited by Chen Shou of the influence of Du Qiong on Qiao Zhou both related to the fall of the Shu-Han and merit closer consideration here. The first case of Qiao Zhou employing the methodology of Du Qiong reads as follows:

> *The [Zuo] Tradition* on the *Spring and Autumn* says that Marquis Mu of Jin 晉穆侯 named the crown prince Chou 仇 (Enemy) and his younger brother Chengshi 成師 (Becoming a General). Shi Fu 師服 said, "These are indeed peculiar names you have given your sons! A good spouse is called a principal wife (*fei* 妃) and a complaining spouse is called an enemy (*chou*). Now you name the crown prince Chou and his younger brother Chengshi. This is the beginning of disorder, and I fear that [the younger brother] will replace [the crown prince]!" Afterward, it turned out just as Shi Fu had said.[155]

> Emperor Ling of Han named his two sons Shihou 史侯 and Donghou 董侯. [Both] were established as emperors and both were dispensed with and made marquises, similar to what Shi Fu had said.[156]

> The Former Sovereign's taboo name was Bei 備, meaning "complete." The Later Sovereign's taboo name is Shan 禪, meaning "to give away." It is like saying that the Lius have already completed [their rule] and are going to give it to another. The significance of this is really like the naming of the sons of Duke Mu and Emperor Ling.[157]

These three prophesies were based on a type of wordplay catagorized in the *Han History* as "inconsistent words" (*yan zhi bu cong* 言之不從).[158] That is, the names chosen by the rulers were meant to convey auspicious meanings, but an alternate reading of these names conveyed the opposite, and these hidden meanings were thought to be prophetic.[159] In the case of the sons of Duke Mu of Jin, the eldest son Chou became the enemy (*chou*) of his brother, who led troops back to Jin in an effort to claim the throne. The hidden meanings of the names of the sons of Emperor Ling of Han were likewise prophetic in a negative sense. The princes were purposely mistitled "marquises" instead of princes to protect them from supernatual elements with evil designs on the heirs to the throne. Ironically, on their removal from the throne as emperors, they were each given benefice as a marquis. The alternate interpretation of the names of the two sovereigns of Shu-Han as explained by Qiao Zhou are obvious, and, ironically, employ the same play on words as the prophesies cited in the memorial urging Liu Bei to claim the throne. In all these examples, Qiao Zhou applied the prophetic techniques learned from Du Qiong to various historical cases with the goal of commenting on the present situation.[160]

A second example of Qiao Zhou's "analogizing and expanding" on Du Qiong's learning is contained in the following *Records of the Three States* narrative:

> Later, the eunuch Huang Hao manipulated power at court. In the fifth year of the Jingyao period (262 CE), a large tree within the palace fell on its own accord without reason. Qiao Zhou was deeply disturbed by this, but had no one to tell. So he wrote upon the tree stump, saying, "Multitudinous and great, the time has come, completed and giving away, how can it be restored" (*zhong er da, qi zhi hui, ju er shou, ruo he fu* 眾而大期之會具而授若何復)? This is to say, "multitudinous" means the Caos. "Great" also refers to a lookout tower (*cao* 曹). The subcelestial realm should gather under that which is multitudinous and great. "Completed and giving away," how can there again be a ruler established [of the Han imperial family]? When Shu-Han was about to be destroyed, some took Qiao Zhou's words as proof. Qiao Zhou said, "Although this is what I have interpreted, I am but an imitator. I have merely taken the words of Gentleman Du Qiong and expanded upon them. I personally have no divine or unique [ability]."[161]

In this anecdote, Qiao Zhou's inscription on the tree stump is an abstruse paraphrase of Du Qiong's explanation of Zhou Shu's interpretation of the "that which faces the path is lofty" prophesy. As explained in the narrative by Chen Shou, Qiao's inscription was based on prophetic wordplay, most notably the various meanings of the word *cao* 曹. The phrase "multitudinous and great" plays on two such meanings: *cao* as a synonym for *zhong* (multitudinous), and *cao* as a synonym for *que* 闕 (lookout tower). The graphs *ju* 具 (complete) and *shou* 授 (to give away) represent the secondary meanings of *bei* 備 (complete) and *shan* 禪 (to give away), both the taboo names of the two rulers of Shu-Han.[162]

In their day, Qiao Zhou's prophesies appear to have been widely accepted. As Lu Zongli has noted, "[Prophesy's] authority and power originate from public acceptance, because real prophesy can be completed only after its public selection and circulation."[163] From the historical postfaces and remarks of the historian-compilers of Qiao's prophetic utterances it is clear that these prophesies were believed by a great many people. In his postface to Qiao Zhou's tree stump prophesy, Chen Shou notes that when Shu-Han was about to fall to Wei, many accepted Qiao's prophesy as proof of the inevitability of the defeat. Furthermore, Chang Qu praises Qiao Zhou as a sage because of the fulfillment of his prophesies.[164]

Following the demise of Shu-Han in 263 CE, the deposed ruler Liu Shan appeared to be happy in his new role as a marquis in residence in the Wei capital at Luoyang. The *Spring and Autumn of the Han and Jin* records a dialogue between Liu Shan and King Wen of Jin, Sima Zhao. At a banquet, Sima asked Liu if he were inclined to think about Shu. Liu replied, "I am happy here and do not think about Shu." This comment was overheard by Xi Zheng, who immediately requested an audience with Liu Shan and instructed him, saying, "If the King asks you again, you should weep and say, 'My ancestors' graves are in Long 隴 and Shu, thus, my heart is sorrowful in the west and there is not a day that I do not think of [Shu].'" Indeed, Sima Zhao did ask again and Liu Shan replied as he had been prompted. Sima Zhao responded, "How is it that these sound like the words of Xi Zheng?" Liu Shan was surprised and admitted the fact. All those in attendance burst out laughing.[165] Liu Shan died in 272 CE and was buried in Luoyang.

For his role in the surrender of Shu Han, Qiao Zhou was treated generously by the Sima clan. Immediately following Liu Shan's relocation to Luoyang, Qiao Zhou—who apparently stayed behind on the Chengdu Plain—and other former Shu-Han officials were given benefices by Sima Zhao. Qiao was made Marquis of Yangcheng commune 陽城亭, though he does not appear to have ever taken up residence there.[166] Chen Shou notes Sima Zhao's high regard for Qiao Zhou and that a letter of appointment was issued summoning Qiao to the Wei court at Luoyang. Chen reports that Qiao began the journey northward, reaching Hanzhong, but was unable to proceed further due to illness.[167] Some time after the establishment of the Jin dynasty in 265 CE, Qiao Zhou's presence at court was again requested. According to Chen Shou, the Jin court "repeatedly ordered those in office [to send] Qiao Zhou [to the capital]."[168] Despite suffering from illness, Qiao traveled to Luoyang, arriving in 268 CE. Qiao was unable to report to court for an audience because of his illness, but was nevertheless appointed chief commandant of the cavalry.[169] Qiao declared himself to be lacking in merit, but was again given benefice at an unspecified location. On receiving this honor, Qiao requested permission to report to his benefice, but the emperor did not consent, hoping to keep Qiao at court in Luoyang.[170] Though permission to leave Luoyang was not initially granted, it appears from the historical records that Qiao Zhou was allowed to return to his home in Baxi commandery.

Chen Shou, in a rare moment of first-person prose, describes his final visit to Qiao Zhou in Baxi in 269 CE. At this time, Chen Shou was serving as rectifier[171] in Baxi. On completion of his official business, he was granted leave to return home. According to the *Records of the Three States*, Chen took opportunity to visit his teacher and bid him farewell. Chen Shou records the following conversation with his master: "Qiao Zhou said to me:

> In the past, Confucius lived seventy-two years. Liu Xiang and Yang Xiong lived seventy-one years, then died. Now my years have exceeded seventy. Perhaps [I will follow] the tradition of Confucius, or maybe the path of Liu or Yang. I fear that I will not emerge from another year, and must then take that long journey. We will not see each other again.[172]

Chen follows the record of this statement with a bit of skepticism: "I doubted whether Qiao Zhou had the means to know this, but it occurred just as he said."[173] The following autumn (270 CE), Qiao received his final appointment as cavalier attendant in regular attendance,[174] but because of poor health did not assume office.

When Qiao refused this post, an edict was issued by Emperor Wu of Jin, ordering enticements be sent to encourage Qiao Zhou to report for duty. The edict, contained in the *Jin yangqiu* 晉陽秋 [*Spring and Autumn of the Jin*] reads, "I am very grieved by this [i.e., Qiao's refusal to take office]. Present [him] one set of court clothes, one suit of garments, and one hundred fifty thousand cash."[175] Qiao Zhou's son, Xi 熙 submitted a response on behalf of his ill father. It reads, "I have long been ill and unable to come to court for an audience. The state graciously presents court clothes, but there is no way to add to my life. When I return to my grave-site, the path is narrow and travel is difficult. Prepare a light casket. My preparations for burial are already complete. I return the items [Your Majesty] has presented."[176] On receiving the epistle, the emperor issued a new edict for the return of the clothing and presented a casket instead. Qiao Zhou died in the winter of 270 CE, and was buried, presumably in the coffin sent by the emperor, near his home, located approximately five *li* north of the commandery seat.[177]

By including his biography of Qiao Zhou in a fascicle devoted to the lives of Shu-Han scholars, Chen Shou presents his mentor as an intellectual; however, much of the biography, not unexpectedly, focuses on the public life of its subject.[178] The lengthy excerpts of Qiao's writings quoted by Chen Shou serve to illustrate Qiao's service to the state of Shu-Han. Although the reader can see glimpses of Qiao's training in the art of political prophesy and his expertise in history in these embedded documents, Chen Shou says precious little about Qiao's scholarship. While this presentation is in harmony with the tradition of "Forest of Classicist" biographies, Chen Shou presents no evidence to support the claims of Chang Qu, Sima Biao, and other early medieval historians that Qiao Zhou was one of the leading intellectual figures of the age. However, following his account of Qiao Zhou's death, Chen appends a brief bibliography of selected scholarly works by his teacher: "His works include *Model Teachings*, *Discourse on the Five Canonical Texts*, *Investigations of Ancient History*, and other works in over one hundred chapters."[179] In his typically understated manner, Chen Shou provides the clues necessary for the interested reader to gather the greater significance of the subject. The works listed here encompass Qiao Zhou's personal teachings (*Model Teachings*), and his critical studies on the canon and history (*Discourse on the Five Canonical Texts*, alternately known as the *Discourse on Truths and Falsehoods in the Five Canonical Texts*, and *Investigations of Ancient History*). Along with titles and fragments of additional works not mentioned by Chen Shou, including his annotations on the *Analects* of Confucius and several volumes of local history, the works listed help to explain the roots of his public intellectual activity, justify the praise offered by Qiao's contemporaries and later historians, as well as illustrate the individual genius of Qiao Zhou and the intellectual vitality of the third-century Chengdu Plain. The following three chapters will examine the private scholarship of Qiao Zhou, situating it within the broader contexts of early medieval Chinese intellectual history.

CHAPTER 4

Critical Approaches to the Canon

THE STATE OF CANONICAL STUDIES

From the early Han through the Three States period, the canon served as the primary curriculum for cultured gentlemen throughout the empire; moreover, exegesis on these canonical texts functioned as one of the major activities of Chinese intellectuals. With the establishment of academic chairs at the Han imperial academy, individual interpretations of canonical texts translated into influence and prestige for exegetes whose views were granted orthodox status, and increased the likelihood of governmental positions for their students.[1] During this period, the craft of exegesis shifted from attempts to gloss difficult terms or phrases to efforts to synthesize the entire Han canon into a unitary expression of truth, to detail-oriented explications of words and passages, returning again to quests for greater meaning from the hallowed texts themselves.[2] Furthermore, the apocryphal-prophetic texts, thought to explicate the hidden meaning of the canon, were increasingly called upon to provide legitimacy for political prophesy.

The late second and third centuries were an age of intellectual transition. From the establishment of the imperial academy with its erudits in the early Han, the struggle to establish orthodox interpretations of canonical texts had linked the intellectual and political worlds. Power and influence came to those who transmitted the accepted canonical traditions, while those who held dissenting views were shut out of the bureaucratic system. The most severe manifestation of this general trend came about in 164 CE when hundreds of scholars were purged from the bureaucracy and banned from any future service. These so-called "Great Proscriptions" (*dangdu* 黨錮) lasted for nearly twenty years, during which time unorthodox scholarly outlooks were forced to find other venues for transmission of their ideas.[3] This came in the form of regional private academies. Although private academies had been in existence for hundreds of years, they proliferated during the last years of the Han.[4]

The intellectual world of the late second century CE has been characterized by two modern scholars as "The Age of Zheng Xuan in Canonical Studies" (Jingxue Zheng Xuan de shi dai 經學鄭玄的時代), indicating the dominance of Zheng's interpretations of the canon.[5] Zheng Xuan himself had sought training with several private teachers, including Diwu Yuanxian 第五元先 of Jingzhao 京兆, Zhang Gongzu 張恭祖 of Dong commandery 東郡, and at the private academy of the noted classicist Ma Rong 馬融 (79–166 CE).[6] There, Ma Rong reportedly ignored Zheng Xuan, leaving Zheng and nearly a thousand other junior students to receive their instruction from Ma's senior disciples. Zheng became disillusioned and left. From these three private teachers, Zheng Xuan gained a mastery of several canonical texts, including the *Jing shi Yi* 京氏易 [Master Jing's *Changes*],[7] the Gongyang and Zuo interpretations of the *Spring and Autumn*, the *Record of Rites*, and *Old Text Hallowed Documents*. After Zheng Xuan was banned from governmental service by the proscriptions, he established his own academy at Gaomi 高密 in Beihai 北海 commandery.[8] Intellectually, Zheng was noted for his synthesis of the orthodox so-called New Text interpretations with the so-called Old Text views. In particular, his exegesis on the rites combined views from both the old and new editions of the *Ceremonials and Rites*. His approach involved the glossing of old names and things and the liberal use of the apocryphal-prophetic texts (often associated with the so-called New Text school) to craft an eclectic and harmonized view of the past as contained in the canon. Zheng Xuan's teachings attracted over a thousand students to his gate, as well as frequent invitations to take office with the various late Han warlord courts. His views were popular in his day, but were vigorously challenged by the adherents of another regional intellectual tradition.

In the last decade of the second century, the intellectual center of the disintegrating Han empire shifted southward to Jing Province. Liu Biao, a distant kinsman of the Han imperial family, entered the city of Xiangyang 襄陽 in 190 CE as the inspector of Jing Province.[9] Shortly after his arrival, Liu Biao commissioned an expert in the *Five Canonical Texts* named Song Zhong to establish a school and teach the canon.[10] Liu Biao's reputation as a patron for scholarship was widely known, and, as a result, several thousand men of letters took refuge in Jing. The *Later Han History* notes, "The scholars from the Guanxi region, Yanzhou and Yuzhou who sojourned in [Jing] numbered several thousand. They could all lead satisfactory lives thanks to the spiritual and economic support extended by Liu Biao."[11] Among these refugee-scholars was the late Han polymath Wang Can 王粲 (177–217 CE),[12] who brought to Xiangyang his massive library, including some ten thousand volumes from the imperial library given to him by Cai Yong 蔡邕 (133–92 CE). These books were copied by Liu Biao and were presumably available at his academy. Wang Can, in a brief history of the Jing academy, writes:

> Those who came from afar carrying books on their backs and ritual implements on their shoulders numbered over three hundred, including Qiwu He 綦毋闓, who was rich in human experience and enjoyed a high reputation as

> a man of virtue. . . . Thus, the *Six Canonical Texts* were taught, lectures on various institutions and artifacts were given, the eight musical tones were made to harmonize, the musical pitches were adjusted, the calendar was prepared, the penal code was framed, books in various fields were collected and the thoughts of all schools were represented.[13]

Little is known of the lives of the academy's founding scholar or other instructors, but something can be said of their range of academic activities. Song Zhong, identified only as a man of Zhangling 章陵 in Nanyang commandery, was said to have compiled a commentary on the *Changes*.[14] From the biography of one of his students, we can add Yang Xiong's *Supreme Mystery* to the list of texts mastered by Song Zhong.[15]

The identities of most of the thousands of students at Liu Biao's academy have been lost, but the names of a few individuals relevant to this study have survived. The most important of Song Zhong's students, Wang Su 王肅 (d. 256 CE),[16] openly challenged the supremacy of Zheng Xuan's interpretations of the canon and, for a time, Wang's opinions eclipsed the views of Zheng as the accepted standard. Wang's biography notes his early study of Yang Xiong's *Mystery* with Song Zhong, and his dislike of the work of Zheng Xuan. Chen Shou's biography of Wang Su notes, "Wang Su compiled the *Sheng zheng lun* 聖證論 [*Discourse on the Veracity of the Sage*] in order to criticize and minimize Zheng Xuan."[17] Unfortunately, the text is now lost. R. P. Kramers has examined the scattered surviving fragments of the work and concludes that it must have been a point-by-point refutation of Zheng Xuan's interpretations of individual passages from the canon, and may have been the artifact of a debate at court adjudicated by the official erudits of the Wei imperial academy sometime shortly before Wang Su's death.[18] Furthermore, Kramers identifies the major points of dispute between Wang Su and Zheng Xuan, namely matters of sacrificial offerings, ancient history, and the length of mourning period.[19]

Wang Su's interpretations of the canon replaced those of Zheng Xuan as the imperially-sanctioned orthodoxy during the Wei and Jin periods. This was due in no small measure to Wang Su's political clout with the Sima clan who dominated the later Wei court and established their own state in 264 CE. Furthermore, as other individuals who studied with Song Zhong at Liu Biao's Jing academy allied themselves with the state of Wei following Liu Biao's death and the surrender of his son Liu Zong 劉琮 to Cao Cao in 208 CE, the ideas propagated in Xiangyang gained wider currency and acceptance. In particular, the metaphysical ethics of Song Zhong's reading of *Supreme Mystery* began to spread and may be viewed as the leaven of the Mystery Learning movement that came to typify Wei-Jin intellectual activity. It was not until the seventh century that the canonical interpretations of Zheng Xuan were accorded orthodox status. Thus, throughout much of Qiao Zhou's lifetime, the ideas of Jing academy scholars were coming to dominate the world of canonical scholarship in the Yangzi River basin and Central Plains.

In order to assess the influence of this intellectual trend on Qiao Zhou's canonical scholarship we must first determine, as much as possible, what access Qiao might have had to these views. Modern scholars have offered conflicting opinions on the effect of Zheng Xuan and Song Zhong's canonical scholarship on the Chengdu Plain, though clearly both views were represented there. Pi Xirui 皮錫瑞 argues that Zheng scholarhip (Zheng *xue* 鄭學) dominated Shu-Han because Zheng Xuan had lived in exile in Xu 徐 Province at the time when Liu Bei served as shepherd of the area (ca. 195/196 CE).[20] Yoshikawa Tadao, on the other hand, credits Xu Ci of Nanyang with bringing Zheng scholarship to the Chengdu Plain.[21] Xu Ci was a student of one of Zheng's fellow commanderymen, Liu Xi, and was said to have been well versed in Zheng-scholarship.[22] He was appointed as an erudit at the Chengdu provincial (and later, imperial) academy. Regardless of their origin on the Chengdu Plain, the views of Zheng Xuan were available in the intellectual community in Chengdu.

The circumstances surrounding the transmission of Song Zhong's views and other Jing academy traditions to the Chengdu Plain are somewhat clearer. The *Records of the Three States* notes the presence of several scholars with connections to the Jing academy. Lai Min was one of the refugee scholars from the Central Plains who found himself in Xiangyang. During the regime of Liu Zhang in Chengdu, Lai Min and his sister, who was married to a distant kinsman of Liu Zhang, were invited to Chengdu. Later, Liu Bei appointed Lai to various offices, including duties in the household of the heir apparent, Liu Shan.[23] Yin Mo, a Chengdu native, was reported to have traveled to Jing to study the "old scholarship" with Song Zhong and Sima Decao where he mastered various canonical and historical texts. Under Liu Bei, Yin Mo was appointed to the office of attendant for the encouragement of education, and later as coachman to the heir apparent Liu Shan, to whom he taught the Zuo interpretation of the *Spring and Autumn*.[24] Finally, Chen Shou noted that Li Ren of Zitong commandery accompanied Yin Mo to study in Jing, and that his son Li Zhuan "continued his father's vocation," as well as mastered the teachings of his father's friend, Yin Mo. Li Zhuan served in the household of the heir apparent Liu Xuan, likely as a tutor. According to his biography, Li Zhuan

> wrote [commentaries] on the old text *Changes*, *Hallowed Documents*, Mao *Odes*, *Three Ritual Texts*, *Mister Zuo's Traditons*, and a *Taixuan zhigui* 太玄指歸 [*Gist of the Supreme Mystery*]. In all of these [writings] he relied upon the [interpretations] of Jia [Kui] 賈逵 (30–101 CE)[25] and Ma [Rong], and took variance with those of Zheng Xuan. Although he was distant from Master Wang [Su] and did not initially see his works, in many instances their ideas were similar.[26]

From these biographical accounts in the *Records of the Three States*, we can see that the views of the Jing academy were well represented in Chengdu, perhaps to a greater degree than those of Zheng Xuan. Moreover, from Yin

Mo's remarks, it would appear that the ideas of the so-called New Text schools dominated the intellectual world of Chengdu prior to Liu Bei's takeover of the political and educational institutions in the region. Yoshikawa makes this claim explicitly, linking the Yang family traditions to the so-called New Text School.[27] However, given the lack of evidence that any sort of canonical scholarship was at the heart of the Yang family enterprise (it was likely political prophesy based on celestial observation), it seems wise to discount the notion that a clash of New Text and Old Text views took place in Chengdu under the reign of the Lius. Rather, it appears that while Liu Bei recognized the importance of the local prophetic traditions and in fact used them to justify his own claim to the imperial title, he also sought to establish (or reestablish) a governmental academy with the canon as its core curriculum. To this end, Chen Shou writes:

> After the Former Sovereign stabilized Shu, the region had been in chaos for dozens of years and scholarly activity was in decline. [The Former Sovereign] thus ordered canonical texts be collected and the academies be put back in good order. [Xu] Ci and [Hu] Qian were named as erudits, and along with Meng Guang, Lai Min, and others, collated old texts. Because things were at an early stage of development, there were many divergent ideas.[28]

As Yoshikawa points out, Liu Bei had spent time under Liu Biao in Jing and had observed Liu Biao's efforts to establish the intellectual foundation for an imperial enterprise, and thus Liu Bei's activities in recruiting scholars and re-ordering the educational infrastructure in Chengdu were in all likelihood based on his observations in Xiangyang.[29]

With the presence of scholars espousing the ideas of both Zheng Xuan and Song Zhong in Chengdu, and with Qiao Zhou serving in posts with these men, it is clear that he would have been exposed to the canonical interpretations of both traditions. However, we know little of Qiao's training in the canon, and, given the fact that he was appointed to education-related posts at roughly the same time these outside traditions entered the region, it seems doubtful that he was a student of either Zheng scholarship or Jing scholarship prior to taking office.

DISCOURSE ON TRUTH AND FALSEHOODS IN THE FIVE CANONICAL TEXTS

Qiao Zhou, like many other intellectuals of the period, was well versed in various canonical texts and compiled extensive commentaries on issues drawn from the canon.[30] Examination of Qiao Zhou's exegesis on the canon reveals a deep skepticism regarding certain canonical texts and their later interpretations. Significantly, Qiao Zhou based much of his criticism of portions of the canon and their interpretations on his understanding of other canonical texts, especially the canonical histories such as the *Hallowed Documents* and the *Zuo*

Tradition. Qiao Zhou's treatment of parts of the canon as history accords with later views on the early unity of canon and history; moreover, the content of Qiao's critical canonical commentaries matches the overall characterization of the early medieval age's preoccupation with issues of ritual.

The surviving historical sources offer spare but useful information on Qiao Zhou's training in the field of canonical studies. Chen Shou's biography of Qiao simply notes that "he was well-versed in the *Six Canonical Texts*," but offers no direct claim as to where or with whom Qiao Zhou might have studied.[31] Earlier, however, in the biography of Qin Mi, Chen Shou mentions that Qiao Zhou often "went to inquire of Qin Mi," hinting that some of Qiao's training in the canon may have come from Qin Mi.[32] In the *Records of the States South of Mount Hua*, Chang Qu goes even further, calling Qiao Zhou a "disciple" of Qin Mi and claiming that "Qiao Zhou transmitted [Qin Mi's] vocation."[33] With the early death of Qiao Zhou's father, a specialist in the interpretation of the canonical *Hallowed Documents*, it seems likely that Qiao Zhou's canonical training was undertaken outside the home and, given both Chen Shou and Chang Qu's brief statements, labeling Qin Mi as Qiao Zhou's teacher in this regard seems a reasonable conclusion.

From Chen Shou's very brief treatment of Qin Mi's intellectual activity, a picture emerges of Qin Mi as a critical interpreter of ancient texts and history. From allusions to outside works in Qin Mi's own writings, it is clear that he possessed a great command of the canon. Moreover, Qin Mi is reported to have challenged various individuals and texts on their views of the past, including traditions included by Sima Qian in *The Grand Scribe's Records*. Unfortunately, the scholarly writings of Qin Mi have been completely lost. But, Chen Shou notes that Qiao Zhou recorded [Qin's] words or ideas in a text entitled *Discourse on Truths and Falsehoods in the Spring and Autumn*.[34]

And while there is no mention of a work by this exact title in the list of works attributed to Qiao Zhou, Chen Shou includes one entitled *Wujing lun* 五經論 [*Discourse on the Five Canonical Texts*] in his bibliography of Qiao's writings.[35] Given Chen Shou's claim of a work dedicated to critical examination of the *Spring and Autumn* and the later bibliographies' attribution of a work on five canonical texts, we can briefly speculate regarding the nature of this work. First, the title *Discourse on the Truths and Falsehoods in the Five Canonical Texts* would seem to encompass the more narrow title offered by Chen Shou in the biography of Qin Mi. The text's arrangement in five fascicles leads to the obvious conclusion that each fascicle was dedicated to the examination of a single work of the late Han canon, but it remains unclear whether the format of the text was that of a discursive commentary or the more common interlinear format.[36] Unfortunately, the *Discourse on Truths and Falsehoods in the Five Canonical Texts* has suffered great textual loss and only fragments related to various aspects of ritual have survived.[37] We thus have no way of knowing whether Qiao Zhou's original work addressed issues related to the *Changes*, *Odes*, or *Music*.[38]

CRITIQUE OF THE RITUAL CANON

The surviving fragments of Qiao Zhou's *Discourse on Truths and Falsehoods in the Five Canonical Texts* deal exclusively with matters of ritual. If Chen Shou's identification of a subordinate work entitled *Discourse on the Truths and Falsehoods in the Spring and Autumn* is an accurate indication of the scope and division of the entire text, then these surviving fragments may have been the portion of the work hypothetically entitled *Discourse on Truths and Falsehoods in the Three Ritual Texts*. In particular, the surviving fragments address three central issues of ritual: capping and marriage rites, offerings and sacrifices, and mourning rites.[39]

Pi Xirui characterizes canonical studies of the early medieval period as intensely focused on funerary ritual.[40] The remnants of Zhou dynasty ritual had recently come into their present forms in the organization of three separate ritual texts: *Yili* 儀禮 [*The Ceremonials and Rites*], also known as the *Lijing* 禮經 [*Canon of Rites*] in seventeen *pian* with appended commentaries; the *Liji* 禮記 [*Record of Rites*] in forty-nine *pian*; and the *Zhouli* 周禮 [*Zhou Rites*], formerly known as the *Zhouguan* 周官 [*Zhou Offices*].[41] Collectively, the three volumes of so-called Zhou rites compiled during the Han came to be known as the *Sanli* 三禮 [*Three Ritual Texts*]. Despite this newly organized ritual canon, there were still serious matters of contention over various points of ritual. The contrast between the Zhou ideal and early medieval reality gave rise to increased interest in the subject of ritual and, in particular, mourning practice.

In his introduction to this topic, Pi Xirui lists some twelve chapters within the *Three Ritual Texts* specifically focused on funerary rites, as well as numerous individual passages scattered throughout the texts. Particularly striking are the number of contradictions on points of ritual across these chapters and passages. As Pi Xirui describes the situation, "The more disputed these points became, the more 'Confucian' scholars argued their opinions."[42] In support of this statement, Pi notes the authors and titles of nineteen pre-Tang works on mourning rites; but Pi Xirui's list is not all-inclusive, for he neglects to mention several other canonical scholars of the period who also left writings on funerary ritual, including Qiao Zhou.

Clearly, Qiao Zhou's writings on ritual were part of a larger intellectual movement in the late Han period to explicate and critique the ritual texts of the canon. But Qiao and other exegetes may have also intended for their scholarship to criticize contemporary institutions and practices as well. As such, one objective of this chapter is to present Qiao Zhou's canonical criticism in its historical and intellectual context. To this end, in the discussion that follows, I will first present the canonical views on a given subject, followed by the views of Qiao Zhou and his contemporaries. Finally, I will analyze the general approach of Qiao Zhou toward the canon, as well as the later influence of his opinions and methods.

Three passages in Qiao Zhou's surviving *Discourse on Truths and Falsehoods in the Five Canonical Texts* address matters of capping and marriage, the important rites that formally delineated the end of childhood and the beginning of adulthood. The *Record of Rites* declares, "As for capping, it marks the beginning of the rites. . . . After capping, one is [called] by his appellative. This is the way of adults (*chengren* 成人)."[43] The political import of this event is also emphasized in the "Guanyi" 冠義 ["Meaning of Capping"] chapter of the *Record of Rites*. It notes, "After the loyal actions of a filial younger brother are established, one can become a man. After becoming a man, one can govern others. For this reason, the sage kings valued [this] rite. Thus is it said, 'As for capping, it marks the beginning of the rites.'"[44] Therefore, in addition to marking the bounds of adulthood, it also marked the bounds of leadership. Protocol for this important rite of passage occupies the head of the *Ceremonies and Rites* and was the subject of much later commentary.

The *Ceremonies and Rites* account of capping is rich in detail concerning the ritual, but lacks one important point: the age at which the rite was to be performed. While the concluding passages of the *Ceremonies and Rites* account touch on the capping of sons of kings, feudal lords, and grandees,[45] no ages are given. Zheng Xuan, however, was of the opinion that the rite should be performed at the age of twenty for the son of an officer.[46]

Qiao Zhou, basing his opinion on the historical precedent of the Duke of Zhou capping the young King Cheng 成, applies his expertise in ancient history to this question of ritual, employing a reconstructed chronology of early Zhou history:

> The old text *Hallowed Documents* says that when King Wu died, King Cheng was only thirteen *sui*. King Wu died in the *gengchen* 庚辰 year. In the *renwu* 壬午 year, the Duke of Zhou went to reside in the east, and in the *guiwei* 癸未 year, he returned.[47] "The Duke's Capping" records that the Duke of Zhou capped King Cheng and ordered the scribes to write words of blessing.[48] This was to remove the mourning cap. Before the Duke of Zhou returned, King Cheng was capped with the leather-trimmed cap. When he opened the metal-bound coffer, he was sixteen. When King Cheng was fifteen, the Duke of Zhou capped him, then departed.[49]

While the actual dates for these events are highly disputed, Qiao Zhou's chronology allowed for King Cheng to complete a three-year mourning for his father prior to receiving the capping rite in the *renwu* year. On the basis of the old text *Documents*' attribution of King Cheng's age of thirteen at the time of his father's death, Qiao then determined his age to have been fifteen at the time of his capping.[50]

Qiao Zhou's calculation of King Cheng's age is also at odds with the earlier opinion of Xu Shen 許慎 (ca. 55–ca. 149 CE). In his *Wujing yiyi* 五經異義 [*Different Meanings of the Five Canonical Texts*], Xu claims that King Cheng was given the leather cap at age fourteen by the grandee, and together they opened the metal-bound coffer at that time. The leather cap, according to Xu, was a mourning cap.[51] Qiao Zhou claims the cap was dark in color and trimmed with leather, typically worn by kings while afield or on hunting expeditions. The bestowal of this cap to King Cheng at this time would have indicated an end to the mourning period.[52] Thus, Qiao Zhou differed from Xu Shen's earlier commentary on both the age and type of capping performed.

Qiao Zhou's opinion that the capping of the son of a king should take place at age fifteen is also expressed in another fragment of his *Discourse on Truths and Falsehoods in the Five Canonical Texts*. Here, Qiao Zhou comments on a passage from the *Guliang Commentary on the Spring and Autumn Annals* that reads, "A son should be capped at age twenty. Once capped, [the marriage] can be arranged. At thirty, a husband takes his wife. A girl should be engaged at age fifteen. At twenty she is given in marriage."[53] Qiao Zhou argues:

> The state cannot long be without an heir. For that reason, the [sons of the] Son of Heaven and the feudal lords are capped at age fifteen. They also take a wife at age fifteen. In order to take a wife, they must be capped. In following the way of husband and wife, the king teaches them the root. One cannot follow the way of children and govern them [according to the] rites. At age fifteen, they are mature children and next are adults. It is desirable that a ruler of men soon have posterity. For that reason, the *Hallowed Documents* says King Cheng was capped at age fifteen. This is written in the metal-bound coffer.[54]

This passage again illustrates Qiao Zhou's acceptance of the old text *Documents* account of the capping of King Cheng. Following this passage, Qiao Zhou offers his criticism of opinions expressed in the newly fixed ritual canon. In particular, he is critical of a passage in the "Mei shi" 媒氏 ["Matchmaker"] chapter of the *Rites of Zhou* that offers the age of thirty and twenty *sui* as the proper ages for men and women to marry, respectively.[55] Citing the "Jia ling" 家令 ["Regulations of the Household"] chapter of the *Record of Rites*, Qiao notes that a girl received the hairpin—the female equivalent of capping—at age fifteen and could immediately become engaged. He also states, "For this reason, males from age twenty to thirty and females from age fifteen to twenty all marry or are given in marriage. Prior to this age, it is too early. After this age, it is too late."[56]

Qiao Zhou's differences in opinion with both canonical texts and previous commentators on the issue of the proper age to perform the capping ritual received some attention from later classical scholars. Yang Shixun's 楊士勛 (Tang period) subcommentary to this passage of the *Guliang Spring and Autumn* recites Zheng Xuan's chronology that claimed King Cheng was ten *sui* at the time of his father's death. Yang then contrasts Zheng's dates to those offered by Qiao Zhou, noting that Zheng Xuan followed the *Zuo Spring and Autumn* while Qiao Zhou's age was based on the *Documents* account.[57]

Attempts to further contextualize Qiao Zhou's writings on capping and marriage with the historical circumstances of the Three States period are frustrated by a lack of sources on these matters. In his study of ritual during this period, Chen Xuguo 陳戍國 notes only one reference to capping in the source materials for the period. Additionally, references to marriage practices in Wei, Wu, and Shu-Han addressed issues such as selection and number of wives and consorts for rulers, the presentation of wives at the ancestral temple, and taboos on marriage with women of the same surname, but the matters of age and engagement periods were not mentioned in the extant sources. Chen Xuguo concludes that neither Wei, Wu, nor Shu-Han strictly observed the received Zhou rites on the matters of marriage.[58] Since the issues addressed by Qiao Zhou in the received fragments of his text did not appear to have been a dominant theme in the ritual activities of Shu-Han, we might surmise that Qiao's writings on the subject of ancient ritual, and in particular the historical precedents for these rites, were part of his broad interest in ancient history and his efforts to investigate and rectify errors in the canonical texts.

A second major point of ritual addressed by Qiao Zhou's *Discourse on Truths and Falsehoods in the Five Canonical Texts* involved sacrifices or offerings made in the ancestral temple. The chapter "Ji yi" 祭義 ["Meaning of Offerings"] in the *Record of Rites* offers the following explanation of sacrificial offerings: "Offerings do not require numerous [repetitions], for in numerous [repetitions] they become bothersome. Offerings do not require infrequency, for in infrequency, they become neglected."[59] Despite this simple scheme, the minutiae of sacrificial offerings continued to accumulate, with specifics on schedule, location, and materials to be offered proliferating widely. These offerings were also closely linked to mourning practice, to be examined next.

Qiao Zhou addresses some of these points in a text entitled "Collected Discourses on Ritual and Offerings." The first fragment from this work deals with the location within the ancestral temple for seasonal offerings. Qiao writes:

> The offerings of the four seasons each [take place] in the sacred places within the chambers of the temple. The *ao* 奥 position is below the west wall, facing east. In the temples of the feudal lords, the wooden spirit tablet was placed south of the body, or above the body—on the east wall, taking south as above.[60]

Prefacing this passage in his *Tongdian* 通典 [*Encyclopedic History of Institutions*], Du You 杜佑 (735–812 CE) cites a now-lost passage from the *Gongyang Spring and Autumn* that reads, "The principal ancestor's [tablet] was buried in the great temple in the west wall of the chamber to protect it from fire."[61] There is no reference to the layout of the ancestral temple of a feudal lord in the surviving ritual texts. Du You's *Encyclopedic History of Institutions* also includes commentaries by Gaotang Long 高堂隆 of Wei and He Xun 賀循,

each offering opinions on specific locations for the placement of shrines in the imperial ancestral temple.[62] In this context, Qiao Zhou's comments appear typical of the exegetical concerns of the time.

Another fragment from Qiao Zhou's "Collected Records on Ritual and Offerings" addresses both the frequency and content of sacrifices presented at the imperial ancestral temple and tombs. Du You collects this passage twice, once in a section discussing seasonal offerings and again in a section dealing with grave offerings. In this passage, Qiao Zhou first lists the schedule and recipients of offerings in the ancestral temple of the Son of Heaven:

> In the temple of the Son of Heaven, from the founding ancestor to the great-great grandfather, the great-grandfather, the grandfather, and deceased father are all presented with offerings of normal food on the first day of the new moon. This is called the monthly offering. In the temple of the two ancestors, offerings are made periodically, but not monthly.[63]

While it is unclear on what source Qiao Zhou based his opinion, Qiao's statement appears to have been influential. The *Encyclopedic History of Institutions* quotes the text of a memorial written by Peng Jingzhi 彭景直 in 707 CE arguing against the current practice of daily offerings at the ancestral tombs. In his memorial, Peng cites Qiao Zhou on the monthly offerings and concludes, "What Qiao Zhou wrote was in accord with the ancient rites and ceremonies. Originally there was no text regarding daily offerings."[64] Peng's suggestion was rejected.

The second portion of this fragment addresses the content of offerings at the imperial ancestral temple:

> The Son of Heaven offers the five grains freshly cooked and precious objects newly fashioned in the imperial ancestral temple. According to the rites, not yet having made an offering, he dares not eat freshly cooked food.[65] This is the way of filial piety. From the new moon offerings to the *la* 臘 offerings,[66] fresh offerings and libations are offered without the body [being present]. For that reason, the [offerings in the] various temples are all completed within the space of a single morning.[67]

The "Monthly Ordinances" chapter of the *Record of Rites* provides a purported account of the Zhou practice of the monthly offerings. While some of the information in Qiao's comments is not specifically contained in the "Monthly Ordinances," the account is generally in harmony with this depiction of the Zhou practice.

Writing at the beginning of the Wei dynasty, Gaotang Long outlines a similar list of products to be presented at the ancestral temple of the Wei rulers. In his description of the monthly offerings, Gaotang Long paraphrases the "Monthly Ordinances" and notes not only the content of the offerings, but also the calendrical differences between Wei and Zhou times in reference to the scheduling of the offerings.[68]

In his study of Three States ritual practice, Chen Xuguo concludes that only the state of Wei had any formal codes or statutes on sacrificial offerings, though these were often at odds with the received Zhou rites. The leaders of Wei offered sacrifices to their dynastic founder Cao Cao at the suburban altar, while offerings to subsequent rulers were made in the ancestral temple. This regular practice by Wei was in sharp contrast to that of Shu-Han. Historical sources indicate only two instances of any type of ritual offerings being made by rulers at the Chengdu court.[69] While it is possible that the sources simply neglected this aspect of Shu-Han court activity, it may also be indicative of a lack of interest or emphasis on the part of Liu Shan. While we might be tempted to read Qiao Zhou's work on regular monthly offerings as a critique of Shu-Han's apparent neglect of these rites, to do so would be presumptuous in the face of scant evidence on the ritual activity of the state as a whole.

The bulk of Qiao Zhou's surviving *Discourse on Truths and Falsehoods in the Five Canonical Texts* consists of writings on mourning practice. These twenty extant fragments address a variety of issues related to mourning, burial, and funerary offerings. In particular, Qiao Zhou seems to have been concerned with two principal aspects of mourning ritual: relationships and reduction of mourning. The issue of relationships is central, for one's relationship with the deceased was the main determinant of how one was to fulfill ritual mourning obligations. Therefore, defining relationships and delineating the practical distinctions within those relationships became an overarching concern of not only Qiao Zhou, but other early medieval scholars writing on mourning rites.

Two passages by Qiao Zhou clearly illustrate his tendency toward definition and distinction. The first involves distinguishing between an adoptive mother (*cimu* 慈母) and a stepmother (*jimu* 繼母). The commentary on the "Sang fu" 喪服 ["Mourning Attire"] chapter of the *Record of Rites* defines an adoptive mother as follows: "When a concubine has no son and the son of a concubine has no mother and the father orders them to be mother and son, she is called an adoptive mother."[70] The *Ceremonies and Rites* also declares, "Mourn for a stepmother as if she was your own mother . . . Mourn for an adoptive mother as if she was your own mother."[71] Qiao Zhou takes issue with the equation of a stepmother and an adoptive mother. In discussing the matter of mourning for an adoptive mother, he first distinguishes an adoptive mother from a stepmother, saying, "A concubine does not receive the name of stepmother. An adoptive mother who adopts without receiving the commandment of the father should not receive in excess of the Lesser Mourning."[72] Qiao's opinion of the low status of an adoptive mother echoes that of Zheng Xuan. For example, the *Encyclopedic History of Institutions* includes a dialogue between Zhao Shang 趙商 and Zheng Xuan in which Zhao asked, "If an adoptive mother remarries, shouldn't one mourn for her as a stepmother?" Zheng Xuan replied, "An adoptive mother is lower in rank than a stepmother. How could she receive the observance of a stepmother?"[73]

In a lengthy passage under the title of "Collected Illustrations," Qiao Zhou continues his criticism of the broad statement equating the adoptive mother with the natural mother found in the "Mourning Attire":

> The regulations on wearing trimmed sackcloth for three years in "Mourning Attire" say, "[Mourn for] an adoptive mother as if she was your own mother." When the father is still alive, this regulation is not observed in mourning for an adoptive mother. The new text ["Mourning Attire"] argues that if adopted by an honored concubine while the father is still alive, [the adopted son] wears the trimmed sackcloth for one year. If adopted by a lesser concubine when the father is still alive, [the adopted son] observes the Greater Mourning for nine months. [Commenting on] the old text, Mister Zheng [Xuan] said,
>
>> This is based on the son of a concubine of a grandee or officer who has been appointed by the father to be adopted as son to a mother. The son of a concubine of a grandee who has been appointed to be adopted by the father observes the Greater Mourning for his mother. The son of a concubine of an officer who has been appointed [to be adopted] mourns for the one year for his mother. A grandee reduces mourning by one level. An officer without rank does not accordingly reduce. When the father dies, all [mourning periods] are extended.[74]
>
> According to the *Canon of Rites*, "When the father is still alive, the son of a grandee by a concubine observes the Greater Mourning for his mother." This does not distinguish between [the rank of] honored or lesser [concubines]. If one is not [descended] from the principal wife, then if a grandee reduces mourning by one level, then the sons of his concubine will likewise reduce one level. As the concubine of a grandee, though honored, she is not of one body with her ruler. How can [mourning for her] not be reduced? On all these distinctions, the new texts do not compare to the old texts.[75]

In this passage, Qiao first negates the "Mourning Attire" claim by arguing that if the father was still alive, the mourning for an adoptive mother was not observed. Then, Qiao Zhou compares the interpretations of the new and old text versions of the "Mourning Attire," noting that the new text's distinctions in mourning an adoptive mother were based on the rank of the concubine ordered to act as the mother. Qiao refutes this claim by quoting Zheng Xuan's commentary on the old text "Mourning Attire" that based its distinctions on the rank of the father, not the concubine. According to Zheng Xuan, the reduction of mourning for an adoptive mother was also based on the status of the father rather than the adoptive mother. Qiao Zhou extends Zheng's opinion by arguing that mourning for all concubines, regardless of rank of father or concubine, should be reduced because the concubine was not of the same body as the father. Finally, Qiao Zhou openly expresses his preference for the old text edition of the "Mourning Attire" over the new text edition.

Later scholars writing on the mourning for an adoptive mother appear to have rejected Zheng Xuan and Qiao Zhou's opinions. The *Encyclopedic History of Institutions* notes that during the Jin, Cui Liang 崔諒 was urged to mourn his adoptive mother as his mother. Liu Zhi 劉智 notes additional situations in which one might establish the relationship of son and adoptive mother, and argues that in all cases the adoptive mother should be mourned, for the son "Dared not disobey the father's command [to be adopted]."[76] Here, the obedience to the father's order superseded any other considerations.

A final example of explaining relationships and their impact on mourning observance also helps to situate Qiao Zhou within the context of early medieval exegesis on mourning. The topic under discussion is the proper manner by which one should mourn a half-brother with a different father but the same mother as one's self. The so-called Zhou precedent for this situation is found in the "Tan gong" 檀弓 ["Sandalwood Bow"] chapter of the *Record of Rites*. In this account, Gongsun Zhu's 公孫朱 half-brother dies and Gongsun Zhu questions Ziyou 子游 about the mourning procedure. Ziyou replies that the half-brother should be mourned according to the Greater Mourning statutes.[77] Zheng Xuan explains Ziyou's reasoning with the following statement: "Since [the half-brother] is considered a relative, then he is to be mourned according to the Greater Mourning."[78] Wang Su takes issue with this blanket statement, arguing, "One should not mourn half-brothers of different fathers and the same mother. Speaking of those living with a stepfather, one should mourn the stepfather, thus the Greater Mourning should be observed for *his* sons.[79] The rites are not clear in this matter, but this is what Ziyou suspected and replied."[80] Wang Su also cites a statement attributed to Confucius contained in the *Kongzi jiayu* 孔子家語 [*Family Teachings of Confucius*] on this question that reads, "One who lives with a stepfather should mourn for his half-brothers. If they do not live together, one does not even mourn for the stepfather, much less his sons!"[81] Thus, Wang Su disputes Zheng Xuan's sweeping statement on the half-brothers as relatives entitled to the Greater Mourning by qualifying the relationship on the basis of living arrangements.

Qiao Zhou's own comments on this situation are brief. He writes: "Now in mourning for half-brothers with a different father after the death of one's [own] father and the remarriage of the mother, the brothers all observe the same degree of mourning as a courtesy."[82] While Qiao does not specify a period or level of mourning to be observed, he notes the equal mourning to be observed by the siblings. The conditions of living together or apart emphasized by Wang Su are absent from Qiao's commentary, and the general nature of his opinion echoes that of Zheng Xuan. However, most later early medieval exegetes followed Wang Su and stressed the issue of cohabitation as the key factor in determining the mourning of half-brothers.[83]

Aside from the all-pervasive theme of relationships—indeed, the core of the rites—perhaps the most important issue in Qiao Zhou's writings on ritual was that of reducing the standard level or time period of mourning observance. While there were mentions of specific circumstances in which mourning was to be reduced in the so-called Zhou ritual texts, the issue came to the fore during the Three States period. The *Encyclopedic History of Institutions* discussion on the topic of reduction of mourning is dominated by commentary from Tian Qiong 田瓊 of Wei.[84] On the subject of the reduction of mourning by the sons of feudal lords and grandees, Tian stresses the connection between the father and son in observing mourning, arguing, "If the ruler does not observe mourning, his son does not dare to observe it . . . If the father reduces the mourning period, then his son does not dare not to reduce it."[85] Xu Zheng 徐整 of Wu held that the observation of the son was based solely on the office held by the father. He argues, "The son of a grandee follows the reduction of mourning of a grandee. When his father dies, he mourns as a person of state."[86] Thus, the privilege of reducing mourning by the son of a grandee was revoked on his father's death.

Qiao Zhou's comments on the matter, while agreeing in principle with those of Xu Zheng, distinguish further between the sons of the principal wife and cadet sons:

> The son of a grandee, while his father is still alive, reduces the mourning for his lateral relatives.[87] If he [the son] is also a grandee, he follows his father in satisfying the mourning. The cadet son of a grandee does not mourn his wife's parents. For his mother and his wife he observes the Greater Mourning. If his father has already died, then he observes mourning for all of them as a person of state.[88]

In this passage, Qiao Zhou notes the loss of reduction privileges for the cadet son of a grandee who has died. However, Qiao's comments do not mention similar loss by the legitimate son.

The same general principle of equal mourning observance by a feudal lord or grandee and his son was to be followed by the wives of these elites. Tian Qiong argues that the wives of feudal lords and grandees followed the same mourning period and practice as their husbands because their level of honor was the same. Tian supports this argument with several situational examples of equal mourning observance by husbands and wives, noting that when the husband reduced mourning, his wife did the same.[89] Similar pronouncements were also made by She Ci 射慈, who notes that daughters of feudal lords who married feudal lords followed their husbands in reducing mourning for both his and her families.[90]

Qiao Zhou adds further stipulations on the reduction of mourning for the wives of feudal lords and grandees:

> The wife of a feudal lord follows her lord in reducing the mourning for her lateral relatives, and thus does not mourn. In mourning for members of her clan, she also reduces the mourning for her lateral relatives. Except for those

> who are feudal lords, she does not mourn for those requiring mourning of less than one year. In mourning her father, mother, or grandparents, she does so as a person of state. The confirmed wife of a grandee mourns for her lateral relatives at the level of a grandee and reduces it one level. After the death of her father, she does not reduce the mourning because of her marriage, but may reduce it one level because of the honor [of becoming the wife of a grandee].[91]

Qiao Zhou notes that the wife of a feudal lord was entitled to forgo mourning for relatives requiring less than one year, and to reduce the mourning for her closest relatives by virtue of her marriage relationship.

A final discussion on reduction of mourning is contained in the *Encyclopedic History of Institutions* under the topic heading of "No reduction of mourning for persons of status." Here Tian Qiong comments on the mourning observed by the wife of a grandee for her children: "The wife of a grandee mourns three years for her eldest son. For a daughter who is married to a grandee, she observes the Greater Mourning."[92] She Ci cites the commentary to the *Record of Rites* in refuting Tian Qiong's statement:

> The *Commentary* said, "If the levels of honor are equal, then one obtains the mourning of relatives."[93] The saying "levels of honor are equal" means if all involved are ministers or grandees, then each mourns as a relative and does not reduce the mourning. The daughter of a feudal lord who is the wife of a feudal lord does not reduce the mourning for her parents or her brothers after the death of her father. The wife of a grandee mourns for her parents and brothers after the death of her father, but does not reduce mourning for the family heir.[94]

Qiao Zhou offers a lengthy explication of this topic, noting various situations among families of feudal lords in which mourning was reduced to the level of a person of state and arguing:

> A feudal lord reduces the mourning for his lateral relatives. If a lateral relative is a feudal lord or if a daughter is married to a feudal lord, he mourns as a person of state. The heir of a feudal lord mourns for his mother, wife, maternal grandparents, and his wife's parents as a person of state. Though the heir has no formal rank, he is of his lord's body. If his appointment has been received from the Son of Heaven, then his mourning for an adult is reduced by one level. If he has not yet received his appointment, then he is a lesser ruler of state. He is the master of his wife. Thus, the heir, in all his mourning, mourns as a person of state.
>
> Anciently, it was said that the maternal grandparents were the legitimate heads of the mother's clan. The wife's parents were the legitimate heads of the wife's clan. The honor of the mother, wife, and self are the same. One does not reduce what they do not reduce. Therefore, the heir does not reduce

> the mourning for his wife's parents. The wife of a feudal lord mourns for her parents and grandparents as a person of state. The confirmed wife of a grandee mourns for her brothers as the successors of her father. If one [brother] was a great clansman, then she observes mourning as a person of state.[95]

Qiao Zhou's opinions are in general agreement with those of Tian Qiong and She Ci.

Reduction of mourning by the upper levels of society seems to have been widely accepted, though it was without classical precedent. But this opinion was not universally held. Yu Xi 虞喜 (fl.late third–fourth century) argues that this practice was a recent development. Yu writes, "The ancients did not reduce mourning. From the top to the bottom, all mourned their relatives. This was prior to the Yin dynasty. The decline and death of the rites began in the Zhou."[96] He Xun also sets up a detailed list indicating which family members a feudal lord, grandee, and the wives of rulers and grandees were permitted to reduce mourning for and which required full observance.[97]

The question of why this high level of interest for a ritual topic with no Zhou antecedent must be addressed. Chen Xuguo has shown in his study of Three States period mourning ritual that none of the states strictly observed the canonically prescribed mourning practices, noting that the received Zhou ritual codes were influential, but, due to political expediencies, they were seldom followed. In particular, burial rites were simplified—often at the request of the soon-to-be deceased—and the time of mourning was greatly reduced. These trends can be clearly seen in the burial of and mourning for Cao Cao, whose last wishes for a simple burial were followed by his son and heir Cao Pi. Additionally, Chen Xuguo's account presents ample evidence to show that Cao Pi did not observe the standard three-year mourning for his father's death, instead accepting the abdication of Emperor Xian, taking additional consorts, and engaging in festive eating and drinking prohibited by the classical mourning codes.[98] As for Shu-Han, Liu Shan was once praised by Qiao Zhou for his filiality in exceeding the three-year mourning for his father,[99] but, like Cao Pi, Liu Shan resumed activities unsuited to one in mourning for the loss of a father prior to the completion of the three years, in particular, changing the year-title before the end of the year in which his father died.[100] Under the political circumstances of the times, the full observation of the received Zhou rites could hardly have been expected to be followed. For this reason, it is not surprising to find scholars of the canon debating the discrepancies between the Zhou ideal and contemporary practice.

THE INFLUENCE OF QIAO ZHOU'S CANONICAL CRITICISM

How, then, should Qiao Zhou's writings on the ritual as contained in the few surviving fragments of his *Discourse on the Truths and Falsehoods in the*

Five Canonical Texts be evaluated? As noted throughout the previous discussion, the issues touched on by Qiao's critical exegesis were not unique, but were in step with some of the general concerns of late Han canonical studies. Moreover, when Qiao Zhou addressed issues covered by the era's two most significant canonical commentators Zheng Xuan and Wang Su, he generally took positions similar to those of Zheng Xuan. Qiao Zhou appears to have been intent on clarifying ambiguous passages or correcting views deemed to be historically incorrect rather than pursuing a larger ethical or metaphysical agenda. In this regard, Qiao Zhou appears to have been more conservative in his approach to the canon than other third-century scholars influenced by Song Zhong's ethical-metaphysical interpretations of the canon and *Supreme Mystery*. With Mystery Learning beginning to prevail in both private intellectual circles as well as the state-run academies of the Central Plains, Qiao Zhou's canonical scholarship was clearly behind the times.

Moreover, Qiao Zhou's scholarship does not appear to have garnered a great deal of attention during the early medieval period. This fact may well be a result of the growing popularity and political orthodoxy of Wang Su's canonical interpretations. Given the closeness in opinion of Qiao Zhou with the then-discredited views of Zheng Xuan, it should come as no surprise to find Qiao's works in this area largely overlooked by intellectuals from the third through seventh centuries. In only one instance do the sources offer accounts of individuals of the third/fourth century commenting directly on Qiao Zhou's views. In this instance, the Jin scholar Yu Xi disagreed with Qiao's opinion on the proper mourning practice of cadet sons.[101]

However, in the early seventh century, Kong Yingda 孔穎達 (574–648 CE) revived the views of Zheng Xuan. Kong's *Wujing zhengyi* 五經正義 [*Orthodox Meanings of the Five Canonical Texts*], elevated Zheng Xuan's interpretations of the canon over those of Wang Su, and soon Kong's exegesis was accepted as the curriculum at the Tang imperial academy.[102] With the rise in Zheng Xuan's interpretations, Qiao Zhou's views were also revisited by several Tang scholars. As noted earlier, Yang Shuxun referenced Qiao's reconstructed chronology for the proper age of the capping ritual, while Peng Jingzhi cited Qiao Zhou as an authority in his opposition to current ritual practice.

The most significant use of Qiao Zhou's canonical criticism during the Tang was the citation of numerous passages from Qiao's writings in the *Encyclopedic History of Institutions* by Du You.[103] The text, completed in 801 CE, was compiled to present the historical foundations of state institutions as models for the current regime. Half of the work's two hundred fascicles are devoted to matters of ritual. Here, Du You presents the views of various ritual authorities of the past ages on a wide range of topics. First, Du You offers the matter under discussion as contained in the canon, then he quotes varying opinions on the issue as if in dialogue with each other. In a sense, by arranging the interpretations of the ritual canon of various scholars in this manner, Du You constructs a debate between these intellectuals. The inclusion of Qiao Zhou in these "debates" shows that by the Tang, Qiao Zhou was again recognized as an authority on matters of ritual and deemed worthy of inclusion in the conversation on the rites with such heavyweights as Zheng Xuan and Wang Su. Du You clearly saw value in Qiao's opinions on capping, marriage, sacrifices, and mourning rites. Moreover, Du You's presentation of Qiao Zhou's writings on ritual in his *Encyclopedic History of Institutions* played a significant role in not only the preservation of Qiao's commentary on the ritual canon, but also in defining the manner in which Qiao Zhou would be regarded as a scholar of the canon by later generations. While it is unclear whether other sections of Qiao's *Discourse on Truths and Falsehoods in the Five Canonical Texts* survived into the the eighth century, Du You's inclusion of only the writings on ritual has dramatically shaped the way later scholars viewed Qiao's text itself.

On the basis of roughly thirty fragments of text from Qiao Zhou's *Discourse on the Truths and Falsehoods in the Five Canonical Texts*, we can reach a few important conclusions regarding the nature of Qiao's canonical criticism. In addition to illustrating his range of expertise on matters of ritual, the surviving passages of Qiao's canonical criticism also demonstrate an acceptance of portions of the canon as historical documents. That is, Qiao Zhou used particular canonical texts as historical evidence with which to refute the claims of other canonical texts or their interpretations. For example, Qiao's discussion on the matter of capping and marriage hinges on an appeal to ancient history for ritual precedence. In this case, the old text *Documents* provides the "proof" needed to refute some unspecified views on the proper age for the performance of the capping ritual.[104] Elsewhere, Qiao Zhou referenced the *Zuo Traditon*, as well as other canonical texts to argue against some of the prescriptions of the Han ritual canon. In these critiques, Qiao clearly believed in the historicity of the *Documents* and *Zuo Traditon* and felt empowered to use the ideas contained within these texts to refute those of other texts within the canon. In short, Qiao Zhou's approach to the canon was selective, eclectic, and historical.

Qiao Zhou's view of the canon as history was very much in accord with the times. As noted by several modern scholars, in the late Han canonical studies and historiography were closely linked. In a lengthy exposition of the development of canonical and historical studies, Qian Mu 錢穆 (1895–1990) recites the traditional view that Confucius was at the root of the canon, having some relationship with the various texts therein, quoting an old saying that claims "Confucius' intent was [expressed] in the *Spring and Autumn*; his actions were [manifest] in the *Classic of Filial Piety*."[105] Qian Mu offers the view that "classical [or canonical] studies were historical studies."[106] Similarly, Lu Yaodong 逯耀東 argues for the early link between these two fields of academic study on the basis of their respective positions in the "Bibliographic Treatise" of the *Han History*, which places historical texts immediately following canonical texts.[107]

Significantly, both Qian Mu and Lu Yaodong date the emergence of historiography as an independent discipline to roughly the second century CE. Lu Yaodong claims that the development of a historiographical consciousness was contemporaneous with the development of literary consciousness, and places this squarely within the context of the Jian'an period of the Later Han. As a result, history began to be treated as a professional discipline and subject of academic inquiry in its own right. Following the split of historical studies from canonical studies, Lu argues, historical exegesis retained the model of canonical commentary as it explored the body of historical writings as if they were canonical texts.[108] With this changing view of textual categories or genres, it should not surprise us to find Qiao Zhou's writings on canonical topics blending his expertise in history with that of the canon, and treating the canon historically. Likewise, in his writings on ancient history, Qiao frequently called on the canon for support of his critique of contemporary views on history.

CHAPTER 5

Critical Approaches to Ancient History

THE STATE OF HISTORICAL STUDIES

As history emerged as an independent discipline separate from canonical studies during the Later Han, a greater number of Chinese intellectuals focused their energies on compiling histories and commenting on earlier historical texts. These early medieval historians applied many of the same methods and techniques associated with the explication of the canon to historical writing and, as such, historical exegesis grew as a legitimate field of scholarship. Evidence from the bibliographic treatises of the *Han History* and the *Sui History* dramatically illustrates the rapid growth of history as an academic discipline in China over the course of the early medieval period.

During the pre-Han period, efforts to record and interpret the past were numerous and varied, as were the motivations behind such efforts. History took the form of odes, speeches, political and philosophical discourse, myth and legend, and chronicle, with each genre functioning as a vehicle for specific rhetorical concerns.[1] Ban Gu's "Bibliographic Treatise" provides a convenient overview of the state of historical studies (or production) through the Former Han period. In this work, derived from Liu Xiang's earlier bibliography, the *Qilüe* 七略 [*Seven Epitomes*],[2] Ban Gu categorized the imperial library in terms of the canon, with generic categories for each canonical text. In this manner he employed the term and text "*Spring and Autumn*" as the category head for historical writing.[3] Under this heading are listed the *Chunqiu gujing* 春秋古經 [*The Ancient Canon Spring and Autumn*] with sixteen commentaries, chronologies, and other supplemental biographies to the canonical text. In addition to these texts directly related to the canonical *Spring and Autumn*, the bibliographic treatise includes collections of speeches, including *Discourses from the States* and *Stratagems of the Warring States*; genealogical histories such as *Shiben* 世本 [*Roots of Generations*]; and a chronological history modeled on the *Spring and Autumn* entitled the *Chu Han chunqiu* 楚漢

春秋 [*Annals of Chu and Han*]. Following these texts, the bibliography lists Sima Qian's *The Grand Scribe's [Records]* with one commentary, and two volumes of annals for the Former Han. In all, the *Han History* "Bibliographic Treatise" includes entries for twenty-three works under the heading "*Spring and Autumn*."[4] From this list we may infer that during the Former Han the canonical *Spring and Autumn* not only lent its name to the whole of historical writings, but also shaped the discipline in terms of form and approach.

This observation is supported by two of the most important commentaries on the *Spring and Autumn* and their influence on later historiography. Specifically, both the *Zuo Tradition* and the *Gongyang Tradition* on the *Spring and Autumn* continued the ancient practice of the historian offering moral judgment through his presentation and evaluation of past persons and deeds. These judgments were based on the worldview of the classisicists (*ru* 儒; often translated as "Confucian"),[5] and in many ways, these historical commentaries legitimized classicist morality by showing its antiquity and efficacy as demonstrated in the past.[6] This model of "praise and blame history" gradually became established as one of the predominant modes of traditional Chinese historiography.

The use of the praise and blame model is quite apparent in Sima Qian's *The Grand Scribe's Records*, without question the most important historical work produced in China. The text, a history of the world as known to Sima Qian covering a period from the legendary Yellow Thearch to the first century BCE, was by the author's own admission an effort to continue the traditions of earlier commentary on the *Spring and Autumn*.[7] Mark Edward Lewis argues that this intent was apparent in the organization and form of the text. Filling the role of "canon" in Sima Qian's history were the annals or chronological accounts of the ruling houses that opened the text. The remaining subsections of the text functioned as commentary: chronological tables; documents or treatises on various topics; hereditary houses, or accounts of the pre-Qin states, Confucius, and important figures from the Han; and biographies of eminent persons from diverse fields as politics, military, scholarship, and so on.[8] In this regard, Sima Qian's work, though a work of "new history" and not a commentary per se, was firmly situated in the tradition of exegesis on canonical history.

However, in terms of scope and format, *The Grand Scribe's Records* was revolutionary. The text was later accepted as the first of the so-called standard histories and served as the general model for the form of all later standard or dynastic histories.[9] Ban Gu's *Han History* retained the basic form (i.e., sequence and subsections) of *The Grand Scribe's Records* while limiting its scope to that of a single dynastic epoch: the Former Han.[10] The *Han History* was similarly moralistic in its approach, assigning praise and blame to historical figures while forwarding various classicist agendas. By the end of the second century CE, these two histories stood as both models for later historians and subjects of exegesis themselves.

The "Bibliographic Treatise" in the *Sui History* documents the vast expansion of historical writing during the six centuries separating the Later Han from the Tang dynasty, illustrating growth in terms of both sheer quantity and conceptual scope. Largely following the model of Ban Gu's "Bibliographic Treatise," the *Sui History* bibliography contains generic headings with detailed lists and descriptions of texts below. As in the earlier bibliographic essay, the *Sui History* bibliography uses the canonical texts *Hallowed Documents* and *Spring and Autumn* as category heads. However, unlike the *Han History* treatise, the *Sui History* bibliography restricts the *Spring and Autumn* category to texts directly related to the canonical history, including entries on over one hundred commentaries and supplemental works. Significantly, *The Grand Scribes Records* and other historical writings subsumed under this heading in the *Han History* treatise are not included.[11]

This omission was rectified by the creation of a broad new generic category: *shi* 史 (History). At the head of the category of "History" stands *The Grand Scribe's Records*, accompanied by four early commentaries on the text. Next was Ban Gu's *Han History* and seventeen commentaries. The placement of these two works at the head of the newly devised bibliographic category speaks to the esteem with which the individual texts were held in the early Tang, while the numerous commentaries on the two histories indicate their status as quasi-canonical historical texts. Following these entries, the *Sui History* bibliography lists titles, authors, and descriptions of nearly seventy histories of various states from the Han through Sui periods.[12] In most cases, these works follow the form and scope established by *The Grand Scribe's Records* and *Han History*.

While the number of "dynastic" histories produced from the Han through Sui is impressive, they were only a small fraction of the total body of historical writing of the early medieval period catalogued by the *Sui History* bibliography under the heading of "History." These dynastic histories are followed in the bibliography by a lengthy list of annals/chronologies, collections of documents and speeches, biographies, genealogies, geographical writings, and associated commentaries. In total, the *Sui History* "Bibliographic Treatise" lists over eight hundred titles of historical works. Clearly, history was conceived as a broad disciplinary category, and was a significant focus of intellectual activity during early medieval China.[13]

Although Qiao Zhou lived during this boom of historical writing and much of his intellectual energies appear to have been directed toward this activity, the vast majority of histories catalogued in the *Sui History* "Bibliographic Treatise" was produced after Qiao Zhou's lifetime. As such, in the history of early medieval historiography Qiao Zhou stands as more a pioneer than follower. In particular, when viewed in the context of late Han historiography, Qiao Zhou appears to have broken with the nascent traditions of the discipline and forged new directions in historical scholarship. Prior to examining those innovations, let us first briefly survey the main threads of late Han historiography.

During the Later Han period, historical writing developed rapidly along several subgeneric lines. The most serious, or perhaps politically legitimate enterprises, were the numerous efforts to compile in-progress histories of the Later Han dynasty, including annals, biographies, and institutional histories.[14] Some of these histories were state-sponsored, but the majority, like their early Han models Sima Qian's *The Grand Scribe's Records* and Ban Gu's *Han History*, were private ventures. Similarly, although most of these texts have been lost or severely fragmented, surviving evidence shows considerable formal similarities to *The Grand Scribe's Records* and *Han History*.

Reflecting the quasicanonical status of *The Grand Scribe's Records* and *Han History*, at least a dozen commentaries on these two historical texts were compiled in the period leading up to and through Qiao Zhou's lifetime.[15] Although biographical information on many of these early historical commentators is lacking and their writings have been seriously fragmented, enough information remains to allow us to sketch a basic picture of early historical exegesis, setting a proper context for Qiao Zhou's own work in this field.

With regards to Sima Qian's *The Grand Scribe's Records*, only one commentary on the work appears to have been compiled prior to the third century CE: Yan Du's 延篤 (d. 144 CE) *Shiji yinyi* 史記音義 [*Sounds and Meanings in The Grand Scribe's Records*]. A brief biography in the *Later Han History* indicates that Yan was a student of the noted late Han classicists Tang Xidian 唐溪典 and Ma Rong, studying the *Zuo Tradition* with Tang.[16] Later, Yan served in the Eastern Palace, the site of official historiographical activity. The four extant fragments of his commentary on Sima Qian's history all cite parallel passages from the *Stratagems of the Warring States* to provide phonetic and explanatory (hence the title "Sound and Meaning") glosses on terms in *The Grand Scribe's Records*. Describing Yan Du's exegetical work, the late Han *Han History* commentator Fu Qian 服虔 said that Yan Du was "one who aimed for correctness."[17]

Interestingly, Ban Gu's *Han History* proved to be a more common base text for historical exegesis during the late Han and Three States period. Scott Galer has identified eleven commentators whose lives and works predate or correspond to that of Qiao Zhou. Those active prior to the third century were Hu Guang 胡廣 (91–172 CE),[18] Ying Shao 應劭 (fl. 165–204 CE),[19] Li Qi 李奇,[20] Wen Ying 文穎,[21] Fu Yan 伏儼,[22] and Fu Qian.[23] An additional five scholars compiled commentaries on the *Han History* during the Three States period: Su Lin 蘇林 (served as an official under Wei),[24] Zhang Yan 張晏 (fl. ca. 264 CE),[25] Meng Kang 孟康 (fl. ca. 264 CE; served as an official under Wei),[26] Wei Zhao 韋昭 (204–273 CE; served as an official under Wu),[27] and Ru Chun 如淳.[28] Significantly, Qiao Zhou and his mentor Qin Mi are the only Shu-Han scholars identified as having engaged in serious historiographical activity and, unfortunately, the writings of Qin Mi in this field have not survived. Despite the dearth of biographical information on many of these exegetes and the lack of detailed bibliographic information on their scholarly works, the surviving commentary by these scholars reflects the concerns of the genre and illustrates what appears to have been the dominant mode of historical exegesis during the second and third centuries CE.

One of the main motivations of commentary, both canonical and historical, during the late Han and Three States period was the clarification of the base text. The explanation of the text was thought to be necessary for a variety of reasons, most related to historical and textual issues. For example, changes in grammar, forms of graphs, pronunciation, and culture and institutions appear to have resulted in a communication gap, of sorts, between the author(s) of the base text and its contemporary readers.[29] This functional need for a commentator to mediate between author and reader can be seen in a few comments regarding the *Han History*. In one instance, the noted canonical exegete Ma Rong sought instruction from Ban Zhao 班昭, sister of Ban Gu and herself a contributing author to the *Han History*. The account reads:

> At this time, the *Han History* began to emerge, but many were not yet able to understand it. Ma Rong, from the same commandery [as Ban Zhao] received tutelege in the pavilion and listened to Ban Zhao read [the *Han History*]. Later, Ma Rong's brother Ma Xu was summoned to succeed Ban Zhao in completing [the history].[30]

Similarly, during the Three States period, the ruler of Wu, Sun Quan, sought a *Han History* tutor for his son.[31] Later scholars have reasoned, on the basis of these anecdotes, that "people of the Han, in reading books, required instruction from a master. Without a master, they could not read."[32]

This need to explain the base text is also illustrated in the content of the commentary itself. Most of the roughly three thousand extant passages of commentary on *The Grand Scribe's Records* and *Han History* by the scholars previously noted employ a "sounds and meaning" approach. That is, these commentaries offer explanatory remarks on the pronunciation of terms, as well as frequently supply identifications of people, places, and objects that had slipped from familiar recognition in the intervening centuries. In most of the surviving annotations, the commentator's sources are not recorded, though in a few instances references to other texts as sources of the commentary are noted.[33] In this manner, most early historical commentary provided the reader with notes needed to make sense of the base text, but largely avoided interpretative intrusions.[34] It is within this context of "sound and meaning" explanatory historical commentary that Qiao Zhou compiled his most well-known scholarly work, an interpretative-critical commentary on ancient history.

INVESTIGATIONS OF ANCIENT HISTORY

Qiao's text, identified in the traditional bibliographic sources by the title *Gushi kao* 古史考 [*Investigations of Ancient History*],[35] is significant for two reasons. First, it is widely regarded as one of the earliest commentaries on Sima Qian's *The*

Grand Scribe's Records. Second, and more important, it stands as one of the earliest works of historical criticism in the Chinese tradition. In this regard, Qiao Zhou ought to be viewed as a founder of the genre of historical writing known as "investigations of history" (*kaoshi* 考史), and his *Investigations of Ancient History* should occupy an important place in the history of Chinese historiography. Though lost as an integral work after the thirteenth century, approximately one hundred fragments from the once-voluminous *Investigations of Ancient History* survive, cited in a variety of sources, including commentaries on *The Grand Scribe's Records*,[36] various other historical works,[37] commentaries on early medieval literature,[38] and medieval encyclopedia such as *Excerpts from Books in the Northern Hall*, *Collection of Literature Arranged by Categories*, *Records of Primary Scholarship*, and *Imperially Reviewed Encyclopedia of the Taiping Period*.[39]

CRITIQUE OF *THE GRAND SCRIBE'S RECORDS* AND OTHER ANCIENT HISTORIES

Despite the lack of a preface or other statement of intent from Qiao Zhou, since at the least the seventh century there has been a general consensus on the motives behind and the objectives of *Investigations of Ancient History*. This opinion is based largely on a single statement recorded in two Tang sources. The earliest statement of Qiao Zhou's motive, found in the *Jin History* biography of the Jin historian Sima Biao, reads:

> Previously, Qiao Zhou considered Sima Qian's *The Grand Scribe's Records* account of the [periods] up to the Zhou and Qin to have sometimes adopted vulgar sayings and the words of the various philosophers, and not relied exclusively upon the orthodox canon. Qiao Zhou then wrote *Investigations of Ancient History* in twenty-five sections, relying on the ancient canon to correct Sima Qian's errors. Sima Biao, in turn considered Qiao Zhou's [work] to be not yet perfect, and thus listed one hundred twenty-two incorrect items in *Investigations of Ancient History*, mostly relying upon the chronicle from Jizhong 汲冢. It [i.e., Sima Biao's corrections] is still in circulation.[40]

A second major Tang source also addresses the issue of Qiao Zhou's intent in compiling *Investigations of Ancient History*. Liu Zhiji 劉知幾 (661–721 CE) quotes the *Jin History* attribution in his *Shitong* 史通 [*Understanding History*],[41] and elsewhere expounds on the issue, arguing:

> Qiao Zhou compiled *Investigations of Ancient History* seeking to reject Sima Qian's *Records* because the master [Sima Qian] had put aside the Confucian canon when writing of the matter of Li Si's removal. [*Investigations of Ancient History*] says, "Qin killed its grandee." [Qiao Zhou] used the title "grandee" of the feudal lords when [Li Si] was the prime minister of the Son of Heaven. By means of this, [Qiao] imitated the *Spring and Autumn*. This is what is called "Similar appearances but different intent."[42]

In this passage, Liu Zhiji strengthens the force of Qiao's intent from "correction" (*jiu* 糾) (as argued in the *Jin History*) to "rejection" (*binyi* 擯抑). Additionally, he provides an illustration of this process, arguing that Qiao was following the historical model of the commentaries on the *Spring and Autumn* in subtly rectifying a perceived error in the earlier text.

Later scholars have widely accepted the attribution that Qiao Zhou's intent was to correct errors in Sima Qian's *Grand Scribe's Records* by appeals to the canon.[43] While this generalization is largely supported, a close examination of the surviving fragments reveals significant exceptions to the rule. First, as Zhang Zongyuan 章宗源 notes in the preface to his reconstruction of the text, a few surviving passages of Qiao's *Investigations of Ancient History* address historical topics beyond the chronological scope of *The Grand Scribe's Records*.[44] Although Zhang Zongyuan presents no examples to support this conclusion, in a passage apparently commenting on the "Biography of Bo Yi and Shu Qi" (*The Grand Scribe's Records* fascicle 61), Qiao Zhou offers up the case of a worthy from Shu commandery named Ren Yong 任永 who was temporarily blinded during the reign of Gongsun Shu but regained his sight after Gongsun's defeat.[45] While in accord with the moral of *The Grand Scribe's Records* narrative, the event it reports occurred much later than the text's chronology. Second, many of Qiao Zhou's "corrections" have no antecedents in the received editions of the canonical texts. This may indicate that Qiao made use of editions of canonical books such as the *Zuo Tradition* and *Hallowed Documents* that are unavailable today, or he may have based his corrections on sources other than the canon. Therefore, on the basis of an examination of the surviving fragments of *Investigations of Ancient History*, the narrow hypothesis of the *Jin History* must be expanded. Nevertheless, the greater number of the surviving fragments of Qiao Zhou's *Investigations of Ancient History* support the *Jin History*'s claim that the work was a commentary on Sima Qian's *The Grand Scribe's Records*, but, in order to further assess the hypothesis's assertion that Qiao Zhou drew on the canon to correct Sima Qian's "reliance upon vulgar sayings" and the "words of the hundred schools of thought," we must first briefly discuss *The Grand Scribe's Records* and its own sources.

Sima Qian's "Postface" to *The Grand Scribe's Records* provides the earliest statement regarding the sources for the compilation of his history. In it, he writes, "Three years after the death [of my father], I, Qian became the Prefect Grand Astrologer and compiled my historical record from the documents of the stone chambers and metal cases."[46] This passage indicates Sima Qian's use of the imperial archives and hints at the diversity of his source material. In his biography of Sima Qian, Ban Gu notes specific works said to have been utilized in the compilation of *The Grand Scribe's Records:* "The Grand Scribe relied upon [the *Traditions* of] Mr. Zuo [Qiuming] and the *Discourses from the States*, and picked from *Roots of Generations*, *Stratagems of the Warring States*, and *Annals of Chu and Han*."[47]

In addition to the remarks by Sima Qian and Ban Gu, several modern studies on the sources of *The Grand Scribe's Records* offer important conclusions on the subject. Studies by Édouard Chavannes, Takigawa Kametarō 瀧川龜太郎 (1865–1946), and Jin Dejian 金德建 examine the various sources employed by Sima Qian, concluding that while certain canonical texts (especially the *Hallowed Documents* and commentaries on the *Spring and Autumn*) were employed in the compilation of *The Grand Scribe's Records*, a greater number of non-canonical materials was used.[48] On the basis of these bibliographical studies, we can see the justification of Qiao Zhou's supposed criticism of *The Grand Scribe's Records*, for while traces of the canon are found throughout *The Grand Scribe's Records*, a large body of non-canonical sources abound.

This quantitative conclusion leads to the obvious question: if *Investigations of Ancient History* used the canonical texts to correct *The Grand Scribe's Records*, then to what extent did Sima Qian himself use these same canonical texts as sources? The *Han History* offers the earliest opinion on this matter. Ban Gu writes, "Sima Qian followed Kong Anguo's inquiries into antiquity. [Sima] Qian's book cited the "Canon of Yao," the "Tribute of Yu," the "Great Plan," the "Prince of Wei," the "Metal-bound Coffer," and other documents. Many of these were the sayings from the old text [*Documents*]."[49] Ban Gu's comment, while significant for its mention of Sima Qian's use of the *Documents*, also points toward a larger question: which editions of the canonical texts were used as sources for *The Grand Scribe's Records?* Three modern studies on the *Documents* and *The Grand Scribe's Records* reach somewhat different conclusions on the matter of editions. For example, Chavannes concludes that Sima Qian evinced a preference for the new text *Documents*.[50] Jin Dejian indicates that Sima Qian utilized both editions of the text, but makes no claim as to which text Sima Qian preferred or cited most often.[51] Finally, Gu Guoshun's 古國順 *Studies on The Grand Scribe's Records citing the Hallowed Documents* concludes that Sima Qian relied mostly on the so-called new text *Documents*.[52] Similarly, a study by Gu Lisan 顧立三 concludes that Sima Qian not only followed the moralizing "praise and blame" format of the *Zuo Tradition*, but also directly incorporated material from the *Zuo Tradition* into his own work.[53]

If, as this survey of recent scholarship indicates, Sima Qian did draw from the canon, in particular the *Hallowed Documents* and the *Zuo Tradition*, then what grounds might Qiao Zhou have for criticizing *The Grand Scribe's Records* for paying insufficient attention to the canon? We have seen that *The Grand Scribe's Records* utilized both old and new text editions of the *Documents*, the *Spring and Autumn* and two of its commentaries, as well as other canonical texts. However, the majority of titles cited in Takigawa's and Jin Dejian's bibliographies are from the works of various Zhou period thinkers outside the canon. Despite the overwhelming number of non-canonical texts listed, Gu Guoshun's, Gu Lisan's and Jin Dejian's research all points to the conclusion that Sima Qian was heavily influenced by selected works from the canon, and suggests that the use of other, non-canonical texts was supplemental in nature.

Still following the attribution that *Investigations of Ancient History* was an effort to correct *The Grand Scribe's Records* by appeals to canonical texts, let us now briefly turn our attention to the sources for Qiao Zhou's work. In only four instances does Qiao Zhou explicitly note the source of his amendments, twice claiming to follow *Roots of Generations*, while citing a commentary of the *Spring and Autumn* and the *Discourses from the States* once each.[54] Additionally, in several instances we have the comments of others indicating where Qiao Zhou's material originated. For example, Sima Zhen claims that certain passages of *Investigations of Ancient History* were based on material found in the *Spring and Autumn*, the *Zuo Tradition*, and the *Discourses from the States*.[55] Attempts to collate these specific fragments of *Investigations of Ancient History* with the sources cited by Qiao Zhou and others have proved unsuccessful. Therefore, the claim that *Investigations of Ancient History* was intended as a correction of *The Grand Scribe's Records* by appeals to the canon is complicated by the attribution of common sources for both Sima Qian's history and Qiao Zhou's criticism and a scarcity of canonical corollaries for Qiao's surviving commentary.

The most troubling of these shared sources is a text entitled *Roots of Generations*, thus described by Ban Gu: "*Roots of Generations* records the ancestors and origins of the thearchs, kings, dukes, feudal lords, ministers, and grandees from the time of the Yellow Thearch to the Spring and Autumn period."[56] The authorship of the text is unclear. While Ban Gu offers no attribution of authorship to the work, the *Sui History* bibliography contains two entries for the work. The first notes the title in two fascicles compiled by Liu Xiang; the other, also in two fascicles, compiled by Song Zhong.[57] The two *Tang History* bibliographies record *Roots of Generations* in four fascicles compiled by Song Zhong.[58] These claims of authorship of *Roots of Generations* are problematic, for if Sima Qian used this work as a source for his history, then it could not possibly have been compiled by either Liu Xiang or Song Zhong since both postdate the compilation of *The Grand Scribe's Records*. Fortunately, other later claims of authorship of the text offer more reasonable conclusions. Fan Ye's brief description of the text in his *Later Han History* reads, "[Zuo Qiuming] also recorded [the lineages] of the thearchs, kings, dukes, feudal lords, ministers, and grandees from the time of the Yellow Thearch to the Spring and Autumn period. [The work] was called *Roots of Generations*, in fifteen sections."[59] Additionally, Yan Zhitui argues forcefully, "*Roots of Generations* was written by Zuo Qiuming."[60] Although the relative lateness of the attribution of the work to Zuo Qiuming is troubling, as is the question of why Ban Gu, writing over a hundred years earlier, did not note this fact, the attribution of authorship of *Roots of Generations* to Zuo Qiuming seems plausible. Given both Sima Qian's and Qiao Zhou's preference for the writings of Zuo Qiuming—both his commentary on the *Spring and Autumn* and the *Discourses from the States*—it would not be unusual for Sima and Qiao to also rely heavily on *Roots of Generations* if they believed it to be the work of Zuo Qiuming.[61] Thus, it seems likely that Qiao Zhou at least regarded Zuo Qiuming as the original compiler of *Roots of Generations*. As we shall see below, this text stands as the source of many of *Investigations of Ancient History* "corrections" to *The Grand Scribe's Records*.

As previously noted, the mainstream of early historical commentary consisted of explanatory glosses on individual graphs or terms in the base text, and these commentaries functioned primarily as reader's guides to the text. A large number of fragments of Qiao's *Investigations of Ancient History* follow this model as they explain things or events in Sima Qian's text. These glosses range from phonetic and phonemic, to identifications of places and personal names, and finally, longer descriptive passages expounding on brief mentions in *The Grand Scribe's Records*.

Many of Qiao Zhou's glosses reflect his expertise in the canon, ritual, and history of the Chengdu Plain. For example, in one instance, Qiao Zhou offers a pronunciation and location of a place name given only brief treatment in *The Grand Scribe's Records*. In fascicle seventy of *The Grand Scribe's Records*, Sima Qian writes, "Ju 苴 and Shu 蜀 attacked each other and each came to inform Qin of its plight."[62] Qiao Zhou's gloss on this passage reads, "Yi Province's Tianju 天苴 is pronounced "bao" as in "Baoli" 包黎. It sounds similar to "ba" 巴 and was likely located in today's Ba commandery."[63] In this example, Qiao offers what appears to be the reading of the graphs for "Tianju" in the local Ba dialect, as well as provides an approximate location for the site, likely based on his own knowledge of his home region.[64]

Most interesting among Qiao Zhou's glosses are the descriptive explanations offered on terse statements in *The Grand Scribe's Records*. For example, Sima Qian writes in the "Hereditary House of the Grand Duke of Qi," "Lü Shang 呂尚 was very poor and old."[65] Qiao Zhou expands and explains, "Lü Wang 呂望 once butchered oxen at Zhaoge 朝歌 and sold drinks at Mengjin 孟津."[66] The source of Qiao Zhou's amendment is unknown. A more detailed explanation on another brief passage is cited in Pei Yin's *Collected Explanations on The Grand Scribe's Records*. Sima Qian's original text states, "This Qin is a land that casts aside propriety and principle and exalts merit that is measured in human heads."[67] Qiao Zhou expounds:

> Qin utilized Wei Yang's 衛鞅 plan[68] and established ranks with twenty levels. In battle, one who obtained the head of a man, according to this plan, received rank. By this means, the men of Qin were always victorious in battle, while the elderly, weak, and women were all killed. Tens of thousands thus received merit through this plan. The subcelestial realm, despising Qin, called it the "Offering-merit-for-heads state."[69]

Again, Qiao's source remains unknown. In these glosses Qiao Zhou's commentary on *The Grand Scribe's Records* appears largely in harmony with other historical exegesis of the period.

The largest body of "sound and meaning" glosses in *Investigations of Ancient History* seeks to rectify perceived errors in personal names found in *The Grand Scribe's Records*. In these passages, Qiao Zhou offers variant names or graphs for personages mentioned in Sima Qian's history.[70] These corrections can be categorized into three broad types. Amendments of the first type simply propose variant graphs for those in Sima Qian's text. For example, in fascicle thirty-two of *The Grand Scribe's Records*, Sima Qian writes, "Tian Chang thus established Duke Jian's younger brother Jing 驁 as Duke Ping."[71] Sima Zhen notes, "*Roots of Generations* and Qiao Zhou both render the graph as Jing 敬, thus [*The Grand Scribe's Records*] is in error."[72] In this case, the graph used by Qiao Zhou and *Roots of Generations*, and favored by Sima Zhen was an alternate form of the more complex graph found in *The Grand Scribe's Records*.[73]

The second type of graphic amendments by Qiao Zhou fall into the category of possible scribal errors. For example, Sima Qian writes, "Duke Yi expired and his son Duke Gui Cimu 癸公慈母 was established."[74] Sima Zhen's commentary notes, "Qiao Zhou said Duke Ji Cimu 祭公慈母."[75] The similarities between the graphs *gui* 癸 and *ji* 祭 are sufficient to raise the question of scribal error. Similarly, in the "Hereditary House of Jin," Sima Qian writes, "In the eighteenth year Marquis Li expired and his son Marquis Xian Ji 獻侯籍 was established."[76] Sima Zhen states, "*Roots of Generations* and Qiao Zhou both rendered this name as Su 蘇."[77] Once again, the similarities between the graphs *ji* 籍 and *su* 蘇 make the possibility of transcription error likely.

The final and most common type of name rectification in Qiao's *Investigations of Ancient History* consists of Qiao Zhou's offering different names for those posited by Sima Qian. In these cases, there appears to be no relationship between the graphs (i.e., alternate forms or possible scribal errors). For example, in the "Hereditary House of Chen Si," Sima Qian notes the establishment of Duke Ping Yu 平公鬱.[78] Sima Zhen adds, "Qiao Zhou said his name was Yulai 郁來."[79] Similarly, we find such conflicting names as "Kangbo" 康伯 and "Moubo" 牟伯[80] and "Juetu" 掘突 and "Tuhua" 突滑.[81] As in the previous cases, there is no additional evidence to determine which name is correct.

The obvious question surrounding these alternate names is: what were Qiao Zhou's sources for these amendments? In several instances Sima Zhen notes the agreement between *Roots of Generations* and *Investigations of Ancient History* accounts. While Qiao's interpretations are largely in harmony with those in *Roots of Generations*, Qiao Zhou sometimes disagrees with the older text. Although the sources of Qiao's amendments in these cases remain unknown, Sima Zhen offers a hint regarding the source for a passage from *Investigations of Ancient History*. Again in the "Hereditary House of Qi," Sima Qian notes the name of Duke Jing's favorite concubine as "Ruiji" 芮姬.[82] Sima Zhen comments, "Qiao Zhou, following Mr. Zuo [Qiuming], rendered the name as Yusi 鬻姒."[83] Utilizing Sima Zhen's clue, we are able to locate the source of this amendment in the *Zuo Tradition* entry for year five of the reign of Duke Ai. It reads, "Of his sons [by concubines] his favorite was Tu, whose mother was Yusi."[84] Unfortunately, the sources for the remaining fragments related to names in *Investigations of Ancient History* cannot be located in the extant historical materials.

In addition to these typical "sound and meaning" glosses, Qiao Zhou's *Investigations of Ancient History* offers several different types of "corrections" to *The Grand Scribe's Records*. These include presenting information that contradicts the accounts contained in Sima Qian's history, as well as adding materials missing from *The Grand Scribe's Records*. In terms of topics of concern, Qiao's *Investigations of Ancient History* covers a wide range of issues, including clans and lineages, biography, chronology, and ancient traditions. Finally, in several instances, Qiao Zhou comments directly on Sima Qian and his history.

One of the largest topics addressed by Qiao Zhou's *Investigations of Ancient History* relates to clan names and lineages. Fifteen fragments scattered about the various Tang commentaries to *The Grand Scribe's Records*, as well as in several Tang encyclopedia address the names and genealogies of not only the rulers of states, but also of the feudal marquises. Several of these passages simply identify clan names, often missing from *The Grand Scribe's Records* account. For example, a fragment contained in the *Record of Primary Scholarship* reads, "The Dating 大庭 clan was surnamed Jiang 姜. They ruled by the virtue of fire. Therefore, [their head] was called by the title of Flaming Thearch (Yan di 炎帝)."[85] While *The Grand Scribe's Records* makes no such statement, the source of Qiao's information is readily available. The *Zuo Tradition* entry for Duke Ai year nine reads, "The Flaming Thearch was the master of fire. His descendents were surnamed Jiang."[86]

In addition to simply identifying clan names, *Investigations of Ancient History* also contradicts information in *The Grand Scribe's Records* on the origins of several clans. The most important such case deals with the lineage of the rulers of Qin, surnamed Ying 嬴. *The Grand Scribe's Records* presents a genealogical statement on the Qin ancestor Bo Yi 柏翳, tracing his lineage back to a granddaughter of Zhuanxu 顓頊, a legendary sage-ruler. Sima Qian notes the supernatural birth of the clan, their efforts in the service of Thearch Shun, as well as the marriage of a son to a daughter of the Shaohao 少昊 [Lesser Heaven] clan—the clan of the Yellow Thearch.[87] Interestingly, Sima Qian traces the lineage through a daughter of Zhuanxu, rather than a son. By doing so, he links the Ying clan to Zhuanxu and, by extension, the Yellow Thearch—the same common ancestor as the Zhou, Yin, and Xia dynasties before. Additionally, in this manner he sidesteps the question of the First Emperor's paternity.[88]

Qiao Zhou, however, presents the lineage of Qin through the paternal line. Qiao writes, "The Qiongsang 窮桑 clan was surnamed Ying. They ruled by the virtue of metal. Therefore, they were called the Metal-heaven (Jintian 金天) clan. Some say their great ancestor followed the Way of the Great

Heaven. Thus, they were called the Shaohao."[89] In ignoring the claims of Sima Qian, which extended the Qin lineage back through a female ancestor to the Yellow Thearch, Qiao Zhou follows the views of the *Zuo Tradition* that contains an anecdote in which the Prince of Tan—a branch of the Qin—states "My exalted ancestor is Shaohao."[90] Regardless of the source of Qiao Zhou's opinion, his position severs the link between the Qin ruling house and the Yellow Thearch as established by Sima Qian.

Yet another strategy employed in *Investigations of Ancient History* involves the retelling of anecdotes from *The Grand Scribe's Records*. Several examples of this practice show Qiao Zhou merely simplifying the earlier account without significant alteration of content or meaning.[91] However, in other instances, Qiao Zhou's version of the anecdote differs from that of Sima Qian in some meaningful manner. For example, twice in *The Grand Scribe's Records*, Sima Qian recounts the story of King Mu 穆 of Zhou's journey to the west and his subsequent rapid return to quash the rebellion led by King Yan of Xu.[92] The account in the "Basic Annals of Qin" notes that King Mu's driver, the Founding Father (Zaofu 造父), "raced nonstop back to Zhou, one-thousand *li* in a day, to avert disorder."[93] Qiao Zhou finds two faults in Sima Qian's narrative: "King Yan of Xu and King Wen of Chu (r. 689–677 BCE) were of the same time period, a great distance from [the time of] King Mu (r. 956–918 BCE). Moreover, as for King Mu traveling in the frontier, how could he have heard of the disorder and ridden a thousand *li* in a day?"[94] Qiao Zhou's criticism turns on both chronological and logistical evidence. First, he notes the nearly three-hundred-year gap between the times of Kings Mu and the so-called rebel King Yan of Xu. Second, Qiao questions King Mu's ability to both receive news of such a rebellion while a great distance from the capital and to travel such a distance in a single day. Thus, on both temporal and spacial grounds, Sima Qian's account is unsatisfactory to Qiao Zhou.

Anecdotes relating to ancient culture bearers constitute the largest single topic of *Investigations of Ancient History* and stand as strong evidence of the need to expand the traditional views on Qiao Zhou's intentions for the work. These thirty-three fragments provide, in varying degrees of detail, information on the origins of several significant cultural inventions. While Western views on culture heroes have emphasized the "concern the gods feel for the physical well-being and nourishment of humans and to the great care they take to teach and show humans how to perform the cultural act,"[95] the writings of Qiao Zhou on the subject make no mention of gods or their benevolence. Rather, Qiao Zhou presents the culture bearers as distinctly human and their innovations as historical fact. Significantly, Qiao Zhou's presentation of these figures engages with views put forth not in Sima Qian's *The Grand Scribe's Records*, but with other accounts of early history.

Qiao Zhou's writings on culture bearers focus on three main types of innovations: culinary, ritual, and tools. On the matter of culinary innovations, Qiao Zhou notes the contributions of four figures: the Fire Driller

(Suiren 燧人), the Divine Farmer (Shennong 神農), the Yellow Thearch, and Yidi 儀狄. In one such passage, Qiao writes:

> As for the ancients, they ate fur and drank blood. The Fire Driller drilled fire and the people began to cook their meat, calling this sauté [or "stir-fry"]. During the time of the Divine Farmer, people ate grains. They placed the grain upon a heated stone and ate it. Then, in the time of the Yellow Thearch, there was the invention of the kettle and earthen rice steamer. The way of cooked food was thus completed.[96]

This fragment conflates several other passages concerning the inventions of the Fire Driller, the Divine Farmer, and the Yellow Thearch. For example, on the Fire Driller, Qiao Zhou also writes:

> At the beginning of antiquity, people sucked dewdrops and ate grass and fruits. They lived in caves in the wilds and lived in the mountains. Thus, they ate birds and beasts, wearing their feathers and skins, drinking blood and eating fur. Those who lived near water ate fish, turtles, snails and clams. Because they did not yet have fire, the stench of rotten [food] caused much harm to their digestive tracts. At that time, a sagacious man ruled by the virtue of fire. He created the fire-bow and made fire. He taught the people how to cook food. He cast metal to make knives. The common people rejoiced greatly. He was called the Fire Driller.[97]

The Divine Farmer was said to have "taught the common people how to farm,"[98] to have "invented the pitchfork and plow,"[99] and to have "invented markets."[100] Three additional passages from *Investigations of Ancient History* note the contributions of the Yellow Thearch to the nourishment of the common people, such as, "The Yellow Thearch first invented the kettle. The Yellow Thearch first invented the earthen rice steamer."[101]

In addition to illustrating the content of Qiao Zhou's *Investigations of Ancient History*, these passages on culture bearers also provide an excellent opportunity to examine the relationship between Qiao Zhou's text and *Roots of Generations*. According to Zheng Xuan's commentary on *Rites of Zhou*, *Roots of Generations* originally contained a section on inventions.[102] A brief comparison between *Investigations of Ancient History* and *Roots of Generations*'s section on inventions reveals much about Qiao's use of the earlier work. Regarding the cultural contributions of the Fire Driller, the two texts are in accord. *Roots of Generations* notes, "The Fire Driller brought forth fire. What was used to create fire was the fire-bow. For that reason, the Fire Driller received his name."[103] However, with regards to the Divine Farmer, the two histories come to different conclusions. While Qiao Zhou claims the Divine Farmer invented the tools and delivery system for agriculture—pitchforks, plows, and markets, *Roots of Generations* attributes these cultural innovations to others. *Roots of Generations* says, "Chui 垂 invented the pitchfork and plow."[104] Additionally, it argues, "Zhurong 祝融 invented markets."[105] Qiao

Zhou's text makes no mention of the figure Chui, although Zhurong's relationship with the institution of markets is noted. Qiao writes, "The Divine Farmer invented markets. When the Gaoyang 高陽 clan declined, the market offices were not repaired. Zhurong repaired the markets."[106] In this case, Qiao Zhou attempts to clarify the terse statement from *Roots of Generations*, offering a different role for Zhurong in the matter of markets. Finally, the extant fragments of *Roots of Generations* make no mention of the Yellow Thearch's invention of cooking utensils.

A comparison of additional topics related to culture bearers reveals similar interplay between Qiao Zhou and *Roots of Generations*. For example, *Roots of Generations* says, "Xi Zhong 奚仲 invented the cart"[107] while Qiao Zhou's text claims, "The Yellow Thearch invented the cart. Heavy loads could be pulled great distances. Later, in the time of the Shaohao, they were pulled by oxen. In the time of Yu, Xi Zhong [introduced] the pulling by horses."[108] Qiao's passage is contained in the *Continued Han History*, where Liu Zhao 劉昭 (fl. 502–520 CE) comments: "Your subject, Zhao, reckons that carts pulled by oxen and horses have been of great benefit to the subcelestial realm. Their origins are quite ancient. How could they have begun with Xi Zhong? *Roots of Generations* is incorrect. The *Investigations of Ancient History* account is correct."[109]

From this brief study of passages on culture bearers in *Investigations of Ancient History*, two points deserve attention. First, it is significant that few of Qiao Zhou's comments on cultural innovations have corollaries in *The Grand Scribe's Records* text. In fact, a large portion of these comments deal with the so-called Three August Ones (Sanhuang 三皇), a subject lacking in Sima Qian's history. Sima Zhen, noting this deficiency, compiled his own "Biographies of the Three August Ones," using the writings of Huangfu Mi, Qiao Zhou, and others as his main sources of information.[110] In addition to writing the biography, Sima Zhen also annotates the work, and his annotations frequently cite *Investigations of Ancient History*. In this sense, Sima Zhen used Qiao's text in his own effort to rectify deficiencies in *The Grand Scribe's Records*. As for Qiao's writings on figures treated extensively in *The Grand Scribe's Records* such as the Yellow Thearch, Shun, and Yu, Qiao Zhou focuses on details not covered by Sima Qian. As such, *Investigations of Ancient History* appears to be supplementing the biographical treatment of these culture heroes in *The Grand Scribe's Records*. Whether this practice can or should be viewed as Qiao Zhou "correcting" or "rejecting" Sima Qian's work remains open for conjecture.

Additionally, in his writings on culture bearers, Qiao Zhou appears to have engaged in more of a dialogue with *Roots of Generations* than with *The Grand Scribe's Records*. While much of the information presented in *Investigations of Ancient History* has corollaries in *Roots of Generations*, Qiao does not always accept the accuracy of the earlier text. Significantly, Qiao Zhou's corrections of *Roots of Generations* are often noted and accepted by later critics like Liu Zhao and Sima Zhen, who both cite preference for Qiao's opinion over that of *Roots of Generations*.[111] On the basis of these two observations, we must expand our appraisal of *Investigations of Ancient History* from the traditional view of the text as a "critique of *The Grand Scribe's Records*" to that of a larger discourse on and engagement with several texts on ancient history.

Qiao Zhou's expression of skepticism toward accounts of several ancient historical legends dealing with the origins of dynastic ancestors further supports the view that Qiao's intent was to rectify a larger body of ancient history, and not just *The Grand Scribe's Records*. In the case of the Yin 殷 dynasty, Sima Qian narrates the tale of the divine paternity of Xie 契, the ancestor of Yin, writing,

> As for Xie of Yin, his mother was called Jiandi 簡狄. She was a daughter of the Yousong 有娀 clan and the secondary wife of Thearch Ku (Di Ku 帝嚳). [One day when] she and two other women went out to bathe, she saw a black bird lay an egg. Jiandi took it and swallowed it. For this reason she became pregnant and gave birth to Xie. After Xie had grown up, he won merit assisting Yu in regulating the waters. Thearch Shun then appointed Xie.[112]

Qiao Zhou rejects this account, arguing,

> Xie was born during the time of Yao. [Since] Shun first promoted him, he could not have been the son of Ku. His paternity was unclear. For that reason, [his father] is not named [in *The Grand Scribe's Records*]. His mother was a daughter of the [You]song clan. Together with the principal wife, the three women went to bathe in the river. A dark bird lay an egg and Jiandi swallowed it. Thus, [the fact] that Jiandi was not the secondary wife of Thearch Ku is obvious.[113]

Qiao Zhou's refutation of this legend hinges on two points of logic. First, Qiao notes the chronological problem with this account. According to the genealogies, Thearch Ku was the father of Yao, who succeeded him on the throne. For Xie to have been born in the time of Yao, after the death of his purported father, would have been highly unlikely. Additionally, that he was first promoted by his so-called brother's successor, Thearch Shun, made the likelihood of Xie's being a son of Thearch Ku even more remote. Thus, Qiao Zhou accepts the attribution that Jiandi was Xie's mother, but contends that his paternity was unclear. Qiao further argues that on the basis of the chronology presented, Jiandi could not have been a consort of Thearch Ku. Qiao's argument is not only at odds with *The Grand Scribe's Records* narrative, but also with *Roots of Generations*, which notes that Thearch Ku had four consorts, including a daughter of the Yousong clan named Jiandi who was the mother of Xie.[114]

In similar fashion, Qiao Zhou also challenges the legend surrounding the Zhou ancestor, Lord Millet (Hou Ji 后稷). In the "Basic Annals of Zhou," Sima Qian notes the parentage of Lord Millet:

> Lord Millet of the Zhou state had the name Qi 棄 [Discarded]. His mother was a daughter of the Youtai 有邰 clan called Jiang Yuan 姜原. Jiang Yuan was the primary wife of Thearch Ku. Once Jiang Yuan went out into the wilderness and saw a giant footprint. She happily rejoiced and had the desire to step in it. When she stepped in it her abdomen moved as if she were carrying a baby inside.[115]

In a brief statement, Qiao Zhou rejects the claims of divine paternity. Qiao writes, "Qi was a scion of Thearch Ku. His father's name is not recorded."[116] However, unlike his refutation of the legend surrounding Xie of Yin, Qiao does not dispute the chronology of *The Grand Scribe's Records* account, but merely asserts that Thearch Ku must have been the father of Lord Millet through his principal wife Jiang Yuan, and that the "footprint story" simply took the place of a clear statement of paternity.[117]

In both of these passages, Qiao Zhou not only disputes *The Grand Scribe's Records* account of the Yin and Zhou ancestors, but the larger traditions as well. The legends surrounding the births of Xie and Lord Millet are each presented in the *Book of Odes*. In Mao 303 we read the following line regarding the divine parentage of Xie: "Heaven commissioned the dark bird to descend and sire the Shang."[118] More detailed poetic accounts of the birth of Lord Millet are found in Mao 245 and 300. In particular, Mao 245 "Birth of Our People" notes:

> She who in the beginning gave birth to our people,
> This was Jiang Yuan.
> How did she give birth to our people?
> Well she sacrificed and prayed
> That she might no longer be childless.
> She trod on the big toe of god's footprint,
> Was accepted and got what she desired.
> Then in reverence, then in awe
> She gave birth, she nurtured;
> And this was Lord Millet.[119]

While Qiao Zhou refutes the claims of divine paternity put forth in the *Odes* and *The Grand Scribe's Records*, he is not completely at odds with the whole of the traditions surrounding Xie and Lord Millet. Qiao's mention of both Xie's and Lord Millet's appointments under Thearch Shun is drawn from a section in the *Hallowed Documents*, the "Canon of Shun," which reads:

> The Thearch [Shun] said, "Qi, the common people are suffering from hunger. You, as the Minister of Agriculture, should sow these hundred grains." The Thearch [Shun] said, "Xie, the people are not friendly with each other and do not follow the five orders of relationships. You, as the Minister of Education, should respectfully set forth the instructions on the five relationships."[120]

From this we can see that Qiao Zhou's rejection of tradition in this case is not completely iconoclastic, but, rather, selective. The more fantastic elements of the stories of Xie and Lord Millet are rejected on grounds of logic, while those more rational elements of the tradition are kept. His "correction" of these accounts as related in *The Grand Scribe's Records* accords Qiao Zhou the opportunity to take on the larger traditions, refuting them with views drawn from selected canonical texts. This adds further credence to the argument that *Investigations of Ancient History* was a larger examination of ancient history, and not simply a critique of Sima Qian's *The Grand Scribe's Records*.

Throughout the preceding discussion of Qiao Zhou's *Investigations of Ancient History*, we have seen numerous points of disagreement between Qiao and Sima Qian. These differences in opinion take many forms, but are generally expressed as amendments to Sima Qian's text by Qiao Zhou. But in three additional instances, Qiao Zhou offers more pointed disagreements, taking issue with Sima Qian's interpretations of history, rather than the details of past events.

In his appraisal to the "Hereditary House of Wei" 魏, Sima Qian comments on the notion of "Heaven's command" and a state's ability to utilize talented individuals. The appraisal reads:

> His Honor the Grand Scribe says, I visited the old site of the hill at Daliang. Someone at the hill said, "As for Qin's defeat of Liang, they followed the rivers and the canals and flooded Daliang. In three months the city wall was destroyed and the king asked to surrender. Thus was the destruction of Wei." Those I spoke to all said because Wei did not utilize the Lord of Xinling the state became weak to the point of destruction. I consider this to be incorrect. It was Heaven's command that Qin pacify the land within the seas. Its work was not yet complete. Even if Wei had obtained the service of Aheng, how could it have been of use?[121]

In this appraisal, Sima Qian ascribes a sort of final authority to "Heaven," and reduces the role of human action on the situation. Qiao Zhou opposes this view, saying: "According to what I have heard, the so-called "Heaven's destruction" is to possess a worthy but not use him. If he were used, how could they have been destroyed? If King Zhou 紂 had used the three benevolent ones, the Zhou would have been unable to rule, how much less the tigers and wolves of Qin?"[122] Here, Qiao Zhou directly disputes Sima Qian's opinion on the efficacy of utilizing men of worth and ability, and their value in averting potential disaster to the state. While Sima Qian's comments make the argument that such disasters were fated to occur on the basis of "Heaven's command," Qiao takes the opposite position. In essence, Qiao sides with the persons interviewed by Sima Qian who ascribe the fall of Wei to its failure to employ the ideas of a worthy.

Another instance of Sima Qian's assigning blame for a political defeat provides a second example of the divergent opinions of Sima Qian and Qian

Zhou. In his appraisal to the "Biography of Lord Pingyuan," Sima Qian criticizes Lord Pingyuan for failing "to see things in the broadest light." Additionally, he writes, "Lord Pingyuan was tempted by Feng Ting's 馮亭 pernicious advice and caused Zhao to lose over 400,000 soldiers at Changping and almost lose Handan."[123] Here, Sima Qian refers to the plan submitted by Feng Ting to turn Shangtang 上黨 in Han over to Zhao in order to forge an alliance against Qin. Lord Pingyuan accepted the proposal, which led to a Qin attack on Shangtang and the defeat of Zhao troops at nearby Changping.[124] Qiao Zhou rejects Sima Qian's evaluation of Lord Pingyuan, saying, "As for the fall of Changping, it was caused by the King of Zhao trusting a spy and changing generals. Why blame Lord Pingyuan for accepting Feng Ting?"[125] In this passage, Qiao argues that the ultimate responsibility for the matter lies in the hands of the ruler himself, and not a subject who had been deceived by another. While Qiao Zhou offers no further justification for his position, this example serves well as evidence of Qiao's differing viewpoint on historiography with Sima Qian.

The final surviving comment by Qiao Zhou on Sima Qian's historiographic approach offers a rare direct judgment on the master historian. In *The Grand Scribe's Records* "Biography of Zou Yan," Sima Qian follows an account of Zou Yan's unconventional methods with the following appraisal:

> Some say Yi Yin carried his cauldrons and urged Tang on to kingship, Baixi fed cows by a cart and through him Duke Mu became the hegemon. In rising, first placate him and then lead him onto the Great Way. As for Zou Yan, although his teachings were not reliable, perhaps he too had the same intentions as the men with cows and cauldrons.[126]

On this matter Qiao Zhou comments: "Seeing this discourse by the Grand Scribe, he certainly had a great love for the strange!"[127] This brief fragment offers the only direct personal comment on Sima Qian by Qiao Zhou. Interestingly, Qiao was not alone in this assessment of Sima Qian, for Yang Xiong once wrote of Sima Qian and his history, "Zhongni (Confucius) loved much—he loved righteousness. Zichang (Sima Qian) loved much—he loved the strange!"[128] Given the fact that both Yang Xiong and Qiao Zhou were natives of Yi Province, and the obvious influence of Yang on other aspects of Qiao's scholarship,[129] it seems quite possible that Qiao Zhou's comment on Sima Qian's "love of the strange" was based on that of his Chengdu predecessor.

THE INFLUENCE OF QIAO ZHOU'S HISTORICAL CRITICISM

Qiao Zhou's critical historical approach as contained in *Investigations of Ancient History* has long been viewed as innovative. However, there is some evidence that points toward Qiao's own inspiration in the matters of historical criticism. As previously noted, the Shu-Han scholar Qin Mi provided some degree of direction in regards to the intellectual development of Qiao Zhou.

While none of Qin Mi's historical writings have survived intact, both Chen Shou and Chang Qu offer comments that provide some indication of Qin's influence on Qiao Zhou in the field of historiography. First, Chen Shou notes a discourse by Qin Mi disputing an earlier discussion on the genealogies of the Three August Ones and Five Thearchs.[130] While the identity of the earlier discourse is unknown, it seems likely that Chen was referring to Sima Qian's "Basic Annals of the Five Thearchs." Unfortunately, Qin Mi's arguments on this matter have not survived, but given the emphasis Qiao Zhou placed on the Three August Ones and Five Thearchs in *Investigations of Ancient History*, we may presume that the influence of Qin Mi was at work in these passages. Despite the lack of solid evidence, it seems likely that Qin Mi's historical criticism influenced Qiao Zhou in some fashion. Qiao's own writings on the lineages and accomplishments of the legendary rulers of high antiquity evince the skepticism of Qin Mi hinted at by Chen Shou. Additionally, if we accept the attribution of Qin Mi's ideas being contained in Qiao's own *Discourse on Truths and Falsehoods in the Five Canonical Texts*, then perhaps the seeds of Qiao Zhou's critical examinations of ancient history also lie in the education he received from Qin Mi.

Although identifying specific influences on Qiao Zhou's *Investigations of Ancient History* remains a highly speculative venture, assessing the work's effect on later generations of historians proves a much easier task. This influence can be seen in both the frequency and manner in which Qiao Zhou's text was cited by later historians, as well as direct evaluations of the work itself. The earliest work to reference Qiao's *Investigations of Ancient History* was Xu Guang's *Sounds and Meanings from The Grand Scribe's Records* [*Shiji yinyi* 史記音義],[131] which cites Qiao Zhou and his *Investigations of Ancient History* on four occasions, generally on matters of dates, lineages, and pronunciation.[132] The next important medieval history to cite Qiao Zhou's *Investigations of Ancient History* was Pei Yin's *Collected Explanations on The Grand Scribe's Records*,[133] which collects explanatory glosses on *The Grand Scribe's Records* by a number of earlier scholars, including Qiao Zhou and Xu Guang. In his commentary, Pei Yin references Qiao's work twelve times on such issues as locations of benefices, details on lineages, names, and other assorted phonetic and descriptive glosses, including three instances in which he quotes Xu Guang quoting Qiao Zhou.[134] Significantly, on one occasion Pei Yin includes Qiao Zhou's dissenting opinion on Sima Qian's appraisal of Lord Pingyuan.[135] In his *Supplemental Annotations* to both Fan Ye's *Later Han History* and Sima Biao's *Continued Han History*, Liu Zhao cites Qiao's *Investigations of Ancient History* several times. In two cases in his commentary on the *Later Han History*, Liu Zhao simply refers his readers directly to the *Investigations of Ancient History* but does not quote the relevant materials.[136] In Liu's commentary on Sima Biao's *Continued Han History*, he quotes passages from *Investigations of Ancient History* seven times on a variety of matters, including geographical concerns and ancient cultural innovations.[137]

Qiao Zhou's *Investigations of Ancient History* had perhaps the greatest impact on Sima Zhen's *Seeking the Obscure in The Grand Scribe's Records*.[138] In this commentary, Sima Zhen cites Qiao Zhou over fifty times, in roughly thirty instances quoting Qiao Zhou's glosses on names, places, and so on. Especially influential on Sima Zhen's work were Qiao's writings on ancient cultural innovations. As noted earlier, Sima Zhen was himself critical of Sima Qian's omission of a "Basic Annals of the Three August Ones," and set out to compile this chapter himself. Qiao Zhou's *Investigations of Ancient History* and *Roots of Generations* provide the bulk of Sima Zhen's source material in both compiling and annotating his history of these legenday figures. In this regard, Sima Zhen's use of *Investigations of Ancient History* is similar to the other medieval exegetes previously examined, with Qiao's *Investigations of Ancient History* serving as source material for Sima Zhen's *Seeking the Obscure in The Grand Scribe's Records*, rather than a methodological model.

Significantly, in the postface to his commentary, Sima Zhen does not mention Qiao Zhou in his brief history of commentary on *The Grand Scribes Records*, indicating that he did not regard Qiao's *Investigations of Ancient History* as a commentary on Sima Qian's history per se.[139] Rather, Sima Zhen acknowledges historical criticism as one of the objectives of *Investigations of Ancient History* and frequently presents quoted passages in opposition to the perceived errors in Sima Qian's work. In fact, the vast majority of passages from *Investigations of Ancient History* cited by Sima Zhen—ranging from glosses offering variant graphs for names to the explicit comments on Sima Qian's historical interpretations—are at odds with *The Grand Scribe's Records*.

While most of Qiao Zhou's rectifications are simply quoted without additional commentary by Sima Zhen, on several occasions the Tang historian adds his own appraisal on both *The Grand Scribe's Records* and *Investigations of Ancient History*. For example, in a comment on *The Grand Scribe's Records* fascicle thirty-six, Sima Zhen notes differing opinions found in *Roots of Generations* and *Investigations of Ancient History*. After citing these two texts in opposition to *The Grand Scribe's Records*, Sima Zhen remarks on what he considers factual errors in *Roots of Generations*, saying, "It must be as Qiao Zhou has said."[140] Similar comments supporting Qiao Zhou's opinion over that of Sima Qian are found throughout Sima Zhen's commentary. However, we also find instances of Sima Zhen's disagreeing with the ideas expressed in *Investigations of Ancient History*. In a gloss on a name found in the "Hereditary House of Zheng," Qiao Zhou offers a personal name missing from Sima Qian's account. Sima Zheng cites Qiao's amendment, but comments, "None of this is correct."[141] Finally, it should be noted that all of Qiao Zhou's surviving direct criticisms of Sima Qian are preserved and reproduced in the *Seeking the Obscure in The Grand Scribe's Records*.

From these examples we can see the methodological influence of *Investigations of Ancient History* on Sima Zhen's *Seeking the Obscure in The Grand Scribe's Records*: the critical examination of earlier historical records. Unlike the preceding historian-exegetes who utilized *Investigations of Ancient History* as source material to provide explanatory reading notes, Sima Zhen follows Qiao Zhou's model of offering critical corrections to the earlier work. And in this spirit of criticism, even portions of Qiao Zhou's own critique of *The Grand Scribe's Records* are disputed by Sima Zhen. In this regard, Sima Zhen's *Seeking the Obscure in The Grand Scribe's Records* may be seen as continuing in the critical exegetic tradition begun by *Investigations of Ancient History*.

Although Qiao Zhou's *Investigations of Ancient History* was frequently cited as a historical source up through the Tang period, the text received little mention in the centuries that followed.[142] It was also during the Song period that the *Investigations of Ancient History* appears to have been lost as an integral work. The overall declining interest in the text corresponds roughly to the same time period in which negative evaluations of Qiao Zhou's political activity increased.[143] While there is no evidence to ascertain that Qiao Zhou was "blacklisted" by Neo-Confucian moralists, the parallel rise in anti-Qiao Zhou rhetoric and the near absence of references to Qiao Zhou's *Investigations of Ancient History* in post-Song sources raises strong suspicions of the sort.

During the Qing, however, Qiao Zhou's critical remarks on *The Grand Scribe's Records* found a new receptive audience. The noted textual critic Liang Yusheng 梁玉繩 (1745–1819) frequently cites Qiao and *Investigations of Ancient History* in his monumental study *Shiji zhiyi* 史記志疑 [*Records of Doubts on The Grand Scribe's Records*].[144] Liang's citations of *Investigations of Ancient History* take a number of forms, and in many instances, Liang openly states his agreement with Qiao's views. For example, citing Qiao Zhou's comments on the chronological problems in *The Grand Scribe's Records* account of Lord Millet, Liang states that his interpretation of this passage is based on that of Qiao Zhou.[145] However, Liang Yusheng does not uncritically accept all of Qiao Zhou's arguments, and he frequently quotes *Investigations of Ancient History*, then expresses his uncertainty or outright disagreement with the positions taken by Qiao.[146] Although Liang Yusheng finds some faults in Qiao Zhou's interpretations of *The Grand Scribe's Records*, he does take *Investigations of Ancient History* as a work of historical criticism and not a mere source of historical trivia. Thus, in many regards, Liang's *Records of Doubts on The Grand Scribe's Records* follows Qiao's *Investigations of Ancient History* down the path of skeptical historical criticism, taking its place as a major work in the historiograhical genre.[147]

This brief survey of citations of Qiao Zhou's *Investigations of Ancient History* by traditional Chinese historians illustrates not only the frequency with which Qiao's text was referenced, but also reveals something of the way the work was viewed. The majority of historians who cited Qiao's history during the period utilized the work as a source for historical information with which to explain other texts, primarily Sima Qian's *The Grand Scribe's Records*. Only Sima Zhen and Liang Yusheng appear to have viewed *Investigations of Ancient History* as a work of interpretative historical criticism and employed it for that purpose.

In addition to citing the text itself, several traditional historians offered critical evaluations of Qiao's *Investigations of Ancient History*. Significantly, most of these appraisals judged the text on the basis of its purported intent to correct *The Grand Scribe's Records* by appeals to the canon. The earliest such critical judgment on *Investigations of Ancient History* is contained in the *Jin History* biography of Sima Biao, which claims that "Sima Biao, considered Qiao Zhou's [work] to be not yet perfect, and thus listed one hundred twenty-two incorrect items in *Investigations of Ancient History*, mostly relying upon the chronicle from Jizhong."[148] Despite the purported need for further correction, Sima Biao reportedly viewed Qiao Zhou as one of the few "good historians" of the age.[149] Later, Liu Zhiji, after citing an example from *Investigations of Ancient History*, concludes, "By means of this [technique, Qiao Zhou] imitated the *Spring and Autumn*."[150] Thus, to Liu Zhiji, Qiao's *Investigations of Ancient History* functioned as a critical and supplemental commentary to *The Grand Scribe's Records* in a manner similar to the commentaries on the canonical *Spring and Autumn*, including that of Zuo Qiuming. This was clearly high praise for Qiao's work. Gao Sisun's 高似孫 (*jinshi* ca. 1174–1190) *Shilüe* 史略 [*Historical Epitome*], in a manner similar to Liu Zhiji, cites an example from *Investigations of Ancient History* that both supplements and critiques Sima Qian's record. Gao then notes, "All of [Qiao's] records were like this."[151]

If in fact all of Qiao's original text contained critical comments like the example cited in the *Historical Summaries*, then the now-lost portions of the text must have been extraordinary. As shown above, the majority of the surviving fragments provide simple explanatory glosses or supplemental comments on various topics of ancient history. But since many of the later historians whose citations of *Investigations of Ancient History* preserved the extant text utilized the work as a historical sourcebook rather than critical commentary, it is possible that many of the more critical historical judgments and explanations of Qiao Zhou's opinions may have been excised in later citations. If this were the case, then the present condition of Qiao's *Investigations of Ancient History* is even more tragic.

Zhang Zongyuan's preface to his reconstruction of *Investigations of Ancient History* offers an expansion of the earlier idea that Qiao's work was a critical commentary on *The Grand Scribe's Records*. Noting the inclusion of material beyond the scope of *The Grand Scribe's Records*, Zhang proposes that *Investigations of Ancient History* is both a historical discourse and correction, arguing that it is an early example of the "investigations on history" genre of historical writing. Furthermore, Zhang disputes the categorization of the work as a commentary on a standard history, supporting the Tang classification of "miscellaneous history" instead.[152]

Despite the widespread citation of the text during the early medieval period and the positive evaluations of the work by noted traditional historians, *Investigations of Ancient History* has received relatively little attention from contemporary historians. For example, Chen Zhi's 陳直 important study on the transmission and appraisal of *The Grand Scribe's Records* by scholars of the Han through Jin periods fails to mention Qiao or his work.[153] In a rare scholarly treatment of Qiao's *Investigations of Ancient History*, Long Xianzhao 龍顯昭 describes the text's tripartite nature (one part history [*shi* 史], one part discourse [*lun* 論], and one part investigation [*kao* 考]), and notes the strengths of the text, most notably in the areas of dates and lineages, details on ritual, and its value in fixing historical accuracy.[154] Long Xianzhao concludes that *Investigations of Ancient History* "was the first systematic study of *The Grand Scribe's Records*," and that "Qiao Zhou's mastery of history and spirit of seeking the truth began the trend of investigations on antiquity and rectifications of history."[155] A similar judgement is later reached by Lu Yaodong, who praises Qiao Zhou and his *Investigations of Ancient History*, saying:

> Using the classics as source material, [Qiao] in China's first work of historiography, carried out a systematic criticism. What Qiao Zhou held to was the position of classical scholarship, but what he engaged in was historical criticism. This truly was the time of the parting of the ways of the canon and history, a unique phenomenon of the era of the blossoming of historical criticism.[156]

On the basis of fewer than one hundred surviving fragments of Qiao Zhou's *Investigations of Ancient History* quoted out of their original context, we can reach a few summary conclusions about the text and Qiao Zhou's activity in the field of historical writing. Although it remains unclear whether Qiao's *Investigations of Ancient History* was originally compiled as a direct commentary on *The Grand Scribe's Records* (i.e., interlinear, or commenting on specific portions of the base text) or as a larger discourse on ancient history, the work as it survives, excerpted and cited in later commentaries, appears largely in step with late Han and Three States period historical exegesis. But, while most early historical commentary from the period functioned primarily as explanatory reading notes, Qiao's glosses and comments often contradict or challenge the base text. For this reason, *Investigations of Ancient History* has long been held to have been an attempt to correct *The Grand Scribe's Records* by appeals to the canon. In this regard, Qiao Zhou's historical approach mirrors that of his canonical criticism. That is, Qiao viewed the texts of the canon as largely historically accurate and as sources of authority to argue the truths of the past. Despite both Sima Qian's and Qiao Zhou's use of the same canonical texts in the compilation of their histories and the greater inability to identify the sources of Qiao Zhou's opinions in the canon or elsewhere, the general view of *Investigations of Ancient History* as a critical rectification of *The Grand Scribe's Records* remains a tenable argument.

However, a large number of fragments from *Investigations of Ancient History* do not support this hypothesis. Anecdotes falling well beyond the chronological and topical scope of *The Grand Scribe's Records* are numerous. Thus, we find additional support for Zhang Zongyuan's proposal that the traditional assessment of Qiao Zhou's *Investigations of Ancient History* be reevaluated in the context of the surviving fragments of the text. Under this charge we find Qiao Zhou not only refuting Sima Qian by means of the canon and other sources (both known and unidentified), but also disputing the views of the canon and other earlier histories. This leads to my general conclusion that Qiao's *Investigations of Ancient History* was an examination of a larger body of writings on ancient history and not simply a commentary on *The Grand Scribe's Records*. Moreover, it was his greater critical engagement with both the canon and earlier histories that distinguished Qiao Zhou and his *Investigations of Ancient History* from his contemporaries in the field of historical exegesis.

CHAPTER 6

New Approaches to Local History

THE STATE OF LOCAL HISTORIOGRAPHY

As part of the late Han proliferation of historical writing, the scope of the genre expanded significantly from the canonical-style annals format and the biographical commentaries of *The Grand Scribe's Records* to include a wide range of approaches and subjects.[1] Among this new wave of historiography were writings that set out to record the history, people, customs, and geography of specifically defined locales, typically identified by the administrative terminology of the day (i.e., province, commandery). By the early Tang period, over two hundred historical texts with local foci were included in the imperial catalog.[2] Although local history writing grew dramatically in practice during the early medieval period, it was not without a few important precedents.

The text entitled "Yu Gong" 禹貢 ["The Tribute of Yu"] contained in the canonical *Documents* may be considered an early prototype of the genre. The "Tribute of Yu," generally thought to date from the late Zhou or even Qin period (ca. third century BCE), presents a catalog of the early Chinese empire framed around the legendary sage-king Yu's efforts to tame the floodwaters.[3] Administrative units are named and their boundaries marked, followed by descriptions of the local geography, people, and produce. Finally, each area is assigned a rank in terms of quality of soil, produce, and so on, and items submitted for tribute to the court are listed. In this brief document, both administrative and cultural concerns are addressed, though, here, the typologies of each area's resources, both human and natural, are framed in the context of their contributions to the state. For example, the "Tribute of Yu" offers the following assessment of the Chengdu Plain:

> [Between] the south side of Mount Hua and the Black Waters (Heishui 黑水) is Liang Province. Mounts Min 岷 and Bo 嶓 were cultivated; the Tuo

> 沱 and Qian 潛 streams were conducted; and Mounts Cai 蔡 and Meng 蒙 were arranged and regulated. In the region of the Heyi 和夷 barbarians, [Yu] effected achievements. [The region's] soil is bluish-black. Its fields are of the upper third class. Its revenues are of the middle third class, with three kinds of admixtures. Its tribute is gold, iron, silver, steel, arrowhead stones, musical stones, black bears, brown and white bears, foxes, and wild cats. The felt-wearing [people of] Xiqing 西傾 following the Huan 桓 River come this way. [Yu] floated on the Qian 潛 River, passed over to the Mian 沔 River, entered the Wei 渭 River, and crossed the Yellow River.[4]

This account marks the earliest surviving description of the Chengdu Plain, with its general characterization of the region as having an abundance of natural resources. The "Tribute of Yu" offers similar appraisals of eight other administrative units. Although the larger objective of the text is not to describe only a specific locale but rather the whole of the empire, the manner in which each administrative unit is presented served as a model for later local writing.

Similarly, while not a local history per se, Ban Gu's "Geographic Treatise" in his *Han History* offers locale-by-locale reports of the whole of the Han empire. Ban Gu's essay, comprised of two fascicles, presents brief accounts on the commanderies and dependent kingdoms, drawing on the census data from the early first century. These accounts are statistically oriented and dry. For example, the entry for Ba commandery reads: "Ba Commandery. 158,643 [registered] households. 708,148 [registered] individuals. Ten districts: Jiangzhou 江州, Linjiang 臨江, Zhi 枳, Langzhong 閬中, Dianjiang 墊江, Quren 朐忍, Anhan 安漢, Dangqu 宕渠, Yufu 魚復, Chongguo 充國, and Fuling 涪陵."[5] In similar fashion, a census of the empire's mountains and waterways is also included in the "Geographic Treatise," where Ban Gu's treatment of the Chengdu Plain geography is taken directly from the "Tribute of Yu" chapter of the *Documents*.[6] But in addition to these matter-of-fact accounts, Ban Gu also offers his own views on some of the empire's locales. In regards to the Chengdu Plain, Ban concludes that the land's bountiful resources led to character flaws among its people.[7] Ban Gu's presentation of both the vital statistics of an area and a judgment of the place and its inhabitants' character provides the model for much of the later local history writing during the early medieval period.

In a study of the development of local history writing in early medieval China and its uses for the study of other aspects of the age, Andrew Chittick notes two major trends in early local historiography. The first direction of the field was that of locale-specific biography. These collections tended to present the lives of local men (and the occasional woman) of political, social, or moral distinction, and may have functioned as forms of local propaganda in terms of imperial recruitment and governmental service.[8] The second major format for local historical writing was geographical or, more precisely, the records of a particular place and its customs. As indicated by Ban Gu's judgment of the Chengdu Plain, during the Later Han places were thought to be embued with a spiritual essence that affected its inhabitants.[9] As such, these local history writings collected both the statistical data of Ban Gu's "Geographic Treatise" as well as more colorful elements designed to illustrate the character of a place. Just as collections of biographies presented the moral character of the residents of a place, geographic writings presented the character of the place itself, which in turn was reflected in the lives of the locals.[10] These two general forms of local history writing dominated the genre during the late Han and early period of disunion. And while the biographical collections were more common early on, by the late fourth century the place-centered approach had become the primary mode of local history writing.

The "Bibliographic Treatise" of the *Sui History* contains a lengthy list of titles that might be considered local histories, both biographical and geographical; moreover, the geographic distribution of these titles is wide-ranging. Not surprisingly, the metropololises and capitals (former and then-current) are well represented in the body of early medieval local histories. Likewise are the ancestral homes of the rulers of state. However, even locales on the periphery of empire came to be documented in local histories. In the case of the Chengdu Plain, the area was the subject of local historical writing during the Later Han as several efforts were made to record the lives of local worthies and the events of the region.

In the "Postface" to his monumental history of the Chengdu Plain, *Records of the States South of Mount Hua*, Chang Qu immediately acknowledges his predecessors in the task of writing the history of southwest China. Chang writes:

> From the beginning of their establishment as states, [the matters of] Ba and Shu are recorded in collected documents. Some are found in apocryphal writings, with others seen in historical records. Distant and hidden, these facts are many, but unreliable . . . Sima Xiangru, Yan Junping, Yang Ziyun, Yangcheng Zixuan 陽城子玄 (fl. first century BCE–CE), Zheng Boyi 鄭伯邑 (fl. first century CE), Yin Pengcheng 尹彭城 (Later Han?),[11] Regular Attendant Qiao [Zhou], Servant Within the Palace Ren [Xi] 任熙 (fl. late third century CE), and others each collected biographies and records and compiled annals, summarizing and praising their corner [of the region]. Their later sages, declared worthies, benevolent men, and ambitious scholars were spoken of to serve as models to the world, and were placed to act as exemplary standards. Their names were noted in the historical records. Gentleman Chen Chengzuo 陳承祚 [Chen Shou] compiled his *Qijiu zhuan* 耆舊傳 [*Biographies of the Elders*], beginning with the Han and concluding with the Wei periods. It is brilliant and can be seen [today]. Only those [personages] of the three provinces were selected. The "Geographic Treatises"[12] are inclined toward mountains and rivers, history, the changing of dynasties, the division of commanderies and

> prefectures, and changes in place names. They are reliable in these [matters], but none goes into the particulars of comprehensively discussing things or places. From the time of Han to the rise of Jin, officers and ministers were arrayed like the stars, and [commandery and district] charts and pamphlets were submitted and collected annually by the minister of works. Therefore, gentlemen and scholars could hide behind the curtains [of the archives and peruse the records]. Those who were sufficiently intimate with the things and places had no need to consult these annals.[13]

This section—the opening lines of the surviving "Postface"—offers a glimpse of the state of local historiography on the Chengdu Plain down to the time of Chang Qu (ca. mid-fourth century CE). In it, Chang hints at both the volume and diversity of historical records, listing several notables who were said to have compiled histories (*benji* 本紀 or "basic annals"), and briefly discussing the scope and importance of these historians' works. Furthermore, here Chang Qu reveals his own standard for a work of local history: a comprehensive discussion of things and places. Thus, Chang Qu's enumeration of prior historians provides a convenient place to begin this brief survey of early Sichuan historiography.

Chang Qu's list includes three of the most important Sichuan intellectual figures of the Former Han: Sima Xiangru, Yan Junping [Zhuang Zun], and Yang Xiong. While all three of these figures have been discussed, a few brief comments about their accomplishments in historiography are in order here. Sima Xiangru, known primarily for his rhapsodies, was a native of Shu commandery. Although he was a local and later served as an imperial envoy in his home region, nothing in his surviving writings nor the standard bibliographic sources indicates that Sima Xiangru compiled a history of his native land. The second figure on Chang Qu's list, Zhuang Zun, was noted primarily for his scholarship on the *Laozi*, and was said to have left behind writings in over 100,000 characters. However, among the accounts of his life and works, there are no references to writings that might be of a historical nature.[14] Rounding out Chang Qu's list of Former Han notables is Yang Xiong. Yang was also a Chengdu native who studied with Zhuang Zun. Yang's writings were voluminous and included rhapsodies, studies on local dialects, a collection of his own sayings, a work based on the *Changes*, and a collection of "admonitions" on twelve provinces.[15] There is no mention of his compiling a work of local history included in the bibliographic notice in his biography. However, by the Tang period, the text entitled *Shu wang benji* 蜀王本紀 [*Basic Annals of the Kings of Shu*] came to be attributed to Yang.

The text of the *Basic Annals of the Kings of Shu* has not survived intact; however, numerous fragments of the work are cited in a variety of sources.[16] These fragments tell the story of the early kings of Shu from legendary beginnings down to the time of the conquest of the area by Qin in 316 BCE. The work also contains a purported genealogy of the earliest of these rulers, supplemented with anecdotes about the kings during the last years prior to Qin annexation, including such memorable tales as the gold-defecating ox and the gender-changing consort of the Shu king.[17]

There is some controversy concerning the attribution of this text to Yang Xiong. Although Chang Qu includes Yang in his list of persons compiling historical records of the area, no linking of a *Basic Annals of the Kings of Shu* to Yang Xiong appears until the Sui and Tang bibliographic treatises.[18] However, despite the late attribution, the entries in the Sui and Tang bibliographic treatises grant legitimacy to the claim of authorship to Yang Xiong. Later scholars like Hong Yixuan, Yan Kejun, and others accepted and furthered this claim by including all extant fragments with the title of "*Basic Annals of the Kings of Shu*" in their compilations of Yang Xiong's writings.[19] Other scholars have been more skeptical. Citing the *Records of the States South of Mount Hua*'s list of multiple compilers of "basic annals" of the region, Zhu Xizu 朱希祖 rejects the claim of single authorship by Yang, arguing that Yang and the others [listed in Chang Qu's "Postface"] each contributed to the collection of fragments that now constitute the text.[20] Xu Zhongshu 徐中舒 cites three types of evidence to argue against crediting the received text to Yang Xiong, placing its date of composition in the third century CE.[21] Yet despite evidence to the contrary, the attribution of the *Basic Annals of the Kings of Shu* to Yang Xiong continues to be widely accepted.

Continuing through Chang Qu's list of southwestern historians, we find little information on the life or works of Yangcheng Zixuan in the standard histories. However, Ren Naiqiang collects fragments of information on this individual and compiles a brief biographical sketch.[22] Based on comments in Huan Tan's 桓譚 (ca. 43 BCE–23 CE) *Xinlun* 新論 [*New Discourses*] and Wang Chong's 王充 (27–ca. 100 CE) *Lunheng* 論衡 [*Balanced Discourses*], Ren Naiqiang concludes that Yangcheng, given name Heng 衡, was a native of Shu commandery and served in Chang'an with his fellow-commanderyman, Yang Xiong. Wang Chong comments somewhat on Yangcheng's scholarly works, noting that he compiled a [commentary on?] the *Canon of Music* that was widely circulated and highly regarded.[23] Though there are no references to Yangcheng compiling a history of the Sichuan area, Ren concedes that such a compilation remained a possibility.[24]

Somewhat more information is available on the historical writings of the next figure appearing on Chang Qu's list of compilers of Chengdu Plain histories, Zheng Boyi. According to the *Records of the States South of Mount Hua*, Zheng, given name Qin 勤, was a native of Linqiong 臨邛 district,[25] served as grand administrator of Hanzhong commandery, and compiled a text entitled *Qijiu zhuan* 耆舊傳 [*Biographies of Elders*].[26] The geographic scope of this collection of biographies is not made explicit from this fragment of information; however, another mention in the *Records of the States South of Mount Hua* biography of Chen Shou provides additional insight. Here, Chang Qu notes,

> In the Yi region, from the Jianwu 建武 period (25–56 CE) onward, Zheng Boyi of Shu commandery, the grand commandant Zhao Yanxin 趙彥信,[27] Chen Shenbo 陳申伯,[28] Zhu Yuanling 祝元靈 of Hanzhong,[29] and Wang Wenbiao 王文表 of Guanghan[30] all used their broad learning and vast knowledge to compile *Ba Shu qijiu zhuan* 巴蜀耆舊傳 [*Biographies of the Elders of Ba and Shu*].[31]

From this reference, it would appear that the biographies compiled by Zheng and others comprised persons from the two commanderies of Ba and Shu. However, the *Records of the States South of Mount Hua* notes Chen Shou's dissatisfaction with this compilation, saying, "[Chen] Shou thought it was not exhaustive enough, and added [figures from] Ba and Han[zhong] to compile the *Yibu qijiu zhuan* 益部耆舊傳 [*Biographies of the Elders of Yi*] in ten *pian*."[32]

There is some apparent contradiction between the name and implied scope of the earlier collection of biographies and Chen Shou's critique and revisions. If the earlier text included accounts of persons from Ba commandery as implied by the received title, why would Chen Shou have needed to add persons from Ba and Hanzhong commanderies to rectify the deficiencies? Additionally, Zhu Gui was noted as having compiled a *Biographies of the Elders of Hanzhong*—one of the areas that Chen Shou specifically addressed. There are several possibile explanations for this problem. First, the title "*Biographies of the Elders of Ba and Shu*" does not appear to reflect accurately the contents of the work, and may not have been the title it was given by its author or authors. In his application of this title, Chang Qu may have conflated various individual, place-specific compilations into a simple, broad generic category. Second, Chen Shou's addition of figures from Ba commandery does not necessarily mean that persons of Ba were entirely excluded from the earlier work. As a native of Baxi commandery, Chen likely was more familiar with the worthies from that area than the compilers of the earlier history and thus may have supplemented that section of the work. The same may hold true for the figures from Hanzhong. Since the text(s) attributed to Zheng Boyi and the others are no longer extant, it is impossible to answer this question definitively.

The final person included in Chang Qu's list of southwest historians is Yin Gong 尹貢 of Yelang 夜郎.[33] A brief biographical sketch of Yin is contained in the fourth fascicle of the *Records of the States South of Mount Hua*. In this account, Yin's service as the grand administrator of Ba commandery and as chancellor of Pengcheng is noted, hence Chang Qu's reference to him as Chancellor Yin. However, there is no surviving record of Yin Gong compiling a history of the region in which he served.[34]

Chen Shu 陳術, appellative Shenbo (fl. mid-third century), stands as one of the later figures on Chang Qu's listing of persons who compiled histories of the region. A brief biographical account in the *Records of the Three States* notes, "At that time [Jingyao 景耀 (258–263 CE)], there was Chen

Shu, appellative Shenbo, of Hanzhong commandery. He was widely learned and had heard many things. He wrote *Shiwen* 釋問 [*Dispelling Questions*] in seven sections, *Yibu qijiu zhuan* [*Biographies of the Elders of Yi Province*], and a [historical] record. He concurrently held the office of grand administrator of three commanderies."[35]

The collection of biographies referenced by Chen Shou does not appear in the bibliographic treatises of the Sui or Tang histories. However, Pei Songzhi's *Commentary on the Records of the Three States* quotes several fragments of this text, citing it under the title of *Yibu qijiu zhuan zaji* 益部耆舊傳雜記 [*Miscellaneous Records of the Elders of Yi Province*]. The seven passages quoted by Pei contain biographical anecdotes on ten figures from the region dating from the late Han through the time of Chen Shu and originating from several commanderies in the area.[36] These anecdotes include the standard features of Chinese biography such as name, appellative, place of origin, offices held, and relationships with other noteworthy figures, while a few also include dialogue. Due to a lack of bibliographic information, it is unclear how broad Chen Shu's original collection of biographies may have been. However, Chen Shou's complaint about its deficiencies (cited earlier) would seem to indicate that the collection was not extensive.

Another third-century collection of biography (not mentioned in Chang Qu's list), Yang Xi's 楊戲 *Ji Han fuchen zan* 季漢輔臣贊 [*Encomia for the Officials of Third Han*] also merits mention. Like Chen Shu's collection, there is no record of the work in the bibliographic treatises of the standard histories and it survives only in fragments quoted in the *Records of the Three States*. Following a brief biographical sketch of Yang Xi, Chen Shou introduces Yang Xi's encomia noting that some of the figures praised by Yang also received further treatment in Chen's own *Records of the Three States*. Nevertheless, Chen Shou reproduces these encomia and adds more detailed biographies to some, often including information on events from these individuals' lives that occurred after Yang Xi's death. It is unclear, however, if the passages quoted by Chen Shou represent the complete text of Yang's encomia, or if some sections of the work were not utilized or had been lost prior to Chen Shou's time. In the surviving text, we find encomia for forty-two persons who served Shu-Han. These figures ranged from Liu Bei himself, eulogized as the Zhaolie Emperor 昭烈皇帝; Zhuge Liang; generals Guan Yu, Zhang Fei, Pang Tong, Fei Yi, and so on; and civil officials such as Xu Jing and Qin Mi. For twenty of the encomia, Chen Shou appends additional biographical sketches.[37]

On the basis of his listing of purported Sichuan historians contained in the "Postface" to the *Records of the States South of Mount Hua*, Chang Qu gives the impression of a flourishing historiographical tradition. However, upon closer examination of the extant writings of these individuals, a somewhat more modest picture emerges. Several of the figures included by Chang Qu in his inventory of prior historians do not appear to have compiled historical writings—or at least writings that were remembered by anyone other than

Chang. However, those works that did survive in fragments or by title offer enough information to piece together a general idea of the early local historiography of the area. While Chang Qu's list claims these historians compiled "basic annals" (*benji*), a review of the works attributed to some of these individuals indicates that their works were not all in the form of chronological histories or annals. In fact, other than the disputed text attributed to Yang Xiong, no bibliographic information exists to confirm the compilation of an annal for the region.[38] As noted by Chittick, biographical writing appears to have been the predominant mode of local historiography prior to the third century throughout China. The scant bibliographic evidence for Chengdu Plain historiography indicates that this larger trend was also the norm in the southwest. While we have no complete collections of Sichuan biographies from this period, the later biographies of these historians list the titles of collections of local lives they compiled. Unfortunately, due to the lack of surviving texts, we can say little of the style or focus of these collections of biographies. The most solid conclusion that can be drawn from this discussion is that the southwest had a tradition of local historiography in which biography dominated the practice.

THE LOCAL HISTORIES OF QIAO ZHOU

In addition, and sometimes in stark contrast to his writings on the canon and ancient history, Qiao Zhou compiled no less than four histories of his native region.[39] Unfortunately, these histories have not survived intact, but a sufficient number of fragments remain to allow us to piece together the scope and focus of Qiao Zhou's contributions to the local historiography of the Chengdu Plain.

Titles and fragments of four works of local history attributed to Qiao Zhou survive in a variety of sources. Qiao Zhou's *San Ba ji* 三巴記 [*Records of the Three Ba Commanderies*], also known by the title *Ba ji* 巴記 [*Records of Ba*], is first referenced under the title of *Records of Ba* in Shen Yue's *Song History* and Liu Zhao's commentary to the *Continued Han History*.[40] The text is listed in the Sui and Tang bibliographic treatises under the title of *Records of the Three Ba Commanderies*, and said to comprise one fascicle.[41] It appears that the title was changed during the Tang, as the Sui bibliographic treatise, Ouyang Xun's *Collection of Literature Arranged by Categories*, and all later works cite it as *Records of the Three Ba Commanderies*. Today only ten direct quotations of the text survive, though it is paraphrased or mentioned several other times.[42]

The second surviving work of local history attributed to Qiao Zhou is a work entitled *Shu ji* 蜀紀／記 [*Annals* (or *Records*) *of Shu*], also known as *Shu benji* 蜀本紀 [*Basic Annals of Shu*]. From the standpoint of textual history, this is perhaps Qiao Zhou's most difficult work to contend with. The work's title has been variously rendered, and several authors have works with this title (or variants thereof) attributed to them.[43] There is no mention of a work with this title attributed to Qiao Zhou in the traditional bibliographic sources. The sole surviving fragment is cited by Pei Songzhi in his *Commentary to the Records of the Three States*.[44]

Perhaps the most interesting hypothesis regarding this work is raised by Xu Zhongshu, who, in an article disputing the claims of authorship of *Basic Annals of the Kings of Shu* to Yang Xiong, posits the claim that Qiao Zhou was in fact the author of the text bearing that title and that the fragment attributed to Qiao with the title *Annals of Shu* was part of that work. Sadly, Xu offers little in the way of evidence to support this claim, merely adding it as a postscript to his convincing argument against Yang Xiong's authorship.[45] This view, though interesting and provocative, is questionable. Addressing Xu Zhongshu's claim, Long Xianzhao argues that the fragment of *Basic Annals of Shu* attributed to Qiao Zhou does not correspond to the text attributed to Yang Xiong, though they discussed an identical matter.[46] Nevertheless, it may be possible that some extant passages attributed to Yang Xiong may in fact be from Qiao Zhou's work.

A third local history attributed to Qiao Zhou proves to be equally difficult in terms of textual history. Qiao's *Yizhou zhi* 益州志 [*Records of Yi Province*] is not mentioned in either the Sui or Tang bibliographies. The only extant fragment from this text was cited in Li Shan's 李善 (d. 689 CE) commentary to Zuo Si's 左思 (ca. 250–305 CE) "Shu Capital Rhapsody."[47]

The final title attributed to Qiao Zhou, *Yizhou yiwu zhi* 益州異物志 [*Record of Strange Things of Yi Province*], is also complex in its history. The *Sui History* bibliography lists six works with the title "Records of Strange Things;" the *Old Tang History* lists five, while the *New Tang History* notes eight.[48] However, there is no mention of a text with this title attributed to Qiao Zhou in these standard bibliographies. Two fragments bearing this title are cited by Li Shan, again in his commentary to Zuo Si's rhapsody, and attributed to Qiao Zhou.[49] An additional fragment of this text attributed to Qiao Zhou is cited in Li Shizhen's 李時珍 (1518–1593) *Bencao gangmu* 本草綱目 [*Outline of Native Plants*].[50] In addition to these three fragments attributed to Qiao, there are four other surviving passages bearing the title of "*Record of Strange Things*" that deal with subject matter within the geographical scope of southwest China. These passages I tentatively attribute to Qiao Zhou, well aware that providing positive proof is impossible at this time.[51]

The twenty-seven surviving fragments of Qiao Zhou's local histories take two distinct forms and demonstrate both his wide base of local knowledge and strong sense of local pride. Although one format employed by Qiao Zhou, that of official administrative history, follows a venerable line of historiographical tradition, his use of the locality story is among the earliest applications of this new model of presenting the local past.

As previously noted, the practice of outlining the political and administrative history of individual locales was one of the earliest forms of history in general and local history in particular. This encyclopedic cataloging of a locale and its place in the larger context of the empire played an important function from both imperial and local perspectives. From the view of the court, control over boundaries, administration, and even naming was a sign of imperial dominance over the periphery. From the view of the local, their subjugation by the imperial was seen as a sign of belonging to the greater imperial enterprise. In this regard, the documentation of local administrative history by official (i.e., court) historians could serve one rhetorical function, while the same narration by a private local historian might serve another role all together.

Of the surviving fragments of Qiao Zhou's writings on the history of the Chengdu Plain, ten passages (direct quotes and references) deal with the administrative history of Ba commandery. An examination of three slightly variant passages addressing the same political event reveals something of both Qiao Zhou's approach to this form of local history, as well as illustrates some problems of working with badly fragmented texts. For example, three passages from Qiao's *Records of Three Ba Commanderies* (or *Records of Ba*) discuss the division of Ba into new administrative units. The first citation of this event is found in the *Song History:*

> Qiao Zhou's *Records of Ba* said: In the first year of the Chuping period (190 CE), the camp major Zhao Wei 趙韙 proposed to divide the prefectures of Ba commandery south of Anhan 安漢, creating Yongning 永寧 commandery. In Jian'an 6 (202 CE), Liu Zhang changed Yongning into Badong 巴東 commandery, dividing Fuling 涪陵 prefecture and establishing Danxing 丹興 and Hanjia 漢葭 prefectures, and establishing a chief commandant of the dependent state of Badong, which later became Fuling commandery.[52]

This same restructuring of the administration is repeated in the *Song History*, again citing Qiao Zhou's *Records of Ba:* "Qiao Zhou's *Records of Ba* [said] in Jian'an 6, Liu Zhang divided Ba commandery [placing] from Dianjiang northward, creating Baxi commandery."[53] The final citation of this passage, contained in Liu Zhao's commentary to Sima Biao's *Continued Han History*, reads:

> Qiao Zhou's *Records of Ba* said: In the first year of the Chuping period, Zhao Wei divided Ba into two commanderies. He wished to use the old name of Ba, therefore, he made Dianjiang 墊江 as the commandery seat [of Ba], and from Anhan southward became Yongning commandery. In Jian'an 6, Liu Zhang divided Ba, making Yongning into Badong and Dianjiang into Baxi commandery.[54]

These three citations of Qiao Zhou's *Records of Ba* account of the division of Ba illustrate one particular aspect of Qiao's approach to local history. In this account, Qiao Zhou sets forth the political or administrative history of the place in question. Simple in approach, he provides the dates, the political actors, and the locations affected by the restructuring of the administrative system. This account reads like a record from a traditional historical annal—simple, straightforward, and devoid of extraneous information.

Qiao's use of this format raises several questions. By the late Han, this type of administrative history had become a standard feature of state-sponsored historical activity, also based on Ban Gu's model of a dynastic history. By documenting the changing administrative structure in the region, Qiao may have been imitating Ban Gu in one of two ways. First, the form of Qiao's narration of local political changes appears identical to accounts in the *Han History* "Geographic Treatise." More important, since there is no indication that Qiao Zhou ever served in the capacity of a state historian, and based on later comments by Chen Shou, it appears doubtful that such an office was ever fully functioning in Shu-Han, Qiao may have followed Ban Gu's lead in compiling a private history in the official format. Significantly, Qiao's account of the region, in all likelihood a private venture, was later used as source material for Shen Yue's *Song History*.

These three citations of Qiao's work also raise some important questions. All three passages appear to cite the same text, *Records of Ba*, on the same matter—the division of Ba commandery. However, the fragments quoted are different. The passages cited in fascicle 37 of the *Song History* and in the "Treatises" of the *Continued Han History* are structurally similar, yet each contains information lacking in the other quotation. The chronologically earlier citation in the *Song History* offers additional details on Zhao Wei's office and prefecture-level changes. The later citation in the "Treatises" of the *Continued Han History* includes information on Zhao Wei's desire to keep the name Ba in the administrative shuffle. The question that immediately comes to mind is which of these accounts, treated as direct quotations in the Zhonghua shuju redactions of the texts, if either, was Qiao Zhou's original text? Are the quoted fragments from the same passage of text, or have Qiao's writings been conflated in the quotations? The problem of the passage cited in fascicle 38 of the *Song History* is somewhat easier to reconcile. It appears to be a paraphrasing of the passage quoted in the "Treatises" of the *Continued Han History*.[55] These textual issues may prove impossible to resolve. Nevertheless, the contents of these passages illustrate Qiao Zhou's practice of the commandery annal style of local historiography.

Additional fragments of Qiao Zhou's local histories introduce another more innovative aspect of his local historiography: the locality story. Andrew Chittick defines the locality story as a short narrative linked to a particular site, selected on the basis of its affiliation with the place, used to illustrate a physical feature or historical event associated with the place, and often serving to link local places with ancient legends of imperial power.[56] More specifically, Chittick identifies three distinct narrative forms taken by these early locality stories. The first simply notes a well-known historical event associated with a given site. Second, a locality story might "anchor" an event of unknown location to a specific place. Finally, they could record new or previously unrecorded events, typically supernatural occurences, associated with a locale.[57] Although these types of stories began appearing in local history writing during the Later Han period, they did not become common until the late third and early fourth centuries. A survey of fragments from forty-two local histories of the Han–Jin period reveals that only one-fourth of these histories employ locality stories or other anecdotes as part of their historical narrratives. The majority of these texts are in the form of administrative histories or biographies.[58] The locality stories included among local histories of the period prior to and contemporary with Qiao Zhou's works tend to focus on connections with both the political and cultural centers of power, including rulers (Yellow Thearch, the First Emperor of Qin, the Han Founder Liu Bang) and intellectual figures (Confucius, Laozi). Qiao Zhou's own use of the locality story should be viewed in the context of this nascent historiographical trend.

Three passages from *Records of Ba* clearly illustrate this feature of Qiao Zhou's local historiography. One such passage, contained in the Tang encyclopedia *Collected Literature Arranged by Category*, cites Qiao Zhou's *Records of Three Ba Commanderies*. It reads:

> *Records of Three Ba Commanderies* said, "In Langzhong 閬中, there is the Yu 渝 River.[59] The Zong 賨 people ardently love to dance. The Exalted Ancestor [Liu Bang] took pleasure in their vigor. Frequently, he went to watch them dance. He sent musicians to practice [this dance].[60] For this reason, it is called the 'Ba Yu Dance' 巴渝舞."[61]

This anecdote fits well with Chittick's general definition of the locality story. The physical setting is fixed at the Yu River that passed through Langzhong in Ba commandery, and the site is linked to the story of the Han founding emperor enjoying the martial dances of the Zong and later ordering his court musicians to learn and perform these dances.[62] Thus, a purported historical event linking the local site to imperial power is also established. As we will see, Qiao's account of this dance would find its way into later local histories of the region.

Another of Qiao Zhou's local anecdotes reached even further into antiquity in its effort to link the Chengdu Plain with the center of political power. This passage, drawn from Qiao's *Basic Annals of Shu* and cited in Pei Songzhi's *Commentary to the Records of the Three States*, seeks to establish one of China's sage-rulers of high antiquity as a native of the area. It reads: "Qiao Zhou's *Basic Annals of Shu* said, "Yu was originally a person of Mt. Min 汶山 in Guangrou 廣柔 prefecture. He was born at Shiniu 石紐, and the name of his land was Ku'er ping 刳兒坪."[63] In this passage, Qiao sites the birthplace of Yu at Shiniu, near present-day Minchuan 汶川 county, Sichuan. This information on Yu's nativity is not included in the traditional accounts of his life found in the *Documents* and *The Grand Scribe's Records*.[64] Considering Qiao's reputation as a classical scholar and his critical comments on Sima Qian's history, it is not surprising to find this type of detail in his writings on local history, though the source of his information is unknown. This anecdote serves, in Chittick's terminology, to "anchor" a classical figure to a local space, lending greater prestige to the site through its association with the ancient sage.

Another anecdote, preserved in the *Records of Shu Notables* describes local scenery and produce, again links the locale to the center of imperial power. The story reads:

> *Records of Three Ba Commanderies* said, "In the lower part of the prefecture, there is Clear-stream Cave 清水穴.The people of Ba use this water to make powder.[65] Thus, brilliant and fragrant, this powder is presented at the capital. Because of this, [the stream] is named Powder Stream 粉水. In olden times, this was called Jiangzhou Fallen-forest Powder 江州墮林粉. Now there is a clear rivulet at the bottom of the mountain. Previously at this site there was the abode of a Daoist called Clear-rivulet Courtyard 清溪院. East of Clear-stream Cave is Dragon-gate 龍門. From a precipice, a divided waterfall is suspended. In the spring, floating boats must weave in and out to pass this crossing. Returning, to the right of the cave is called Begonia Rivulet 海棠溪. It is blocked by the rivulet's plants and trees. At the time of the summer floods, one can pole a boat several *li* overcoming these [obstacles]."[66]

Like the previous anecdote, this story from Qiao's text connects a local place and activity to the political center. Here, the local stream is used to produce a cosmetic power that was presented at the capital. In addition to providing the link between the local and the capital, Qiao Zhou also offers a more detailed discussion of the place, noting its natural and man-made landmarks.[67]

Though by definition a locality story should link the local to the center, the severely fragmented nature of Qiao Zhou's local writings often make identification of the link impossible. Several surviving fragments from Qiao's writings on the Chengdu Plain, while missing these connections, offer important information on local produce and customs, which functioned in similar fashion to biographies of human subjects. That is, these colorful descriptions of a locale provide evidence of the character of the place.

The first anecdote, taken from Qiao's *Records of Yi Province*, describes the practice of washing brocade silk in Chengdu. Cited in Li Shan's commentary to Zuo Si's "Shu Capital Rhapsody," this passage reads: "Qiao Zhou's *Records of Yi Province* said, "In Chengdu, after the woven brocade is finished, it is rinsed in the river's water and its pattern is much more distinct than when it is first finished. Rinsing it in another river is inferior to [this] river."[68] While the passage does not link the local site to larger imperial concerns, it provides interesting information about a commercial practice of the area—one that would be referenced again by several later historians writing about Chengdu.

The three passages from *Record of Strange Things of Yi Province* expressly attributed to Qiao Zhou deal with local geography and produce. A passage cited in Li Shan's commentary to Zuo Si's "Shu Capital Rhapsody" describes a prominent natural landmark:

> Qiao Zhou's *Record of Strange Things* said, "The Inverted Pond (Dianchi 滇池) is near the border of Jianning 建寧.[69] It has a large marsh-lake and is over two-hundred *li* in circumference. Its inlet is deep and wide, but its lower reaches are shallow and narrow like an overturned pond. Therefore, it is popularly called the 'Inverted Pond.'"[70]

In addition to cataloging the region's natural features, Qiao also notes the utility of local produce. Li Shizhen's *Outline of Native Plants* quotes Qiao's *Record of Strange Things from Ba and Shu* (a variant title) regarding a plant known as "white thistle" (*baici* 白刺) or "patterned grass" (*wenzhang cao* 文章草), including a poetic appraisal of the plant by Qiao. The verse reads:

> [When using] patterned grass to prepare wine, one can perfect its flavor.
>
> Using money to buy the grass, not speaking of its expense.[71]

Qiao's appraisal of the grass hints at its use in preparing tinctures. Mixed with ferment, the grass flavored the liquor and also promised medicinal benefits. The exact site at which this grass was located is unfortunately missing in the received fragment.

The final passage of *Record of Strange Things* specifically attributed to Qiao, again contained in the commentary to Zuo Si's rhapsody, discusses turtles of the Fuling area.[72]

> Qiao Zhou's *Record of Strange Things* said, "Fuling has many large turtles. Their shells can be used for divination. Among them are those like the hawksbill. They are commonly said to be numinous. There are also swamps and marshes. In Badong, there is a marsh-lake. The people say it has a divine dragon and one must not cry out or [beat on] drums. If one cries out or beats on drums, then there will be more rain."[73]

This anecdote records the type of turtles found in the region and their use—divination. Additionally, Qiao mentions the local belief in the divine nature of these turtles and their companion, a dragon of a marsh-lake in Badong commandery.[74]

This element of the supernatural also occurs in several fragments of texts entitled *Record of Strange Things* of unknown authorship but directly linked to sites on the Chengdu Plain. While it is impossible to ascertain whether they are from Qiao Zhou's work, I include one example here to illustrate the focus of these stories and hold open the possibility that they were compiled by Qiao Zhou. The following passage, cited in the *Records of Shu Notables*, relates a tale associated with a local spring. The anecdote reads:

> The *Record of Strange Things* said, "Previously, there was a drought and the springs were dried up. A man of the Gu 姑 clan was ill and wished to drink of the sweet spring. His wife wandered about, reaching the foot of Zhouwang 周望 mountain, where she encountered an old man who said, 'If you give me

> your hairpin, the sweet [water] can be had.' The wife plucked out her hairpin and gave it to [the old man]. He threw it to the ground and the spring emerged. To this day, there is a plentiful source of water from this fissure. It is five or six *chi* in circumference and shaped like a pair of hairpins. To the west is Zhou Rivulet 周溪. The wife's surname was Zhou 周."[75]

The precise location of this spring is not known. Nevertheless, the anecdote is representative of those collected by Qiao Zhou and others under the category of "Records of Strange Things."[76]

Concluding our examination of Qiao Zhou's local histories, we must briefly visit the issue of source materials. At no point in his writings does Qiao Zhou state explicitly the sources of his information on the region. Furthermore, a comparison of Qiao's writings with fragments of earlier local histories reveals no evidence of borrowing from previous texts. While not precluding some adaptation from unknown earlier textual sources, this fact strengthens the hypothesis that the bulk of Qiao's local historiography was based on personal knowledge of his native region and its traditions and lore. As a native of Baxi commandery, Qiao would likely have heard the stories surrounding local sites, and his writings may be regarded as an early attempt to collect these stories under the rubric of local historiography.

A comparison of the passages of Qiao's text relating to administrative geography with those containing locality stories yields interesting observations. First, nearly all the administrative passages are gleaned from the treatises and commentaries to standard histories compiled prior to the Tang. The sole exception, a passage preserved in the *Records of Shu Notables* citing Qiao's *Records of Three Ba Commanderies*, presents the history of the establishment of Linjiang 臨江 prefecture.[77] Additionally, the treatises of and the commentaries on the standard histories all cite Qiao's text as "*Records of Ba*." Finally, all the passages containing locality stories—including those not cited in this chapter—are drawn from Tang and later collectanea or encyclopedia and use the name "*Records of Three Ba Commanderies*." It would appear that the pre-Tang historians were primarily interested in Qiao's local histories for their details on administrative geography, while interest in his locality stories did not rise until the Tang.

From this brief look at Sichuan local historiography of the third century, we can clearly see both continuity with previous approaches to local history as well as the development of a new direction for the craft. In the biographical writings of Chen Shu and Yang Xi, the focus remained on local actors on the national stage. The nativity of these actors was less important than the role they played and only served as a common thread with which to bind their collected lives together. The writings of Qiao Zhou, on the other hand, emphasize the place over its people. In fact, there is no mention of any sort of biographical writings in Qiao Zhou's historiographical works. Some of Qiao Zhou's local histories continued the earliest format of historiography, that of the annal, with several fragments of his *Records of Ba* narrating the administrative history of the area in a chronological fashion. However, it is the inclusion of the locality story that sets Qiao Zhou apart in the field of Sichuan local historiography. These anecdotes describe the physical and cultural features of local sites, often establishing links between the places and the political center. Additionally, the range of subjects touched on by Qiao Zhou in his writings on the Chengdu Plain illustrate the breadth of his knowledge of the region. Subjects ranging from local produce, flora and fauna, music and dance, ancient landmarks (both natural and man-made), and current beliefs and legends are all sited within the bounds of his geographic writings. Qiao was not the first Chinese historian to include locality stories in his historical writings, nevertheless, he was part of a growing trend toward incorporating these types of stories into local histories. Furthermore, he was the first to include the locality story in writings on the Chengdu Plain. As such, Qiao's local histories both directly and indirectly influenced the later compilation of Sichuan histories.

THE INFLUENCE OF QIAO ZHOU'S LOCAL HISTORIES

The impact of Qiao Zhou's historiographical innovations was not immediately felt by Chengdu Plain historians. Qiao's student, Chen Shou clearly surpassed his teacher as the most important historian from the region, but Chen's mark was made in the area of official or dynastic, not local history. Though his *Records of the Three States* treats each of the immediate post-Han political entities in a separate *Records* (*zhi* 志) or *Documents* (*shu* 書), the overall structure is based on the annals-biography format of *The Grand Scribe's Records* and *Han History*. But in addition to this important history, Chen Shou also compiled a collection of biographies of eminent persons from the area entitled *Biographies of the Elders of Yi Province*. As noted earlier, Chen Shou was reportedly dissatisfied with earlier collections of local lives and set out to rectify their deficiencies with a collection of his own. Though the work is no longer intact, a number of fragments are quoted by Pei Songzhi in his *Commentary on the Records of the Three States*, as well as in other encyclopedia.[78] None of the persons included in *Biographies of the Elders of Yi Province* is treated in any detail in the *Records of the Three States*—this is not surprising given that most of these individuals predated the independent state of Shu-Han. In this work, Chen Shou clearly continues in the tradition of biographical writing as a mode of local historiography.

In addition to Chen Shou's work on local history, a Shu native of the Western Jin period, Chang Kuan 常寬, also figures in the development of early medieval Sichuan historiography. Chang was said to have compiled two works of local history. One entitled *Shu houzhi* 蜀後志 [*Later Records of Shu*] was described as a continuation of Chen Shou's *Records of the Three States*. The text is no longer extant. The second work was a collection of biographies entitled *Liang Ba qijiu zhuan* 梁巴耆舊傳 [*Biographies of the Elders of Ba in Liang*

Province], said to be a continuation of Chen Shou's *Biographies of the Elders of Yi Province*.[79] Again, this collection is no longer extant and record of it is only made by Chang Kuan's descendent, Chang Qu.[80]

In the cases of these two historians, Qiao Zhou's key local historiographical innovation, the locality story, was ignored as Chen Shou and Chang Kuan followed traditional models of writing the local past. However, other historians of the late third century (and beyond) picked up on this developing feature of local historiography.

Chang Qu's *Records of the States South of Mount Hua* stands as the most comprehensive history of the Chengdu Plain, as well as the work that most clearly reflects Qiao Zhou's historiographical innovations.[81] Generally speaking, the *Records of the States South of Mount Hua* deals with the geography, political history, and lives of the people of the Chengdu Plain from earliest times through the Eastern Jin period.[82] In his treatment of the independent regimes of the region, Chang Qu traces the histories of the various independent rulers of the area: Gongsun Shu, Liu Yan and Liu Zhang, the Two Sovereigns of Shu-Han (Liu Bei and Liu Shan), and Li Shi's Cheng-Han dynasty, presenting chronological accounts of the leaders and their affairs in a manner similar to a "basic annals" account of a ruler from *The Grand Scribe's Records*, *Han History*, or *Records of the Three States*.[83] The lives of the subjects of these independent regimes along with other notable persons from the region are treated chronologically and by geographic location.[84] The first four fascicles of the history are generally regarded as the most important. Drawing on a variety of prior works of local history, Chang Qu narrates the history of Ba, Shu, Hanzhong, and Nanzhong, noting each area's administrative history, physical landmarks, unique customs, and important figures. These sections are innovative in their comprehensive treatment of each particular place, and while continuing the format of the earlier geographic treatise, they significantly expand the genre, eventually serving as a model for later local histories and gazetteers.[85] It is in this regard that we find the influence of Qiao Zhou most pervasive.

The frequent addition of the locality story to the geographic treatise sets Chang's sections on local geography apart from earlier efforts. As we have observed, Qiao Zhou was the first Sichuan historian to include locality stories in his local histories of the region. A cursory reading of the geographic fascicles of the *Records of the States South of Mount Hua* easily shows Chang Qu to have continued this process. However, a closer look—especially at the section on Ba commandery—demonstrates that Chang Qu did much more than merely incorporate this new element into his history. He relied heavily on Qiao's stories, often quoting them verbatim, though offering no credit to his predecessor.[86]

For example, Qiao Zhou's account of the Ba Yu Dance from his *Records of Three Ba Commanderies* is quoted with some additional detail inserted in Chang Qu's account of early Han period Ba.

QIAO ZHOU: In Langzhong there is the Yu River. The Zong people ardently love to dance. The Exalted Ancestor took pleasure in their vigor. Frequently, he went to watch them dance. He sent musicians to practice it. For this reason, it is called the "Ba Yu Dance."[87]

CHANG QU: In Langzhong there is the Yu River. Many of the Zong people live along the river. Their temperament is active and brave. Previously they served as the vanguard of the Han [army], breaking through the enemy lines. They ardently love to dance. The Emperor admired this, saying, "These are the songs that King Wu attacked [King] Zhou by." He then sent musicians to practice and study it. Now it is called the "Ba Yu Dance."[88]

The details added by Chang Qu strengthen the anecdote's effect as a locality story, stressing the connection between the place, a historical event, and the center of power. While Qiao Zhou's account only links the Yu River and the dance tradition of the Zong with the Han founding emperor, Chang Qu's version of the story extends the link between the local and the imperial back to the founding of the Zhou dynasty.

In some cases, Chang Qu abbreviates Qiao Zhou's earlier locality story. For example, Qiao Zhou's account of an unidentified site in Ba commandery describes a local stream where powder was produced and presented to the capital. Following this link between the place, its produce, and the capital, Qiao Zhou describes additional scenery at the site: a Daoist abode, another stream, a waterfall, and so on. However, in the *Records of the States South of Mount Hua*, Chang Qu directly quotes Qiao Zhou to a fixed point in the narrative, then truncates the remainder of the anecdote. Chang Qu's account of this site reads:

In the lower part of the prefecture, there is Clear-stream Cave. The people of Ba use this water to make powder. Thus, brilliant and fragrant, this powder is presented at the capital. Because of this, [the stream] is named Powder Stream. In olden times, this was called Jiangzhou Fallen-forest Powder.[89]

Apart from two variant graphs, the accounts are identical to a point. Chang's abbreviation of Qiao's longer anecdote may be explained as part of Chang Qu's historiographical agenda: linking the Chengdu Plain to the center of political power. In the passages following his quotation of Qiao Zhou's anecdote, Chang Qu describes rice from the region that was also presented at court, as well as a location where the local aristocracy gathered to drink in the shade on hot days. These additional details would all seem to further Chang's purpose, while Qiao Zhou's description of local religious sites and scenery would not.

However, this is not always the case. In one instance, Chang Qu's account appends a fantastic local legend to Qiao Zhou's simpler narrative. Writing on the matter of the marsh-lake in Jianning, Qiao Zhou says:

The Inverted Pond is near the border of Jianning. It has a large marsh-lake and is over two-hundred *li* in circumference. Its inlet is deep and wide, but its lower reaches are shallow and narrow like an overturned pond. Therefore, it is popularly called the Inverted Pond.[90]

Chang Qu largely follows Qiao's account:

> Dianchi prefecture: The commandery seat is the old Dian village. It has a marsh-lake over two-hundred *li* in circumference. Its inlet is deep and wide, but its lower reaches are shallow and narrow like an overturned pond. Therefore, it is called the Inverted Pond. An old legend says there is a divine horse in the pond. It mated [with a local's mare] and [the mare] gave birth to a fabulous colt. It is customarily called the "Inverted Pond Colt," and it is said that it can travel five-hundred *li* in a day.[91]

Here, Chang Qu offers supernatural origins for the fine horses of the region, a characterization that began in the early Han and continued throughout the medieval period.[92] This additional information is reminiscent of the comments at the conclusion of Qiao Zhou's remarks on the turtles of Fuling. After describing the turtles and their use, Qiao appends an anecdote about the dragon who lived in another marsh-lake. While there is no direct evidence to support such a claim, it seems possible that the entire story related in the *Records of the States South of Mount Hua* account of the Inverted Pond may in fact be from Qiao Zhou's earlier work.

From these examples, we can clearly see the influence of Qiao Zhou's local histories on Chang Qu's work. Tracing an anecdote from Qiao Zhou to the *Records of the States South of Mount Hua* and beyond allows us to follow his indirect influence on later local historiography. The passage on the rinsing of brocade in a Chengdu river from Qiao's *Records of Yi Province* provides a good example of this influence:

> In Chengdu, after the woven brocade was finished, it was rinsed in the river's water and its pattern was much more distinct than when it was first finished. Rinsing it in another river is inferior to [this] river. Yellow Sheen was called the "fine cloth in a tube."[93]

A similar account in the *Records of the States South of Mount Hua* account reads:

> The road [of the provincial academy] was west of the wall [near] the site of the former Brocade Office. The Brocade River was where, after weaving brocade, it was then rinsed in [the river]. The brocade was then more brilliant. Rinsing it in another river was not as good. For this reason, this area was called the Brocade Quarter.[94]

In Chang Qu's retelling of this anecdote, additional details are added. In particular, the problematic term *jiangshui* 江水 in Qiao Zhou's account is properly identified as the Brocade River (Jin jiang 錦江), not the Yangzi which passes to the west of Chengdu. Finally, Chang's anecdote adds important details about the Chengdu brocade industry, noting the location of the Brocade Office and the designation of this particular neighborhood in Chengdu as the Brocade Quarter.

The story transmitted in the *Records of the States South of Mount Hua* was subsequently adapted and reproduced in Li Daoyuan's *Commentary on the Classic of the Waterways*. Here the passage reads:

> The [provincial] academy moved to the west of Yi [Barbarian] Quarter road, near the site of the former Brocade Office. This refers to the Brocade River. After weaving brocade, then it is rinsed in the river's flow. The brocade was then more brilliant. If it was rinsed in another river, then the brocade's color would be weak. For this reason, this area was called the Brocade Quarter.[95]

Again, a few additional details are added by the later historian to the core account by Qiao Zhou.

The story was next cited by Li Shan in his commentary to Zuo Si's rhapsody—chronologically the earliest attribution of this story to Qiao Zhou (and treated in this study as the base text). It is unclear, however, whether Li Shan's citation of Qiao was in fact a direct quotation or a paraphrase.

A final retelling of this practice is contained in Yue Shi's 樂史 (fl. early nineteenth century CE) *Taiping huanyu ji* 太平寰宇記 [*Records of the World of Great Peace*]. This passage strips away the accrued details and returns it to a simpler form. It reads:

> Rinsing Brocade River, also known as the Shu River, is where they came to rinse brocade. The brocade became more brilliant and lustrous in this water. Therefore, it is called Rinsing Brocade River 濯錦江.[96]

Thus, we can see how Qiao Zhou's early account of a particular practice current in his time became the kernel around which later accounts of the practice were based. This appears in large measure as a result of the inclusion of this fragment in Chang Qu's history and its subsequent influence. Yet, in all of these transmissions, only Li Shan attributes this anecdote to Qiao Zhou. While the Chengdu silk-washing practice may well have been common knowledge in Qiao's time and later, the similarities between Qiao Zhou's written record of the silk-washing and later writings on the area hint at the influence of Qiao's earlier account of the practice.[97]

In the *Records of the States South of Mount Hua*, Chang Qu reproduces passages of Qiao Zhou's earlier local histories nearly a dozen times. The liberal quoting and paraphrasing of Qiao's own writings in Chang's *Records of the States South of Mount Hua* is ample evidence of the high regard in which Qiao was held by Chang Qu. Chang's remark in the "Postface" of his history regarding historians "sufficiently intimate with the things and places [having] no need to consult these annals [i.e. "Geographic Treatises"]"[98] seems to refer to individuals like Qiao Zhou. Furthermore, Chang Qu's praise of local histories that "comprehensively discuss things or places"[99] also aptly applies to Qiao's writings. Given Chang Qu's strong implicit support for Qiao Zhou's scholarship, that the general characteristics of local historiography praised by Chang should mirror the strengths of Qiao and his writings should come as no great surprise. We may cautiously postulate the thesis that while Chang Qu followed the established models of geographical history writing (i.e., the "Geographic Treatises" of Ban Gu's *Han History*) and the earlier trend of biography as historical commentary and local history, Qiao Zhou was a significant influence on the expansion of Chang's work from basic administrative history and biography to the sweeping historical–cultural record of the southwest that is the complete *Records of the States South of Mount Hua*.[100] While this discussion has identified a few examples of this influence, there are undoubtedly many other passages in the *Records of the States South of Mount Hua* that are also from the brush of Qiao Zhou; however, these are likely to remain unidentified.

Shifting from the preceding examination of historical texts to a summary view of historical contexts, I would like to briefly address the question of purpose. Specifically, why did Qiao Zhou compile his local histories? The fragments of Qiao's local histories seem oddly out of place in the context of his intellectual background and oeuvre. Qiao Zhou was a dedicated classicist, trained in both the orthodox canon and the regional mantic traditions of astronomical observation and prophesy. Qiao's writings on ritual and ancient history demonstrate a devotion to a classicist vision of antiquity and a belief that this worldview was in fact relevant in the chaotic times of the third-century Chinese civil war, while his prophesies illustrate a firm belief in the principles of correlative cosmology. Surprisingly, neither his classicist ideology nor his faith in the heavens played a significant role in his writings on local history.

We find few clues regarding the purpose of Qiao's local histories from the historical–political context. Qiao Zhou spent nearly his entire adult life as a subject of the state of Shu-Han. As such, one might expect to find evidence of partisanship in his writings about his own state. However, there is no real evidence that his local histories (or other scholarly writings) were designed as propaganda for the imperial enterprise of the Liu clan and Shu-Han. His political writings tended to exhort Liu Shan toward moral behavior both individually and for the welfare of the people of the state, supporting the notion that Qiao's support for the Lius' regime was heavily based on the classical ideal of a sage-king. Thus, his local histories did not tend to favor the Lius or their state over the other contenders for the remains of the shattered Han empire. After the surrender of Shu-Han, Qiao Zhou finally accepted a post offered by the Jin, though, due to failing health, he did not take office.

Unfortunately, none of Qiao's local histories can be accurately dated and thus we do not know whether they were compiled under the administration of Shu-Han or Jin. The chronology might prove significant in assessing the purpose of these writings. As previously noted, the objective of the locality story appears to be in linking the local to the national. If Qiao's local histories were compiled under Shu-Han, his links to the central imperial authority might be seen as undermining the local imperial authority of the Lius. Were the histories compiled under Jin, then they could be read in a manner that argues for a reconciliation between the local and the new imperial power. But without any clear indication of the circumstances surrounding the writing of these histories, we can be certain of little regarding the political implications of Qiao Zhou's local writings.

Moreover, Qiao's surviving local histories demonstrate a greater interest in the matters of place in his home region than the particular political body reigning over the landscape. It is this sense of regional pride that pervades the local histories of Qiao Zhou and provides the strongest evidence of Qiao's purpose in compiling these local records. While the Chengdu Plain and its surrounding mountainous regions had been integrated into the political sphere of the central plains by the state of Qin in 316 BCE and subsequent campaigns increased the empire's control of the region during the Former Han, the Chengdu Plain remained to some extent culturally apart from the center of imperial power concentrated in the Yellow River heartland. The views expressed by Ban Gu in his "Geographic Treatise," quoted earlier, that the bounty of the land resulted in the weak character of its inhabitants perhaps best exemplifies the Central Plains view of the Chengdu Plain. And while Ban Gu's prejudice against the south may have been somewhat extreme, despite over three hundred years of Qin and Han influence in the area, many outsiders were still unconvinced that the region was an equally cultured part of the empire.

Both Qiao Zhou's and Chang Qu's local histories function as counterbalances to these views. As indicated in the preceding discussion, many of the locality stories in Qiao's histories attempt to link the region to the centers of power in both high antiquity and the recent past. Tying both the sage-king Yu and the Han founder Liu Bang to the region, Qiao argues that the Chengdu Plain was both cultured and integrated into the larger Chinese sphere from ancient times and, by extension, remained so in his own time. His discussions of imperial demand for local produce emphasize the economic and cultural impact of the region on the empire. While some of the extant anecdotes in the local histories of Qiao Zhou do not explicitly link the Chengdu Plain to the center, the fragmentary nature of these surviving texts does not permit us to draw solid conclusions about the possible purposes of these passages.

Writing nearly one hundred years after Qiao Zhou, Chang Qu also seems to be fighting similar prejudices. In fact, an overriding theme of the *Records of the States South of Mount Hua* is the argument that the region was cultured at an early date and had long played a role in the affairs of the empire. It is important to remember that both the local histories of Qiao Zhou and Chang Qu were likely compiled in Chengdu during periods when the area was politically independent of the dominant regimes of the central plains and eastern Yangzi. Under politically separate entities, Qiao's and Chang's arguments for cultural legitimacy might have safely been advanced without appearing to be disloyal to their regional sovereigns. The cultural links between the Chengdu Plain and the center might thus be appreciated by both the independent rulers as a possible justification for campaigns against their rivals, and seen by those outside of the Chengdu Plain as evidence of the region's cultural and historical unity with the greater Chinese cultural sphere. Were these attempts to legitimize the Chengdu Plain's place in the cultural empire successful? While it is unclear how Qiao Zhou's local histories were received either in Chengdu or without, it appears that Chang Qu's history met with mixed reactions in the north and east. Regardless of their receptions, we may rightly view Qiao Zhou's local histories and Chang Qu's *Records of the States South of Mount Hua* as powerful arguments for cultural inclusion and statements of regional pride.

Epilogue

This book has attempted to illustrate the vitality of the intellectual world of early medieval Sichuan through a survey of various scholarly traditions of the region, including an in-depth examination of the life and works of a representative figure, Qiao Zhou. In one sense, I have tried to disprove the nagging generalization that Sichuan lacked serious scholarship during the Three States period. In another, I have sought to present the misrepresented figure of Qiao Zhou as both an exemplar of Sichuan scholarship and as a significant intellectual in China at large. In light of the traditional and received views of intellectual activity in third-century Sichuan and of Qiao Zhou, these tasks are interrelated.

EVALUATING THE LIFE OF QIAO ZHOU

From the fourth century onward, numerous individuals have offered their assessments of Qiao Zhou's life and character. The earliest appraisals of Qiao Zhou came in the form of encomia and commentary from various Jin dynasty intellectuals who were either natives of the Chengdu Plain or were holding public office in the region and tended to look favorably on the intellectual accomplishments of Qiao Zhou. But positive evaluations quickly faded with harsher appraisals emerging and gaining widespread acceptance. Most later judgments took Qiao Zhou's political activity, especially his role in the surrender of Shu-Han, as the basis for their damning criticisms. Sadly, many of these negative evaluations were based less on the historical record of Qiao Zhou's life than the fictional representations contained in the *Three Kingdoms*. Furthermore, few later evaluations had much in the way of historical or scholarly intent, but rather employed Qiao Zhou as a rhetorical figure for contemporary debates.

Although most appraisals of Qiao Zhou, both traditional and modern, have focused on his political activity, generally in negative terms, the earliest evaluations in fact judged Qiao on the merits of his scholarship. The first such appraisal of Qiao Zhou is contained at the conclusion of Chen Shou's "Forest of Classicists" fascicle. Here Chen Shou praises his mentor as follows: "Qiao Zhou's words and principles were deep and penetrating. He was a great scholar of his generation, possessing the principle of Dong [Zhongshu] and Yang [Xiong]."[1] Given the close relationship between Chen Shou and his teacher, his laudatory remarks are not at all surprising. However, the comparison between Qiao Zhou and the two early Han syncretic scholars provides a glimpse of how Chen viewed the intellectual aspects of Qiao: as a broadly learned syncretic classicist.

In addition to his own appraisal of Qiao Zhou, Chen Shou also cites two other early positive assessments. First, in his *Biographies of the Elders of Yi Province*, Chen notes the commission of a portrait of Qiao Zhou for the provincial academy by the inspector of the province Dong Rong 董榮. Following the completion of the portrait, Dong ordered his assistant Li Tong 李通 to compose an encomium for Qiao to accompany the image.[2] Li Tong's piece reads:

Lofty was the Marquis Qiao.	抑抑譙侯
He loved antiquity and transmitted classical [scholarship].	好古述儒
He treasured the Way and embraced the truth.	寶道懷真
He scrutinized the age and filled the void.	鑒世盈虛
He refined his name and beautified his footsteps.	雅名美跡
His entire life was [devoted to] books.	終始是書
Our future generations will revere his worth.	我后欽賢
There are no words that do not praise him.	無言不譽
Grasp hold of the wisdom that has gone before.	攀諸前哲
I have painted this portrait.	丹青是圖
O' you coming generations,	嗟爾來葉
Reflect on this manifest exemplar![3]	鑒茲顯模

The purpose of this portrait and verse is clear: Qiao Zhou was to serve as an example for students in the academy where he himself had taught for many years, with his portrait joining the images of other standard classicists and local worthies depicted in the Chengdu school.[4] In the judgment of the provincial inspector Dong Rong, Qiao Zhou ranked among these great men of letters and scholarship.

The final assessment quoted by Chen Shou comes from the noted historian Yang Xi. Although there is no mention of Qiao Zhou in the surviving fragments of Yang's *Encomia for the Officials of Third Han*, Chen Shou did not reproduce passages of Yang's text related to individuals for whom he had compiled biographies. This would include Qiao Zhou. Thus, it is unknown whether Yang Xi's original text included materials on Qiao Zhou or not. Regardless, Chen Shou quotes Yang Xi on Qiao Zhou:

> At that time there were some people who said that Qiao Zhou was not among the talents of the age, and few followed or respected him. Only Yang Xi esteemed him. [Yang Xi] once said, "None of us or those of later generations, in the end, will be the equal of this eminent one" (*zhang'er* 長兒). Those who knew [Qiao Zhou] respected Yang Xi because of this.[5]

It is unclear when Yang Xi's remark was made or under what context. Nevertheless, his respect for Qiao Zhou's scholarly achievements is clear, as is his sense of humor. Fang Beichen 方北辰 notes the term "*zhang'er*" literally means "tall child," and is a punned reference to Qiao Zhou's stature.[6]

The final early judgment of Qiao Zhou's intellectual abilities comes in the form of an encomium by Chang Qu, contained in his *Records of the States South of Mount Hua*. Here, Chang directly borrows the language of Chen Shou's own appraisal, saying, "Deep and penetrating, the Cavalier Attendant in Regular Attendance Qiao Zhou, appellative Yunnan. He was the son of Qiao Bing. During the reigns of the Lius he was Imperial Household Grandee."[7] Although Chang's encomium employs the language of Chen Shou regarding Qiao's intellect, the bulk of the appraisal focuses on Qiao's political appointments, noting the highest offices held under Jin and Shu-Han. As previously noted, Chang's history does not contain a full biography of Qiao Zhou, though both Qiao Zhou and his father are included in lists of the region's most accomplished intellectuals, and Chang frequently cites Qiao's local histories within his own work. In one case, after relating the fulfillment of one of Qiao Zhou's prophesies, Chang Qu declared him to be a sage.[8] These citations and the declaration of Qiao as sage stand as evidence of the high regard in which Chang Qu held Qiao Zhou.

Unfortunately, these early positive assessments of Qiao Zhou's intellectual achievements have been largely overlooked and replaced by numerous evaluations of Qiao Zhou's political activity. The two earliest judgments on Qiao Zhou's political life are presented in Pei Songzhi's *Commentary* and illustrate the varying degrees in which Qiao's role in the surrender of Shu-Han were evaluated during the Jin dynasty. Placed immediately following Chen Shou's comment attributing the safety of Liu Shan and his family to Qiao Zhou's plan to surrender, Pei Songzhi quotes dissenting opinions by Sun Chuo 孫綽 (ca. 301–80 CE) and Sun Sheng.[9] Sun Chuo's passing comments about Qiao Zhou note only that Qiao Zhou persuaded the Later Sovereign to surrender. In the appraisal that follows, Sun Chuo primarily criticizes Liu Shan's refusal to die along with his state and places the blame for the splintering of the empire on Liu Bei. No explicit judgment of Qiao Zhou is made.[10] Sun Sheng, on the other hand, places ultimate blame on Liu Shan for the downfall of the Shu-Han imperial enterprise, offering a harsh criticism of Qiao Zhou in the process. Sun Sheng writes:

> The principle of the *Spring and Autumn* is that a ruler dies with the Altars of Soil and Grain (i.e., the state) and a noble minister dies with his office. How can one who is called the Son of Heaven be [thus] disgraced by other men? Qiao Zhou told the leader of a ten-thousand carriage state to save his own life and shirk responsibility, forgetting the rites, striving for profit, and hoping for some small glory. How deluded![11]

In his denunciation of the surrender, Sun Sheng depicts Qiao Zhou as self-serving and seeking personal benefit in encouraging his ruler to surrender. According to Sun, the principled action for both Liu Shan and Qiao Zhou would have been to die along with the state of Shu-Han. Sun Sheng continues his criticism of Qiao Zhou's proposal by noting that Liu Shan, while a mediocre ruler, was not as bad as the archetypal last rulers of previous dynasties and argues that, given Shu-Han's geographic conditions, even a military solution was possible, offering historical examples of leaders who were successful in recovering lost territory from exile. Sun's final appraisal of Qiao Zhou is scathing. He declares, "Qiao Zhou was truly a worn-out minister!"[12]

Finally, Pei Songzhi paraphrases the views of another Jin historian, Zhang Fan 張璠:

> Zhang Fan considered Qiao Zhou's plan to surrender to Wei a result of Liu Shan's weak essence, but that [Liu Shan's] heart had no injurious nature. For this reason, [Qiao's plan] was carried out. If he [Liu Shan] encountered an angry or reckless person, though he had no other plan, he still had compassion on the despised and shamed. Sometimes he was angry and would rashly put a person to death, establishing for a time, fear. But this was but for an instant. His plans were destroyed by the misfortunes of the Yi tribes.[13]

Here, Zhang Fan attributes Liu Shan's acceptance of Qiao Zhou's plan to his compassionate nature—not wishing to expose his subjects to almost-certain slaughter at the hands of the approaching Wei forces—and makes no explicit judgment of Qiao Zhou. Zhang Fan's views are similar to those of Sun Chuo, and together they stand in stark contrast to the opinions of their contemporary, Sun Sheng. Clearly, the verdict on Qiao Zhou's political career was mixed in the generation immediately following the fall of Shu-Han.

Although Qiao Zhou's intellectual accomplishments were frequently noted during the Tang, his political life does not appear to have been of great concern to scholars between the fourth and twelfth centuries. For example, while Sima Guang frequently mentions the activities of Qiao Zhou in his *Comprehensive Mirror for Aid in Governing,* he offers no personal appraisal of Qiao or his role in the events of Shu-Han. The popular abridgement of Sima Guang's history, the *Outline to the Comprehensive Mirror for Aid in Governing,* attributed to Zhu Xi 朱熹 (1130–1200), presents only one brief assessment. Echoing the general tone of the earlier views of Sun Chuo and Zhang Fan, the *Outline* claims: "The Later Sovereign was of moderate talent and did not know that the ruler of a state should die along with the Altars of Soil and Grain. Qiao Zhou and the others were petty, and cast his state to the bandits."[14] While not a particularly harsh criticism, the *Outline's* view of Qiao Zhou as "petty" gained further voice and legitimacy as the influence of the *Outline to the Comprehensive Mirror for Aid in Governing* grew in late imperial China.

Taking a decidedly negative turn, the Yuan dynasty commentator on Sima Guang's history, Hu Sanxing, criticizes Qiao Zhou's political activity on philological grounds. In the *Comprehensive Mirror for Aid in Governing*, Sima Guang narrates Qiao Zhou's proposal to personally go to Luoyang and negotiate a favorable benefice for Liu Shan after the surrender of Shu-Han, quoting directly the *Records of the Three States* account of Qiao's argument.[15] Commenting on this passage, Hu Sanxing focuses on the term used for the capital, "*jingdu*" 京都, claiming that it manifests Qiao Zhou's hidden agenda opposing the Liu clan and Shu-Han. Hu argues: "'*Jingdu*' refers to Luoyang, the Wei capital. King Jing 景 of Jin's [Sima Shi] taboo name was Shi 師, thus people of Jin avoided using it, changing '*jingshi*'京師 [capital] to '*jingdu*' 京都. When Shu was suggesting surrender, Qiao Zhou was already acting as a person of Jin in observing this taboo!"[16]

Hu Sanxing's harsh implication that Qiao Zhou's loyalties were already fixed on the Sima clan prior to the surrender is groundless and based on a poor understanding of the historiography of the Three States period. The recommendation to surrender by Qiao Zhou was first recorded in the *Records of the Three States* by Chen Shou who compiled the history primarily as a subject of the Jin dynasty. Thus observation of the taboo on the graph *shi* would likely have been by Chen Shou in his representation of Qiao Zhou's speech and not Qiao Zhou himself.[17] Nevertheless, Hu's conclusion is significant in its illustration of the view that Qiao's actions were motivated by an already displaced loyalty to a state other than Shu-Han—in this case, the yet-to-be-established Jin. Thus, while the *Comprehensive Mirror for Aid in Governing* itself makes no judgment on Qiao Zhou, the commentary attached to it by Hu Sanxing and the moralizing abridgment attributed to Zhu Xi both offered unfavorable opinions of Qiao Zhou. The affect of these assessments can be seen in later appraisals of Qiao Zhou.

Without question, the most influential assessment of Qiao Zhou's political career and personal character is contained in the Ming dynasty fictional account of the Three States period, the *Three Kingdoms*. Expanding on the historical framework provided by Chen Shou's *Records of the Three States*, the novel treats Qiao Zhou as both a historical figure and literary prop, attributing motive but generally refraining from passing judgment on Qiao's political activity, and setting him as a "bookend figure" to illustrate the symmetry of fate and history.

As with the historical account in the *Records of the Three States*, the *Three Kingdoms* presents Qiao Zhou's role in Shu-Han politics within three broad contexts: the founding of the state of Shu-Han, debates over military policy, and the surrender of Shu-Han to Wei. The literary account, as one might expect, takes subtle but significant liberties with the historical record in its presentation of Qiao Zhou in these events. First, the novel places Qiao Zhou's entrance into the world of politics some seven years earlier than the historical records, claiming a role for Qiao as a public official in influencing Liu Zhang to surrender to Liu Bei in 214 CE (at which point Qiao would have been approximately fourteen *sui!*). This recommendation, based on Qiao's reading of celestial portents, presages Qiao's later role in the surrender of Liu Shan and Shu-Han.[18] The *Three Kingdoms* similarly affords Qiao Zhou credit with convincing Liu Bei to claim the title of emperor, again on the basis of celestial portents, and in playing a central role in the accession ceremony.[19] This treatment in the novel establishes Qiao Zhou as a "skilled reader of the stars"[20] and early supporter of Liu Bei and his dynastic enterprise. However, the fictional account of his encouragement of Liu Zhang to surrender also sets Qiao as a traitor of sorts. This aspect of the literary portrayal of Qiao Zhou resurfaces as the novel presents Qiao opposing the military campaigns of Zhuge Liang and Jiang Wei, casting his opposition in terms of both fate and personal enmity against the two military commanders.[21] Qiao's arguments against aggressive campaigns lead to his ultimate act of "betrayal," the recommendation that Liu Shan surrender to the rapidly advancing troops of Wei. Following Liu Shan's acceptance of the plan, the novel passively offers its strongest (yet indirect) judgment on Qiao Zhou. In one of the most dramatic scenes in the novel, immediately following Liu Shan's acceptance of the plan to surrender, a prince suddenly emerges from behind a screen and says to Qiao, "Rotten pedant! Irresponsibly arguing the fate of our sacred grain altars just to save your miserable skin! What Son of Heaven has ever surrendered?"[22] Liu Shan quickly rebukes his son, Liu Chen, to which the prince responds, "While your father lived, Qiao Zhou never dared to meddle in government policy. Now he rashly offers counsel in matters of state, presuming to give voice to subversive opinions, which have neither reason nor justification. . . . Why heed these rotten pedants and casually cast aside the late Emperor's patrimony?"[23] His mind fixed, the Later Sovereign has his attendants remove the prince from court and orders Qiao Zhou to prepare the documents of surrender. Following his expulsion from court, Liu Chen kills his wife and children, offers their heads at the shrine of Liu Bei, then kills himself in the shrine.[24] The novel, in its final mention of Qiao Zhou, tersely claims that after the surrender, Qiao Zhou, Xi Zheng and others "were awarded lordships and titles" by Wei.[25]

The *Three Kingdoms* employs the character of Qiao Zhou to support two main themes of the novel. First, Qiao stands as the embodiment of the principle of symmetry. He is depicted as the persuader for both Liu Zhang and Liu Shan to surrender. Following the surrenders of these two rulers, Qiao is shown to have quickly taken office with their successors. Qiao's role in both the founding and demise of Shu-Han also illustrates the theme of symmetry. In these regards, Qiao functions as a "human bookend" in the rise and fall of dynastic enterprises on the Chengdu Plain during the third century CE. The other major theme supported by the literary representation of Qiao Zhou is that of the triumph of fate over human will. In this regard, Qiao as a "skilled reader of the stars" continually demonstrates his superior ability to predict the future (fate), and the repeated accuracy of his predictions in the face of valiant will as manifest by Zhuge Liang and Jiang Wei.

While the *Three Kingdoms* presents Qiao Zhou primarily in the guise of a fatalist and offers a relatively neutral assessment of Qiao's political activity, evaluations of Qiao Zhou from the seventeenth century onward took a much more critical view, often basing their arguments on the literary rather than historical Qiao Zhou. The harshest critics of Qiao Zhou expressed their views in inflammatory fashion and employed the figure of Qiao Zhou in debates on issues far removed from Three States history. A few other scholars and critics viewed Qiao in a more objective manner, offering justifications for his political actions.

Even in the early years of the twenty-first century, Qiao Zhou continues to receive mixed evaluations. During a year-long stay in Sichuan in 2000, reactions to the news that I was conducting research on Qiao Zhou resulted in one of two responses: "Who?"—signaling Qiao's status as a lesser-known figure of the period, or "The traitor! Why?"—illustrating the enduring view of Qiao as the instrument of destruction to the state of Shu-Han. That these replies came in roughly equal numbers from university professors, students, and taxi drivers speaks somewhat to the popular views of Qiao in China today. Equally telling is the view of Qiao held by participants in an online forum for the discussion of Three States history and culture, who in a recent poll named Qiao Zhou the twelfth most-hated figure of the period.[26] This reading, of course, was based largely on the characterization of Qiao Zhou by not only the *Three Kingdoms*, but by video and computer game representations of the history of the period. In short, contemporary concerns have significantly colored later assessments of Qiao Zhou, and often have more to do with the literary depiction of Qiao than historical evidence.

The views of Qiao Zhou as a "fortune-teller," "traitor," and "rotten pedant" that became common and widely accepted after the fifteenth century obscure his position as an important and influential intellectual in the early medieval period. In particular, Qiao's activities as a historian were lost in the frenzy to denounce him as a political opportunist and use him as a rhetorical figure for contemporary debates on loyalty and legitimacy. However, the Qiao Zhou known to the Chinese intellectual community prior to the Song period was highly regarded as a critical classicist and historian, as well as an innovative chronicler of his native Sichuan. Qiao's works were widely cited by scholars during the period of disunion and the Tang with no hint of shame over Qiao's political activities.

Few direct assessments of Qiao Zhou's scholarship have survived. Regarding his writings on the ritual canon, there are few citations or appraisals.

Records of one traditional scholar agreeing and another disagreeing with Qiao's interpretations of points of ritual are contained in Du You's *Encyclopedic History of Institutions*, itself the largest repository for Qiao's writings on the rites. Qiao's *Investigations of Ancient History* attracted considerably more attention from traditional historians, including a few very favorable assessments. Sima Biao, while offering his own "corrections" to Qiao's work, still regarded Qiao Zhou as one of the few "good historians" of the late Han and Three States period.[27] Later, the noted Tang historical critic Liu Zhiji praised *Investigations of Ancient History* for following the model of the *Spring and Autumn*.[28] More recently, Long Xianzhao argued "Qiao Zhou's mastery of history and spirit of seeking the truth began the trend of investigations on antiquity and rectification of history."[29] Similarly, Lu Yaodong praised *Investigations of Ancient History* as "China's first work of historical criticism," and claimed that the text marks the separation of the disciplines of canonical studies and history.[30] In regards to Qiao Zhou's works of local history, while there are no surviving direct evaluations of his work in this field, the fact that his histories were widely quoted in later histories and gazetteers speaks to their importance in the development of the genre. Unfortunately, Qiao Zhou's scholarly activity has been largely overlooked, and these comments by traditional and modern scholars stand in relative isolation from the popular opinions regarding Qiao Zhou. How, then, should we evaluate Qiao Zhou's scholarship and intellectual activity, both as a representative of third-century Sichuan and as a scholar in his own right?

By virtue of his training, Qiao Zhou stands at the tail of an influential regional intellectual lineage and at the head of another significant scholastic tradition. As such, he embodies the intellectual transitions of the late Han and Three States periods, especially as they unfolded in Sichuan. From Du Qiong, Qiao Zhou was educated in the mantic-prophetic traditions of the Yang family of Guanghan commandery. This distinguished intellectual lineage practiced the arts of prophesy based on celestial observation and the interpretation of prophetic wordplay. Members of the lineage had been active in political affairs since the early Han and were frequently called on by both the imperial court and local bureaucracy to explicate natural phenomena and offer advice for dispelling disasters. During the turmoil at the end of the Han, their prophetic skills were sought and employed by would-be dynasts to legitimize their political ambitions. Qiao Zhou found himself in a similar situation as he participated in the presentation of numerous omens and prophesies to Liu Bei in an effort to convince him to take the throne after the formal fall of the Han dynasty. Moreover, Qiao's skills in prophesy were often manifest during his lifetime of service to the state of Shu-Han. His students appear to have been instructed in these arts, but there is no evidence that the methods of the Yang family continued in practice beyond Qiao Zhou. As such, Qiao stands as the final major practitioner of this important regional intellectual tradition.

From Qin Mi, Qiao Zhou developed a critical attitude toward both the classical canon and history. While the details on Qin Mi's scholarly activities are unfortunately brief, he appears to have been a skeptic regarding commonly accepted academic traditions. However, Qin was not a total iconoclast. Rather, he esteemed and trusted certain canonical and historical texts, and employed these texts to criticize and correct others that he deemed deficient. These views were passed on to Qiao Zhou, whose writings demonstrate these purported traits of his teacher.

In the field of canonical studies, Qiao Zhou appears from some perspectives to be conservative, but from another angle demonstrates the budding criticism that would appear in fullbloom in his writings on history. His surviving writings on the canon focus on ritual, particularly matters of sacrifical offerings and mourning practice. As such, Qiao was among the first wave of early medieval scholarship on ritual. But given the late Han and Three States general intellectual tendency toward metaphysical ethics as manifest in the hallmark movement of Mystery Learning, Qiao's canonical exegesis appears behind the times. However, while lacking the metaphysical embellishments of the new wave of scholarship that Qiao was most likely exposed to during the course of his career in Chengdu, his writings on the canon demonstrate a view of the canon as history, and a view that the individual books of the canon were not all equally historical or accurate. Rather, Qiao Zhou frequently employed the positions of selected canonical texts to refute the views of other canonical texts. He also applied his understanding of history to argue for or against positions in the canon or its contemporary interpretation. Unfortunately, given the severely fragmented state of Qiao's writings on the canon, we are unable to identify any larger political or ethical agendas that may have been present.

Qiao's view of the canon as history carried over into his work on ancient history, where he regularly offered "corrections" to prior histories on the basis of his understanding of the vision of early China presented in the canonical histories. Qiao's critique of Sima Qian's *The Grand Scribes Records* is among the earliest commentaries on the text and is the only early commentary to provide more than simple explanatory notes. As such, his *Investigations of Ancient History* has been regarded as the founding work of Chinese historical criticism. Finally, Qiao Zhou's compilations of Sichuan history also show Qiao as an innovator in the field of local historiography. In this regard, Qiao incorporated "locality stories" into his accounts of the southwest in order to illustrate the character of the place, as well as to assert the region's long-standing role in imperial affairs. This method was widely followed by later local historians and eventually developed into a standard feature of traditional local histories and gazetteers.

In all his scholarly writings Qiao demonstrated a devotion to tradition and a pedantic desire for an accurate representation of the past. He appears to have had no driving agenda, either philosophical or political. As such, he may rightly be viewed as a conservative intellectual figure. Additionally, viewing his scholarship in light of the late Han and Three States intellectual traditions, we find Qiao's work to have been innovative, but not stylishly so. The more "interesting" developments of Mystery Learning, Pure Conversation, Daoism, and Buddhism have drawn much more scholarly attention for their colorful deviations from the norm. This study has attempted to illustrate the mainstream of scholarly activity in Chengdu during this time and contributes a different perspective to the usual view of third-century Chinese intellectual history.

TOWARD AN INTELLECTUAL HISTORY OF THIRD-CENTURY CHINA

In part, offering an informed reevaluation of the scholarly and political activity of Qiao Zhou is one major objective of this book. More important, I have endeavored to present a clearer view of intellectual activity in Sichuan during the late Han and Three States period. Under normal circumstances, I would only be combating the unknowns of early medieval intellectual history, but in the case of the Three States period Sichuan, my task is complicated by "misknowns," the popular false familiarity of the age based largely on later literary views. As such, the findings presented here may be new information to one audience, and may run counter to the accepted understanding of another. The larger objective of this book has been to contribute to the intellectual history of early medieval China through a detailed study of a representative figure from a place and tradition that have received little attention in prior scholarship. This has been accomplished incrementally through examinations of various aspects of Qiao Zhou's life and scholarship.

Seeking to counter the views propagated by traditional Central Plains historians of the Chengdu Plain as an uncultured backwater, I have presented evidence of scholarly activity in the region over the span of roughly four centuries, from the Former Han through the Three States period. From this study, it is clear that the region developed several distinct intellectual traditions, and that this activity was recognized by the political and cultural power-brokers at the imperial court and regional headquarters. During the Former Han, the literary genre of *fu* flourished in the region, with its greatest practitioners receiving accolades and low-ranking positions from the Han court. By mid-dynasty, eclectic scholarly traditions developed in Chengdu. Zhuang Zun and Yang Xiong blended moralistic canonical studies with the mystic elements of the early Daoist traditions to lay the foundation for the early medieval intellectual movement of Mystery Learning. However, in harmony with their Daoist forebears, both Zhuang and Yang evinced a preference for reclusion over activity at court. Over the next two centuries, the traditions of the Yang clan from Guanghan dominated Sichuan intellectual activity. Ten generations of scholars mastered the Yang's techniques of reading both celestial signs and prophetic speech and demonstrated varying degrees of willingness to use those skills for political ends. Many members of this intellectual lineage answered calls from the imperial court and offered their interpretations of the signs of the times, occasionally with prescriptions for restoring order or averting disaster. Others, however, avoided the inherent dangers of political involvement and opted to decline official summons. With the establishment of the Shu-Han court in Chengdu, Liu Bei recruited various intellectuals to staff his academy and tutor his sons. Liu Bei's stable of scholars included men trained in the local Yang family traditions, as well as individuals versed in interpretative traditions on the canon from outside the region. Chen Shou's account of the collision of these various intellectual traditions at the Shu-Han court offers an interesting view of scholarly life at court, despite Chen's fairly obvious bias toward the local traditions in which he too had been instructed. In this setting we see Liu Bei's employment of a wide variety of scholars in an effort to construct a functioning imperial bureaucracy in Chengdu. The surviving accounts often note the generally low quality of some of these intellectual recruits, standing in stark contrast to the types of intellectuals who entered the service of Liu's rival, the Caos in Wei.

It is the intellectual community of Wei in north China that has received the most attention from modern scholars. The decline of traditional scholasticism at the late Han court, itself a result of the factional struggles between scholar-bureaucrats and eunuchs that culminated in the Great Proscriptions of the mid-second century, led to the growth of the self-conscious literary, philosophical, and academic pursuits of the Wei court—lyric poetry, Pure Conversation, and Mystery Learning. Because of their dramatic break from the older Han scholastic traditions, these northern activities have come to represent the intellectual traditions of the third century as a whole.[31] Scholars who continued to practice canonical exegesis and traditional historiography tended to be either criticized for being "conservative," "ossified," or were overlooked entirely. In this manner, the avant garde has been taken for the mainstream, which did not dry up immediately upon the arrival of the new wave. Lost in this northern-centric and nouveux-centric scholarly focus are the primary currents of third-century scholarly activity that focused on the explication of the canon and the continued preparation of histories, most often of the Han dynasty itself.

This book has presented views of both another place and another scholarly stream. The intellectual activity of Sichuan as represented by Qiao Zhou is important not only for the counterbalance it provides against the well-documented new wave of Wei Mystery Learning, but for its own contributions to the intellectual world of third-century China. The scholarly traditions of the Han were continued and expanded on by Qiao Zhou and others, working in a place long held to have no real intellectual traditions. The prophetic skills of the Yang family dramatically illustrate the intersection of the academic and political worlds, and Qiao's lifelong use of these methods in the service of the state testifies to the continued vitality of this intellectual tradition. Qiao's incorporation of criticism to the study of the canon and history was regarded as innovative by later scholars, as were his contributions to the compilation of local history. His critical approach to the classical and historical canon marks a sharp departure from the late Han norm of providing explanatory glosses on difficult graphs of passages of texts, demonstrating a new level of canonical analysis. Similarly, Qiao's critique of earlier efforts to document China's ancient past, including Sima Qian's *The Grand Scribe's Records* show Qiao to have moved beyond mere explanation into the realm of critical interpretative analysis. While these critical innovations were largely overlooked both in his day and ours, they proved to be highly influential to later scholars who are now credited as leading practitioners of historical criticism.[32] In contrast, Qiao's use of the locality story in his documentation of Sichuan's history was widely imitated in the years immediately following his death. As this innovation became the norm in local history writing, its origin gradually fell into obscurity.

It has been my intent in preparing this revisionist intellectual history and biography to depict the Chengdu Plain as a vibrant intellectual place, and to show Qiao Zhou as one of its most accomplished scholars, arguing that both locale and man deserve to be considered when a comprehensive intellectual history of China's exciting and transitional third century is finally written.

Chronology: The Life of Qiao Zhou

DATE (CE)	EVENT
ca. 200	Qiao Zhou born in Baxi commandery.
221	Signs memorial urging Liu Bei to take throne.
223	Appointed as Attendant for the Encouragement of Education.
234	Appointed as Attendant for Direction of Education.
238	Serves as Coachman of the Heir Apparent and Prefect of the Household of the Heir Apparent.
246	Criticizes Liu Shan's excursions. Demoted to Palace Attendant Grandee.
258	Participates in debates over Shu-Han military policy. Writes "Discourse on Enemy States." Promoted to Imperial Household Grandee.
263	Urges Liu Shan to surrender.
265	Wen Li visits Qiao Zhou in Shu.
268	Travels to Luoyang. Appointed Chief Commandant of the Cavalry. Given benefice as Marquis of Yangcheng commune.
269	Chen Shou visits Qiao Zhou in Baxi. Qiao foretells his own death.
270	Autumn: Appointed Cavalier Attendant in Regular Attendance. Winter: Dies.

Notes

TERMS AND CONVENTIONS

1. Although "Sichuan" is a relatively late name for the region, it provides a convenient though anachronistic term of reference. For a study on the origins of the name "Sichuan," see Zhang Zhigao 張至臯, "Sichuan de mingcheng youlai he xiaqu yanbian" 四川的名稱由來和轄區演變 ["On the Origins and Evolution of the name 'Sichuan'"], in *Shehui kexue yanjiu* 社會科學研究, 5 (1979): 35–36.

2. Tan Qixiang et al., *Zhongguo lishi dituji* 中國歷史地圖集 [*The Historical Atlas of China*] (Shanghai: Ditu chubanshe, 1982).

3. Tung Tso-pin, *Chronological Tables of Chinese History* (Hong Kong: Hong Kong University Press, 960); Fang Shiming and Fang Xiaofen, *Zhongguo liri he Zhong-Xi liri duizhao biao* (Shanghai: Shanghai cishu, 1987).

4. Jiang Liangfu (b. 1901), comp., *Lidai renwu nianli beizhuan zongbiao* (Beijing: Zhonghua shuju, 1959).

5. Zhang Shunhui et al., eds., *Sanguo zhi cidian* (Ji'nan: Shandong jiaoyu chubanshe, 1992).

6. Hans Bielenstein, *The Bureaucracy of Han Times* (Cambridge: Cambridge University Press, 1980).

7. Charles O. Hucker, *A Dictionary of Official Titles in Imperial China* (reprint; Taipei: Southern Materials Center, 1986); Sun Fengji, *Zhiguan fenji* (*Siku quanshu* 四庫全書 edition) (reprint; Beijing: Zhonghua shuju, 1988).

INTRODUCTION

1. While the term "Sanguo" is commonly rendered in English as "Three Kingdoms," the designation as such is technically incorrect. By the time the three independent polities were established, none of the rulers claimed the title of "king" (*wang* 王). See Rafe de Crespigny, "The Three Kingdoms and Western Jin: A History of China in the Third Century A.D." in *East Asian History* v. 1 (June 1991): 14 n. 36. As such, the term "state" seems more appropriate, and will be used throughout.

2. This troubled time has been well documented in the traditional sources, and several later synoptic narratives provide accessible accounts of the age and its events. While the standard histories of the period, the *Later Han History* and the *Records of the Three States*, offer detailed views of individual participants in the history, their narratives are broken and do not provide a satisfactory chronological account. The most accessible record remains Sima Guang's *Comprehensive Mirror for the Aid in Government*, which recounts the events of the age in a year-by-year fashion. Translations of the relevant sections of the *Comprehensive Mirror* can be found in *Emperor Huan and Emperor Ling: being the Chronicle of Later Han for the years 157 to 189 AD as recorded in Chapters 54 to 59 of the* Zizhi tongjian *of Sima Guang*, translated and annotated by Rafe de Crespigny. Asian Studies Monographs, New Series No. 12 (Canberra: Faculty of Asian Studies, Australian National University, 1989); *To Establish Peace: being the Chronicle of the Later Han dynasty for the years 189 to 220 AD as recorded in Chapters 59 to 69 of the* Zizhi tongjian *of Sima Guang* [volume 1: Chapters 59–63, 189–200], translated and annotated by Rafe de Crespigny. Asian Studies Monographs, New Series No. 21 (Canberra: Faculty of Asian Studies, Australian National University, 1996); *To Establish Peace: being the Chronicle of the Later Han dynasty for the years 189 to 220 AD as recorded in Chapters 59 to 69 of the* Zizhi tongjian *of Sima Guang* [volume 2: Chapters 64–69, 201–220], translated and annotated by Rafe de Crespigny. Asian Studies Monographs, New Series No. 21 (Canberra: Faculty of Asian Studies, Australian National University, 1996). A detailed synopsis of the age can be found in B. J. Mansvelt Beck, "The Fall of the Han," in *CHC*, 1: 317–356.

3. The name "Shu-Han," as used throughout, is anachronistic. While the state refered to itself as "Han," the principle sources from the period refer to it as "Shu," referencing the Han-era commandery located at Chengdu, the capital of the state. For a detailed study on the rhetoric of the naming of the state, see J. Michael Farmer, "What's in a Name? On the Appellative 'Shu' in Early Medieval Chinese Historiography," *Journal of the American Oriental Society* 121 (2001): 44–59.

4. For a concise overview of the Three States period, see de Crespigny, "Three Kingdoms and Western Jin." Detailed studies of the period in Chinese can be found in He Ziquan 何茲全, *Sanguo shi* 三國史 [*History of the Three States*] (Beijing: Beijing shifan daxue chubanshe, 1994) and Ma Zhijie 馬植杰, *Sanguo shi* 三國史 [*History of the Three States*] (Beijing: Renmin chubanshe, 1997).

5. The novel is attributed to a noted late-Yuan 元 dramatist Luo Guanzhong 羅貫中(ca. 1315/18–ca. 1400), though these claims are considerably later than the earliest edition of the text and the issue of authorship remains hotly debated. The standard edition of the text is *Sanguo yanyi*, ed. Mao Zonggang 毛宗崗 (fl. 1660) (Shanghai: Shanghai guji, 1989). For English translations, see C. H. Brewitt-Taylor, *Romance of the Three Kingdoms*, 2 vols. (Shanghai, 1925; reprint, Rutland,Vermont: C. E. Tuttle, 1959); Moss Roberts, trans., *Three Kingdoms: A Historical Novel*, 2 vols. (Berkeley: University of California Press, 2004) (hereafter cited as *TK*).

For general introductions to the work, see C. T. Hsia, "The Romance of the Three Kingdoms," in *The Classic Chinese Novel* (New York: Columbia, 1968), 34–74; Andrew Lo, "San-kuo yen-i," in *The Indiana Companion to Traditional Chinese Literature*, ed. William H. Nienhauser, Jr., 2nd rev. ed. (Taipei: SMC Publishing, 1986), 668–671; Andrew H. Plaks, *The Masterworks of the Ming Novel* (Princeton: Princeton

University Press, 1987), 361–495; and the "Afterward" to Moss Roberts' translation. The entry by Andrew Lo in *The Indiana Companion* contains a useful bibliography of editions, translations, and studies of the *Three Kingdoms*. An updated bibliography is contained in volume 2 of *The Indiana Companion to Traditional Chinese Literature* (1996), 396–398.

Throughout I will refer to the text by Roberts's abbreviated title *Three Kingdoms*, altering other renderings of the title in quoted passages.

6. For comics, see the simply illustrated children's comic version published under the title *Sanguo yanyi* (n.p.: Jiangsu shaonian ertong chubanshe, 1994), and the more graphic ten-volume series published in Chinese and English by Asiapac Publications: *Romance of the Three Kingdoms*, adapted by Zhang Qirong and translated by Wu Jingyu (Singapore: Asiapac, 1995).

Purportedly, even Chairman Mao was an avid reader of a comic book edition of the text. According to a brief online article, Mao Zedong "was too interested in [the comic] to remember his meals." When called to supper, the Chairman lectured his attendant saying, "Chinese comics are great, simple but meaningful. Many complicated things were stated vividly with a few words. It's easy to understand." Yi Jingshan, "Chairman Mao Liked the Chinese Comic 'Romance of the Three Kingdoms,'" online source: http://eng.cartoonwin.com/articles/articles004.html, accessed August 2005. I have been unable to locate additional sources to support this claim that Mao was a fan of the comic versions of the Three States stories.

Online comic versions of the Three States epic have also appeared. See "Sanguo manhua" 三國謾畫, online source: http://www.shiji.cc/san/index.php, accessed August 2005. This rendition offers an irreverent take on Three States story laced with references to contemporary Western popular culture. For a more formal comic version, see "Three Kingdoms," online source: http://china-on-site.com/pages/comic/comiccatalog2.php, accessed August 2005.

A recent influential television adaptation is the eighty-four-part television drama produced by China Central Television that first aired in 1994. The series has been frequently rebroadcast, and is widely distributed for home viewing in China, Hong Kong, and the West.

For computer/video games, see Koei's "Romance of the Three Kingdoms," "Dynasty Warriors," and "Kessen II."

7. Liu Bei's political and military activities are chronicled in his official biography in the *Records of the Three States*, where he is referenced by the posthumous designation of "Former Sovereign" (Xianzhu 先主). See Chen Shou, *Sanguo zhi* 三國志 [*Records of the Three States*] (Beijing: Zhonghua shuju, 1959) (hereafter cited as *Sgz*), 32.871–892.

8. For the official biographies of Guan Yu and Zhang Fei, see *Sgz*, 36.939–944.

9. For the official biography of Zhuge Liang, see *Sgz*, 35.911–969.

10. For the official biography of Cao Cao, posthumously designated as the Martial Emperor of Wei (Wei Wudi 魏武帝), see *Sgz*, 1.1–56.

11. For the official biography of Sun Quan, referenced as Sovereign of Wu (Wu zhu 吳主), see *Sgz*, 47.1115–1150. For a detailed study of the Suns and the state of Wu, see Rafe de Crespigny, *Generals of the South* (Canberra: Faculty of Asian Studies, Australian National University, 1990).

12. On Mi Heng's mockery of Cao Cao and other powerful military men, and his subsequent execution, see *Sgyy*, 23.287–294; *TK*, 180–183.

13. For example, the novel cites a later poem lamenting Yang Xiu, which reads:

> Brilliant and all-seeing was Yang Xiu;
> His family always wore the cap of state.
> Words from his brush sprang magically to life;
> And poetry took shape within his breast.
> He starts to speak: all hearers are amazed;
> His swift replies confound a brilliant throng.
> Alas, he died by his own talent wronged;
> Cao Cao's retreat was not the cause at all.

See *TK*, 552–554; Sgyy 72.942–943.

14. For the official biography of Zhou Yu, see *Sgz*, 54.1259–1267.

15. Several studies have examined the manner in which the *Three Kingdoms* adapted the historical records to achieve its own ends, whether literary or political. For example, see Hsia, "Romance," 41–48; Paul W. Kroll, "Portraits of Ts'ao Ts'ao: Literary Studies on the Man and the Myth" (Ph.D. dissertation, University of Michigan, 1976); Winston Yang, "The Literary Transformation of Historical Figures in the *San-kuo chih yen-i*: A Study of the Use of the *San-kuo chih* as a Source of the *San-kuo chih yen-i*," in *Critical Essays on Chinese Fiction*, Winston L. Y. Yang and Curtis P. Adkins, ed. (Hong Kong: Chinese University Press, 1980), 47–84; and Plaks, *Masterworks*, 406–473.

16. Although the Daoist religion has its roots in Sichuan with the Celestial Masters (Tianshi dao 天師道) community of the mid-second century ce, it will not be treated in this study for two reasons. First, the movement was largely lower-class and communal, having little impact on high thought or scholarship in the region. Second, the bulk of the community was forcibly moved to the northwest in the early third century and thus were not of great significance in the area for much of the time period under consideration here. However, when these Daoist exiles returned to the Chengdu Plain in the fourth century ce, they played a significant role in regional politics. For an overview of the Celestial Masters Daoist movement, including history and practice, see Isabelle Robinet, *Taoism: Growth of a Religion*, Phyllis Brooks, trans. (Stanford: Stanford University Press, 1997), 53–77. Also see Barbara Hendrichke, "Early Daoist Movements," in *Daoism Handbook*, Livia Kohn, ed. (Leiden: Brill, 2000), 138–141. For the activity of the newly returned Daoists, see Terry F. Kleeman, *Great Perfection: Religion and Ethnicity in a Chinese Millennial Kingdom* (Honolulu: University of Hawai'i Press, 1998).

17. For the official biography of He Yan, see *Sgz*, 9.292. For the official biography of Wang Bi, see *Sgz*, 28.795–796 n. 1. Several recent studies on He Yan and Wang Bi are worth noting. First, Wang Xiaoyi's 王曉毅 *Wang Bi pingzhuan* 王弼評傳 [*Critical Biography of Wang Bi*] (Nanjing: Nanjing daxue chubanshe, 1996) offers thorough treatments of not only the life and works and Wang Bi, but also He Yan. In English, one should consult Rudolf G. Wagner's recent series of monographs on Wang Bi. See Rudolf G. Wagner, *The Craft of a Chinese Commentator: Wang Bi on the* Laozi (Albany: State University of New York Press, 2000); *Language, Ontology, and Political Philosophy in China: Wang Bi's Scholarly Exploration of the Dark (Xuanxue)* (Albany:

State University of New York Press, 2003); and *A Chinese Reading of the Daodejing: Wang Bi's Commentary on the* Laozi *with Critical Text and Translation* (Albany: State University of New York Press, 2003).

18. For an overview of poetry of the period, see Robert Joe Cutter, "Poetry from 200 B.C.E. to 600 C.E.," in Victor Mair, ed., *Columbia History of Chinese Literature* (New York: Columbia, 2001), 248–273. On Cao Zhi and the Seven Masters of the Jian'an Period, see Robert Joe Cutter, "Cao Zhi (192–232) and His Poetry," Ph.D. dissertation (University of Washington, 1983); Hans Frankel, "Fifteen Poems by Ts'ao Chih: An Attempt at a New Approach," *Journal of the American Oriental Society*, 84 (1964): 1–14. For a study of the philosophical contributions of one member of this intellectual circle, Xu Gan 許幹 (170–217 CE), see John Makeham, *Name and Actuality in Early Chinese Thought* (Albany: State University of New York Press, 1994); and Makeham, trans., *Balanced Discourses* (New Haven: Yale University Press, 2002).

19. Balazs treats the members of this informal group in his "Nihilistic Revolt or Mystical Escapism: Currents of Thought in China During the Third Century A.D.," in H. M. Wright, trans., *Chinese Civilization and Bureaucracy* (New Haven: Yale University Press, 1964), 236–242. The article originally appeared as "Entre Révolte nihiliste et évasion mystique. Les courants intellectuels en Chine at IIIe siècle de notre ère," *Etudes Asiatiques*, 2 (1948): 27–55. Another important treatment of the Seven Sages is Donald Holzman, "The Place of the Seven Sages of the Bamboo Grove in Chinese History," *Occasional Papers Kansai Asiatic Society*, no. 3 (1955): 1–13. Also see Holzman, "Les Sept Sages de la Forêt des Bambous et la société de leur temps," *T'oung Pao*, 44 (1956): 317–346. Anecdotes concerning these figures are scattered throughout Liu Yiqing's 劉義慶 (403–444 CE) *Shishuo xinyu* 世說新語 [*New Account of Tales of the World*]. See Yu Jiaxi 余嘉錫 (1833–1955), ed., *Shishuo xinyu jianshu* 世說新語箋疏 (Reprint. Shanghai: Shanghai guji, 1993). For a translation, see Richard B. Mather, *Shih-shuo Hsin-yü: A New Account of Tales of the World* (Minneapolis: University of Minnesota Press, 1976). For a detailed study of the philosophy of one "member" of this group, Ji Kang 嵇康, see Robert Henricks, *Philosophy and Argumentation in Third-Century China: The Essays of Hsi K'ang* (Princeton: Princeton University Press, 1983).

20. Etienne Balazs' "Nihilistic Revolt or Mystical Escapism," 226–254.

21. Makeham, *Name and Actuality*, 3.

22. These traditional biases against the south are discussed in chapter 1.

23. For studies on the Yangzi region, see Yoshikawa Tadao, "Scholarship in Ching-Chou at the End of the Later Han Dynasty," *Acta Asiatica*, 60 (1991): 7; and Andrew Chittick, "The Life and Legacy of Liu Biao: Governor, Warlord, and Imperial Pretender in Late Han China," *Journal of Asian History* 37 (2003): 155–186. Liu Biao and the intellectual activity centered at his academy at Jingzhou is discussed in greater detail in chapter 4.

To date, only four brief studies have examined the intellectual history of the Chengdu Plain. In Chinese, see Cheng Yuanmin 程元敏,"Dong Han Shu Yang Hou jingwei xue zongchuan" 東漢蜀楊厚經緯學宗傳 ["The Classics and Apocryphal Family Traditions of Yang Hou of the Eastern Han"], *Guoli bianyiguan guankan* 國立編譯館館刊, 17.1 (1988): 31–48; 17.2 (1988): 19–39; and Cheng Yuanmin, *Sanguo Shu jingxue* 三國蜀經學 [*Canonical Studies in Three States Shu*] (Taibei: Xuesheng shuju, 1997). In Japanese, see Yoshikawa Tadao 吉川忠夫, "Shuku ni okeru shin'i no gaku no dentō"

蜀における讖緯の學の傳統 ["The tradition on the study of the books on prophesy (ch'en-wei) in the Shu region"], in Yasui Kōzan 安居香山, ed. *Shin'i shisō no sōgōteki kenkyū* 讖緯思想の綜合的研究 [Collected Studies on Prophetic Thought] (Tokyo: Kokusho Kankōkai, 1984), 105–136. In English, see Michael Nylan, "The Legacies of the Chengdu Plain," in Robert Bagley, ed. *Ancient Sichuan: Treasures from a Lost Civilization* (Seattle: Seattle Art Museum, 2001), 309–325.

24. Sadly, the majority of these writings have been lost. See *Sgz*, 35.929.

25. Much has been written on Zhuge Liang in Chinese, Japanese, and Western languages. In English, most studies have addressed historiographical issues, typically the manner in which Zhuge Liang was treated in various histories and literature. For representative scholarship, see Eric Henry, "Chu-ko Liang in The Eyes of His Contemporaries," *Harvard Journal of Asiatic Studies* 52.2 (December 1992): 589–612. Hoyt Tilllman has written numerous articles on this matter. For example, see, Tillman "Historic Analogies and Evaluative Judgments: Zhuge Liang as Portrayed in Chen Shou's *Chronicle of the Three Kingdoms* and Pei Songzhi's Commentary," in "Dimensionen der historischen Kritik in China," a special issue edited by Achim Mittag for *Oriens Extremus* (Hamburg, Germany), Vol. 43, 2002 [2004], 60–70; "Textual Liberties and Restraints in Rewriting China's Histories: The Case of Ssu-ma Kuang's Re-Construction of Chu-ko Liang's Story," in Thomas H. C. Lee, ed., *The New and the Multiple: Sung Senses of the Past* (Hong Kong: The Chinese University Press, 2004), 61–106; and "Some Historical and Philosophical Sources of the *Sanguo yanyi*: Sima Guang and Chen Liang on Zhuge Liang," in Kimberly Besio and Constantine Tung, eds., *Three Kingdoms and Chinese Culture* (Albany: State University of New York Press, 2006). For the military activities of Zhuge Liang, see John Killegrew, "Zhuge Liang and the Northern Campaign of 228–234," in *Early Medieval China* 5 (1999): 55–91.

In Chinese, the tone of much academic writing on Zhuge Liang is laudatory, ignoring the surviving historical evidence. Such is the high quantity and general tenor of Chinese writings on Zhuge Liang that one can easily imagine a large factory complex situated outside of Chengdu in which graduate students of Chinese history are chained to desks and required to type up panegyric essays on the thought and consciousness of Zhuge Liang, sufficient to place one or two such essays in each issue of every *xuebao* [academic journal] in China! For a rare example of serious scholarship on Zhuge Liang, see Zhu Dawei 朱大渭 and Liang Mancang 梁滿倉, *Wuhou chunqiu* 武侯春秋 [*The Annals of the Martial Marquis*] (Beijing: Tuanjie chubanshe, 1998). An exhaustive collection of traditional and modern biographies of Zhuge Liang, his complete extant writings, and mentions of him in traditional essays and poems has been compiled by Wang Ruigong 王瑞功. See Wang Ruigong, ed., *Zhuge Liang yanjiu jicheng* 諸葛亮研究集成 [*Collected Researches on Zhuge Liang*] (Ji'nan: Qi Lu chubanshe, 1997).

In Japanese, the tone of writings on Zhuge Liang often mirrors the praise offered by Chinese scholars. For a comprehensive bibliography of Japanese scholarship on Zhuge Liang, see Nakabayashi Shiro 中林史朗 and Watanabe Yoshihiro 渡邊義浩, ed., *Sangokushi kenkyu yoran* 三國志研究要覽 [*Essential Research on The Record of the Three States*] (Tokyo: Jinbutsu Oraisha, 1996), 100–105.

26. For a study of the *fangshi* tradition and translations of biographies of various mantic artists, see Kenneth J. DeWoskin, *Doctors, Diviners, and Magicians of Ancient China: Biographies of Fang-shi* (New York: Columbia University Press, 1983).

27. The primary source for the life of Qiao Zhou is the biography written by his student Chen Shou contained in Chen's history of the age, *Records of the Three States*. See *Sgz*, 42.1027–1034. For a translation of this biography, see J. Michael Farmer, "The World of the Mind in Early Medieval Sichuan," Ph.D. dissertation (University of Wisconsin–Madison, 2001), 425–455. The only other scholarly study of Qiao Zhou remains Long Xianzhao's "Qiao Zhou," in Jia Shunxian 賈順先 and Dai Dalu 戴大祿 eds., *Sichuan sixiang jia* 四川思想家 [*Sichuan Thinkers*], (Chengdu: Ba-Shu chubanshe, 1987), 67–93.

Chen Shou's history has long circulated with commentary prepared by Pei Songzhi. Pei's commentary collates passages from numerous other historical records with Chen's base text. These additional sources sometimes support, and other times contradict Chen Shou's history. Occasionally Pei Songzhi offers his own views on the materials he presents. His commentary is especially valuable in that Pei cites all of his sources and, as such, the commentary has preserved many otherwise lost works of early medieval history.

Two other important editions of the *Sanguo zhi* are Lu Bi, *Sanguo zhi jijie* 三國志集解 [*Collected Explanations on the Records of the Three States*] (1936. Reprint, Taipei: Yiwen yinshuguan, n.d.) (hereafter cited as *Sgzjj*); and Fang Beichen, *Sanguo zhi zhuyi* 三國志注譯 [*Records of the Three States, Annotated and Translated*] (Xi'an: Shaanxi renmin chubanshe, 1996) (hereafter cited as *Sgzzy*).

For a detailed study of Chen Shou's life and the compilation of the *Records of the Three States*, see Robert Joe Cutter and William G. Crowell, trans., *Empresses and Consorts* (Honolulu: University of Hawai'i Press, 1999), 61–81. Also see Yang Yaokun 楊耀坤 and Wu Yechun 伍野春, *Chen Shou Pei Songzhi pingzhuan* 陳壽裴松之評傳 [*Critical Biographies of Chen Shou and Pei Songzhi*] (Nanjing: Nanjing daxue chubanshe, 1998).

While not containing a complete biography of Qiao Zhou, Chang Qu's *Records of the States South of Mount Hua* offers important information and judgments regarding Qiao and his career. The most important modern edition of this work is Ren Naiqiang 任乃強, ed., *Huayang guo zhi jiaobu tuzhu* 華陽國志校補圖注 [*Records of the States South of Mount Hua Collated, Supplemented with Illustrations and Annotations*] (Shanghai: Shanghai guji chubanshe, 1987) (hereafter cited as *Hygz*). Ren's copious notes and comprehensive introduction make this edition essential to the study of this text. In fact, Ren's introductory materials form the most comprehensive study on the life and works of Chang Qu. A second modern annotated edition is also available. See Liu Lin 劉琳, ed., *Huayang guo zhi jiao zhu* 華陽國志校注 [*Records of the States South of Mount Hua, Collated and Annotated*] (Chengdu: Ba-Shu shushe, 1984). Liu's notes are useful, but not as voluminous as those compiled by Ren Naiqiang.

28. The term "Central Plains" (*zhongyuan* 中原) refers to the general area encompassing present-day Henan Province and parts of Shandong, Hebei, Shanxi, Anhui, and Jiangsu provinces. For scholarship on this region as the origin of Chinese civilization, see Ho Ping-ti, *The Cradle of the East* (Chicago: University of Chicago Press, 1975); David N. Keightly, ed. *The Origins of Chinese Civilization* (Berkeley: University of California Press, 1983). As we will see, these Yellow-River-centric views have been greatly displaced by recent archeological discoveries in the southwest and elsewhere.

29. For the official biography of Zheng Xuan, see *HHs*, 35.1207–1213. The activities of Zheng Xuan are treated in chapter 4.

30. See *Hygz*, 1:45; *Js*, 82.2142.

CHAPTER 1

1. *Yijing zhengyi* 易經正義 [*Orthodox Meanings of the Canon of Changes*] (*Shisan jing zhushu* ed.), 2.26. For a translation, see Richard John Lynn, trans., *The Classic of Changes: A New Translation of the* I Ching *as Interpreted by Wang Bi* (New York: Columbia University Press, 1994), 185.

2. *Shangshu zhengyi* 尚書正義 [*Orthodox Meanings of the Hallowed Documents*] (*Shisanjing zhushu* ed.), 2.119; Bernhard Karlgren, trans., "Book of Documents," in *Bulletin of the Museum of Far Eastern Antiquites* 22 (1950): 1.

3. Ban Gu, *Han shu* (Beijing: Zhonghua shuju, 1962) (hereafter cited as *Hs*), 28A.1523. The final quoted passage is from *Shangshu*, "Yu gong" 禹貢 ["The Tribute of Yu"]; Karlgren, "Documents," 12.

4. Changes in the administrative nomenclature of this region will be noted throughout this study. The region encompassed parts of present-day Shaanxi, Sichuan, and Yunnan provinces.

5. *Shangshu*, "Yu gong.'" Karlgren, "Documents," 15.

6. The term "Heaven's Storehouse" was originally applied to the Guanzhong 關中 region; that is, the "Land-within-the-Passes" near Chang'an 長安. When the Han founder was contemplating a location for his new capital, an advocate for the Chang'an site argued that the area was surrounded by agriculturally productive lands, irrigating rivers, and protective mountains, and was thus a "Heaven's Storehouse." Later, the designation shifted, and from the third century onward, the term became synonymous with the Chengdu Plain. See *Sj*, 55.2043–2044 and *Sgz*, 35.35.912–913.

7. The first four fascicles of the *Records of the States South of Mount Hua* treat the geography, economy, culture, and history of the Ba, Hanzhong, Shu, and Nanzhong regions and their respective administrative subunits (commanderies, kingdoms, and districts).

Michael Nylan notes four recurring elements in early descriptions of the Chengdu Plain: wealth; diverse population; favorable strategic location; and advanced industrial capacity. See Nylan, "Legacies of the Chengdu Plain," 310.

8. English-language accounts of the early history of the Chengdu Plain are found in the following works: Jeannette L. Faurot, *Ancient Chengdu* (San Francisco: Chinese Materials Center, 1992); Steven Sage, *Ancient Sichuan and the Unification of China* (Albany: State University of New York Press, 1992), 83–156; and Robert Bagley, ed. *Ancient Sichuan: Treasures from a Lost Civilization*.

9. For example, early Han texts mention the involvement of states bearing the names of entities later found on the Chengdu Plain in the political and military affairs of the Shang-Zhou transition; the state of Qin used the region as a testing ground for its own social and political reforms that later resulted in the overthrow of the Zhou and the establishment of the short-lived Qin dynasty; and, finally, the Han founder Liu Bang utilized local troops and mounted his final campaign to unify the empire from a base in northeastern Sichuan and southern Shaanxi.

A good general study of early relations between the Chengdu Plain and the Central Plains is Gu Jiegang's 顧頡剛 *Lun Ba-Shu yu zhongyuan de guanxi* 論巴蜀與中原的關系 [*The Relationship Between Ba-Shu and the Central Plains*] (Chengdu: Sichuan renmin chubanshe, 1981).

10. *Hs*, 28B.1645. Ban Gu also make similarly disparaging remarks about Chu. See *Hs*, 28B.1666.

11. The exact timeframe of Wen Weng's tenure in Shu is unclear. *Han History* 89 claims Wen was sent to Chengdu in the last year of the reign of Emperor Jing (141 BCE). *Han History* 28 makes a contradictory claim that Wen went to Shu in the interval between Emperors Jing and Wu (ca. 141–140 BCE). The *Records of the States South of Mount Hua* notes that Wen arrived in Shu in the later years of the reign of Emperor Wen (r. 180–157 BCE). Yves Hervouet analyzes these dates and reaches the conclusion that Wen arrived in Chengdu in the latter years of Emperor Wen's regency. Hervouet, however, accepts the claim that the success of Wen Weng's academy in Chengdu led to an imperial edict ordering the establishment of similar academies across the empire (Hervouet, *Un poète de cour sous les Han*, 14–17). This claim is disputed by Yu Qiding (see note 21).

12. See *Hs*, 89.3625–3627. Translations of Wen Weng's biography can be found in John K. Shryock, *The Origin and Development of the State Cult of Confucius* (1933; reprint, New York: Paragon, 1966), 68; Witold Jablonski, "Wen Wong," *Rocznik Orientalistyczny* 21 (1957): 135–136; and Édouard Biot, *Essai sur l'histoire de l'instruction publique en Chine* (Paris: Benjamin Duprat, 1947), 121–124.

13. On Shu book knives, see Tsuen-hsuin Tsien, "A Study of the Book Knife in Han China, (206 BC–AD 220)," *Chinese Culture* 12.1 (1971): 87–101.

14. The former states of Qi and Lu were generally regarded as the centers of classical learning.

15. *Hs*, 89.3626.

16. *Hs*, 28B.1645.

17. *Hygz*, 3.141.

18. Although the Chengdu academy frequently changed administrative hands, it has operated almost continuously until the present day, boasting an impressive gallery of Sichuan intellectuals who either studied or taught at the school. Many of the figures we will examine passed though the gates of this institution. *Hygz*, 3.151. For a detailed study on the academy and its hallmark illustrations, see J. Michael Farmer, "Art, Education, and Power: Illustrations in the Stone Chamber of Wen Weng," *T'oung Pao* 86, no. 1 (2000): 1–36.

19. An amazing amount of Chinese scholarship continues to support the myth of Wen Weng. For example, see Liu Dingsheng 柳定生, "Wenjiao de yuanyuan" 文教的淵源 ["Origins of Education"] in *Sichuan shihua* 四川史話 [*History Talks on Sichuan*] (Taibei: Zhengzhong shuju, 1975), 18–19; Gao Wen 高文 et al., "Wen Weng," in *Sichuan lishi renwu mingsheng cidian* 四川歷史人物名勝詞典 [*Dictionary of Famous Historical Figures from Sichuan*] (Chengdu: Sichuan renmin chubanshe, 1989), 92; Xu Caian 徐才安, "Wen Weng zhi Shu" 文翁治蜀 ["Wen Weng's Rule in Shu"] in *Sichuan gudai shihua* 四川古代史話 [*History Talks on Ancient Sichuan*] (Chongqing: Chongqing chubanshe, 1992), 39–40; Yan Gengwang 嚴耕望, "Han dai junxian xuexiao zhidu" 漢代郡縣學校制度 ["Organization of Commandery and District Schools in the Han"], in *Dalu zazhi* 大陸雜誌 v. 6, no. 10 (May 1953), 310, 319, 326; and Meng Mo, Liu Lin, et al., *Sichuan gudai shigao*, 106–107. For a rare critical view of Wen Weng, see Meng Wentong 蒙文通, *Ba-Shu gushi lunshu* 巴蜀古史論述 [*Essays on the Ancient History of Ba and Shu*] (Chongqing: Sichuan renmin chubanshe, 1981), 87.

20. Yves Hervouet notes the chronological problems attending the claim that Wen Weng sent Sima Xiangru to study at the capital as related to the two dates for Wen's arrival in Chengdu presented in the *Han History*. Dismissing these claims, Hervouet concludes that the reference to Sima Xiangru as Wen's student (*Sj*, 117.2999 n. 3) is metaphorical, and intended to portray Sima as a later contributor to the cultural development of the region. See Hervouet, *Un poète de cour sous les Han* (Paris: Presses Universitaires de France, 1964), 14–17.

21. Yu Qiding 俞啟定 strongly argues against the tradition that such an order was ever issued. No surviving texts of such an edict exists for either the reigns of Emperor Jing or Wu. Furthermore, Yu cites the difficulty of managing the resources to establish even one imperial academy and postulates that the charge to establish regional academies may have been an order in principle only. Noting the uneven development of regional academies well into the Later Han period, Yu argues that the establishment of local schools was likely more dependent on local resources and initiative than on any type of imperial mandate. See Yu Qiding, *Xian Qin Liang Han rujia jiaoyu* 先秦兩漢儒家教育 [*Pre-Qin–Han Classical Education*] (Ji'nan: Qi-Lu shushe, 1987), 148–155.

22. On the claim that illustrations in the Chengdu academy originated with Wen Weng, see Farmer, "Art, Education, and Power."

23. Despite the weight given to the traditions surrounding Wen Weng, there is ample evidence to show that the southwest had an active intellectual life prior to Wen's arrival in Chengdu. In fact, the ancient achievements of the southwest and its people is one of the broad themes of Chang Qu's *Records of the States South of Mount Hua*. His history is in one sense an attempt to refute the biases expressed by Ban Gu and others throughout the years, and to present the region as a part of the larger empire. In the "Postface" to the *Records of the States South of Mount Hua*, Chang directly challenges Ban Gu's assertion that civilization was brought to the southwest by Wen Weng, listing several pre-Han cultural and political figures from the area as evidence for early local culture and involvement in national affairs. See *Hygz*, 896.

24. As much has been written on the life and works of Sima Xiangru, both in China and the West, a brief introduction and discussion will suffice here. The major Western language study of Sima Xiangru is Yves Hervouet, *Un poète de cour sous les Han*. Hervouet has also translated the *Grand Scribe's Records* biography of Sima Xiangru. See Yves Hervouet, *Le Chapitre 117 du Che-ki (Biographie de Sseu-ma Siang-jou)* (Paris: Presses Universitaires de France, 1972). For a translation into English, see Burton Watson, *Records of the Grand Historian of China*, 2 vols. (New York: Columbia University Press, 1961), 259–306. Also see William H. Nienhauser, Jr., "An Interpretation of the Literary and Historical Aspects of *Hsi-ching tsa-chi*" (Miscellanies of the Western Capital), unpublished Ph.D. dissertation (Indiana University, 1972). For representative Chinese scholarship, see Gong Kechang 龔克昌, *Han fu yanjiu* 漢賦研究 [*Studies on the Han Rhapsody*] (Ji'nan: Shandong wenyi chuban she, 1984). For an English translation, see Gong Kechang, *Studies on the Han Fu*, trans., David R. Knechtges et al. (New Haven: American Oriental Society, 1997).

25. The title gentleman (*lang* 郎) is a generic term for court attendants, typically granted to men awaiting appointment or reappointment to a specific office. There were three salary ranks for gentlemen during the Han. However, it is unclear to which rank Sima Xiangru was appointed. See Hucker, *Official Titles*, 301.

26. I have been unable to locate any details on the post of martial regular mounted attendant (*wuqi changshi* 武騎常侍).

27. The story of Sima Xiangru's relationship with Zhuo Wenjun 卓文君 is well known and is considered one of the more romantic tales in the early Chinese tradition. See *Sj*, 117.3000–3001; Watson, *Records*, 260–261; Hervouet, *Chapitre 117 du Che-ki*, 5–8.

28. Gong Kechang addresses the question of which of Sima Xiangru's rhapsodies caught Emperor Wu's attention. *The Grand Scribe's Records* account claims that Sima Xiangru composed the "Zixu fu" 子虛賦 ["Rhapsody on Sir Vacuous"] while in residence at the court of the king of Liang. A poem of the same title appears in the *Selections of Refined Literature*, presented in that anthology as the first part of Sima's "Tianzi youlie fu" 天子遊獵賦 ["Excursion Hunt of the Son of Heaven"]. Gong Kechang argues that the rhapsody on the hunt is incorrectly divided into two separate poems in the *Selections of Refined Literature*, giving the impression that the "Rhapsody on Sir Vacuous" that appears in the anthology is the same poem noted by title in *The Grand Scribe's Records* biography. See *Sj*, 117.3002; Gong Kechang, *Han fu yanjiu*, 68–73; Gong Kechang, *Studies on the Han Fu*, 132–138. For translations of the rhapsodies, see Watson, *Records*, 2:301–321; Hervouet, *Le Chapitre 117 du Che-ki*, 11–142; David R. Knechtges, trans., *Wen xuan, or Selections of Refined Literature*, 3 volumes (Princeton: Princeton University Press, 1982–1996), 2:53–114.

29. The post of general gentleman of the palace (*langzhong jun* 郎中軍) was likely an ad hoc assignment with no set duties. See Hucker, *Official Titles*, 301.

30. See Hervouet, *Un poète*, 69–134.

31. The preceding biographical discussion follows *Sj*, 117.2999–3074; *Hs*, 57A–B.2529–2611.

32. One of the more notable among these was Wang Bao 王褒 (d. ca. 61 BCE) who served as a court poet under Emperor Xuan 宣 of Han (r. 74–48 BCE) and was appointed to the post of grandee remonstrant (*jiandaifu* 諫大夫), a largely honorific censorial position. Biographies of Wang Bao can be found in *Hs*, 64B.2821–2830; and *Hygz*, 10A.534. For an English introduction, see Sharon S. J. Hou, "Wang Bao," in *Indiana Companion*, 1:871–892. For details on the post of grandee remonstrant, see Bielenstein, *The Bureaucracy of Han Times*, 26; 30.

33. See Gong Kechang, *Studies on the Han Fu*, 72–74.

34. *Hs*, 28B.1645.

35. Ban Gu presents Zhuang Zun's surname as "Yan" 嚴 to avoid a taboo on the personal name of Emperor Ming 明 of Han, Liu Zhuang 劉莊. It is under the name "Yan Junping" that Zhuang Zun is most commonly known. See *Hs*, 72.3056–3058; *Hygz*,10A.532–533. There are three important articles on Zhuang Zun. See Zhong Zhaopeng 鐘肇鵬, "Yan Zun," in Jia Shunxian and Dai Dalu, *Sichuan sixiang jia*, 2–34; Aat Vervoorn, "Zhuang Zun: A Daoist Philosopher of the Late First Century B.C.," *Monumenta Serica* 38 (1988–1989): 69–94; and Alan K. L. Chan, "The Essential Meaning of the Way and Virtue: Yan Zun and 'Laozi Learing' in Early Han China," *Monumenta Serica*, 46 (1998): 105–127.

36. *Hs*, 72.3056. Vervoorn notes Zhuang Zun's "reclusion in the market" (*shiyin* 市隱) as strict adherence of Zhuangzi's admonition for "the sage to live inconspicuously

among the common people, unnoticed by all and in externalities indistinguishable from them, set apart only by his detachment from the world around him." See Vervoorn, "Zhuang Zun," 71.

37. *Hygz*, 10A.532. His most important writing, *Daode zhenjing zhigui* 道德真經指歸 [*The Gist of the Veritable Classic of the Way and Its Potency*], has been fragmented, but surviving portions are contained in the Daoist canon. A recent reprint of this text is Yan Zun, *Laozi zhigui* 老子指歸 (Beijing: Zhonghua shuju, 1997).

38. *Hs*, 72.3056.

39. Li Quan was was executed by Liu Yan as part of Liu's efforts to intimidate the local elites of the Chengdu Plain. See *Hygz*, 5.340.

40. *Sgz*, 38.973.

41. See Yan Kejun 嚴可均, *Quan Han wen*, 52.8b–10a, in *Quan shanggu, Sandai, Qin, Han, Sanguo, Liuchao wen* 全上古三代秦漢三國六朝文 [*Complete Prose from High Antiquity, the Three Dynasties, Qin, Han, Three States, and Six Dynasties*] (Beijing: Zhonghua shuju, 1995). For a translation of this letter, see David R. Knechtges, "The Liu Hsin/Yang Hsiung Correspondence on the *Fang yen*," *Monumenta Serica* 33 (1977–1978): 309–325.

42. The principle biography of Yang Xiong is located in *Hs*, 87A–B. For an English translation, see David R. Knechtges, *The Han shu Biography of Yang Xiong (53 B.C.–A.D. 18)* (Tempe: Center for Asian Studies, Arizona State University, 1981). The *Records of the States South of Mount Hua* also contains a brief biography. See *Hygz*, 10A.533. The claim that Yang Xiong himself was a native of Chengdu has been disputed. See Huang Kaiguo 黃開國, "Yang Xiong," in Jia and Dai, *Sichuan sixiang jia*, 37–38.

43. On the rhapsodies of Yang Xiong, see Gong Kechang, *Han fu yanjiu*, 92–119; David R. Knechtges, *The Han Rhapsody : A Study of the Fu of Yang Hsiung (53 B.C.–A.D. 18)* (Cambridge: Cambridge University Press, 1976).

44. *Hs*, 87A.3514.

45. Modeled on the collected teachings of Confucius, the *Analects*, Yang's *Model Sayings* is a collections of aphorisms responding to questions on a number of matters. The responses are terse and witty, written in an archaic style. The primary targets of Yang Xiong's wit are the eclectic thinkers of the pre-Qin and Han periods whose teachings were contrary to those of the Confucian classics. For an introduction to the text, see David R. Knechtges, "Fa yen," in *ECT*, 100–104. Huang Kaiguo also deals with the *Model Sayings* in his article on Yang. See Huang, "Yang Xiong," 55–62.

46. *Hygz*, 10A.533. Yang Xiong's *Regional Sayings* demonstrates his abilities in language, linguistics, and philology. The text is the result of nearly thirty years of collected notes on regional dialects and exegesis. This work was highly regarded at the time of its completion, and is today an important source in the study of Han period dialects. See Paul L-M Serruys, *The Chinese Dialects of Han Time According to* Fang Yen (Berkeley: University of California Press, 1959). For the authenticity of Yang Xiong's authorship, see, Knechtges, "The Liu Hsin/Yang Hsiung Correspondence," 309–325.

47. For an introduction to the text, see Michael Nylan, "T'ai hsuan ching" 太玄經, in *ECT*, 460–466. A detailed introduction to the text and its philosophy can be found in Michael Nylan and Nathan Sivin, "The First Neo-Confucianism: an Introduction to Yang Hsiung's 'Canon of Supreme Mystery' (*T'ai hsuan ching*, c. 4 B.C.)," in

Charles Le Blanc and Susan Blader, eds., *Chinese Ideas about Nature and Society* (Hong Kong: Hong Kong University Press, 1987), 41–99. For a translation of the text into English, see Michael Nylan, *The Canon of Supreme Mystery by Yang Hsiung* (Albany: State University of New York Press, 1993). Also see Huang, "Yang Xiong," 44–54.

48. Nylan and Sivin, "The First Neo-Confucian," 42.

49. Nylan and Sivin, "The First Neo-Confucian," 57–58.

50. Michael Nylan positions Yang Xiong's *Mystery* as one of the earliest works of Mystery Learning. See Nylan, "Legacies," 314–316.

51. Ma Rong and Song Zhong are discussed in greater detail in chapter 4.

52. For a brief summary, see Nylan, "Legacies," 314–316. For a detailed examination of the importance of the Jingzhou academy, see Yoshikawa Tadao, "Scholarship in Ching-Chou."

53. *Hs*, 28B.1645.

54. The political factors behind the traditional views of Han intellectual activity are discussed in Hans Van Ess's "The Old Text/New Text Controversy: Has the 20th Century Got it Wrong?" *T'oung Pao* 80 (1994): 146–170. For some of the classic accounts, see Feng Youlan 馮友蘭, *Zhongguo zhexue shi* 中國哲學史 [*History of Chinese Philosophy*] (Beijing: Zhonghua shuju, 1961); Gu Jiegang 顧頡剛, *Han dai xueshu shilue* 漢代學術史略 [*Summary History of Han Scholarship*] (Shanghai: Shanghai dongfang shushe, 1941); Pi Xirui, *Jingxue lishi* 經學歷史 [*History of Canonical Studies*] (Taibei: Yiwen yinshuguan, 1966); Qian Mu, *Liang Han jingxue jingu wen pingyi* 兩漢經學今古文平議 [*Evaluation of the Old and New Text Canonical Studies in the Han Dynasty*] (Taibei: Sanmin shuju, 1971). Also see Robert Kramer's summary in CHC, 1: 747–765.

55. See Kidder Smith, "Sima Tan and the Invention of Daoism, 'Legalism,' et cetera," *Journal of Asian Studies* 62, no. 1 (February 2003): 129–156; and Mark Csikszentmihalyi and Michael Nylan, "Constructing Lineages and Inventing Traditions through Exemplary Figures in Early China," *T'oung Pao* 89 (2003): 87–97.

56. See Van Ess, "Old Text/New Text," and Michael Nylan, "The Chin Wen/Ku Wen Controversy in Han Times," *T'oung Pao* 80 (1994): 83–145.

57. Csikszentmihalyi and Nylan, "Constructing Lineages," 75.

58. For an overview of the prophetic-apocryphal texts, see Itano Chōhachi, "The t'u-ch'an prophetic books and the establishment of Confucianism," in *Memoirs of the Research Department of the Toyo Bunko* 34 (1976): 47–111; 36 (1978): 85–107; Liu Zehua 劉澤華, "Handai 'weishu' zhong shen, ziran, ren yitihua de zhengzhi guannian" 漢代僞書中神自然人一體化的政治觀念 ["The Han Dynasty political View of the Unification of Spirits, Nature, and Human Beings in the Weft Texts"], in *Wenshizhe* 1993.1: 35–42; Zhong Zhaopeng 鐘肇鵬, *Chenwei lunlüe* 讖緯論略 [*Summary Essays on Prophetic-Apocryphia*] (Shenyang: Liaoning jiaoyu chubanshe, 1991).

The widely accepted view that the prophetic-apocryphal traditions were intimately linked with the "New Text school" of classical studies (see Jack Dull, "A Historical Introduction to the Apocryphal (ch'an-wei) Texts of the Han Dynasty," Ph.D. dissertation (University of Washington, 1966); Hans Van Ess, "The Apocryphal Texts of the Han Dynasty and the Old Text/New Text Controversy," *T'oung Pao* 85 (1999): 29–64) has been challenged. Michael Nylan argues against the stark characterizing link between New Texts and the prophetic-apocryphal learning, noting scholars specializing in Old

Texts interpretations were also practitioners of the prophetic-apocryphal arts, claiming, "For every *jinwen* [New Text] scholar associated with 'superstitions' we can find a comparable *guwen* [Old Text] scholar." See Nylan, "Chin Wen/Ku Wen," 108–112.

59. Lu Zongli defines *chen* as "subtle, esoteric, and portentous words foretelling events; the revelation of Heaven's will through human language." He furthermore argues that this form of prophesy relied on public acceptance and circulation for its authority and power. See Lu Zongli, *Power of the Words:* Chen *Prophesy in Chinese Politics* A.D *265–618* (Bern: Peter Lang, 2003), 15; 23–24.

60. For a list of the bans, see Lu, *Power of the Words*, 38–39. Lu Zongli treats each prohibition in greater detail in the pages that follow his list (39–70).

61. See Csikszentmihalyi and Nylan, "Contructing Lineages," 89–92.

62. Guanghan commandery was located north of Chengdu in present-day Guanghan, Sichuan.

63. Two excellent studies on the Yang's and their impact on prophetic-apocryphal learning on the Chengdu Plain have been written. See Yoshikawa, "Shuku ni okeru shin'i no gaku no dentō," 105–136; Cheng Yuanmin, "Dong Han Shu Yang Hou jingwei xue zongchuan," 19–39.

64. Located in present-day Shanxi Province.

65. *HHs*, 30A.1048 n. 2. This title refers to the interpretative tradition of Xiahou Sheng 夏侯勝 (fl. 70 BCE) and his son Xiahou Jian 建. The *Xiahou Tradition* was based on the earlier interpretations of the *Documents* by Fu Sheng 伏勝. See Edward Shaughnessy, "Shang shu," in *ECT*, 381.

66. *HHs*, 30A.1048 n. 2.

67. Gongsun Shu, appellative Ziyang 子陽, was a man of Maoling 茂陵 in Fufeng 扶風 commandery (located near present-day Xianyang, Shaanxi). See *Hygz*, 5.329–340; *HHs*, 13.533–548. For an English summary, see Bielenstein, "Wang Mang," in *CHC*, 1:240–256.

68. *HHs*, 30A.1047.

69. Little is known of these figures; in fact, Zhou Xun and Zheng Boshan are only mentioned in conjunction with Yang Tong.

70. The *River Chart* was said to be presented to the ancient culture bearer Fuxi by a dragon-horse emerging from a tributary of the Yellow River. Its patterns formed the basis of the Eight Trigrams and the *Changes*. According to Michael Saso, the *River Chart* is a "genre of religious or mystical symbols for expressing the unchanging state of the Dao." See Michael, Saso, "What is the Ho-t'u?" *History of Religions*, 17: 1 (August 1977): 399–416.

The *Luo Documents* were said to have been revealed to the sage-king Yu on the back of a turtle emerging from the Luo River. The diagrams assisted Yu in controlling the floods. Later, the diagrams influenced the hexagrams of the *Changes*. See Julian F. Pas, *Historical Dictionary of Taoism* (Lanham, Maryland: Scarecrow Press, 1998), 211–212.

71. *HHs*, 30A.1047; *Hygz*, 10A.561.

72. Cheng Yuanmin argues that the Yang family secret teachings were based on the Xiahou interpretations of the *Documents*. See Cheng, "Dong Han Shu," 36.

Yoshikawa Tadao concludes that the Yang family teachings were a combination of written and oral instructions, and that Yang Tong was forced to seek out additional teachers to provide the oral component. Yoshikawa also speculates that Yang Tong's teachers must have received instruction in the family traditions from Yang Guang or some other member of the Yang family. See Yoshikawa, "Shuku," 107–108.

73. The *Records of the States South of Mount Hua* notes the titles of these works as *Jiafa zhangzhu* 家法章注 [*Chapters and Verses Commentary on the Family Methods*] and *Jie shuo* 解說 [*Explanations of Sayings*]. See *Hygz*, 10A.561 and *HHs*, 30A.1047.

74. *HHs*, 30A.1047.

75. Ren Naiqiang, in a lengthy biographical note on Yang Tong, discusses the primary sources for the two surviving biographies. He claims the *Later Han History* account was drawn from the *Records of the Han from the Eastern Lodge*, while the *Records of the States South of Mount Hua* biography was based on Chen Shou's *Biographies of the Elders of Yi Province*. See *Hygz*, 569–570 n. 3.

76. The graph 序 (Xu) is mistakenly transcribed as 厚 (Hou) in the *Later Han History*. All extant versions of the *Records of the States South of Mount Hua* use the graph 序. Ren Naiqiang, citing several classical allusions, notes the relationship between the graphs 序 and 桓 (Huan) that appears in Yang's appellative, Zhonghuan 仲桓, and argues that the *Later Han History* is in error. My transcription of Yang's name follows that of the *Records of the States South of Mount Hua* and Ren Naiqiang. See *Hygz*, 570 n. 5.

The *Records of the States South of Mount Hua* mentions Yang Tong's eldest son Yang Bo 博, appellative Zhongda 仲達, and notes his service as imperial palace grandee. See *Hygz*, 690. There is no surviving encomium for Yang Bo. Cheng Yuanmin argues that Yang Bo, like his younger brother, would also have been instructed in the family teachings. See Cheng, "Dong Han Shu," 37–38.

77. *HHs*, 30A.1048. The title of palace attendant (*shizhong* 侍中) encompassed a number of suboffices, all authorized to enter the restricted areas of the palace. See Hucker, *Official Titles*, 423.

78. *Hygz*, 10B.742–743. The *Later Han History* provides a more detailed account of each of these prophesies and their ultimate fulfillment. See *HHs*, 30A.1048–1049.

79. *HHs*, 30A.1049.

80. For Liang Ji, see *HHs*, 6.271–282; *CHC*, 1:285–286.

81. *HHS*, 30A.1050.

82. He most likely received this appellative for his ability to discern the celestial patterns (*wen* 文), although perhaps the title could also be rendered "Father of Culture."

83. *HHs*, 30A.1050.

84. *Hygz*, 10B.562. There is little additional information on many of these figures. The *Records of the States South of Mount Hua* "Listing of Men and Women of Yi, Liang, and Ning Provinces" identifies Zhao Yue and Kou Huan only as "high-minded gentlemen" (*gaoshi* 高士), along with noting their appellatives, native places, and tutelage under Yang Xu (*Hygz*, 960). Hou Qi receives a similarly scant mention. Chang describes him as a "beloved high-minded gentleman" (*du'ai gaoshi* 篤愛高士), and notes Hou as a native of Fan 繁 prefecture (*Hygz*, 669). There is no biographical record of He Chang, though brief notices on two of his students survive in the *Records of the*

States South of Mount Hua. Here, Chang Qu notes that Yang Ban 楊班, appellative Zhongheng 仲桓 was a native of Chengdu, while Luo Heng 羅衡, appellative Zhongbo 仲伯, was a native of Pi 郫 district, and that both studied with the summoned scholar He Youzheng. Yang served as prefect of Maoling 茂陵 and Langzhong 閬中 prefectures and was regarded as a good administrator (*Hygz*, 10A.537). Luo served as the prefect of Wannian 萬年 prefecture, and under his leadership the local families' cows and horses "flourished on the sides of the roads." He was later made chief of Guanghan (*zhang* 長). According to Chang Qu, each of these local administrators had shrines erected to their memory by the people of the prefectures where they served. Ren Naiqiang speculates that there had been a biography of He Chang at one time with these brief accounts of Yang Ban and Luo Heng appended to the account of their teacher's life. Ren also believes that the account of He Chang was passed over by Chen Shou as he compiled his *Biographies of the Elders of Yi Province*, but these mentions of Yang and Luo were extracted at that time. Chang Qu simply followed Chen's record. These details are not found among the extant fragments of Chen Shou work. See *Hygz*, 547 n. 28.

85. *Sgz*, 42.1020.

86. The *Prophesies of the Spring and Autumn* is mentioned briefly in several biographical accounts of figures from the Later Han period, however, no further bibliographical information is available on the text.

87. A detailed explanation of this interpretation is found in the biography of Du Qiong, *Sgz*, 42.1021–1022. I will discuss this in some detail on pages 39–40. Chang Qu praises Zhou Shu in an encomium that reads, "Mysterious and Loyal, the appointed scholar Zhou Shu, appellative Shubo of Langzhong." *Hygz*, 680. The activities of Zhou Shu's son, Qun are discussed on pages 23–24.

88. See *Sgz*, 31.866 n. 4; *HHs*, 79A.2551. Both the Meng *Changes* and Ouyang *Documents* were officially recognized interpretations of their respective canonical texts and, as such, were taught by erudits at the imperial academy. The Meng interpretation of the *Changes* linked the ancient divination text to the cyclical changes of *yin* and *yang* and the five functions theories of the early Han, and was highly valued for its use in the interpretation of portents and prophesies. The Ouyang *Documents* was the sole orthodox interpretative tradition until the traditions associated with the Xiahou family were established at the academy during Emperor Xuan's reign. It retained its official sanction through the Eastern Han as well. It is unclear what role the Ouyang *Documents* might have played in the mantic arts.

89. The time frame of their study with Yang Xu is not clearly indicated, and thus we do not know if this training preceded or followed their study at the imperial academy.

90. *HHs*, 80B.2734. Also see *Sgz*, 31.865.

91. *HHs*, 80B.2734. For a translation, see DeWoskin, *Doctors, Diviners, and Magicians*, 74.

92. *Hygz*, 10B.564. The only post mentioned by name was that of erudit at the imperial academy. Chen Shou's *Biographies of the Elders of Yi Province* mentions that Ren briefly held office at the commandery and provincial levels. Cited in Pei Songzhi's *Commentary*, in *Sgz*, 38.972 n. 1.

93. *HHs*, 79A.2551. Another saying went, "He lives in the present and walks in the past—Ren Dingzu!" *HHs*, 79A.2551. When asked about Ren An by Shu-Han

chancellor Zhuge Liang, Qin Mi replied, "He remembered a man's good and forgot his faults." *Sgz*, 38.972 n. 1. Chang Qu's joint encomium for Ren and Dong read, "Dong and Ren were upright in their ambitions, as [valued as] great quantities of bound silk." *Hygz*, 10B.564.

94. Huangfu Mi, *Gaoshi zhuan*, 3.9a (*Bbcs* edition).

95. *Hygz*, 10B.579.

96. For example, Cheng Yuanmin, following Bi Yuan's 畢沅 (1730–1797) *Chuanjing biao* 傳經表 [*Tables of the Transmission of the Canonical Texts*] (*Congshu jicheng chupian* edition), 55–62, argues that "there were none [in this lineage] who did not master the canonical texts, including the Xiahou *Hallowed Documents*," and "all definitely mastered the New Text Xiahou tradition of the *Documents*." See Cheng, "Dong Han Shu," 2:36. This argument, along with Bi Yuan's graphical representation, is based on the false equation of instruction of a student by a teacher with the transmission of a single canonical text. The tendency of students to seek out multiple teachers during the Later Han, combined with the lack of mention of transmission of a canonical text in the biographical accounts of the Yang family lineage, makes this assumption difficult to accept.

97. It is interesting to note that the Yang family lineage did not appear to practice other significant elements of the *fangshi* tradition, including medicine and alchemy.

98. For discussions on the early traditions of reclusion, see Aat Vervoorn, *Men of the Cliffs and Caves: The Development of the Chinese Eremitic Tradition to the End of the Han Dynasty* (Hong Kong: Chinese University Press, 1990); Alan J. Berkowitz, *Patterns of Disengagement: The Practice and Portrayal of Reclusion in Early Medieval China* (Stanford: Stanford University Press, 2000).

99. Especially Yang Xu and Feng Hao. Whether there is an academic link between Han Daoism and the prophetic-apocryphal learning traditions is an intriguing question that has yet to be fully investigated. Yoshikawa suggests such a link is evinced in Du Qiong's rhapsody "Chongsi fu" 重思賦 ["Rhapsody on Deep Thought"], suggesting that "Du Qiong might have been attracted to things 'mysterious.'" See Yoshikawa, "Shuku," 116.

100. The collected biographies of classical scholars originates in Sima Qian's *The Grand Scribe's Records*, where he prefaces his accounts of the scholarly and official activities of four major scholars with a brief discussion of the relationship between scholarship and the state, and outlines the history of this relationship from the Zhou times down to the founding of the Han, noting the decline of scholastic activities under Qin and their revival under "the sage-ruler" Liu Bang. See *Sj*, 121.3115–3129.

Ban Gu continues this historiographical tradition by including his own "Forest of Classicists" fascicle in his *Han History*. Ban offers a similar historical preface, noting his desire to "present the actions of twelve masters, binding them to the Way of King Wu [of Zhou], completing a single Kingly Method (*wang fa* 王法)." Following this introduction, Ban presents biographies of twelve scholars of the Former Han, again focusing on their scholarly and official activities. See *Hs*, 88.3589–3622.

101. The biography of Zhuge Liang is located in *Sgz*, 35.911–937; while that of Qin Mi is located in *Sgz*, 38.971–976.

102. See *Sgz*, 42.1019–1020. A biography and encomium for Du Wei are also contained in *Hygz*, 10B.614; 707.

Appended to Chen Shou's biography of Du Wei is a brief notice on Wu Liang 五梁, appellative Deshan 德山, of Nan'an 南安 prefecture in Qianwei commandery. Wu was commended for his classical learning and moral integrity. He served as gentleman consultant, grandee of instructional consultants, and general of the gentlemen-of-the-household for all purposes. It is unclear whether Wu Liang was connected to the Yang intellectual lineage. See *Sgz*, 42.1020.

103. *Sgz*, 42.1020.

104. *Sgz*, 42.1020. While Chen Shou attributes Zhou Qun's accuracy in prognostication to his careful observations, Wang Jia's 王嘉 *Shiqian ji* 拾遺記 [*Collected Records*] contains an anecdote claiming supernatural origins of Zhou's art. In this story, Zhou Qun was traveling on Mount Min, picking medicinal herbs, when a large white baboon came down from a steep precipice, then changed into an old man. The old man presented Zhou Qun with a jade tablet and instructed him in the mantic arts. Cited in *Sgzjj*, 42.2b. Wang Jia's text is mentioned in the *Old Tang History* bibliography. See *JTs*, 46.1995.

105. The seat of Yuexi commandery was located near present-day Xichang 西昌 city, in southern Sichuan Province.

106. *Sgz*, 42.1020 n. 1.

107. *Sgz*, 42.1020–1021 n. 1. The Quail Tail is one of the twelve Jupiter stations. The "Treatise on Astronomy" in the *Jin History* notes, "From the 17th degree of Zhang (26th lunar mansion) to the 11th degree of Zhen (28th lunar mansion) is the *chunwei* (station), associated with (the terrestrial branch) *su*. This division corresponds to [the state of] Chu and Jingzhou (prefecture) (present-day Guizhou, Hunan and Hupei)." See *Js*, 11.309; Ho Peng Yoke, *The Astronomical Chapters of the* Chin Shu (Paris and The Hague: Mouton and Co., 1966), 115.

108. The *Jin History* "Treatise on Astronomy" notes, "North of the Dong Jing (the 22nd lunar mansion) lie the five "Five Marquises" stars, which govern the prosecution of offenders and the preparation for emergencies. They are said to regulate the (two *qi* of) *Yin* and *Yang*, and discriminate between success and failure, and (also) said to influence the will of the Emperor. One of the stars among them is called Di Shi 帝師 ("the Emperor's Teacher"), another called Di You 帝友 ("the Emperor's Friend"), a third called San Gong 三公 ("Three Dukes"), a fourth called Bo Shi 博士 ("Professor"[sic]) and a fifth called Tai Shi 太史 ("Astronomer-Royal"). The five normally assist the Emperor in the discussion and clarification of doubtful matters. Peace will come to the country when these stars appear large, bright and lustrous, but internal trouble will start when they send out pointed beams." See *Js*, 11.298; Ho, *Astronomical Chapters*, 92–93.

109. *Sgz*, 42.1020–1021 n. 1. These episodes are not found in the extant "Treatises" from the *Continued Han History*.

110. Zhou Qun was named Preceptor Companion Attendant by Liu Zhang. Later, after Liu Bei established his base in Yi Province, Zhou Qun was named colonel of the Forest of Classicists. The colonel of the Forest of Classicists (*Rulin xiaowei* 儒林校尉) was responsible for the administration of a local academy. See Hucker, *Official Titles*, 273.

111. This attack took place in Jian'an 23–24 (219–20 CE). See *Sgz*, 32.884.

112. *Sgz*, 42.1020.

113. The only information on Zhang Yu is contained in this anecdote.

114. *Sgz*, 42.1021. Lu Bi notes that over 80,000 people moved from Hanzhong to Luoyang after Liu Bei's invasion. See *Sgzjj*, 42.3a.

115. Chen Shou provides an extremely brief notice of Zhou Qun's son, Zhou Ju 巨. Appended to Zhou Qun's biography is the statement, "[His] son, Ju, had inclinations toward [Zhou Qun's] art." *Sgz*, 42.1021.

116. *Sgz*, 42.1021.

117. *Hygz*, 10A.539.

118. These posts included grandee of instruction and consultation (*jianyi daifu* 諫議大夫), general of the gentlemen-of-the-household-of-the-left (*zuozhonglang jiang* 左中郎將), grand herald (*da honglu* 大鴻臚), and grand master of ceremonies (*taichang* 太常). The grandee of instruction and consultation attended and advised the emperor. See Hucker, *Official Titles*, 148. The general of the gentlemen-of-the-household-of-the-left was in charge of groups of expectant officials, or gentlemen. See Hucker, *Official Titles*, 191. The grand herald appears to have been part of the governmental office charged with receiving diplomatic envoys, hence the literal title "making loud announcements." See Hucker, *Official Titles*, 264. The grand master of ceremonies was in charge of state sacrificial rites. See Hucker, *Official Titles*, 476.

119. *Sgz*, 42.1021.

120. *Hygz*, 10A.539.

121. *Hygz*, 10A.539.

122. Jiang Wan succeeded Zhuge Liang as the leader of Shu-Han's military forces. See *Sgz*, 44.1057–1060.

123. For the official biography of Fei Yi, see *Sgz*, 44.1060–1062.

124. *Sgz*, 42.1021.

125. *Sgz*, 42.1022.

126. This biographical notice is appended to the longer biography of Li Mi. See *Hygz*, 11.639.

127. Gao Wan was recommended as filial and incorrupt, and appointed as prefect of Quyang 曲陽 prefecture, and later appointed as prefect grand astrologer under the Jin. *Hygz*, 11.639.

128. It may be the case that Chen Shou is subtly advancing the cause of his own teacher as an heir to the teachings of Du Qiong over Gao Wan. It is unclear whether Gao was a major disciple of Du or merely consulted with him as did Qiao Zhou. The influence of Du Qiong on Qiao Zhou is discussed in detail in chapter 2.

129. *Sgz*, 42.1023.

130. Nanyang was located near present-day Nanyang, Henan Province.

131. Lu Bi identifies Liu Xi as having his home of record in Beihai, having served as the prefect of Nan'an, authored a treatise on posthumous titles, and being a master of ancient phonology. See *Sgzjj*, 42. 5a–6b.

132. Xu Jing, a native of Runan, was invited to take office in Ba and Guanghan commanderies under the provincial administration of Liu Zhang. After Liu Bei's seizure of Yi Province, Xu Jing was retained in various offices. Following the establishment of Liu Bei as emperor, Xu was appointed as minister over the masses

(*situ* 司徒), one of the three highest civil offices. For Xu Jing's biography, see *Sgz*, 38.963–969.

133. *Sgz*, 42.1022–1023.

134. *Sgz*, 42.1023.

135. *Sgz*, 42.1023.

136. *Sgz*, 42.1023.

137. Sun Sheng, appellative Anguo 安國, was a Jin dynasty historian. His most important works were *Wei shi chunqiu* 魏氏春秋 [*The Spring and Autumn of the House of Wei*] and *Jin yangqiu* 晉陽秋 [*The Spring and Autumn of the Jin*]. After the compilation of these works, the Jin general Huan Wen 桓文 was infuriated over the depiction of his family and demanded a retraction. Sun Sheng refused. However, his son secretly made the revisions. As a result, there are two versions of this text. See *Js*, 82.2147–2149.

138. *Sgz*, 42.1023 n. 1.

139. Xinye prefecture was located near the provincial capital of Jing Province (present-day Xinye city, Hebei Province).

140. In Chen Shou's *Collected Works of Zhuge Liang*, cited in Pei Songzhi's commentary. *Sgz*, 42.1025–1026 n. 2.

141. *Sgz*, 42.1026.

142. Chen Shou singles out Mr. Zuo [Qiuming]'s *Spring and Autumn* as the principle object of Yin Mo's expertise.

143. Liu Xuan, appellative Wenheng 文衡, was the eldest son of Liu Shan. He was named heir apparent in 238. After the defeat of Shu-Han in 264 CE, he was killed by rioting troops in Chengdu. See *Sgz*, 34.908.

144. *Sgz*, 42.1027.

145. The biography of Xi Zheng appears in *Sgz*, 42.1034–1041.

146. Huang Hao was a childhood companion of Liu Shan. See *Sgz*, 39.986. The role and influence of Huang Hao are discussed in greater detail in chapter 3.

147. *Sgz*, 42.1034.

148. A copiously annotated translation and close reading of this essay, rendered as "Rejecting Slander," is contained in Dominik Declercq, *Writing Against the State* (Leiden: Brill, 1998), 102–119.

149. *Sgz*, 42.1041.

150. *Sgz*, 42.1041.

CHAPTER 2

1. Xichongguo prefecture was located near present-day Nanchong 南充, Sichuan.

2. On the calculation of Qiao Zhou's year of birth, see pages 37 and 72.

3. The reading for the graph 峅 is unknown. Its sole occurrence is in this name, and modern dictionaries that contain the graph are united in their assessment that there is no known reading. Based on similarities with other graphs containing the phoenetic component *bing* 并, it seems possible that the reading may have been 峅 b'ieŋ.

4. *Sgz*, 42.1027–1034. For a fully annotated translation, see Farmer, "The World of the Mind," 425–455.

5. Yu Ying-shih offers a thorough examination of the development of the *shi* during the Han and early medieval period. See Yu Ying-shih 余英時 *Shi yu Zhongguo wenhua* 士與中國文化 [*The* Shi *and Chinese Culture*] (1987. Reprint. Shanghai: Shanghai renmin chubanshe, 2003). See especially chapters 4–6. For a detailed discussion of the *shi* mentality and its transformation during the early medieval period, see Peter Bol, *"This Culture of Ours": Intellectual Transitions in T'ang and Sung China* (Stanford: Stanford University Press, 1992), 32–75.

6. *Hygz*, 1.46.

7. *Hygz*, 1.45.

8. The three powers were Heaven, Earth, and Man. This passage refers to the knowledge of the Way of Heaven (*Tiandao* 天道), geography, and human affairs. See *Yijing zhengyi* 易經正義, 9.81.

9. *Hygz*, 1.45.

10. The post of Shanglin *ling* 上林令 drew a small salary of six hundred bushels.

11. This passage is contained in *Ywlj*, 48.865. An identical passage is also found in *Tpyl*, 219.8b. Ren Naiqiang added this anecdote to an appendix to fascicle 10A of the *Records of the States South of Mount Hua*. Ren noted that this passage did not appear in any of the surviving editions of the text and speculated it may have originally belonged to the biographies appended by Chang Qu to the text's original encomia for Qiao Long, but was subsequently excised from the text. See *Hygz*, 555.

12. For Sima Xiangru's remonstrance, presented in the form of a rhapsody, see *Sj*, 117.3002; *Hs*, 27A.2533, 2575. For Dongfang Shuo's objections, see *Hs*, 35.2847–2851.

13. *Hygz*, 12.678.

14. *HHs*, 81.2666.

15. The gentleman consultant (*yilang* 議郎) was the title for officials at court without regular adminstrative duties. See Hucker, *Official Titles*, 267.

16. Lady Zhao was established as empress in Yongshi 永始 1 (16 BCE). See *Hs*, 10.319. The biography of Empress Zhao is contained in *Hs*, 97B.3988–3993. She has been characterized as licentious and extremely jealous. See Liu Xiang 劉向 (79–8 BCE), *Lienü zhuan* 列女傳 [*Biographies of Exemplary Women*], 8.8b–9a (*Sbby* ed.). For an English translation, see Albert O'Hara, *The Position of Woman in Early China According the* Lieh Nü Chuan (Taipei: Mei Ya Publications, 1971), 235–238.

17. *HHs*, 81.2666. The implication of this line is that Empress Zhao killed the infant sons of other imperial consorts.

18. *HHs*, 81.2666.

19. *HHs*, 81.2666–2667.

20. The *Later Han History* account offers no details on the nature of these anomalies or how they were interpreted by Qiao Xuan. See *HHs*, 81.2667.

21. The assistant grand master of ceremonies (*taichang cheng* 太常丞) aided the grand master of ceremonies in the arrangements for state sacrificial ritual. The assistant's salary was one thousand bushels. See Hucker, *Official Titles*, 476.

22. For a brief overview of Wang Mang and the Xin, see Hans Bielenstein, "Wang Mang, the Restoration of the Han Dynasty, and Later Han," in *CHC*, 1: 223–290.

23. *HHs*, 81.2667.

24. The grand administrator (*taishou* 太守) was the chief civil and military officer of the commandery administrative unit, drawing a salary of two thousand bushels. See Hucker, *Official Titles*, 482.

25. The claim that the poison was only to frighten Qiao Xuan comes from the account in *Hygz*, 1.17. The *HHs* account omits this detail.

26. Xu You was a minister of the sage-emperor Yao. Yao wished to give the throne to Xu, but he declined and fled. See *Zhuangzi*, 1.5b–6a. *Sbby*. Also see *Sj*, 61.

27. Bo Yi and his brother Shu Qi 叔齊 were noted for their objection to the regicide committed by King Wu of Zhou in his overthrow of the last Shang king. In protest, they starved themselves to death rather than live under the Zhou. See *Sj*, 61.2121–2127. For an English translation, see William H. Nienhauser, ed., *The Grand Scribe's Records*, vols. 1, 7 (Bloomington: Indiana University Press, 1994), 7:1–8.

28. *HHs*, 81.2668.

29. See *Hygz*, 1.17. The *HHs* account puts the figure at one million cash. See *HHs*, 81.2668. I have chosen to follow Chang Qu's earlier narrative on this matter. The fact that Qiao Xuan's son could immediately product eight (or even one) million cash to offer to the grand administrator indicates the financial resources the family commanded.

30. *HHs*, 81.2668.

31. *Hygz*, 1.17. The poem is also contained in Lu Qinli 逯欽立, ed., *Xian Qin, Han, Wei, Jin, Nanbei chao shi* 先秦漢魏晉南北朝詩 [*Poems from the Pre-Qin, Han, Wei, Jin, Northern and Southern Dynasties*] (Beijing: Zhonghua, 1983), 12.325.

This short poem employs matched allusions to the *Han History* and *Analects*, forming a chiasmus. Line 1 borrows language from *Hs*, 72.3097; line 2 from *Lunyu* 19.2; line 3 alludes again to *Lunyu* 14.12; and line 4 is taken from *Hs*, 73.3112. The first three allusions refer to persons firm in virtue and willing to sacrifice their own lives to hold firm to their moral standards. The final allusion borrows the term *lingsheng* 令聲 (honorable reputation) from a lament by a father to a son who had lost his virtue through immoral actions.

32. *HHs*, 81.2668.

33. For Qiao Ying, see *HHs*, 81.2668; *Hygz*, 12.678.

34. *Sgz*, 42.1027.

35. *Hygz*, 1.45.

36. *Hygz*, 12.681. In this translation, the asterisks indicate the lacunae in the original Chinese text.

37. The *Han History* notes several Central Plains clans who were resettled on the Chengdu Plain following the conquest of their home states by Qin. Among the cases mentioned by Ban Gu was that of the Zhuo 卓 clan who were relocated from the state of Zhao. On their arrival in Shu, they settled in an iron-rich area of the basin and greatly increased their fortunes, with their wealth equalling that of the Central Plains nobility. Ban Gu presents similar scenarios for the Cheng 程 clan, as well as the rise in the fortunes of an individual named Luo Pou 羅裒 who served as a middleman in the

business dealings of wealthy immigrant clans in the region. See *Hs*, 91.3690. These episodes are translated in Nancy Lee Swann, *Food and Money in Ancient China* (Princeton: Princeton University Press, 1950), 452–454.

Ma Feibai 馬非百 placed the total number of households resettled to the Chengdu Plain by Qin as "over four thousand." He also noted nearly fifty forced moves of powerful Central Plains families to various other locations. See Ma Feibai, *Qin ji shi* 秦集史 [*Collected Histories of Qin*] (Beijing: Zhonghua shuju, 1982), 916–929.

That the Qiaos may have been a part of these migrations remains a distinct possibility.

38. Ren Naiqiang speculated that the family derived its wealth from commercial interests relating to the Zong people in the area; however, there is no evidence to support or reject such a claim. *Hygz*, 1.18 n. 2.

39. *Sgz*, 42.1027–1034.

40. Strangely enough, the *Records of the States South of Mount Hua* does not contain a full biography of Qiao Zhou, though Chang Qu mentions Qiao in highly favorable terms on numerous occasions, frequently cites passages of Qiao's writings, and includes an encomium.

41. *Sgz*, 42.1033. This prophesy is discussed on page 72.

42. *Sgz*, 42.1027.

43. *Sgz*, 42.1027.

44. *Sgz*, 42.1027.

45. *Hygz*, 1.45.

46. See chapter 1.

47. *Sgz*, 42.1022.

48. *Sgz*, 42.1022.

49. *Sgz*, 42.1027.

50. Chang Ming 常明, comp. *Sichuan tongzhi*, prefaced dated 1816 (reprint; Chengdu: Ba-Shu chubanshe, 1984), 52.4a. Also see Cao Xuequan 曹學佺, *Shu zhong mingsheng ji* 蜀中名勝記 [*Record of Shu Notables*] (Preface dated 1618; Reprint, Taipei: Xuehai chubanshe, 1969), 27.4a.

51. *Nanchong xianzhi* (n.p., 1929), 4.91a–b.

52. See chapter 1.

53. This refers to the prophesy that read "Dang tu gao zhe, Wei ye" 當塗高者魏也. See chapter 1.

54. *Sgz*, 42.1022.

55. While the historical record provides no date for this discussion between Qiao Zhou and Du Qiong, the references to the Cao's state of Wei would seem to indicate that the exchange took place after 220 CE and the establishment of Wei.

56. *Sgz*, 42.1022.

57. *Sgz*, 38.971.

58. These texts included, from the Han canon, the *Documents*, *Changes*, *Li ji* 禮記 [*Record of Rites*], *Chunqiu* 春秋 [*Spring and Autumn Annals*], and *Shi jing* 詩經 [*Book*

of Odes]; historical texts *The Grand Scribe's Records*, *Han History*, and *Zhanguo ce* 戰國策 [*Stratagems of the Warring States*]; and works by various masters such as *Lun yu* 論語, *Xiao jing* 孝經 [*Canon of Filial Piety*], *Laozi*, *Zhuangzi*, *The Gist of the Laozi*, and Yang Xiong's *Model Sayings* and *Supreme Mystery*. Chen Shou's limited discussion of Qin Mi's intellectual activities centers on Qin's innovations in the field of historical criticism and their influence on Qiao Zhou.

59. *Sgz*, 38.971–972.

60. See chapter 1, note 39.

61. *Sgz*, 38.976.

62. Wang Shang was a native of Mianzhu in Guanghan commandery and served as commandery administrator of Shu under the regime of Liu Zhang. A biography is contained in Chen Shou's *Biographies of the Elders of Yi Province*, cited in Pei Songzhi's *Commenatry* to the *Records of the Three States*. See *Sgz*, 38.967 n. 1.

63. Li Hong was a Chengdu native, remembered for his rebuke of a local administrator during the trial of Li's son for murder. He is referenced in Yang Xiong's *Model Sayings*. A brief biography is contained in the *Records of the States South of Mount Hua*. See *Hygz*, 10A.533.

64. *Sgz*, 38.973.

65. Pei Songzhi notes: "The *River Chart*'s "Images of the Collected Lands" ["Kuodi xiang" 括地象] says, 'The land of Mount Min: Its top is the Eastern Well. The Celestial Lord used [this place] to gather felicity. The divinities used [this place] to establish blessings. Its top is the Well of Heaven.' Zuo Si's "Rhapsody on the Shu Capital" says, 'In the distant past, the spiritual essence of the Min mountains ascended to become the Well Network (*jingluo* 井絡). The Celestial Lord controlled the cycles and gathered felicity in his land. Great Blessings profusely spread, rising and emanating from all directions.'" See *Sgz*, 38.975 n. 2.

66. Minshan commandery was located west of Shu commandery, its seat south of present-day Minchuan 汶川 on the Yangzi River.

67. Pei Songzhi notes: "The *Annals of the Ages of Thearchs and Kings* says, 'Gun married a daughter of the You Xin 有莘 clan named Zhi 志, who was known as Xiuji 修己 [Cultivate One's Self]. As she walked at the top of the mountain, she saw a comet in the *ang* 昂 astral sector. She dreamed that she was close to the comet and was moved by it. She swallowed a divine pearl. Her belly and mind expanded and she gave birth to Yu at Shiniu.'" Pei also cites Qiao Zhou's *Basic Annals of Shu* on this topic. See *Sgz*, 38.975 n. 3.

68. The astral sector (*fenye* 分野) system linked celestial sections with corresponding earthly regions, including links between heavenly and earthly objects such as stars, planets, mountains, and rivers. Events in the celestial sector were believed to have significance for the corresponding terrestial sector. See Joseph Needham and Wang Ling, eds., *Science and Civilisation in China, Vol. 3: Mathematics and the Sciences of the Heavens and the Earth* (Cambridge: Cambridge University Press, 1959), 545.

69. Pei Songzhi notes: "The *Records of Shu* says, 'The Three August Ones rode their carriages out of Gukou.' I do not know how [Qin] Mi knew this was Xiegu." *Sgz*, 38.975 n. 4. The Xiegu valley followed the Wugong 武功 River between present-day Fufeng 扶風 and Taibai 太白 in Shaanxi Province.

70. *Sgz*, 38.975.

71. This refers to Sima Qian's narrative in *The Grand Scribe's Records*. See *Sj*, 1.

72. *Sgz*, 38.976.

73. *Sgz*, 38.976.

74. *Hygz*, 10B.567.

75. This work is discussed in greater detail in chapter 4.

CHAPTER 3

1. The title of the chief provincial official during the Han alternated between inspector (*cishi* 刺史) and shepherd (*mu* 牧). During the Later Han, the post carried a salary of two thousand bushels. See Bielenstein, *Bureaucracy of Han Times*, 90.

2. The standard biographical account of Liu Yan is contained in *Sgz*, 31.865–868. Also see *Hygz*, 5.340–346.

3. For Zhang Lu, see *Sgz*, 8.263–266.

4. *Yingxiong ji* 英雄記 [*The Record of Heroes*], cited in Pei Songzhi's *Commentary*, notes the influx of refugees from the Central Plains, who "encroached on and ravaged the old inhabitants." This activity left the locals in a state of severe agitation. See *Sgz*, 31.869 n. 2.

5. See *Sgz*, 31.869–870. These events are treated in great detail in the respective biographies of the participants in the *Later Han History* and *Records of the Three States*, as well as the *Comprehensive Mirror for Aiding in Government*. Rafe de Crespigny offers a concise summary in "The Three Kingdoms & Western Jin," part 1, 1–14.

6. Liu Bei was said to have been the descendant of a son of Emperor Jing 景 of Han. His father died while Liu Bei was still young, and his mother wove mats and sandals to support the family. Additionally, various kinsmen assisted the young Liu Bei, paying his tuition and offering other material support. See *Sgz*, 32.871.

7. According to the *Records of the Three States*, when Liu Bei took control in Chengdu, "Shu was affluent and prospering. The Former Sovereign prepared liquor and a great banquet for the officers and soldiers and repaid [the common people] with grain and silk." *Sgz*, 32.882.

8. The text of this memorial is contained in *Sgz*, 32.886–887. It was signed by eleven named officers and one-hundred-twenty unnamed individuals.

9. Mianyang was located northwest of present-day Hanzhong, Shaanxi.

10. The text of the memorial is reproduced in *Sgz*, 32.886–887.

11. This event is recorded in *Sgz*, 2.61–76. For detailed studies on the establishment of Wei, see Carl Leban, "Ts'ao Ts'ao and the Rise of Wei: the Early Years," Ph.D. diss., Columbia, 1971; Carl Leban, "Managing Heaven's Mandate: Coded Communications in the Accession of Ts'ao P'ei, A.D. 220," in *Ancient China*, eds., David Roy and Tsuen-hsuin Tsien (Hong Kong: The Chinese University Press, 1978), 315–341; Howard L. Goodman, *Ts'ao P'i Transcendent: The Political Culture of Dynasty-Founding in China at the End of the Han* (Seattle: Scripta Serica, 1998).

12. *Sgz*, 2.76.

13. Though Cao Pi ended the Jian'an period in its twenty-fifth year, changing the year-title to Huangchu 黃初, Liu Bei refused to recognize this calendrical change, thus his use of "Jian'an 26"—a year not found on most dynastic chronological tables.

14. For a succinct account of these events in English, see de Crespigny, "Three Kingdoms and Western Jin," part 1, 1–36; in Chinese, see He, *Sanguo shi*; and Ma, *Sanguo shi*.

15. The *Three Kingdoms* claims an earlier entrance into political activity for Qiao Zhou. See *Sgyy*, 65.850; *TK*, 777–778.

16. The twelve officials were the gentlemen consultants Liu Bao 劉豹 and Xiang Ju 向舉; lieutenant generals Zhang Yi 張裔 (d. 230 CE) and Huang Quan 黃權 (d. 240 CE); [officer] under the command of the commander-in-chief Yin Chun 殷純; Yi province aide-de-camp attendant Zhao Zuo 趙莋; headquarters attendant Yang Hong 楊洪 (d. 228 CE); attendant libationer He Zong 何宗; bureau of consultation attendant Du Qiong; and the attendants for the encouragement of education Zhang Shuang 張爽, Yin Mo 尹默, and Qiao Zhou. See *Sgz*, 32.887.

17. *Sgz*, 32.887–888.

18. *Sgz*, 32.887.

19. Four other Eastern Han emperors, each ruling only a short period, are not included in this tally. See Fang, *Sgzzy*, 32.1597, n. 11.

20. *Sgz*, 32.887.

21. An additional prophetic text cited in the memorial also employs the term *bei*/complete, again linking Liu Bei to the prophesy.

22. *Sgz*, 32.887.

23. The four planets listed, plus Mercury.

24. *Sgz*, 32.887–888.

25. Originally named Xu, the city was renamed Xuchang 許昌 after the relocation of the Han court to the site in 196 CE. Xuchang was located near present-day Xuchang, Henan province.

26. *Zhou Yi*, hexagram 1/5; Lynn, *I-ching*, 138.

27. *Sgz*, 32.888.

28. The six officials were Xu Jing, Mi Zhu 糜竺, Zhuge Liang, Lai Gong 賴恭, Huang Quan, and Wang Mo 王謀.

29. The document read by Liu Bei at his accession ceremony notes the crimes of Cao Cao and Liu Bei's own reluctance to take the throne. "Awed by Heaven's bright mandate," however, Liu Bei made offerings and asked for Heaven's blessings on his house of Han. The text of this document is contained in *Sgz*, 32.889. For a translation and discussion of the rhetoric of the accession document, see Farmer, "What's in a Name?" 46–47.

30. *Sgzjj*, 32.31b. Also see Gu Yanwu, *Rizhi lu* 日知錄 [*Record of Daily Knowledge*] (rpt., Taipei: Wenshizhe, 1979), 27.746.

31. Shen Jiaben argues that the individual should be Zhou Qun, while Qian Yiji makes a case for Zhou Qun's son, Zhou Ju. See *Sgzjj*, 32.31b.

32. Ren accepts the claim of textual corruption in both the *Records of the Three States* and *Records of the States South of Mount Hua*. See *Hygz*, 6.376–377, n. 3.

33. See Zhu Dawei 朱大渭, "Wei Jin Nanbei chao zhengjie mingren chengcai nianling jiegou pouxi" 魏晉南北朝政界名人成才年齡結構剖析 ["A Structural Analysis of the Ages Upon Taking Office of Famous Persons from the Political World of the Wei, Jin, and Northern and Southern Dynasties"], in *Liuchao shilun* 六朝史論 [*Essays on Six Dynasties History*] (Beijing: Zhonghua shuju, 1998), 141–157.

34. See chapter 2.

35. Apparently Zhuge Liang was quite taken with Qiao Zhou's intellectual talents despite Qiao's homely appearance. Pei Songzhi's *Commentary* quotes the *Shu ji* 蜀記 [*Records of Shu*] on the first meeting of the two men: "When Qiao Zhou first met Zhuge Liang, the attendants all laughed. When [Qiao] had left, a director asked to expel those who had laughed. Zhuge Liang replied, 'I too cannot endure [the sight of him], how much less so the attendants?'" *Sgz*, 42.1027, n. 1.

36. All three are listed as signatories of the memorial urging Liu Bei to take the throne. There is no additional information available on Zhang Shuang.

The title attendant for the encouragement of education (*quanxue congshi* 勸學從事) does not appear in either the *Han History* or *Later Han History*, indicating that the office may have been the creation of officials in Yi Province and not a common post during the earlier Han period.

37. *Sgz*, 42.1026.

38. Hucker translates the title as "educational assistant" and describes the post as "one of several school officials on the staffs of regional [i.e., provincial] inspectors." Hucker, *Official Titles*, 198.

39. *Sgz*, 42.1027.

40. Hucker claims the office of attendant for direction of education (*dianxue congshi* 典學從事) was responsible for all educational activities in the province. See Hucker, *Official Titles*, 503.

41. The post of coachman (*pu* 僕) carried a salary of one thousand bushels. See Hucker, *Official Titles*, 484.

42. The post of prefect of the household of the heir apparent (*taizi jialing* 太子家令) carried a variable salary of three hundred to one thousand bushels. Given the supervisory nature of the office, we may presume that Qiao Zhou was at the upper end of the salary scale. See Hucker, *Official Titles*, 138.

43. The post of palace attendant grandee (*zhongsan daifu* 中散大夫) carried a salary of six hundred bushels.

44. According to Hucker, the imperial household grandee (*guanglu daifu* 光祿大夫) was "an intimate imperial aide and advisor, in residence in the palace," with a rank of two thousand bushels. See Hucker, *Official Titles*, 288.

45. Colonel for the direction of education (*dianxue xiaowei* 典學校尉). *Sgz*, 42.1025.

46. *Sgz*, 42.1026.

47. Cadet (*shuzi* 庶子). *Sgz*, 42.1026–1027.

48. *Sgz*, 32.1027.

49. The bibliographic treatises of the *Sui History*, *Old Tang History*, and *New Tang History* were united in their assessments of *Model Teachings*. See *Sui*, 34.998; *JTs*, 47.2025; *XTs*, 59.1511. Fragments of Qiao's *Model Teachings* were contained in the Tang encyclopedia *Collection of Literature Arranged by Categories* (one fragment), *Imperially Reviewed Encyclopedia of the Taiping Period* (eighteen fragments), and the *Record of Primary Scholarship* (six fragments). Aside from these encyclopedia, additional portions of the text survived cited in the commentaries of Liu Jun on the *New Account of Tales of the World* (one fragment) and Li Shan on the *Selections of Refined Literature* (one fragment). A single fragment each was preserved in Jia Sixie's 賈思勰 (sixth-century) preface to his *Qimin yaoshu* 齊民要術 [*Essential Arts of the Common People*] and Feng Yan's 封演 (*jinshi* 756) *Wenjian ji* 聞見記 [*Records of Things Heard and Seen*]. Finally, Ma Zong's 馬總 (d. 823 CE) *Yilin* 意林 [*Forest of Ideas*] originally contained five fragments of the *Model Teachings*. The extant edition of Ma's work does not contain these fragments, but Zhou Guangye's 周廣業 (1730–1798) *Yilin yiwen* 意林逸文 [*Missing Texts from the Forest of Ideas*] collected these fragments under the title of *Model Teachings*. See Zhou Guangye, *Yilin yiwen*, in *Yilin*, 6.3a (*Sibu beiyao* ed.). The twenty-eight extant passages of the *Model Teachings* were cited in these sources a total of thirty-five times.

Recompilations of the text are contained in Tao Zongyi 陶宗儀 (b. 1316), recomp., *Master Qiao's Model Teachings*, 1.1a–b, in *Shuofu* 說郛 (*Gujin shuobu congshu* 古今說部叢書 ed.) (Shanghai: Shanghai yiwen chubanshe, 1991); Yan Kejun, *Quan Jin wen*, 70.4a–5b, in *Quan Shanggu, Sandai, Qin, Han, Sanguo, Liuchao wen*; and Ma Guohan, recomp., *Qiaozi Faxun*, 1.1a–4b, in *Yuhanshanfang jiyi shu*.

50. Other questions in the text appear to have come from persons other than the heir, perhaps Qiao Zhou's students. For a more detailed discussion of Qiao's *Model Teachings*, see Farmer, "The World of the Mind," 329–346.

51. *Tpyl*, 607.7b.

52. See *Sgz*, 42.1024–1025.

53. *Tpyl*, 156.5b.

54. *Lunyu*, 2.1; translation in Lau, *Analects*, 63.

55. The graph for Luo's given name was sometimes rendered as 獻. The earliest surviving biographical information comes from the *Xiangyang ji* 襄陽記 [*Records of Xiangyang*] as quoted in Pei Songzhi's *Commentary*. See *Sgz*, 41.1008, n. 1. A later biography is included in the *Jin History*. See *Js*, 57.1551.

56. The graph for Li's given name was rendered as 密 in pre-Song times, but was later rendered as 宓. His name is sometimes given as "Li Qian" 李虔. Ren Naiqiang notes that this was a scribal error for the graph *fu* 虙, itself a variant reading for the graph *mi/fu* 宓. See *Hygz*, 11.640 n. 13. The earliest biographical information is contained in the *Records of the States South of Mount Hua*. See *Hygz*, 11.637–641. A later biography in the *Jin History* follows closely the *Hygz* account. See *Js*, 88.2274–2276.

57. The earliest biographical account of Du Zhen is located in the *Records of the States South of Mount Hua*. See *Hygz*, 11.641–644. The *Jin History* account is largely based on the *Hygz* biography. See *Js*, 90.2331–2332.

58. The *Records of the States South of Mount Hua* provides the basic biographical account, though the *Jin History* biography includes details from unknown sources. See

Hygz, 11.623–624; *Js*, 91.2347–2348. Pei Songzhi quotes portions of the *Hygz* biography in *Sgz*, 42.1032, n. 1. The *Jin History* biography appears to have been based on Pei's abridgment of Chang Qu's text rather than the lengthier extant *Hygz* version.

59. Biographical information on Chen Shou can be found in both the *Records of the States South of Mount Hua* and the *Jin History*. While the *Jin History* narrative focused primarily on Chen's official career and the circumstances surrounding the compositon of the *Records of the Three States*, the *Records of the States South of Mount Hua* account provided more detail on Chen's early training and other intellectual activities. See *Hygz*, 11.634–637; *Js*, 82.2137–2138. A lengthy critical biography of Chen Shou can be found in Yang and Wu, *Chen Shou Pei Songzhi pingzhuan*.

60. *Hygz*, 11.623.

61. *Sgz*, 42.1030.

62. The *Records of the States South of Mount Hua* notes that Li Mi wrote a now-lost work entitled "Shuli lun" 述理論 ["Discourse on Propagating Principles"] that discussed matters of loyalty and righteousness, and "the matter of the Daoist transformation of classicist studies" that was highly regarded by Jin intellectuals such as Huangfu Mi. From this description, it appears that Li Mi may have been influenced by the current of Mystery Learning; rare for Sichuan intellectuals of the third century. See *Hygz*, 11.638.

63. *Js*, 57.1551.

64. *Sj*, 67.2195. This characterization was based on the *Analects*' classification of Zigong under the category of "Speech." *Lun yu*, 11/3.

65. *Js*, 88.2274.

66. *Lun yu*, 11/3.

67. *Lun yu*, 11/3. Also see *Sj*, 67.2187–2188; Nienhauser, *Grand Scribe's Records*, 7:64–65.

68. *Sgz*, 42.1032.

69. This information is not contained in the *Jin History* biography of Chen Shou, but rather in that of Wen Li. Given the age difference between Chen Shou and the older students of Qiao Zhou, one wonders who might have given this nickname to Chen or even if it was self-bestowed. See *Js*, 91.2347.

70. For Luo Xian's dismissal, see *Sgz*, 41.1008 n. 1; *Js*, 57.1551. For Chen Shou's dismissal, see *Js*, 82.2137.

71. After the fall of Shu-Han, there is also evidence to indicate that Qiao Zhou's students recommended each other for posts under the Jin. Luo Xian's recommendation of Du Zhen and Chen Shou to Emperor Wu of Jin is a prime example. The *Records of Xiangyang* notes that these men all received appointments on the basis of Luo's recommendation. See *Sgz*, 41.1008 n. 1.

72. *Js*, 88.2275–2276.

73. *Hygz*, 11.624.

74. *Sgz*, 39.986.

75. For a biography of Dong Yun, see *Sgz*, 39.985–987.

76. *Sgz*, 39.986.

77. *Sgz*, 33.897. Some scholars have ascribed the purpose of this journey to the inspection of waterworks; others have interpreted the trip as the referent for the later criticisms of Liu Shan's exucrsions. See *Sgzjj*, 33.10b–11b. Hu Sanxing, commenting on this passage in the *Comprehensive Mirror for Aid in Governing* says, "At the death of Zhuge Liang, the Han sovereign ventured out sightseeing, and no one dared to stop him." See *Zztj*, 73.2315.

78. *Sgz*, 42.1028.

79. *Sgz*, 42.1028.

80. *Sgz*, 42.1028.

81. Yao Qi was a supporter of Liu Xiu and accompanied him on his campaigns against Wang Lang, the Bronze Horses, and the Red Eyebrows. After the establishment of the Later Han, he served in a number of military and civil posts. See *HHs*, 20.731–734.

82. *Sgz*, 42.1028.

83. The *Hallowed Documents* says, "But when a deceased father, wishing to build a house, had laid out the plan, if his son be unwilling to raise up the hall, how much less will he be willing to complete the roof!" *Shang shu*, "Da gao," 11. See Karlgren, "Documents," 37–39; James Legge, trans., *The Chinese Classics*, 5 volumes (1861–1872. Reprint; Hong Kong: Hong Kong University Press, 1960), 3:371–372.

84. *Sgz*, 42.1028.

85. *Zztj*, 75.2368. Fang, *Chronicle*, 2:4.

86. Jiang Wei , appellative Boyue 伯約, was a native of Ji prefecture in Tianshui. His father, Jiang Jiong 姜冏, had been a general under Cao Cao, but, in 228 CE, Jiang Wei returned to Shu where he was made general upholding righteousness by Zhuge Liang. On Zhuge's death, Jiang took charge of military affairs of Shu. After Liu Shan surrendered to Deng Ai, Jiang was ordered to surrender to Zhong Hui 鍾會. Zhong plotted to rebel against Wei, and Jiang joined the rebellion, hoping to reestablish Shu. The plot was unsuccessful and Jiang was killed in battle. See *Sgz*, 44.1062–1069.

87. Cited in Pei Songzhi's *Commentary*. See *Sgz*, 44.1064, n. 1.

88. For a summary of these events, see Xu Zhaoren 徐兆仁, *Sanguo taolüe* 三國韜略 [*Summary of Three States Military Affairs*] (Beijing: Zhongguo renmin daxue chubanshe, 1995), 849.

89. For a biography of Zhang Ji, see *Sgz*, 45.1073–1075.

90. *Sgz*, 45.1075.

91. Didao was located on the Tao River near present-day Lintao 臨洮, Gansu.

92. For a biography of Wang Jing, see *Sgz*, 9.304–305.

93. The Tao River is a tributary of the Yellow River. It flows eastward from northwest Sichuan until it reaches present-day Min county, Gansu, where it turns northward. It conjoins the Yellow River west of present-day Lanzhou, Gansu.

94. *Sgz*, 45.1075.

95. For a biography of Chen Tai, see *Sgz*, 22.638–642.For a summary of these events, see Xu, *Sanguo taolüe*, 861.

96. For a biography of Deng Ai, see *Sgz*, 28.775–783.

97. Duangu was located on the Wei 渭 River near present-day Dashui 大水, Gansu.

98. See *Sgz*, 44.1064. Also see Xu, *Sanguo taolüe*, 862.

99. The Mang River is a tributary joining the Wei River west of Chang'an.

100. For a biography of Sima Wang, see *Js*, 37.1085–1087.

101. See *Sgz*, 44.1065; Xu, *Sanguo taolüe*, 868.

102. See *Sgz*, 44.1065; Xu, *Sanguo taolüe*, 874.

103. See *Laozi* 60.

104. *Sgz*, 44.1069.

105. *Zztj*, 77.2451. For "crafty heart seeking to enlarge the borders of the state," see *Zuo zhuan*, Cheng 8. Hu also notes, "Because of his many campaigns, Jiang Wei lost Shu and died just as Qiao Zhou said." *Zztj*, 77.2441.

106. For a biography of Liao Hua, see *Sgz*, 45.1077.

107. See *Zuo zhuan*, Yin 4. Legge translates this passage as "Military weapons are like fire; if you don't lay the fire aside, you will burn yourself." Legge, *Chinese Classics*, 5:16.

108. I.e., in this time of distress. See Mao 192. Karlgren, *Book of Odes* (Stockholm: Museum of Far Eastern Antiquities, 1974), 135–137.

109. Cited in Pei Songzhi's *Commentary*. See *Sgz*, 45.1077, n. 1.

110. *Sgz*, 42.1029–1030.

111. *Sgz*, 39.987.

112. *Sgz*, 39.986. The post of assistant of the Yellow Gates presumably refers to the aide to the prefect of the Yellow Gates, a eunuch in charge of eunuchs who attended the emperor. The prefect's salary was six hundred bushels, but no mention of the assistant's salary is made. The post was clearly low in rank and status. See Hucker, *Official Titles*, 261.

113. *Sgz*, 39.987.

114. *Sgz*, 39.987.

115. *Sgz*, 38.963–969.

116. *Sgz*, 39.987.

117. *Sgz*, 39.987.

118. *Hygz*, 7.417.

119. *Zztj*, 77.440–441. Fang, *Chronicle*, 2:265–266. The *Comprehensive Mirror for Aid in Governing* also quotes a large poriton of Qiao's treatise, though it eliminates the names of the interlocutors. Long Xianzhao follows the *Records of the States South of Mount Hua*, dating the text from 257 CE. See Long, "Qiao Zhou," 73.

120. For a biography of Zhuge Dan, see *Sgz*, 28.769–774.

121. *Hygz*, 7.417.

122. The name of Chen Zhi's dramatic persona is multi dimensional. The first graph, *gao*, can mean "tall," "lofty," "exalted," etc., and function as a surname. The remaining two graphs are generally rendered as "worthy" (*xian*) and "minister" (*qing*). Therefore, other possible translations of the name could be "Mr. Exalted-worthy Minister,"

"Mr. Exalted Minister," "Worthy Minister Gao," or even, treating it as an untranslated Chinese name, "Gao Xianqing." The translation possibilities are even more free for the pseudonym Qiao Zhou attaches to himself in the "Discourse": "Mr. Falling-down Fool." Here, the first graph *fu* also contains several possible meanings: "to fall down," "prostrate," "to embrace," "a recluse," and a surname. The second graph, *yu*, is generally rendered as "fool" or "stupid." Finally, the graph *zi* simply denotes a person, often rendered "Master" in early Chinese philosophical texts. Thus, Qiao's dramatic persona could be translated in a number of different ways: "Mr. Falling-down Fool," "Master Who Embraces Stupidity," "Master Who Secludes Himself in Stupidity," "Fu the Fool," "Mr. Prostrate Stupid," or again, be rendered untranslated as a Chinese name "Fu Yuzi."

123. *Sgz*, 42.1029.

124. *Sgz*, 42.1029. Structurally, the principle is expressed in two sets of parallel lines. Lines 2–3 are near perfect opposites: large state–small state; no worries–has worries; indolence–good. Lines 4–5, while repeating the conditions stated in the preceeding two lines, also conclude with polar opposites: chaos and order. In addition to the parallel structure of this passage, lines 2–4 also end with a common rhyme.

125. For King Wen, see *Sj*, 4.116–118; Nienhauser, *Grand Scribe's Records*, 1:58. For Gou Jian, see *Sj*, 66.2177–2181; Nienhauser, *Grand Scribe's Records*, 7:55–59.

126. *Sgz*, 42.1029.

127. For a concise summary of these events, see de Crespigny, "The Three Kingdoms and Western Jin," 1:33–36. Also see Fang, *Chronicle*, 1:635–698; Ma, *Sanguo shi*, 165–180; He, *Sanguo shi*, 209–222; and Zhou Yiliang, "Cao shi Sima shi zhi douzheng" 曹氏司馬氏之鬥爭 ["The Conflict Between the Cao and Sima Clans"], in *Wei Jin Nanbeichao shi zaji* 魏晉南北朝史雜記 [*Miscellaneous Notes on the History of the Wei, Jin, and Northern and Southern Dynasties*] (Beijing: Zhonghua shuju, 1985), 26–37.

128. *Sgz*, 42.1029.

129. *Sgz*, 42.1030.

130. Hucker, *Official Titles*, 288. It should be noted that Chen Zhi, as prefect of the masters of writing, drew a salary of one thousand bushels.

131. *Sgz*, 42.1030.

132. The *Records of the States South of Mount Hua* account of the debate concludes with the statement, "No one questioned this." See *Hygz*, 7.417.

133. He Ziquan graphically describes the situation as follows: "The people were famished, the ruler was muddleheaded, everyone was seeking a moment's peace, the great officers charged with assisting the ruler did not dare to live in the capital, but fled to the frontier to cultivate millet. These were the circumstances of Shu-Han. These were the circumstances of [a state] waiting for destruction." See He, *Sanguo shi*, 264.

134. For a summary of these events, see He, *Sanguo shi*, 259–270; and Ma, *Sanguo shi*, 185–192.

135. *Sgz*, 42.1030.

136. *Sgz*, 42.1030.

137. *Sgz*, 42.1030.

138. *Sgz*, 42.1030.

139. *Zhou Yi*, hexagram 1, 9/6.

140. *Sgz*, 42.1031.

141. King Zhou is regarded as an archetypical "last bad king." The prince of Wei was said to have recognized his brother's corruptness and asked his tutors for advice. The Prince was urged to flee the state. See *Shangshu*, "Wei zi;" Legge, *Chinese Classics*, 3:273–279. After his brother's death, the prince submitted to King Wu of Zhou. See *Zuo zhuan*, Xi, 6; Legge, *Chinese Classics*, 5:146–147.

142. *Sgz*, 42.1031.

143. See Xu Heping 徐鶴屏, "Shixi Shu-Han dui shaoshu minzu de zhengce" 試析蜀漢對少數民族的政策 ["An Examination of the Shu-Han Policy Toward Ethnic Minorities"], in *Zhongnan minzu xueyuan xuebao: Zhexue kexue ban* 中南民族學院學報:哲學科學版 (1988): 4, 34–38. This article paints an overly positive picture of Shu-Han's policies and their acceptance by the indigenous populations of Nanzhong and, as such, stands in stark contrast to the conditions described by Qiao Zhou.

144. For a summary account of the southern campaign and Shu-Han–minority relations, see He, *Sanguo shi*, 176–183. Specific details can be found in the biographies of Zhuge Liang, Liu Hui, Ma Zhong, and others.

145. *Sgz*, 33.900.

146. Liu Chen was the fifth son of Liu Shan. In 259 CE he was ennobled as King of the Northern Territories (Beidi wang 北地王). See *Sgz*, 34.908, n. 1.

147. Cited in Pei Songzhi's *Commentary*. See *Sgz*, 33.900–901, n. 1.

148. Cited in Pei Songzhi's *Commentary*. See *Sgz*, 33.900–901, n. 1.

149. *Sgz*, 33.900.

150. The title of general of the agile cavalry (*piaoji jiangjun* 飄騎將軍) was bestowed on either military officers on assignment or favored courtiers with no military significance. Deng Ai's conferral of this title of Liu Shan was clearly a case of the latter. See Hucker, *Official Titles*, 379.

151. Liu Shan's sons and grandsons were also given benefices and official posts. In all, over fifty members of the former Shu-Han imperial family received such honors. See *Sgz*, 33.902.

152. The primary accounts of the surrender of Shu-Han are located in *Sgz*, 33.900–903; *Hygz*, 7.424–425; *Zztj*, 78.2472–2474.

153. In his postface to the collected writings of Zhuge Liang, Chen Shou seems to defend Zhuge against these charges, arguing that he was dealing with common people and thus his writings tended to be direct and instructive rather than embellished and ornamental. See *Sgz*, 35.931.

154. *Sgz*, 42.1022.

155. Chou succeeded his father as Duke Wen 文 of Jin. Upon Duke Wen's death, his son Duke Zhao 昭 took the throne and enobled his uncle Chengshi as earl of Quwo 曲沃. In 739 BCE, Duke Zhao was murdered and Chengshi was invited to return to Jin, but his troops were defeated. He then returned to Quwo, and three generations later, his grandson Duke Wu 武 of Quwo conquered Jin in 678 BCE. See *Zuozhuan*, Huan, 2. For a translations, see Legge, *Chinese Classics*, 5: 40–43.

156. Shihou was the designation of Liu Bian 劉辨, Emperor Shao 少 of Han (r. 189 CE). He was removed from the throne by Dong Zhuo the same year as his accession. He was replaced by his half-brother Liu Xie, who ruled as Emperor Xian and later abdicated to Cao Pi. See *HHs*, 10B.449–450.

157. *Sgz*, 42.1022.

158. Liu Xiang described this as "when the orders from the superior disagree with the common people's will, the ruler would then be unable to regulate his empire." See *Hs*, 27B.1376.

159. See Lu Zongli, "Heaven's Mandate," Ph.D. dissertation (University of Wisconsin, 1995), 171.

160. The *Song History* and *Jin History* treatises also record this prophesy, though with minor modifications. Neither account provides the portion of the prophesy noting the historical cases of Duke Mu or Emperor Ling. They each render Qiao Zhou's closing remarks as "This is really like the omens of the meaning of the naming of the sons of Duke Mu and Emperor Ling." See *Js*, 28.834; *Song*, 31.899. Only Shen Yue's narrative in the *Song History* offers a historical postface, which reads, "Shu was subsequently lost. This is an example of inconsistent words." *Song*, 31.899.

161. *Sgz*, 42.1023.

162. In their accounts of this prophesy, both the *Song History* and *Jin History* include Chen Shou's explanation as part of the prophesy itself, adding the appearance that Qiao Zhou himself provided the interpretation of the prophesy. Both histories offer the following postface: "Shu was lost like Qiao Zhou had said. The [tree falling] was a grass omen (*cao yao* 草妖)." See *Js*, 28.858; *Song*, 32.938.

163. Lu, *Power of the Words*, 23–24.

164. *Hygz*, 9.516.

165. Cited in Pei Songzhi's *Commentary*. See *Sgz*, 33.902, n. 1.

166. The *Records of the States South of Mount Hua* lists Qiao's place of benefice as "Chengyang" 城陽 commune. See *Hygz*, 596. The *Sui History* lists it as "Yiyang" 義陽 commune. See *Sui*, 33.953.

167. *Sgz*, 42.1032.

168. *Sgz*, 42.1032.

169. The office of chief commandant of the cavalry (*qiduwei* 騎都尉) was a functional military post, apparently given on an ad hoc basis. See Hucker, *Official Titles*, 134. Because Qiao Zhou possessed no military background, it seems likely that the title was honorary and that no real military duties were implied.

170. *Sgz*, 42.1032.

171. The rectifier (*zhongzheng* 中正) was a local dignitary appointed to register and classify all males within his jurisdiction who were eligible for governmental service on the basis of their social status. See Hucker, *Official Titles*, 189.

172. *Sgz*, 42.1033.

173. *Sgz*, 42.1033.

174. The office of cavalier attendant in regular attendance (*sanqi changshi* 散騎常侍) was an honorific title that accorded the bearer access to the ruler. See Hucker, *Official Titles*, 395.

175. Cited in Pei Songzhi's *Commentary*. See *Sgz*, 42.1033, n. 1.

176. Cited in Pei Songzhi's *Commentary*. See *Sgz*, 42.1033, n. 1.

177. Present-day Nanchong 南充, Sichuan. A brief history of Qiao Zhou's grave has been compiled by Wang Hua 王化. The grave has been moved several times, and now rests in a city park in Nanchong. See Wang Hua, "Qiao Zhou mu" 譙周墓 ["Qiao Zhou's Grave"], in Wang Zhihou 王稙厚, ed., *Mingren mingsheng* 名人名勝 [*Famous People and Famous Things*] (Chengdu: Sichuan cidian chubanshe, 1990), 22–24.

178. A fundamental principle of early Chinese historical writing was to offer moral commentary on the past and provide exemplars of virtue to guide the present. These commentaries and admonitions generally focused on the larger political enterprise: the rise and fall of rulers and states. Biographies in historical writings, thus, provided a powerful vehicle for this task, offering one case study after another testifying to the power of individuals to benefit or ruin the grand enterprise of statecraft. See Denis Twitchett, "Chinese Biographical Writing," in W. G. Beasley and E. G. Pulleyblank, eds., *Historians of China and Japan* (London: Oxford University Press, 1961), 95–114; Twitchett, "Problems of Chinese Biography," in Arthur Wright and Denis Twitchett, eds., *Confucian Personalities* (Stanford: Stanford University Press, 1962), 24–39; and chapter 8 of Twitchett, *The Writing of Official History Under the Tang* (Cambridge: Cambridge University Press, 1992), 62–83.

179. *Sgz*, 42.1033.

CHAPTER 4

1. For a concise yet nuanced overview of the canon and its cultural significance, see Michael Nylan, *The Five "Confucian" Classics* (New Haven: Yale University Press, 2001), 1–71. The remainder of Nylan's book treats the individual texts of the Han canon. On the history of Chinese canonical studies, see Pi, *Jingxue lishi*. For English-language overviews of the state of classical studies during the Han, see Robert P. Kramers, "The Development of the Confucian Schools," in *CHC*, 1:747–765; Ch'en Ch'i-yün, "Confucian, Legalist, and Taoist Thought in Later Han," in *CHC*, 1:766–807.

2. For a study of the forms and significance of canonical commentary in China, see Daniel K. Gardner, "Confucian Commentary and Chinese Intellectual History," *Journal of Asian Studies*, 57.2 (May 1998): 397–422. Other useful studies include Wagner, *The Craft of a Chinese Commentator;* Martin Kern, "Ritual, Text, and the Formation of the Canon," *T'oung Pao* 87 (2001): 43–91.

3. The "Great Proscriptions" were more than just intellectual purges, and were only one part of a larger struggle between various interest groups at court, including imperial in-laws, eunuchs, and bureaucratic officials. On the "Great Proscriptions," see *CHC*, 1: 328–330.

4. Yoshikawa Tadao posits that the imperial academy was restricted to the so-called New Text interpretations of the canon, and that those wishing to teach or study the "Old Text" interpretations were forced to travel to these private schools. For an overview of the general situation and a detailed study of the academy in Jing, see Yoshikawa, "Scholarship in Ching-chou," 1–6.

5. Xie Xianghao 謝祥皓 and Liu Zongxian 劉宗賢, *Zhongguo ruxue* 中國儒學 [*Chinese Classical Studies*] (Chengdu: Sichuan renmin chubanshe, 1998), 279–297.

6. For the official biography of Ma Rong, see *HHs*, 60A.1953–1978.

7. Jing Fang 京房 (77–37 BCE) was a second-generation disciple of Meng Xi 孟喜 (ca. 90–40 BCE). Meng's interpretation of the *Changes* linked the ancient divination text to the cyclical changes of *yin* and *yang* and the five conducts theories of the early Han, and was highly valued for its use in the interpretation of portents and prophesies. Jing Fang continued this view of the text.

8. Gaomi was located near present-day Gaomi, Shandong Province. For a brief discussion of Zheng's academy, see Yoshikawa, "Scholarship in Ching-chou," 4.

9. For the official biographies of Liu Biao, see *Sgz*, 6.210–217; *HHs*, 74B.2419–2426. Liu Biao's academy is treated in great detail in Yoshikawa, "Scholarship in Ching-chou." For a recent study on Liu Biao's political ambitions, see Chittick, "Liu Biao."

10. While Song Zhong has no biography in the standard histories, a brief account is found in Lu Deming's 陸德明 (556–627 CE) *Jingdian shiwen* 經典釋文 [*Explaining the Canon*], 1.18 (*Congshu jicheng chubian* ed).

11. *HHs*, 74B.2421. Translated in Yoshikawa, "Scholarship in Ching-chou," 7.

12. The official biography of Wang Can is located in *Sgz*, 21.597–598. For a study of Wang, see Ronald Miao, *Early Medieval Chinese Poetry: The Life and Verse of Wang Ts'an (A.D. 177–217)* (Wiesbaden: Steiner, 1982).

13. In *Ywlj*, 38.693; *Tpyl*, 607.8a–b. Translated in Yoshikawa, "Scholarship in Ching-chou," 11.

14. See the bibliographic treatises in the *Sui* and *New Tang Histories*. *Sui*, 32.909; *XTs*, 57.1424.

15. *Sgz*, 13.414.

16. For the official biography of Wang Su, see *Sgz*, 13.414–423. For a translation, see R. P. Kramers, *K'ung Tzu Chia Yu: The School Sayings of Confucius* (Leiden: E. J. Brill, 1950), 54–72.

17. *Sgz*, 13.419; Kramers, *School Sayings*, 71.

18. Kramers, *School Sayings*, 79–89.

19. See Kramers, *School Sayings*, 84. All of these issues were also addressed by Qiao Zhou.

20. Pi, *Jingxue lishi*, 145.

21. The *Records of the Three States* dates Xu Ci's arrival to "the Jian'an period." See *Sgz*, 42.1023.

22. For the biography of Xu Ci, see *Sgz*, 42.1022–1023. Also see chapter 1.

23. See *Sgz*, 42.1025. See chapter 1. For the possible educational duties of this post, see chapter 1.

24. *Sgz*, 42.1026. See chapter 1.

25. Jia Kui was a descendent of the noted early Han scholar Jia Yi 賈誼 and a master of several canonical texts. He is most noted for his eclectic approach and commentaries on the *Zuo Tradition* and *Discourses from the States*. Fan Ye's appraisal for Jia notes that "the scholarship of Zheng Xuan and Jia Kui has been transmitted for several hundred years, and is much revered by all classicists." For his official biography, see *HHs*, 36.1234–1241.

26. *Sgz*, 42.1027.

27. Yoshikawa, "Scholarship in Ching-chou," 23.

28. *Sgz*, 42.1023. Chen Shou's account in *Records of the Three States* offers a somewhat tragi-comic account of early scholarship under Liu Bei, including petty feuds, fistfights, and public performances mocking various scholars. See chapter 1.

29. Yoshikawa, "Scholarship in Ching-chou," 24.

30. Unfortunately, only a limited amount of Qiao Zhou's canonical studies have survived, and that which has is in very poor condition. The resulting body of work thus lends itself only to tentative analysis.

31. *Sgz*, 42.1027.

32. *Sgz*, 38.976.

33. *Hygz*, 10B.567.

34. *Sgz*, 38.976.

35. *Sgz*, 42.1033. Later bibliographies record a work under the title *Wujing ranfou lun* 五經然否論 [*Discourse on the Truths and Falsehoods in the Five Canonical Texts*], in five fascicles. See *Sui*, 32.938; *JTs*, 46.1983; *XTs*, 57.1445. It seems likely that these two titles reference the same text. Qiao's *Discourse on the Truths and Falsehoods in the Five Canonical Texts* appears to have circulated into the Song period, for references to the *Discourse on Truths and Falsehoods in the Five Canonical Texts* are found in the bibliographic essays of the Sui and Tang standard histories, but no later mention of the text is found in either the bibliographies of the standard histories or in private bibliographic catalogs, leading to the conclusion that the text as a whole was lost during the Song period.

36. See Gardiner for a discussion of the appeal and practice of interlinear commentary. Gardiner, "Confucian Commentary," 400–404.

37. Despite the loss of the complete text, a number of fragments have survived, quoted in a variety of sources. The primary repository of *Discourse on Truths and Falsehoods in the Five Canonical Texts* fragments is Du You's *Encyclopedic History of Institutions*; see Du You, *Tongdian* (Beijing: Zhonghua shuju, 1996) (hereafter cited as *Td*). Additional portions of Qiao's text are quoted in Li Fang's 李昉 (925–996 CE) *Taiping yulan* 太平御覽 [*Imperially Reviewed Encyclopedia of the Taiping Period*] (Li Fang, et al., eds. *Taiping yulan* (Beijing: Zhonghua shuju, 1998) (hereafter cited as *Tpyl*), the treatises of the *Continued Han History* (for an English-language study, see B. J. Mansvelt Beck, *The Treatises of the Later Han, Their Authorship, Sources, Contents, and Place in Chinese Historiography* (Leiden: Brill, 1990)); and *Song History*, and in later commentaries on several canonical texts.

Fragments of Qiao Zhou's *Discourse on Truths and Falsehoods in the Five Canonical Texts* were collected and recompiled by several scholars. Most notable are two Qing reconstructions of the text by Wang Mo 王莫 and Ma Guohan 馬國翰 (1794–1857 CE). Huang Shi 黃奭 also includes a reconstruction in his collection of recompiled ancient texts, *Huang shi yishu kao* 黃氏逸書考 [*Mr. Huang's Examination of Lost Books*], but it appears that Huang's work is actually a reproduction of Ma Guohan's, including Ma's collation notes.

For a detailed textual history of the work, see Farmer, "World of the Mind," 162–165.

38. One fragment of the *Discourse on the Truths and Falsehoods in the Five Canonical Texts* was gleaned from the *Shi zhengyi* 詩正義 [*Orthodox Meaning of the Odes*], and while dealing with matters of ritual, may have been from an original section of Qiao's work dealing with the *Odes*. From Qiao Zhou's writings on ancient history, we are able to see something of his approach to the *Spring and Autumn*. See below.

Yan Zhitui 顏之推 (531–ca. 591 CE) mentions a commentary on the *Changes* by an individual known as "The Talent of Shu" (Shu cai 蜀才). The standard bibliographies of the *Sui History* and two *Tang Histories* each note the existence of a "*Zhou Changes* in ten fascicles with Commentary by The Talent of Shu." The *Sui History* bibliography also contains an entry for "*Laozi's Canon of the Way and Its Potency* in two fascicles with Commentary by The Talent of Shu; lost." The two *Tang Histories* also note this commentary, but make no reference to its condition. Today some twenty-six fragments of *The Talent of Shu's Commentary on the Zhou Changes* survive, incorporated into later commentaries on the base text. These fragments are all in the form of brief character glosses, employed by the later commentators as examples of textual variants in the *Zhou Changes*. In its current form, little can be said about the original work. While Yan Zhitui makes no claims as to the identity of "The Talent of Shu," he includes the opinions of several others, including Xie Gui 謝炅 and Xiahou Kai 夏侯該, who argue that "The Talent of Shu" was Qiao Zhou. See Yan Zhitui, *Yan shi jiaxun* 顏氏家訓 [*Family Teachings of Mr. Yan*] (Beijing: Zhonghua shuju, 1996), 17.440.

39. Of the twenty-eight extant passages of Qiao's text, three address issues of capping and marriage, five discuss offerings, and twenty deal with various matters of mourning and burial.

40. See Pi Xirui, *Jingxue tonglun* 經學通論 [*Comprehensive Discourses on Canonical Studies*] (1954. Reprint, Beijing: Zhonghua shuju, 1998), 3.1. Also see Pi, *Jingxue lishi*; and Robert Kramers' summary of classical studies during the Han in *CHC*, 1: 747–765.

41. For concise introductions to these texts, see William G. Boltz, "Chou li," in *ECT*, 24–32; William G. Boltz, "I li," in *ECT*, 234–243; Jeffrey K. Riegel, "Li chi," in *ECT*, 293–297.

42. Pi, *Jingxue tonglun*, 3.40.

43. *Liji zhengyi*, 61.453–454.

44. *Liji zhengyi*, 61.454.

45. During the Zhou, the era purportedly represented in the ritual texts, the title of grandee (*daifu* 大夫) designated the second highest category of officials. The office of grandee fell below the rank of minister (*qing* 卿), but ranked above that of an ordinary officer (*shi* 士). See Hucker, *Official Titles*, 465.

46. *Yili zhushu*, 1.1.

47. *Renwu* and *guiwei* are successive years in the *jiazi* sixty-year cycle.

48. There is no extant section with this title in the current *Ceremonies and Rites*, though the text does briefly mention the capping of a ducal heir. Moreover, the received edition of the *Rites* contains no mention of the Duke of Zhou capping King Cheng. The words of blessing were presumably those ordered by the Duke of Zhou upon King Wu's illness. See *Sj*, 33.1510.

49. *Td*, 56.1571.

50. This information is not contained in the received edition of the *Documents*. Also see Sun Xingyan 孫星衍, *Shangshu jingu wen zhuzhu* 尚書今古文注疏 [*Commentary and Subcommentary on the Old and New Text Hallowed Documents*] (Beijing: Zhonghua shuju, 1986), 232–241.

51. Cited in *Td*, 56.1571.

52. See *Zhouli zhushu*, 21.782.

53. *Guliang zhuan*, Wen, 12.

54. Cited in commentary to *Guliang zhuan*, Wen, 12 (*Shisan* ed.).

55. *Zhouli zhushu*, 14.95.

56. Cited in commentary to *Guliang zhuan*, Wen, 12 (*Shisan* ed.).

57. *Guliang zhuan*, Wen, 12. In *Shisan*, 1408–1409.

58. Chen Xuguo, *Wei, Jin, Nanbei chao lizhi yanjiu* 魏晉南北朝禮制研究 [*Studies on Ritual during the Wei, Jin, and Northern-Southern Dynasties*] (Changsha: Hunan jiaoyu chubanshe, 1995), 67–74.

59. *Liji zhengyi*, 47.364.

60. *Td*, 48.1347.

61. *Td*, 48.1347.

62. *Td*, 48.1347.

63. *Td*, 49.1369. For a detailed discussion of these temples, see *Liji zhengyi*, 46.360–361.

64. *Td*, 52.1450.

65. This information is not contained in the received editions of the ritual texts.

66. La, or New Year's.

67. *Td*, 49.1369.

68. *Td*, 49.1368–1369.

69. See Chen, *Wei, Jin, Nanbei chao lizhi yanjiu*, 25–32.

70. *Yili zhushu*, 30.159.

71. *Yili zhushu*, 30.159.

72. *Td*, 94.2555.

73. *Td*, 94.2555.

74. *Yili zhushu*, 30.159. The passage quoted by Qiao Zhou differs somewhat from the passage as it appears in the *Shisan jing zhushu* edition, but there are no substantial differences in meaning between the two quotes.

75. *Td*, 94.2556.

76. *Td*, 94.2556.

77. *Liji zhengyi*, 8.62. For a translation, see Legge, *Li Ki*, 1:151.

78. *Liji zhengyi*, 8.62.

79. Emphasis added.

80. *Td*, 91.1494–1495.

81. *Td*, 91.1495. See Wang Su, ed., *Kongzi jiayu*, 10.3a (Sbby ed.). For an introduction to the texts, see R. P. Kramers, "K'ung tzu chia yü," in *Early Chinese Texts*. Also see Kramers, *K'ung Tzu Chia Yu*, 1–200.

82. *Td*, 91.1495.

83. The *Encyclopedic History of Institutions* cites several examples from the Jin and Song period following Wang Su. See *Td*, 91.1495–1496.

84. Yoshikawa notes that Tian Qiong was a student of Zheng Xuan. See Yoshikawa, "Scholarship in Ching-chou," 9. I have not been able to locate additional biographical information on Tian.

85. *Td*, 93.2532.

86. *Td*, 93.2532.

87. This refers to persons with a common ancestor outside the direct parent–child line, including brothers and sisters, cousins, aunts and uncles, and their spouses. The term *pangqin* 旁親 was introduced by Zheng Xuan in his gloss on a passage in the *Records of Rites*. See *Liji zhengyi*, 33.273; Legge, *Li Ki*, 2:53.

88. *Td*, 93.2532.

89. *Td*, 93.2532–2533.

90. *Td*, 93.2533.

91. *Td*, 93.2533.

92. *Td*, 93.2533.

93. *Yili zhushu*, 32.171.

94. *Td*, 93.2533.

95. *Td*, 93.2533.

96. *Td*, 93.2533–2534.

97. *Td*, 93.2534.

98. Chen, *Wei, Jin, Nanbei chao lizhi yanjiu*, 32–37.

99. *Sgz*, 42.1028.

100. Chen, *Wei, Jin, Nanbei chao lizhi yanjiu*, 37–38.

101. *Td*, 88.2422.

102. For a brief overview of Kong Yingda and his *Orthodox Meanings of the Five Canonical Texts*, see Xie and Liu, *Zhongguo ruxue*, 454–457.

103. For a brief overview of Du You and his *Encyclopedic History of Institutions*, see Xie and Liu, *Zhongguo ruxeu*, 461–463.

104. See *Td*, 56.1571; *Guliang zhuan*, Wen, 12.

105. Qian Mu, "Jingxue yu shixue" 經學與史學 ["Canonical Studies and Historiography"], in ed. Du Weiyun 杜維運 and Huang Jinxing 黃進興, *Zhongguo shixue shi lunwen xuanji* 中國史學史論文選集 [*Selected Essays on the History of Chinese Historiography*] (Jingmei, Taiwan: Huashi chubanshe, 1976), 121.

106. Qian, "Jingxue yu shixue," 121.

107. Lu Yaodong, *Wei-Jin shixue de sixiang yu shehui jichu* 魏晉史學的思想與社會基礎 [*Wei-Jin Historiographical Thought and its Social Foundations*] (Taipei: Dongda tushu, 2000), 253.

108. Lu, *Wei-Jin shixue sixiang*, 256. Later, Lu cites Qiao Zhou's *Investigations of Ancient History* as the earliest independent work of historical criticism (267). I discuss the *Investigations of Ancient History* in detail in chapter 5.

CHAPTER 5

1. See Mark Edward Lewis, *Writing and Authority in Early China* (Albany: State University of New York Press, 1999), 99–146. Lewis offers detailed analysis of each of these forms for historical expression and their uses.

2. For a discussion of this text, see Lewis, *Writing and Authority*, 325–332.

3. A separate category of *Documents* was also included.

4. See *Hs*, 30.1712–1715.

5. Anthony DeBlasi concisely articulates some of the problems with the term "Confucian," noting our inability to define what intellectual concepts or even individuals that the label should include, and what and whom should be excluded. DeBlasi opts to use the term "classical" as his translation of "*ru*." See Anthony DeBlasi, *Reform in the Balance: The Defense of Literary Culture in Mid-Tang China* (Albany: State University of New York Press, 2002), 14–16. For a more detailed treatment, see Michael Nylan, "Han Confucianism," in *Imagining Boundaries: Changing Confucian Doctrines, Texts, and Hermeneutics*, ed. Kai-wing Chow, On-cho Ng, and John B. Henderson (Albany: State University of New York Press, 1999), 17–56.

6. See Lewis, *Writing and Authority*, 130–144. A detailed study of the *Zuo Tradition* and its place in Chinese historiography can be found in David Schaberg, *A Patterned Past: Form and Thought in Early Chinese Historiography* (Cambridge: Harvard University Asia Center, 2001).

7. This intent is drawn from Sima Qian's famous letter to his friend Ren An, as reproduced in the *Han History*. See *Hs*, 62.2735.

8. Lewis, *Writing and Authority*, 311–312.

9. For a concise introduction to the text, see A. F. P. Hulsewé, "Shih chi," in Loewe, *ECT*, 405–414. A lengthier account is found in Édouard Chavannes, *Les Mémoires Historiques de Se-Ma Ts'ien: Traduits et Annotés*, v. 1 (Paris: Librairie d'Amérique et d'Orient, 1967), I–CCXLIX. Also see Nienhauser, *Grand Scribe's Records*, 1: v–xxii.

10. For a concise introduction to the text, see A. F. P. Hulsesé, "Han shu," in Loewe, *ECT*, 129–136.

11. *Sui*, 32.928–932.

12. These included fifteen histories of the Later Han, seven histories of the Three States period, eight histories of the Jin, three histories of the Song, three histories of the Qi, three histories of the Liang, two histories of the Later Wei, one history of the Chen, and one history of the Zhou. See *Sui*, 33.953–956.

13. Several detailed and accessible accounts of the development of historical commentary during the early medieval period have been written by both Chinese and Western scholars. Two such studies merit special mention: a chapter entitled "The Separation of Canon and History and the Rise of Historical Criticism" in Lu Yaodong's monograph on early medieval historiography, and a chapter entitled

"Historical Commentary from the 2nd to 4th Century" from Scott Galer's doctoral dissertation. Lu, *Wei-Jin shixue sixiang*, 253–276; Scott W. Galer, "The Foundation of Text Critical *Shiji* Commentary: Xu Guang and the *Shiji yinyi*" (Ph.D. diss., University of Wisconsin–Madison, 2003), 9–77.

14. For lists of such efforts, see Hans Bielenstein, "The Restoration of the Han Dynasty, with Prolegomena of the Historiography of the *Hou Han shu*," 4 vols., *Bulletin of the Museum of Far Eastern Antiquities*, 26 (1954): 13; Mansvelt Beck, *Treatises of the Later Han*, 17–18. While Qiao Zhou's name is sometimes included among those said to have compiled histories of the later Han, this attribution is erroneous. See J. Michael Farmer, "How I Came to Doubt Qing Scholarship: The Case of Yao Zhenzong and Qiao Zhou's *Records of the Later Han*," *Monumenta Serica* 51 (2003): 237–251.

15. Scott Galer has compiled a detailed study on these early historical exegetes and their commentaries. The brief discussion here closely follows Galer's work. See Galer, "The Foundation of Text Critical *Shiji* Commentary," 9–77.

16. *HHs*, 64.2103–1208. For a more thorough discussion of Yan Du and his work, see Galer, "The Foundation of Text Critical *Shiji* Commentary," 27–32.

17. *HHs*, 64.2108.

18. No title is given for Hu Guang's *Han History* commentary, and only twelve fragments have survived. See Galer, "The Foundation of Text Critical *Shiji* Commentary," 36–39. For Hu Guang's official biography, see *HHs*, 44.1504–1512.

19. Ying Shao's commentary was contained in a work entitled *Hanshu jijie yinyi* 漢書集解音義 [*Collected Explanations Sounds and Meanings of the Han History*]. See Galer, "The Foundation of Text Critical *Shiji* Commentary," 40–42. For Ying Shao's official biography, see *HHs*, 48.1609–1615.

20. No title is given for Li Qi's *Han History* commentary, though over three hundred glosses survive, quoted in Yan Shigu's 嚴師古 (581–645 CE) commentary. Li Qi does not have a biography in the official histories. See Galer, "The Foundation of Text Critical *Shiji* Commentary," 42–43.

21. No title is given for Wen Ying's *Han History* commentary, and he was not accorded a biography in the official histories. See Galer, "The Foundation of Text Critical *Shiji* Commentary,"43–44.

22. Thirteen glosses from Fu Yan's *Qian Hanshu jiumiu* 前漢書糾謬 [*Rectifying Errors in the Former Han History*] survive. He has no official biography. See Galer, "The Foundation of Text Critical *Shiji* Commentary," 44–47.

23. Fu Qian's *Hanshu yinxun* 漢書音訓 [*Sounds and Explanations of the Han History*] was cited over five hundred times in Yan Shigu's commentary. For Fu Qian's biography, see *HHs*, 79.2582–2583. See Galer, "The Foundation of Text Critical *Shiji* Commentary," 47–49.

24. No title is attached to the over three hundred glosses attributed to Su Lin, though he was said to have compiled a *Hanshu yinyi* 漢書音義. A brief biographical note is found in *Sgz*, 21.621, n. 1. See Galer, "The Foundation of Text Critical *Shiji* Commentary," 49–51.

25. Over four hundred of Zhang Yan's glosses from his *Xi Hanshu yinshi* 西漢書音釋 [*Sounds and Explanations of the History of the Western Han*] were cited, and sometimes

criticized, in Yan Shigu's commentary. See Galer, "The Foundation of Text Critical *Shiji* Commentary," 51–54.

26. Meng Kang's *Hanshu yinyi* 漢書音義 was cited over five hundred times by Yan Shigu. No official biography exists, though Yan Shigu lists several offices that Meng Kang held under the Wei. See Galer, "The Foundation of Text Critical *Shiji* Commentary," 54–56.

27. Wei Zhao compiled several volumes of commentary on various canonical and historical texts. His *Hanshu yinyi* 漢書音義 was cited over five hundred times by Yan Shigu. For his official biography, see *Sgz*, 65.1460–1464. See Galer, "The Foundation of Text Critical *Shiji* Commentary," 56–60.

28. Few biographical details are available on Ru Chun, other than a brief note by Yan Shigu indicating that Ru served under the Wei. No title is attached to the over seven hundred glosses attributed to Ru Chun on the *Han History*. See Galer, "The Foundation of Text Critical *Shiji* Commentary," 60–63.

29. See John Henderson, *Scripture, Canon, and Commentary: A Comparison of Confucian and Western Exegesis* (Princeton: Princeton University Press, 1991), 75.

30. See *Hs*, 84.2784. Translation in Galer, "The Foundation of Text Critical *Shiji* Commentary," 32–33.

31. See *Sgz*, 59.1362.

32. This saying is attributed to Wang Mingsheng 王鳴盛 (1722–1798), and cited in Lu Bi's *Sanguo zhi jijie*, 59.1b. Translation in Galer, "The Foundation of Text Critical *Shiji* Commentary," 34.

33. Here, Meng Kang's text-critical approach stands against the norm, with its concern for identifying variants between *The Grand Scribe's Records* and *Han History* accounts of parallel events, and in its use of non-canonical texts to gloss the histories. See Galer, "The Foundation of Text Critical *Shiji* Commentary," 54–56.

34. Zhang Yan's commentary on the *Han History* is exceptional in its explication of lengthier passages of the base text, rather than the typical glosses of individual graphs or terms, as well as its provision of a few critical and interpretative comments. See Galer, "The Foundation of Text Critical *Shiji* Commentary," 51–54.

35. The work is mentioned in Chen Shou's bibliography attached to his biography of Qiao Zhou. Entries in the *Old Tang History* and *New Tang History* "Bibliographic Treatises" note the work in twenty-five fascicles under the heading of "Miscellaneous History" (see *JTs*, 46.1994; *XTs*, 58.1463). The text appears to have survived into the thirteenth century, where it was examined and commented on by Gao Sisun in his *Historical Epitome* (see Gao Sisun, *Shilüe* (*Bbcs* ed.), 1.18a–b). The traditional bibliographic sources make no further mention of *Investigations of Ancient History* until the Qing period, when several scholars collected the surviving fragments of the text and attempted to reconstruct the work.

36. Including works by Xu Guang, Gan Bao 干寶 (ca. 340 CE), Pei Yin, and Sima Zhen.

37. Such as Sima Biao's *Continued Han History*, Fan Ye's *Later Han History*, and Liu Zhiji's *Understanding History*.

38. Including commentaries to the *Selections of Refined Literature* and *New Account of Tales of the World*.

39. Several reconstructions of the text by Qing and more recent scholars exist. The most notable of these efforts is that of Zhang Zongyuan, who assembled ninety fragments, organizing them by the source of each fragment. In his preface to the work, Zhang discussed the generic classification of Qiao's *Investigations of Ancient History* in the traditional bibliographies, questioning the *Sui History*'s treatment of the work as commentary on a standard history, siding with the Tang histories' classification of the text as miscellaneous history. See Zhang Zongyuan, "Preface to Qiao Zhou's *Investigations of Ancient History*," *Pingjin guan congshu* 平津觀叢書 (*Bbcs* ed.), 1.2a–b. The biography of another noted Qing bibliographer, Tang Qiu 湯球 (CE 1803–1881) indicates that Tang recompiled a number of fragmented texts, including Qiao Zhou's *Investigations of Ancient History*, but this edition is no longer extant (see *Qing shi gao*, 486.13424). Huang Shi's collection of recompiled texts contains a text identical to that of Zhang Zongyuan, including verbatum reproductions of Zhang's collation notes. See chapter 4, note 37. Most recently, Cheng Jinzao 程金造, in a study of books cited in Sima Zhen's commentary on Sima Qian's *The Grand Scribe's Records*, collects fifty-two brief fragments of glosses from Qiao's text, organizing them by the chapter of *The Grand Scribe's Records* that they appear to comment on. Most of the fragments listed by Cheng are included among the unclassified fragments in Zhang Zongyuan's recompilation. See Cheng Jinzao, *Shiji suoyin yinshu kaoshi* 史記索隱引書考實 [*Investigation of Documents Cited in Seeking the Obscure in The Grand Scribe's Records*] (Beijing: Zhonghua shuju, 1998), 536–542. For an annotated translation of the surviving fragments, see Farmer, "The World of the Mind," 501–555.

40. *Js*, 82.2142. For the chronicle unearthed at Jizhong, see David Nivison, "Chu shu chi nien," in Loewe, *ECT*, 39–47.

41. Liu, *Shitong*, 12.6b.

42. "*Mao tong xin yi* 貌同心異." See Liu, *Shitong*, 8.1a–b.

43. For example, Gao Sisun quoted the *Jin History* statement in his *Historical Epitome*.

44. Zhang, "Preface," 1.2a.

45. This fragment is contained in the commentary to *Wen xuan*, 46.2060.

46. *Sj*, 130.3296.

47. *Hs*, 62.2737.

48. Chavannes notes the inclusion of material taken from numerous philosophical texts, official documents (memorials, edicts, etc.), inscriptions, and popular songs. See Chavannes, *Les Mémoires Historiques*, CIX–CLXXI. Takigawa offers an annotated bibliography of some fifty sources for the work. See Takigawa Kametarō, "Shiki shizai" 史記資材, in *Shiki kaichū kōshō fu kōho* 史記會注考證附校補 [*Collected Annotations and Examinations of* The Grand Scribe's Records, *with Collations and Appendices*] (Rpt. of Tokyo: Tōhō Bunka Gakuin 東方文化學院, 1934 ed. Taipei: Wenshizhe chubanshe, 1993), 1363–1368. Finally, Jin Dejian's bibliography notes eighty-seven textual sources for *The Grand Scribe's Records*. See Jin Dejian, *Sima Qian suojian shukao* 司馬遷所見書考 [*Investigation of Documents Seen by Sima Qian*] (Shanghai: Shanghai renmin chubanshe, 1963).

49. *Hs*, 88.3607.

50. Chavannes, *Les Mémoires Historiques*, CXXVI.

51. Jin, *Sima Qian suojian shukao*, 61–80.

52. Gu Guoshun, *Shiji shu Shangshu yanjiu* 史記述尚書研究 (Taipei: Wenshizhe chubanshe, 1985), 1–40. See especially page 6. Gu's basic arguments are supported with generous citations from the *Hallowed Documents* and *The Grand Scribe's Records*.

53. Gu Lisan, *Sima Qian zhuanxie* Shiji *caiyong* Zuozhuan *de yanjiu* 司馬遷撰寫史記採用左傳的研究 [*Studies on Sima Qian's Use of the* Zuo Tradition *while Compiling* The Grand Scribe's Records] (Taipei: Zhengzhong shuju, 1980), 4–11.

54. *Sjsy*, 34.1551 n. 1; *Sjjj*, 36.1576 n. 2; *Sjsy*, 43.1798 n. 1.

55. *Sjsy*, 46.1885 n. 1; 34.1552 n. 1; 4.113 n. 2. Pei Yin makes similar attributions in his commentary. See *Sjjj*, 34.1552 n. 1.

56. *Hs*, 62.2737.

57. *Sui*, 33.988.

58. *JTs*, 46.2012; *XTs*, 58.1499.

59. *HHs*, 40A.1325.

60. Yan Zhitui, *Yan shi jaixun*, 17.484. Yan cites his source for this information as Huangfu Mi's *Diwang shiji* 帝王世紀 [*Generations and Annals of Thearchs and Kings*]. See Yan Zhitui, *Yan shi jiaxun*, 17.487 n. 12.

61. Later scholars, while not universally accepting the claim of authorship by Zuo Qiuming, have followed the view that Liu Xiang and Song Zhong were not the text's authors, but were rather editors or commentators. See *Shiben bazhong* 世本八種 [*Eight Recompilations of the Roots of Generations*] (Beijing: Shangwu, 1957).

62. *Sj*, 70.2281.

63. *Sjjj*, 70.2281 n. 1.

64. Further examples of Qiao Zhou's glossing of place names can be found in the surviving fragments. Sima Qian, in the "Basic Annals of the Five Thearchs" notes, "Yao's son Danzhu 丹朱 and Shun's son Shangjun 商均 were allowed to have their own territories in order to offer sacrifices to their ancestors." See *Sj*, 1.44; Nienhauser, *Grand Scribe's Records*, 1: 16. Qiao Zhou provides the names of these benefices, writing, "Yao's son was given benefice at Tang 唐. Shun's son was given benefice at Yu 虞" (*Sjjj*, 1.45 n. 8). Interestingly enough, Qiao does not offer the locations of these benefices. Sima Zhen's *Seeking the Obscure in The Grand Scribe's Records* cites the Tang period gazetteer the *Record of Collected Territory* [*Kuodi zhi* 括地志] that sites Danzhu's benefice in Tang county of Ding 定 Province and Shangjun's benefice in Yucheng 虞城 county of Song 宋 Province. See *Sjsy*, 1.45 n. 8. The source of Qiao Zhou's information is unknown.

65. *Sj*, 32.1477.

66. *Sjsy*, 32.1478 n. 1.

67. *Sj*, 83.2461; Nienhauser, *Grand Scribe's Records*, 7: 282.

68. This refers to the revised laws and ordinances proposed by Lord Shang 商君, Wei Yang. See *Sj*, 68.2230–2231; Nienhauser, *Grand Scribe's Records*, 7: 89–90.

69. *Sjjj*, 83.2461 n 3.

70. Most of these amendments occurred within the Hereditary Houses section of *The Grand Scribe's Records*. Several fascicles contained multiple notes by Qiao—Qi

(four), Wu (three), Chu (two)—while the Hereditary Houses of Chen, Wei, Song, Jin, and Zheng each contained a single amendment. It is also significant to note that all these fragments were preserved in Sima Zhen's *Seeking the Obscure in The Grand Scribe's Records*, and that Pei Yin did not mention these passages in his commentary.

71. *Sj*, 32.1512.

72. *Sjsy*, 32.1512 n. 2. Also see Mao, *Shiben*, 1.11a.

73. Here, the graph offered by Sima Qian was not a substitute for the simple form offered by Qiao Zhou, though the simple form was an acceptable substitute for the complex form. There is no supporting evidence for the correctness of either claim.

74. *Sj*, 32.1481.

75. *Sjsy*, 32.1481 n. 3.

76. *Sj*, 39.1637.

77. *Sjsy*, 39.1637 n. 1. Also see Mao, *Shiben*, 1.11b.

78. *Sj*, 36.1585.

79. *Sjsy*, 36.1585 n. 6.

80. *Sj*, 37.1590; *Sjsy*, 37.1590 n. 1.

81. *Sj*, 42.1759; *Sjsy*, 42.1759 n. 2.

82. *Sj*, 32.1505.

83. *Sjsy*, 32.1505 n. 1.

84. *Zuozhuan*, Ai 5; Legge, *Classics*, 5: 806–807.

85. Xu Jian 徐堅 (659–729 CE) et al., *Chuxue ji* 初學記 [*Record of Primary Scholarship*] (Beijing: Zhonghua, 1962) (hereafter cited as *Cxj)*, 9.202.

86. *Zuozhuan*, Ai, 9. Legge misreads this passage as "The emperor Yan (Shinong) had his fire-master from whom the House of Jiang descended." Legge, *Classics*, 5: 819. Similar types of comments can be found in fragments from *Investigations of Ancient History* preserved in *Zuozhuan zhengyi*, 20.1861; *Tpyl*, 79.9a; and *Tpyl*, 80.2a.

87. *Sj*, 5. 173.

88. According to *The Grand Scribe's Records* biography of Lü Buwei, the First Emperor's mother was already pregnant by Lü Buwei when she was presented to King Zhuangxiang 莊襄 of Qin. Owing to a "long pregnancy," the child was believed to be the son of the king. See *Sj*, 85.2508. The biography of the First Emperor does not include this detail. See *Sj*, 6.223. Derk Bodde argues that detail is an interpolation by a later author intended to slander the First Emperor. See Bodde, "The State and Empire of Ch'in," in *CHC*, 1:42–44; 95. Nevertheless, the idea remains current. For example, see Chen Kaige's recent film, *The Emperor and the Assassin*.

89. *Tpyl*, 79.8b. Kong Yingda comments on this matter, saying, "The Metal-heaven clan was able to cultivate the Great Heaven's methods. Thus they were called the Lesser Heaven." See *Zuozhuan zhengyi*, Wen, 18.

90. *Zuozhuan*, Zhao, 17. The link between the surname Tan and Qin is expressed in Sima Qian's appraisal to "The Basic Annals of Qin," *Sj*, 5.221.

91. For example, see *Sj*, 33.1520 and *Sjsy*, 33.1520 n. 1; *Sj*, 76.2370; *Sj*, 84.2484 and *Cxj*, 7.160.

92. *Sj*, 43.1779; 5.175–176.

93. *Sj*, 5.175; Nienhauser, *Grand Scribe's Records*, 1: 88.

94. *Sjsy*, 43.1780 n. 6.

95. Mircea Eliade, cited in Anne Birrel, *Chinese Mythology* (Baltimore: Johns Hopkins, 1993), 40.

96. *Zztj*, 10.338. This fragment was not included in Zhang Zongyuan's recompilation of *Investigations of Ancient History*.

97. This passage as recompiled by Zhang Zongyuan conflates fragments drawn from *Tpyl*, 12.10a; *Liji zhengyi*, 1.1; *Tpyl*, 78.2b–3a; *Sjsy*, Sima Zhen, comp., "Sanhuang benji," 1, in Takigawa, *Shiki kaichū kōshō fu kōho* (hereafter cited as "Sanhuang"); and *Liji zhengyi*, 1.1. See Zhang, *GSK*, 1.11b.

98. *Btsc*, 10.2b; Zhang, *GSK*, 1.10a.

99. *Btsc*, 17.3a; Zhang, *Gsk*, 1.10a. These claims were also noted in *Tpyl*, 823.1a.

100. *Tpyl*, 191.5a; Zhang, *Gsk*, 1.11a.

101. *Btsc*, 17.3a; *Tpyl*, 757.3a; Zhang, *Gsk*, 1.10a.

102. *Zhou li zhengyi*, 39.268. Fragments of *Roots of Generations* text related to various inventions have been collected by Mao Panlin 茆泮林 in an attempt to reconstruct this section of the text. See Mao Panlin, "*Shiben* zuo pian" 世本作篇 ["*Roots of Generations*, Chapter on Inventions"], in *Longxi jingshe congshu* 龍溪精舍叢書, 1.1a–14a.

103. Mao, "*Shiben* zuo pian," 1.1a.

104. Mao, "*Shiben* zuo pian," 1.7a.

105. Mao, "*Shiben* zuo pian," 1.6a.

106. *Cxj*, 24.591.

107. Mao, "*Shiben* zuo pian," 1.8a.

108. *XHsz*, 29.3642 n. 3; Zhang, *Gsk*, 1.3b. For an additional example on ritual institutions and implements, see a passage from *Investigations of Ancient History* cited in *Liji zhengyi*, 1.1 and the *Roots of Generations* account in Mao, "Shiben zuo pian,"1.2a.

109. *XHsz*, 29.3642 n. 3.

110. This biography is not contained in the Zhonghua recension of *The Grand Scribe's Records*, but is found in Takigawa's edition.

111. *XHsz*, 29.3642 n. 3; *Sjsy*, 1.1–2 n. 1.

112. *Sj*, 3.91–92; Nienhauser, *Grand Scribe's Records*, 1: 41.

113. *Sjsy*, 3.91–92 n. 4.

114. Mao, *Shiben*, 1.3b.

115. *Sj*, 4.111; Nienhauser, *Grand Scribe's Records*, 1: 55.

116. *Sjsy*, 4.111 n. 3. This fragment was also quoted in *Sjzy*, 4.112 n. 5.

117. The *Roots of Generations* also notes that Jiang Yuan was the wife of Thearch Ku and the mother of Lord Millet. Mao, *Shiben*, 1.3b.

118. Mao 303.

119. Mao 245. Translation based on Arthur Waley, *The Book of Songs* (New York: Grove Press, 1996), 244–247.

120. *Shangshu zhengyi*, 3.18; Karlgren, "Documents," 7; Legge, *Classics*, 3: 44–45.

121. *Sj*, 44.1864.

122. *Sjsy*, 44.1864 n. 1. In this case, Sima Qian's position in regard to the fall of Wei is different from the one he adopted elsewhere in his history regarding the defeat of Xiang Yu. In that episode, Xiang Yu blames his political misfortune on Heaven, to which Sima Qian comments, "What error! To excuse himself by claiming 'Heaven destroyed me, it was not any fault of mine in using troops!' How absurd!" See *Sj*, 7.338; Nienhauser, *Grand Scribe's Records*, 1: 208.

123. *Sj*, 76. 2376; Nienhauser, *Grand Scribe's Records*, 7: 212. *The Grand Scribe's Records* offers two accounts of this matter. The first, from the perspective of Qin, is found in fascicle 73, and the second, from the perspective of Zhao, is found in fascicle 76.

124. See *Sj*, 73.2332–2333.

125. *Sjjj*, 76.2376 n. 1. cf., Nienhauser, *Grand Scribe's Records*, 7: 212 n. 34.

126. *Sj*, 74.2346; Nienhauser, *Grand Scribe's Records*, 7: 182.

127. *Sjsy*, 74.2346 n. 8.

128. Wang Rongbao 汪榮寶, ed. *Fayan yishu*, 法言義疏 [*Meaning and Subcommentary on Model Sayings*] (Beijing: Zhonghua, 1987), 18.507.

129. I.e., Qiao Zhou's *Model Teachings*. See chapter 3.

130. *Sgz*, 38.976.

131. Xu's commentary on *The Grand Scribe's Records* circulated through the Tang and was subsequently lost. Virtually all the surviving fragments are contained in the Three Scholar's Commentary to *The Grand Scribe's Records*. The only scholarly article on Xu's work is Zhu Dongrun 朱東潤, "*Shiji* Xu Guang ben yiwen kaozheng" 史記徐廣本異文考證 ["Xu Guang's Basic Examination on the Text of *The Grand Scribe's Records*"] in *Shiji kaosuo* 史記考索 [*Investigations on The Grand Scribe's Records*] (Shanghai: Huadong shifan daxue chubanshe, 1996), 106–131. Additionally, Scott Galer's dissertation provides an introduction to and systematic study of this important text.

132. *Sjjj*, 4.121 n. 2; 34.1551 n. 2; 43.1832 n. 1; and 70.2281 n. 1.

133. For more on Pei's commentary, see Zhu Dongrun, "Pei Yin *Shiji jijie* shuoli" 裴駰史記集解說例 ["Discussion on Pei Yin's *Collected Explanations on The Grand Scribe's Records*"], in *Shiji kaosuo*, 132–140.

134. *Sjjj*, 4.121 n. 2; 34.1549 n. 1; 70.2281 n. 1.

135. *Sjjj*, 76.2376 n. 1.

136. In each instance, Liu wrote, "For this matter, see *Investigations of Ancient History*." See *HHs*, 16.620 n. 7; 16.636.

137. *XHsz*, 19.3403 n. 2; 20.3422 n. 1; 20.3429 n. 3; 29.3642 n. 3.

138. For a critical discussion of Sima Zhen and his commentary, see Zhu Dongrun, "Sima Zhen *Shiji suoyin* shuolie" 司馬貞史記索隱說例 ["Discussion on Sima Zhen's *Seeking the Obscure in The Grand Scribe's Records*"], in *Shiji kaosuo*, 141–163.

139. See Sima Zhen, "*Shiji* suoyin houxu" 史記索隱後序 ["Postface to *Seeking the Obscure in The Grand Scribe's Records*"], contained in the supplemental materials in the Zhonghua edition of the *Shiji*. See *Sj*, vol. 10, 9–10. I am grateful to Scott Galer for calling this fact to my attention.

140. *Sjsy*, 36.1584 n. 3.

141. *Sjsy*, 42.1759 n. 2.

142. It merits mention at this point that the final of the Three Scholars' Commentaries on *The Grand Scribe's Records*, Zhang Shoujie's *Orthodox Meanings of The Grand Scribe's Records*, does not cite Qiao Zhou or *Investigations of Ancient History*. However, the Song historian Sima Guang cites *Investigations of Ancient History* twice in his *Comprehensive Mirror for Aid in Governing*. Each of Sima Guang's citations reference Qiao's writings on ancient culture bearers, and was used as source material rather than interpretative commentary. See *Zztj*, 45.1450; 47.1769.

143. See Epilogue.

144. Liang Yusheng, *Shiji zhiyi*, in *Shixue congshu* 史學叢書 (*Baibu congshu* ed.).

145. Liang, *Shiji zhiyi*, 3.2a–b, 19.1a.

146. For example, see Liang, *Shiji zhiyi*, 17.18a, 20.25b, 21.2a; and 31.5b.

147. Long Xianzhao also expresses similar sentiments. See Long, "Qiao Zhou," 83.

148. *Js*, 82.2142.

149. *Js*, 82.2142.

150. Liu Zhiji, *Shitong tongshi*, 8.1a–b.

151. Gao Sisun, *Shilüe*, 1.18a–b.

152. Zhang Zongyuan, "Preface to Qiao Zhou's *Investigations of Ancient History*," 1.2a–b.

153. Chen Zhi, "Han Jin ren dui *Shiji* de chuanbo ji qi pingjia" 漢晉人對史記的傳播及評價 ["Han–Jin Scholars on the Transmission and Value of *The Grand Scribe's Records*"], in *Sichuan daxue xuebao* 四川大學學報, no. 3 (1957); reprinted in *Zhongguo shixue shi lunji* 中國史學史論集 [*Collected Essays on the History of Chinese Historiography*] (Shanghai: Shanghai renmin chubanshe, 1980), 234–258.

154. Long, "Qiao Zhou," 82–86.

155. Long, "Qiao Zhou," 89.

156. Lu, *Wei-Jin shixue sixiang*, 268.

CHAPTER 6

1. An earlier version of this chapter was previously published as "Qiao Zhou and the Historiography of Early Medieval Sichuan," in *Early Medieval China* 7 (2001): 39–77. I am grateful to the publishers for permission to reprint that material here.

2. *Sui*, 28.963–996, passim.

3. For a brief discussion, see Edward L. Shaughnessy, "*Shang shu*," in Loewe, *ECT*, 376–389.

4. *Shangshu*, "Yu gong."' Translation adapted from Karlgren, "Documents," 15.

5. Although Ban Gu's list contains eleven entries, only ten were classified as districts. Chongguo was classified as a dependent kingdom. *Hs*, 28A.1603.

6. *Hs*, 28A.1531.

7. See *Hs*, 28B.1645, translated above in chapter 1.

8. See Andrew Chittick, "The Development of Local Writing in Early Medieval China," in *Early Medieval China* 9 (2003): 38–40.

9. Chittick's discussion of this aspect is particulary insightful. See Chittick, "Development of Local Writing," 49–52.

10. Chittick, "Development of Local Writing," 48–52.

11. Taniguchi Fusao 谷口房男 identifies Yin as a person of the later Han period, but offers no evidence to support this claim. See Taniguchi Fusao, *Kayōkoku shi jinmei sakuin* 華陽國志人名索引 [*Index to Persons in the Records of the States South of Mount Hua*] (np: Tosho kankokai, 1981), 4.

12. I.e., Ban Gu's "Geographic Treatise." See *Hs*, 28A–B.1523–1674.

13. *Hygz* 12.723–739.

14. *Hs*, 72.3056–3058; *Hygz*, 10A.532–533.

15. Yang's "admonitions" can be found in Yan Kejun, *Quan Han wen* 54.1a–4a; *Ywlj*, 6.110–116.

16. For a reconstruction of the text, see Hong Yixuan 洪頤煖, ed., *Shu wang benji*, in *Jingdian jilin* 經典籍林 (*Baibu congshu jicheng* ed.) (Taipei: Yiwen yinshu guan, n.d.).

17. Hong, *Shu wang benji*, 1.2a–2b; 1.2b–3a.

18. *Sui*, 33.983; *XTs*, 58.502.

19. See Yan, *Quan Han wen*, 53.4b–7b; Zhang Zhenze 張震澤, ed., *Yang Xiong jijiao zhu* 揚雄集校注 [*The Collected Works of Yang Xiong, Collated and Annotated*] (Shanghai: Shanghai guji chubanshe, 1993), 243–259.

20. Zhu Xizu, "*Shu wang benji* kao" 蜀王本紀考 ["An Investigation of the *Basic Annals of the Kings of Shu*"] in *Shuowen yuekan* 說文月刊, 3.7 (1942): 117–120.

21. Xu Zhongshu, "Lun *Shu wang benji* chengshu niandai ji qi zuozhe" 論蜀王本紀成書年代及其作者 ["Essay on the Completion Date and Authorship of the *Basic Annals of the Kings of Shu*"], in Xu Zhongshu, ed., *Lun Ba Shu wenhua* 論巴蜀文化 [*Essays on the Culture of Ba and Shu*] (Chengdu: Sichuan renmin chubanshe, 1981), 138–149.

22. My summary follows Ren's investigations. Ren also noted that Chang Qu's use of the name "Zixuan" was likely an error, as the other sources all refer to Yangcheng as "Zizhang" 子張. See *Hygz*, 12.724–725 n. 5.

23. Wang Chong, *Lunheng* (*Zhuzi jicheng* 諸子集成 ed.) (Hangzhou: Zhejiang guji chubanshe, 1999), 1216; 1180.

24. *Hygz*, 12.725, n. 5.

25. Located near present-day Qiongxia 邛峽, Sichuan.

26. *Hygz*, 11B.670.

27. Zhao Qian 謙, appellative Yanxin, was made grand commandant in Chuping 1 (190 CE). Together with the minister of works Xun Shuang 荀爽, Zhao opposed Dong Zhuo's plan to relocate the emperor to Chang'an. See *Hygz*, 10A.536.

28. See discussion on Chen Shu 術, pages 126–127.

29. Zhu Gui 龜, appellative Yuanling, was a person of Nanzheng 南鄭 district (near present-day Hanzhong, Shaanxi). Zhu was said to be especially skilled at writing, and refused to accept an appointment by the shepherd of Yi Province, Liu Yan.

According to Chang Qu, Zhu compiled a collection of biographies entitled *Hanzhong qijiu zhuan* 漢中耆舊傳 [*Biographies of the Elders of Hanzhong*]. See *Hygz*, 10C.601.

30. For Wang Shang, see *Hygz*, 10B.564; 573–574 n. 20. Also see page 41 and chapter 2, n. 62.

31. *Hygz*, 11.634.

32. *Hygz*, 11.634.

33. Yelang was located near present-day Guanling 關岭 county, Guizhou.

34. *Hygz*, 4.260.

35. *Sgz*, 42.1027.

36. These persons were Li Quan 李權 (d. ca. 190 CE) (native place unknown), *Sgz*, 31.867 n. 1; Zhang Su 張肅 (d. ca. 212 CE) of Shu commandery, *Sgz*, 32.882 n. 2; Zhang Ren 張任 (d. 214 CE) of Shu commandery, *Sgz*, 32.882 n. 2; 32.883 n. 1; He Zhi 何祇 (fl. mid-third century CE) of Shu commandery, *Sgz*, 41.1015 n. 1; Li Fu 李福 (d. ca. 238 CE) of Zitong 梓潼 commandery, *Sgz*, 45.1087 n. 1; Li Chao 李朝 (d. 222 CE) of Guanghan commandery, *Sgz*, 45.1088 n. 1; Wang Si 王嗣 (d. mid-third century CE) of Qianwei commandery, *Sgz*, 45.1091 n. 1; Chang Bo 常播 (d. mid-third century CE) of Shu commandery, *Sgz*, 45. 1091 n. 1; Wei Ji 衛繼 (d. ca. 263 CE) of Hanjia 漢嘉, *Sgz*, 45.1091 n. 1.

37. Yang Xi's encomia with Chen Shou's supplements are found in *Sgz*, 45.1079–1091.

38. This is not to say that the persons listed by Chang did not compile chronological historical records of the area. It is possible that Chang Qu relied on now-lost texts, bibliographic records of texts, or local traditions to compile his list. Significantly, Chang made no claim to having access to these records himself. He may have been creating a lineage of prior southwest historians to lend credibility to his own endeavor. In fact, an overarching theme of the *Records of the States South of Mount Hua* was to establish legitimacy for the region by creating links between the southwestern periphery and the centers of political power—both in the Central Plains and Eastern Yangzi regions. Chang's list of early historians fits into this overall theme.

39. B. J. Mansvelt Beck proposes that Qiao Zhou compiled only one volume of local history—*Shu benji* 蜀本紀 [*Basic Annals of Shu*]—and that the other works attributed to him were merely variant titles of this lone work. See Mansvelt Beck, *Treatises*, 30.

40. *Song*, 37.1120; 38.1170, 1171, 1209; *XHsz*, 23.3507 n. 1, 7.

41. *Sui*, 33.983; *JTs*, 46.2016; *XTs*, 58.1503.

42. These include citations in the *Imperially Reviewed Encyclopedia of the Taiping Period* and *Comprehensive Mirror for Aid in Governing*.

43. Note the attribution of "basic annals" to the figures listed in Chang Qu's "Postface," as well as the later text by Wang Yin 王隱 (fl. 317 CE), entitled *Shu ji* [*Records of Shu*], cited in Pei Songzhi's *Commentary to the Records of the Three States*. See *Js*, 82.2141–2143.

44. *Sgz*, 38.975 n. 3.

45. Xu Zhongshu, "Lun *Shu wang benji*," 149.

46. Long, "Qiao Zhou," 79–80.

47. *Wenxuan*, 4.185.

48. *Sui*, 33.993; *JTs*, 46.2014; *XTs*, 58.1502.

49. *Wenxuan*, 4.179, 188.

50. Li Shizhen, *Bencao gangmu* (Shanghai: Weigu zhai, 1885), 36.46a.

51. Fragments from three of Qiao Zhou's four local histories have been collected and published in Liu Weiyi 劉緯毅, *Han–Tang fangzhi jiyi* 漢唐方志輯佚 [*Recompiled Local Records from the Han through Tang*] (Beijing: Beijing tushuguan chubanshe, 1997), 38–40. Liu omits the fragment bearing the title of *Annals of Shu*.

52. *Song shu*, 37.1120.

53. *Song shu*, 38.1170.

54. *XHsz*, 23.3507 n. 1.

55. Shen Yue also paraphrases the *Records of Ba* in another passage from the same chapter. See *Song shu*, 38.1171.

56. Andrew B. Chittick, "Pride of Place: The Advent of Local History in Early Medieval China" (Ph.D. dissertation, University of Michigan, 1997), 123.

57. Chittick, "Development of Local Writing," 53–54.

58. See Liu Weiyi, *Han-Tang fangzhi jiyi*, passim.

59. Located at present-day Langzhong, Sichuan. The Yu River is presently known as the Jialing 嘉陵 River.

60. The term *yueren* 樂人, translated here as "musicians," refers to those who later came under the administrative command of the Music Bureau (Yuefu 樂府) and included instrumentalists, vocalists, dancers, and other entertainers.

61. *Ywlj*, 43.768. For more on the Zong people, see Kleeman, *Great Perfection*, 25–46. For the Yu Dance, see Dong Qixiang 董其祥, "Ba Yu wu yuanliu kao" 巴渝舞源流考 ["On the Origins of the Ba Yu Dance"], in Xu Zhongshu, ed., 巴蜀考古論文集 [*Collected Essays on Ba Shu Archeology*] (Beijing: Wenwu chubanshe, 1987), 167–177; Kleeman, *Great Perfection*, 45–46.

62. This information is not contained in the official biography of Liu Bang in *The Grand Scribe's Records*, however, Yan Shigu's commentary on the *Han History* "Treatise on Ritual and Music" notes Liu Bang's enjoyment of the music of the people of Yu and its motivational effect on Liu's troops. See *Hs*, 22.1074 n. 7.

63. *Sgz*, 38.975 n. 3.

64. cf. *Shangshu*, "Yao dian;" *Sj*, 2.49–84.

65. The precise role of this stream's water in the production of the cosmetic powder is unclear. For a discussion of pigments and cosmetics, see Edward H. Schafer, "The Early History of Lead Pigments and Cosmetics in China," in *T'oung Pao*, 44 (1956): 413–438.

66. Cao, *Shu zhong mingsheng ji*, 17.4b–5b.

I have been unable to fix the precise location of this site. The *Shu zhong mingsheng ji* does not specify which prefecture Qiao Zhou refers to in this passage. The name "Jiangzhou" mentioned in the passage may refer to Jiangzhou prefecture, located near present-day Chongqing.

67. A word of caution must be issued regarding this fragment and others preserved exclusively in *Shu zhong mingsheng ji*. Cao Xuequan does not provide a source for these passages attributed to Qiao's *Record of Three Ba Commanderies*. Given the highly fractured nature of Qiao's history, it is very unlikely that Cao had direct access to the complete text in the seventeenth century. Rather, he was probably quoting a citation from an unknown intermediary source. As such, we may rightly question the authenticity of the fragment, though not necessarily completely disregard it.

68. *Wenxuan*, 4.185. In his translation of this passage, David Knechtges rendered the term "river's waters" (*jiangshui* 江水) as "Yangzi." See David R. Knechtges, Wen xuan *or Selections of Refined Literature*, v. 1, *Rhapsodies on Metropolises and Capitals* (Princeton: Princeton University Press, 1982), v. 1, 360, l. 271 n.

69. Near present-day Kunming 昆明, Yunnan Province.

70. *Wenxuan* 4.188.

71. See Li Shizhen, *Bencao gangmu*, 36.46a. Also see Huang Tzu-ch'ing and Chao Yün-ts'ung, trans., "The Preparations of Ferments and Wine," in *Harvard Journal of Asiatic Studies* 9 (1945): 24–44; Edward H. Schafer, "Tang," in K. C. Chang, ed., *Food in Chinese Culture* (New Haven: Yale University Press, 1977), 119–122; Yü Ying-shih, "Han," in Chang, *Food in Chinese Culture*, 68–69; Xu Yiping 徐希平, ed., *Gaoshang de tianlu—xiang, cha, yao, jiu* 高尚的天祿香茶藥酒 (Chengdu: Sichuan renmin chubanshe, 1997), 168–219.

72. Near present-day Pengshui 彭水, Sichuan.

73. *Wenxuan* 4.179.

74. Near present-day Fengjie 奉節, Sichuan.

75. Cao, *Shu zhong mingsheng ji*, 17.11b.

76. There are no apparant reproductions of Qiao Zhou's history of strange things from the Chengdu Plain in either of the two major early medieval collections of this type of information, Zhang Hua's 張華 *Bowu zhi* 博物志 [*Record of Various Things*] or Gan Bao's *Soushen ji* 搜神記 [*Seeking the Supernatural*], though Gan Bao does cite one of Qiao Zhou's prophesies.

77. Cao, *Shu zhong mingsheng ji*, 19.11a.

78. In particular, the *Yiwen leiju* contains fourteen passages of this text. Pei's *Commentary* contains ten. There are no duplicated passages in the *Yiwen leiju* and Pei's *Commentary* collections.

79. Chang Kuan's title reflects the Jin period renaming of Yi Province as Liang Province.

80. *Hygz*, 11.659–660.

81. Little is known of Chang Qu's life. Ren Naiqiang collected scattered fragments of information on Chang Qu's life and compiled a brief biography that covers his family background, public life, and the circumstances surrounding the compilation of the *Records of the States South of Mount Hua*. See *Hygz*, 1–3.

82. Ren Naiqiang notes that each section of the text states a concluding date for the material it discusses; however, the dates recorded and the actual dates of the events in the text often do not match. *Hygz*, 3.

83. *Hygz*, fascicles 5–9.

84. *Hygz*, fascicles 10–12. Ren Naiqiang argues that these biographies were originally encomia, with the fuller treatments of the individuals' lives added at a later date. See *Hygz*, 3–5.

85. Cf. Ban Gu's treatises in *Hs*, 28A–B.1523–1674; and Sima Biao's treatises in *XHsz*, 19–23.3385–3554.

86. Chang also quotes Qiao Zhou's administrative account of the division of Ba. As noted earlier, the fragments of Qiao Zhou's passage on this matter quoted in the "Treatises" of the *Continued Han History* and the *Song History* are not identical. Chang Qu's account included elements from both of these accounts, while adding a few additional details. It is impossible to determine how much of Chang's narrative is a direct quotation of Qiao Zhou's history. See *Hygz*, 1.26. It merits mention that Chang Qu rarely identified the sources of his information.

87. *Ywlj*, 43.768.

88. *Hygz*, 1.14. Ren Naiqiang includes a lengthy note on the Ba Yu Dance. See *Hygz*, 1.16, n. 7.

89. *Hygz*, 1.30.

90. *Wenxuan*, 4.188.

91. *Hygz*, 4.267–268.

92. For similar characterizations of quality horses from other regions, see Edward H. Schafer, *The Golden Peaches of Samarkand: A Study of T'ang Exotics* (Berkeley: University of California Press, 1963), 58–70.

93. *Wenxuan*, 4.185.

94. *Hygz*, 3.153.

95. Yang Shoujing 楊守敬 and Xiong Huizhen 熊會貞, ed., *Shuijing zhushu* 水經注疏 [*Commentary and Subcommentary on the Classic of the Waterways*] (Nanjing: Zhejiang guji chubanshe, 1999), 33.2754.

96. Yue Shi, *Taiping huanyu ji* (preface dated 1803; reprint, Taipei: Wenhai chubanshe, 1963), 72.10a.

97. Despite the overwhelming evidence of Qiao Zhou's influence on Chang Qu's *Huayang guo zhi*, there are no surviving references to Qiao's histories or anecdotes contained therein in fourteen local histories of the southwest compiled between the Jin and Tang periods. Recompilations of the following Sichuan local histories are located in Liu Weiyi, *Han–Tang fangzhi jishi*: Anon., *Yongchang jun zhuan* 永昌郡傳 [*Biographies from Yongchang Commandery*], 40–41; Yuan Xiuming 袁休明 (Jin period), *Ba Shu zhi* 巴蜀志 [*Records of Ba and Shu*], 147; Anon., *Ba Han zhi* 巴漢志 [*Records of Ba and Hanzong*], 147–148; Ren Yu 任預 (Jin period), *Yizhou ji* 益州記 [*Records of Yi Province*], 257–259; Li Ying 李膺 (Jin period), *Yizhou ji* 益州記 [*Records of Yi Province*], 305–310; Anon., *Yizhou ji* 益州記 [*Records of Yi Province*], 310–313; Anon., *Shu jun tu jing* 蜀郡圖經 [*Map Classic of Shu Commandery*], 360; Anon., *Shu jun ji* 蜀郡記 [*Records of Shu Commandery*], 360–361; Zheng Wei 鄭暐 (Tang period), *Shu ji* 蜀記 [*Records of Shu*], 406–407; Anon., *Shu zhong ji* 蜀中記 [*Records of Shu*], 407; Anon., *Yizhou dili zhi* 益州地里志 [*Yi Province Geographic Treatise*], 407; Bo Minzhong 白敏中 and Lu Qiu 盧 求, eds. (Tang period), *Chengdu ji* 成都記 [*Records of Chengdu*], 408–409; Anon., *Yuzhou tujing*

渝州圖經 [*Map Classic of Yu Province*], 409–410; Anon., *Ba nan shanchuan ji* 巴南山川記 [*Records of Mountains and Rivers of South Ba*], 415.

98. *Hygz*, 12.739.

99. *Hygz*, 12.723.

100. A survey of surviving fragments from other local histories of the Chengdu Plain prior to Chang Qu's *Records of the States South of Mount Hua* reveals no evidence that Chang Qu was significantly influenced by these works.

EPILOGUE

1. *Sgz*, 42.1042.

2. There is no additional biographical information on either Dong Rong or Li Tong.

3. This passage is cited in Pei Songzhi's *Commentary*, *Sgz*, 42.1033 n. 2.

4. For a detailed study of the images in the Chengdu academy, see Farmer, "Art, Education, and Power."

5. *Sgz*, 45.1078.

6. Qiao was said to be eight *chi* tall, or about six feet two inches. Fang, *Sgzjy*, 1957; 1976. Other modern Chinese translations of the passage do not note the pun.

7. *Hygz*, 681.

8. *Hygz*, 9.516.

9. Sun Chuo, appellative Xinggong 興公, was a Western Jin dynasty scholar-official, noted for his skill in composing rhapsodies. See *Js*, 56.1544–1549. For Sun Sheng, see chapter 1, note 137.

10. Cited in Pei Songzhi's *Commentary*. See *Sgz*. 42.1030, n. 1.

11. Cited in Pei Songzhi's *Commentary*. See *Sgz*, 42.1031, n. 1.

12. Cited in Pei Songzhi's *Commentary*. See *Sgz*, 42.1031, n. 1.

13. Cited in Pei Songzhi's *Commentary*. See *Sgz*, 42.1031, n. 1. Although not a direct quote of Zhang Fan's text, I have treated this passage as a paraphrase of Zhang Fan by Pei Songzhi rather than the ideas of Pei himself. Pei Songzhi is careful to preface his own comments with the phrase "Your subject, Songzhi reckons." His usual self-identifying preface is missing in this instance.

14. Zhu Xi, attr., *Zizhi tongjian gangmu*, 16.38b.

15. *Sgz*, 42.1030; *Zztj*, 78.2473.

16. *Zztj*, 78.2473.

17. See *Sgz*, 42.1030.

18. *TK*, 500; *Sgyy*, 65.850.

19. *TK*, 609; *Sgyy*, 80.1037.

20. The novel twice refers to Qiao Zhou in this fashion. See *TK*, 500; 787–788; *Sgyy*, 65.850; 102.1328.

21. See the episodes in *TK*, 701; *Sgyy*, 91.1186; *TK*, 785–786; *Sgyy*, 101.1323–1324; *TK*, 787–788; *Sgyy*, 102.1328; and *TK*, 868–869; *Sgyy*, 112.1453–1454.

22. *TK*, 909; *Sgyy*, 118.1522.

23. *TK*, 909–910; *Sgyy*, 118.1522.

24. *TK*, 910–911; *Sgyy*, 118.1522. *The Annals of the Han and Jin* records the historical antecedent for this act. See *Sgz*, 33.900–901 n. 1.

25. *TK*, 920; *Sgyy*, 119.1537.

26. Topping the list were Liu Shan and Huang Hao. Commentary on Qiao Zhou's entry reads: "some astrologer guy or something, advised Liu Shan to surrender as well." Posted at www.3kingdoms.net/forums (Accessed 15 February 2004).

27. *Js*, 82.2142.

28. Liu Zhiji, *Shitong tongshi*, 8.1a–b.

29. Long, "Qiao Zhou," 89.

30. Lu, *Wei-Jin shixue sixiang*, 268.

31. For representative scholarship, see the Introduction.

32. For example, Liu Zhiji, Sima Zhen, and Liang Yusheng.

CHRONOLOGY

A detailed *niannpu* for Qiao Zhou can be found in Yi Lang 一郎, "Qiao Zhou nianpu" 譙周年譜 ["Chronology of Qiao Zhou"], in *Sanguo zhi shuyuan yuankan* 三國志書院院刊 (2000): 44–46.

Bibliography

LIST OF ABBREVIATIONS

CHC — *The Cambridge History of China, vol. 1, The Ch'in and Han Empires, 221 B.C.–A.D. 220*. Ed., Denis Twitchett and Michael Loewe. Cambridge: Cambridge University Press, 1986.

ECT — *Early Chinese Texts*. Ed., Michael Loewe. Berkeley: The Society for the Study of Early China and the Institute of East Asian Studies, University of California, 1993.

HHs — Fan Ye 范曄 (398–445 CE). *Hou Han shu* 後漢書 [*Later Han History*]. Beijing: Zhonghua shuju, 1965.

Hs — Ban Gu 班固 (32–92 CE). *Han shu* 漢書 [*Han History*]. Beijing: Zhonghua shuju, 1962.

Hygz — Chang Qu 常璩 (ca. 291–ca. 361 CE). Ed., Ren Naiqiang 任乃強. *Huayang guo zhi jiaobutuzhu* 華陽國志校補圖注 [*Records of the States South of Mount Hua, Supplemented with Illustrations and Annotations*]. Shanghai: Shanghai guji, 1987.

Js — Fang Xuanling 房玄齡 (578–648 CE) et al. *Jin shu* 晉書 [*Jin History*]. Beijing: Zhonghua shuju, 1974.

JTs — Liu Xu 劉昫 (887–946 CE) et al. *Jiu Tang shu* 舊唐書 [*Old Tang History*]. Beijing: Zhonghua shuju, 1975.

Sgyy — Luo Guanzhong 羅貫中 (ca. 1315/18–ca. 1400), attr. *Sanguo (zhi) yanyi* 三過志演義 [*Extended Meanings of the Records of the Three States*]. Edited by Mao Zonggang 毛宗崗 (fl. 1660). Shanghai: Shanghai guji, 1989.

Sgz — Chen Shou 陳壽 (233–297 CE). *Sanguo zhi* 三國志 [*Records of the Three States*]. Beijing: Zhonghua shuju, 1959.

Sgzjj — Lu Bi 盧弼 (1876–1967). *Sanguo zhi jijie* 三國志集解 [*Collected Explanations on the Records of the Three States*]. 1936. Reprint. Taipei: Yiwen yinghuguan, n.d.

Sgzzy — Fang Beichen 方北晨, ed. *Sanguo zhi zhuyi* 三國志注釋 [*Records of the Three States Annotated and Translated*]. Xi'an: Shaanxi renmin chubanshe, 1996.

Sj Sima Qian 司馬遷 (c. 145–86 BCE). *Shi ji* 史記 [*The Grand Scribe's Records*]. Beijing: Zhonghua shuju, 1959.

Song Shen Yue 沈約 (441–513 CE). *Song shu* 宋書 [Song History]. Beijing: Zhonghua shuju, 1974.

Ssjzs *Shisan jing zhushu* 十三經注疏 [*Thirteen Canonical Texts with Commentary and Subcommentary*]. Ed., Ruan Yuan 阮元 (1764–1849). Reprint. Beijing: Zhonghua shuju, 1980.

Sui Wei Zheng 魏徵 (580–643 CE) et al. *Sui shu* 隋書 [*Sui History*]. Beijing: Zhonghua shuju, 1973.

Td Du You 杜佑 (735–812 CE). *Tongdian* 通典 [*Encyclopedic History of Institutions*]. Beijing: Zhonghua shuju, 1996.

TK Roberts, Moss, trans. *Three Kingdoms: A Historical Novel*. 2 vols. Berkeley: University of California Press, 2004.

Tpyl Li Fang 李昉 (925–996 CE). *Taiping yulan* 太平御覽 [*Imperially Reviewed Encyclopedia of the Taiping Period*]. Beijing: Zhonghua shuju, 1998.

XTs Ouyang Xiu 歐陽修 (1007–1072), Song Qi 宋祁 (998–1061) et al. *Xin Tang shu* 新唐書 [*New Tang History*]. Beijing: Zhonghua shuju, 1975.

Ywlj Ouyang Xun 歐陽詢 (557–641 CE) et al. Yiwen leiju 藝文類聚 [*Collection of Literature Arranged by Categories*]. Shanghai: Shanghai guji chubanshe, 1999.

Zztj Sima Guang 司馬光 (1019–1086). *Zizhi tongjian* 資治通鑑 [*Comprehensive Mirror for Aid in Governing*]. Beijing: Zhonghua shuju, 1956.

PRIMARY SOURCES

Ban Gu. *Bohu tong* 白虎通 [*The Comprehensive Discussions in the White Tiger Hall*]. *Sbck* edition.

Bi Yuan 畢沅 (1730–1797). *Chuanjing biao* 傳經表 [*Tables of the Transmission of the Canonical Texts*]. In *Congshu jicheng chu pian*.

Cao Xuequan 曹學佺. *Shu zhong mingsheng ji* 蜀中名勝記 [*Record of Shu Notables*]. Preface dated 1618. Reprint. Taipei: Xuehai chubanshe, 1969.

Chang Ming 常明, ed. *Sichuan tongzhi* 四川通志 [*Comprehensive Gazetteer of Sichuan*]. Preface dated 1816. Reprint. Chengdu: Ba-Shu chubanshe, 1984.

Chen Shou. *Yibu qijiu zhuan* 益部耆舊傳 [*Biographies of the Elders of Yi Province*]. In *Taiping yulan*.

Cheng Rong 程榮 (fourteenth century). *Han Wei congshu* 漢魏叢書 [*Collectanea of Han and Wei Works*]. Taipei: Xinxing shuju, 1966.

Congshu jicheng chupian 叢書集成初篇 [*Complete Collection of Collected Books, First Series*] Beijing: Zhonghua shuju, 1985.

Congshu jinghua 叢書菁華 [*Choice Selections from Collected Books*]. Taibei: Yiwen yinshu guan, n.d.

Ershiwu shi bu bian 二十五史補編 [*Supplements to the Twenty-five Histories*]. 6 vols. 1936. Reprint. Beijing: Zhonghua shuju, 1994.

Feng Yan 封演 (*jinshi* 756 CE). *Wenjian ji* 聞見記 [*Records of Things Heard and Seen*]. In *Congshu jicheng chupian*.

Gao Sisun 高似孫 (*jinshi* ca. 1174–1190). *Shilüe* 史略 [*Historical Epitome*]. In *Congshu jicheng chupian*.

Gao You 高誘 (ca. 168–212 CE), comm. *Lü shi chunqiu* 呂氏春秋 [*Master Lü's Spring and Autumn*]. In *Jingxuntang congshu* 經訓堂叢書, *Baibu congshu* edition.

Guoyu 國語 [*Discourses fromf the States*]. Shanghai: Shanghai guji, 1988.

Heyin Siku quanshu zongmu tiyao ji Siku weishou shumu Jinhui shumu 合印四庫全書總目提要及四庫未收書目禁燬書目 [*Combined Printing of the General Bibliography and Précis of the Complete Writings of the Four Treasuries, Books Not Included in the Four Treasuries, and Banned Books*]. 5 vols. Taibei: Shangwu yinshuguan, 1985.

Hong Yixuan 洪頤烜, ed. *Shu wang benji* 蜀王本紀 [*Basic Annals of the Kings of Shu*]. In *Jingdian jilin* 經典籍林. *Baibu congshu jicheng* edition. Taipei: Yiwen yinshu guan, n.d.

Hou Kang 侯康 (1798–1837). *Bu Sanguo yiwen zhi* 補三國藝文志 [*Supplement to Treatise on Three States Bibliography*]. In Shixue congshu 史學叢書 (Bbcs edition).

Huang Shi 黃奭 (nineteenth century), recomp. *Huang shi yishu kao* 黃氏逸書考 [*Mister Huang's Examinations of Lost Books*]. In *Congshu jinghua* 叢書菁華.

Huangfu Mi 皇甫謐 (215–282 CE). *Gaoshi zhuan* 高士傳 [*Biographies of High-Minded Gentlemen*]. In *Longxi jingshe congshu* 龍溪精舍叢書. Zheng Yaochen 鄭堯臣, ed. Beijing: Zhongguo shudian, 1991.

Li Shizhen 李時珍 (1518–1593). *Bencao gangmu* 本草綱目 [*Outline of Native Plants*]. Shanghai: Weigu zhai, 1885.

Liang Yusheng 梁玉繩 (1745–1819). *Shiji zhiyi* 史記志疑 [*Records of Doubts on* The Grand Scribe's Records]. In *Shixue congshu* 史學叢書, *Baibu congshu* edition.

Liu Lin 劉琳, ed. [Chang Qu's 常璩] *Huayang guozhi jiaozhu* 華陽國志校注 [*Records of the States South of Mount Hua, Collated and Annotated*]. Chengdu: Ba-Shu shushe, 1984.

Liu Xiang 劉向 (79–8 BCE). *Lienü zhuan* 列女傳 [*Biographies of Exemplary Women*]. *Sibu beiyao* edition.

Liu Xie 劉勰 (ca. 465–ca. 520 CE). *Wenxin diaolong* 文心雕龍 [*Embellishments on the Heart of Literature*]. Taipei: Liren shuju, 1994.

Liu Zhiji 劉知幾 (661–721 CE). *Shi tong* 史通 [*Understanding History*]. In *Sibu beiyao*.

Lu Deming 陸德明 (556–627 CE). *Jingdian shiwen* 經典釋文 [*Explanations on the Canon*]. In *Congshu jicheng chupian*.

Lu Qinli 逯欽立, ed. *Xian Qin, Han, Wei, Jin, Nanbei chao shi* 先秦漢魏晉南北朝詩 [*Poems from the Pre-Qin, Han, Wei, Jin, Northern and Southern Dynasties*]. Beijing: Zhonghua, 1983.

Ma Guohan 馬國翰 (1794–1857). *Yuhanshan fang ji shenshu* 玉函山房輯佚書 [*Recompiled Books from Jade Case Studio*]. Reprint. Taipei: Wenhai chubanshe, 1967.

Mao Panlin 茆泮林, ed. *Shiben* 世本 [*Roots of Generations*]. In *Longxi jingshe congshu* 龍溪精舍叢書.

Mao Zonggang 毛宗岡 (fl. mid-seventeenth century), ed. Luo Guanzhong 羅貫中 (ca. 1330–ca. 1400) attr. *Sanguo yanyi* 三國演義 [*The Extended Meaning of the Three States*]. Taipei: Sanmin shuju, 1988.

Nanchong xianzhi 南充縣志 [*Gazetteer of Nanchong County*]. N.p., 1929.

Shiben bazhong 世本八種 [*Eight Recompilations of the* Roots of Generations] Beijing: Shangwu, 1957.

Sibu beiyao 四部備要 [*Complete Core Works of the Four Categories*].

Sibu congkan 四部叢刊 [*Collective Printing of the Four Categories*].

Sima Biao 司馬彪 (240–315 CE). *Xu Han zhi* 續漢志 [*Continued Treatises on the Han*]. In *HHs*.

Sun Fengji 孫逢吉. *Zhiguan fenji* 職官分紀 [*Official Positions Arranged Chronologically*]. In *Siku quanshu*.

Sun Xingyan 孫星衍. *Shangshu jingu wen zhuzhu* 尚書今古文注疏 [*Commentary and Subcommentary on the Old and New Text Hallowed Documents*]. Beijing: Zhonghua shuju, 1986.

Takigawa Kametarō 瀧川龜太郎 (1865–1946). *Shiki kaichū kōshō fu kōho* 史記會注考證附校補 [*Examination of the Collected Commentaries on* The Grand Scribe's Records, *with Supplemental Collation Notes*]. Reprint of Tokyo: Tōhō Bunka Gakuin 東方文化學院, 1934 edition. Taipei: Wenshizhe chubanshe, 1993.

Tao Zongyi 陶宗儀 (b. 1316), recomp. *Shuofu* 說郛 [*Sayings Within a City Wall*]. In *Gujin shuobu congshu* 古今說部叢書. Shanghai: Shanghai yiwen chubanshe, 1991.

Tuo Tuo 脫脫 (1313–1355) et al. *Song shi* 宋史 [*Song History*]. Beijing: Zhonghua shuju, 1977.

Wang Chong 王充 (27–ca. 100 CE). *Lunheng* 論衡 [*Discourses in the Balance*]. Reprint. Taipei: Shijie shuju, 1990.

Wang Guowei 王國維 (1877–1927). *Shuijing zhu jiao* 水經注校 [*Collated Commentary on the Classic of the Waterways*]. Reprint. Taipei: Xinwenfeng chubanshe, 1987.

Wang Liqi 王利器. *Shiji zhuyi* 史記注譯 [*The Grand Scribe's Records: Annotated and Explained*]. Xi'an: San Qin chubanshe, 1988.

Wang Mo 王莫 (*jinshi* 1778), recomp. *Han Wei yishu chao* 漢魏遺書鈔 [*Exercpts from Lost Books of the Han and Wei*]. In *Congshu jinghua* 叢書菁華.

Wang Renjun 王仁俊 (1866–1913). *Shuofu* 說郛 [*Sayings Within a City Wall*]. In *Gujin shuobu congshu* 古今說部叢書.

Wang Rongbao 汪榮寶, ed. *Fayan yishu*, 法言義疏 [*Meaning and Subcommentary on Model Sayings*]. Beijing: Zhonghua, 1987.

Wang Su 王肅 (d. 256 CE), ed. *Kongzi jiayu*. *Sibu beiyao* edition.

Wang Xianqian 王先謙 (1842–1918). *Han shu buzhu* 漢書補注 [*Supplementary Commentary to the Han History*]. Reprint. Taibei: Yiwen yinshu guan, n.d.

———. *Hou Han shu jijie* 後漢書集解 [*Later Han History with Collected Commentaries*]. Reprint. Taibei: Yiwen yinshu guan, n.d.

Wu Shijian 吳士鑑 (1873–1933). *Jin shu jiaogzhu* 晉書斠注 [*Collation Notes to the Jin History*]. Reprint. Taibei: Yiwen yinshu guan, n.d.

Wu Shuping 吳樹平, ed. Liu Zhen 劉珍 et al. *Dongguan Han ji jiaozhu* 東觀漢記校注 [*Records of the Han from the Eastern Lodge, Collated and Annotated*]. Henan: Zhongzhou guji chuban she, 1987.

Xi Zuochi 習鑿齒 (ca. 318–395 CE). *Han Jin chunqiu* 漢晉春秋 [*Spring and Autumn Annals of the Han and Jin Dynasties*]. Recompiled by Huang Shi. In *Huang shi yishu kao*.

Xiao Tong 蕭統 (501–531 CE), comp. *Wenxuan* 文選 [*Selections of Refined Literature*]. Commentary by Li Shan 李善 (d. 689 CE). Shanghai: Shanghai guji chubanshe, 1986.

Xu Jian 徐堅 (659–729 CE) et al. *Chuxue ji* 初學記 [*Record of Primary Scholarship*]. Beijing: Zhonghua, 1962.

Xu Tianlin 徐天麟 (d. 1226). *Dong Han huiyao* 東漢會要 [*Collected Essentials of the Eastern Han*]. Taibei: Shijie shuju, 1971.

Xue Juzheng 薛居正 (912–981 CE). *Jiu Wu dai shi* 舊五代史 [*Old Five Dynasties History*]. Beijing: Zhonghua shuju, 1976.

Xun Yue 荀悅 (148–209 CE). *Han ji* 漢紀 [*Annals of the Han*]. In *Sibu congkan*.

Yan Kejun 嚴可均, ed., *Quan shanggu, Sandai, Qin, Han, Sanguo, Liuchao wen* 全上古三代秦漢三國六朝文 [*Complete Prose from High Antiquity, the Three Dynasties, Qin, Han, Three States, and Six Dynasties*]. Beijing: Zhonghua shuju, 1995.

Yan Zhitui 顏之推 (531–ca. 591 CE). *Yan shi jiaxun* 顏氏家訓 [*Family Teachings of the Yan Clan*]. Beijing: Zhonghua shuju, 1993.

Yan Zun 嚴遵. *Laozi zhigui* 老子指歸. Beijing: Zhonghua shuju, 1997.

Yang Shoujing 楊守敬 and Xiong Huizhen 熊會貞, eds., *Shuijing zhushu* 水經注疏 [*Commentary and Subcommentary on the Classic of the Waterways*].

Yao Zhenzong 姚振宗 (1842–1906). *Sanguo yiwen zhi* 三國藝文志 [*Three States Bibliographic Treatise*]. In *Ershiwu shi bubian* 二十五史補編. Beijing: Zhonghua shuju, 1998.

Yu Jiaxi 余嘉錫 (1833–1955), ed. *Shishuo xinyu jianshu* 世說新語箋疏 [*New Account of Tales of the World*]. Reprint. Shanghai: Shanghai guji, 1993.

Yu Shinan 虞世南 (558–638 CE). *Beitang shuchao* 北堂書鈔 [*Excerpts from Books in the Northern Hall*]. Beijing: Xueyuan chubanshe, 1998.

Zhang Zhenze 張震澤, ed. *Yang Xiong jijiao zhu* 揚雄集校注 [*Collected Works of Yang Xiong, Collated and Annotated*]. Shanghai: Shanghai guji chubanshe, 1993.

Zhang Zongyuan 章宗源. "Qiao Zhou *Gushi kao* xu" 譙周古史考序 ["Preface to Qiao Zhou's *Investigations of Ancient History*"]. In *Pingjin guan congshu* 平津觀叢書. *Baibu congshu* edition.

Zheng Qiao 鄭樵 (1104–1162). *Tong zhi* 通志 [*Comprehensive Encyclopedia of Institutions*]. Beijing: Zhonghua shuju, 1990.

Zhao Erxun 趙爾巽(1844–1927) et al. *Qing shi gao* 清史稿 [*Draft Qing History*]. Beijing: Zhonghua shuju, 1976–1977.

Zhou Guangye, 周廣業 (1730–1798). *Yilin yiwen* 意林逸文 [*Missing Texts from the Forest of Ideas*]. In *Yilin* 意林 [Forest of Ideas]. In *Sibu beiyao*.

Zhu Xi 朱熹 (1130–1200), attr. *Zizhi tongjian kangmu* 資治通鑑綱目[*Outline of Comprehensive Mirror for Aid in Governing*]. In *Siku quanshu*.

WORKS IN CHINESE AND JAPANESE

Cao Wenzhu 曹文柱. *Baihua Sanguo zhi* 白話三國志 [*Vernacular Records of the Three States*]. Beijing: Zhongyang minzu xueyuan chubanshe, 1994.

Chen Qiankang 陳乾康. "Lun Sanguo shudai de Wu-Shu tongmeng" 論三國時代的吳蜀同盟 ["Essay on the Oath between Wu and Shu during the Three States Period"]. In *Sichuan shifan daxue xuebao* 四川師範學學報 vol. 24, no. 4 (1997).

Chen Yinke 陳寅恪. *Wei Jin Nanbei chao shi jiangyan lu* 魏晉南北朝史講演錄 [*Record of Lectures on Wei Jin Northern-Southern Dynasties History*]. Hefei: Huangshan shushe, 1987.

Chen Xuguo 陳戍國. *Wei, Jin, Nanbei chao lizhi yanjiu* 魏晉南北朝禮制研究 [*Studies on Ritual during the Wei, Jin, and Northern-Southern Dynasties*]. Changsha.: Hunan jiaoyu chubanshe, 1995.

Chen Zhi 陳直. "Han-Jin ren dui Shiji de chuanbo ji qi pingjia" 漢晉人對史記的傳播及其評价 ["Han–Jin Scholars on the Transmission of *The Grand Scribe's Records*, Including Their Critical Evaluations"]. In Wu and Yuan. *Zhongguo Shixue shilun ji* 中國史學史論集. Shanghai: Shanghai renmin chubanshe, 1980.

Cheng Jinzao 程金造. "Lun Shiji Pei Yin Jijie, Sima Zhen Suoyin, Zhang Shoujie Zhengyi Sanjia zhujie" 論史記裴駰集解司馬貞索隱張守節正義三家注解 ["Essay on the Three Scholar's Commentaries on *The Grand Scribe's Records*: Pei Yin's *Collected Explanations on The Grand Scribe's Records*, Sima Zhen's *Seeking the Obscure in The Grand Scribe's Records*, and Zhang Shoujie's *Orthodox Meanings of The Grand Scribe's Records*"]. In *Wenshi*, no. 7 (1979).

———. *Shiji suoyin yinshu kaoshi* 史記索隱引書考實 [*Investigation of Documents Cited in Seeking the Obscure in The Grand Scribe's Records*]. Beijing: Zhonghua shuju, 1998.

Cheng Shunying 程舜英. *Liang Han jiaoyu zhidu shi ziliao* 兩漢教育史資料 [*Resources on the History of Education in the Han Dynasty*]. Beijing: Beijing shifan daxue chubanshe, 1983.

Cheng Yuanmin 程元敏. "Dong Han Shu Yang Hou jingwei xue zongchuan" 東漢蜀楊厚經緯學宗傳 ["The Classics and Apocryphal Family Traditions of Yang Hou of the Eastern Han"]. *Guoli bianyiguan guankan* 國立編譯館館刊. 17.1 (1988): 31–48; 17.2 (1988):19–39.

———. *Sanguo Shu jingxue* 三國蜀經學 [*Canonical Studies in Three States Period Shu*]. Taipei: Xuesheng shuju, 1997.

Dong Qixiang 董其祥. "Ba Yuwu yuanliu kao" 巴渝舞源流考 ["Investigations on the Origins of the Ba Yu Dance"]. In Xu Zhongshu 徐中舒, ed. *Ba Shu kaogu lunwenji* 巴蜀考古論文集 [*Collected Essays on Ba-Shu Archeology*]. Beijing: Wenwu chubanshe, 1987.

Fang Beichen 方北辰. "Qianqiu shusheng yidai qingliu: Jin shu Wang Xizhi zhuan xuandu" 千秋書聖一代清流：晉書王羲之傳選讀 ["The Calligraphic Sage of a Thousand Autumns, The Pure Flowing of a Generation: Selections from the *Jin History* Biography of Wang Xizhi"]. In *Zhonghua huoye wenxuan* 中華活頁文選, no. 33 (1999): 1–2.

Fang Shiming 方詩銘 and Fang Xiaofen 方小芬. Zhongguoshi liri he Zhong-Xi liri duizhao biao 中國史曆日和中西曆日對照表 [*Chinese Historical Calendar Days and a Calendrical Concordance of Chinese and Western Days*]. Shanghai: Shanghai cishu, 1987.

Feng Youlan 馮友蘭. *Zhongguo zhexue shi* 中國哲學史 [*History of Chinese Philosophy*]. Beijing: Zhonghua shuju, 1961.

Gao Wen 高文 et al. *Sichuan lishi renwu mingsheng cidian* 四川歷史名勝詞典 [*Dictionary of Sichuan Historical Personages and Events*]. Chengdu: Sichuan renmin chubanshe, 1989.

Ge Jianxiong 葛劍雄. *Xi Han renkou dili* 西漢人口地理 [*Population and Geography of the Western Han*]. Beijing: Renmin chubanshe, 1986.

Gong Kechang 龔克昌. *Han fu yanjiu* 漢賦研究 [*Studies on the Han Rhapsody*]. Ji'nan: Shandong wenyi chuban she, 1984.

Gu Guoshun 古國順. *Shiji shu Shangshu yanjiu* 史記述尚書研究 [*Studies on* The Grand Scribe's Records *Citations of the* Hallowed Documents]. Taipei: Wenshizhe chubanshe, 1985.

Gu Jiegang 顧頡剛. *Han dai xueshu shilue* 漢代學術史略 [*Summary History of Han Scholarship*]. Shanghai: Shanghai dongfang shushe, 1941.

———. *Lun Ba-Shu yu zhongyuan de guanxi* 論巴蜀與中原的關系 [*The Relationship Between Ba-Shu and the Central Plains*]. Chengdu: Sichuan renmin chubanshe, 1981.

Gu Lisan 顧立三. *Sima Qian zhuanxie Shiji caiyong Zuozhuan de yanjiu* 司馬遷撰寫史記採用左傳的研究 [*Studies on Sima Qian's Citing the* Zuozhuan *in the Compilation of* The *Grand Scribe's Records*]. Taipei: Zhengzhong shuju, 1971.

Guo Yundao 郭允蹈. *Shu jian* 蜀鑑 [*Mirror of Shu*]. Reprint. Taipei: Zhonghua shuju, 1968.

He Ziquan 何玆全. *Sanguo shi* 三國史 [*History of the Three States*]. Beijing: Beijing shifan daxue chubanshe, 1994.

Huayang xian zhi 華陽縣志 [*Gazetteer of Huayang County*]. Taipei: Hsüeh-sheng shuchü, n.d.

Huang Desheng 黃德聲 and Fu Dengzhou 傅登舟 eds. *Zhongguo fangzhi xuejia yanjiu* 中國方志學家研究 [*Studies on Authors of Chinese Local Histories*]. Wuhan: Wuhan chubanseh, 1989.

Huang Kaiguo 黃開國. "Yang Xiong" 揚雄. In Jia Shunxian 賈順先 and Dai Dalu 戴大祿 eds. *Sichuan sixiang jia* 四川思想家 [*Sichuan Thinkers*]. Chengdu: Ba-Shu chubanshe, 1987.

Huang Wei 黃葦. *Fangzhi lunji* 方志論集 [*Collected Essays on Gazetteers*]. Hangzhou: Zhejiang renmin chubanshe, 1983.

———. *Fangzhi xue* 方志學 [*Studies on Gazetteers*]. Shanghai: Fudan daxue chubanshe, 1993.

Jia Shunxian 賈順先 and Dai Dalu 戴大祿 eds. *Sichuan sixiang jia* 四川思想家 [*Sichuan Thinkers*]. Chengdu: Ba-Shu chubanshe, 1987.

Jiang Liangfu 姜亮夫, comp. *Lidai renwu nianli beizhua zongbiao* 歷代人物年里碑傳綜表 [*Table of Dates and Places of Birth, Dates of Death, with Epitaphs and Biographical Sketches Referenced of Historical Personages*]. Beijing: Zhonghua shuju, 1959.

Jin Dejian 金德建. *Sima Qian suo jian shu kao* 司馬遷所見書考 [*Examination of Documents Seen by Sima Qian*]. Shanghai: Shanghai renmin chubanshe, 1963.

Li Hengmei 李衡眉. *Lun zhaomu zhidu* 論昭穆制度 [*Essay on the Organiztion of Funerary Offerings*]. Taipei: Wenjin chubanshe, 1992.

Li Yingke 李穎科. "Lun Pei Songzhi de shixue sixiang" 論裴松之的史學思想 ["Essay on Pei Songzhi's Historiographical Thought"]. In *Lishi xue* 歷史學 no. 4 (1996): 62–66.

Li Youming 李有明 and Chen Hongtao 陳紅濤 eds. *Sichuan gudai mingren* 四川古代名人 [*Famous Persons of Ancient Sichuan*]. Chengdu: Sichuan sheng shehui kexue yuan chubanshe, 1984.

Li Zefen 李則芬. "Ping Chen Shou Sanguo zhi" 評陳壽三國志 ["Critique of Chen Shou's *Records of the Three States*"]. In *Dongfang zazhi* 東方雜誌 14.7 (1917): 19–24. Reprinted in Li Zefen, *Sanguo lishi lunwen ji* 三國歷史論文集 [*Collected Essays on Three States History*]. Taipei: Liming wenhua, 1982.

Li Zongtong 李宗侗. *Zhongguo shixue shi* 中國史學史 [*A History of Chinese Historiography*]. Taipei: Zhonghua wenhua chuban shiye weiyuan hui, 1953.

Lin Yongren 林永仁 and Lai Cenglin 來層林. *Ba-Chu wenhua* 巴楚文化 [*Ba-Chu Culture*]. Beijing: Huawen chubanshe, 1999.

Liu Dingsheng 柳定生. *Sichuan shihua* 四川史話 [*Historical Talks on Sichuan*]. Taipei: Cheng-chung shu-chü, 1975.

Liu Guihui 劉國輝 et al. *Sanguo zhi (xiandai wen ban)* 三國誌(現代文版) [*Records of the Three States (Modern language edition)*]. 2 vols. Beijing: Hongqi chubanshe, 1992.

Liu Lin 劉琳. "Chang Qu ji qi Huayang guozhi" 常璩及其華陽國志 ["Chang Qu and his *Records of the States South of Mount Hua*"]. In Huang Desheng 黃德聲 and Fu Dengzhou 傅登舟, eds. *Zhongguo fangzhi xuejia yanjiu* 中國方志學家研究 [*Studies on Authors of Chinese Local Histories*]. Wuhan: Wuhan chubanseh, 1989.

———. "*Huayang guozhi* jianlun" 華陽國志簡論 ["A Basic Essay on the *Records of the States South of Mount Hua*"]. In *Sichuan daxue xuebao* 四川大學學報. 2 (1979): 82–87.

Liu Rulin 劉汝霖. *Han Jin xueshu biannian* 漢晉學術編年 [*A Chronology of Han–Jin Scholarship*]. Beijing: Zhonghua shuju, 1987.

Liu Weihang 劉偉航. "Yizhou menfa chutan" 益州門閥初探 ["A Preliminary Investigation on the Great Families of Yi Province"]. In *Wei Jin Nanbei chao Sui Tang shi* (1986.10): 21–27. First appeared in *Nanchong shifan xueynan xuebao* 南充師範學院學報 (1986: 2): 98–101.

Liu Weiyi 劉緯毅. *Han Tang fangzhi jiyi* 漢唐方志輯佚 [*Recompiled Local Records from the Han through Tang*]. Beijing: Beijing tushuguan chubanshe, 1997.

Liu Xianxin 劉咸炘. *Sanguo zhi zhiyi* 三國志知意 [*Meaning of the* Records of the Three States]. In *Tuishi shu* 推十書. Reprint. Chengdu: Chengdu guji, 1996.

Liu Zehua 劉澤華. "Handai 'weishu' zhong shen, ziran, ren yitihua de zhengzhi guannian" 漢代偽書中神自然人一體化的政治觀念 ["The Han Dynasty political View of the Unification of Spirits, Nature, and Human Beings in the Weft Texts"]. In *Wenshizhe* 1993.1: 35–42.

Long Xianzhao 龍顯昭. "Qiao Zhou" 譙周. In Jia Shunxian 賈順先 and Dai Dalu 戴大祿, eds. *Sichuan sixiang jia* 四川思想家 [*Sichuan Thinkers*]. Chengdu: Ba-Shu chubanshe, 1987.

Lu Yaodong 逯耀東. *Wei-Jin shixue de sixiang yu shehui jichu* 魏晉史學的思想與社會基礎 [*Wei-Jin Historiographical Thought and its Social Foundations*]. Taipei: Dongda tushu, 2000.

Lü Zhiyi 呂志毅. "Li Jifu ji qi Yuanhe junxian tuzhi" 李吉甫及其元和郡縣圖志 ["Li Jifu and his *Illustrated Record of Commanderies and Districts of the Yuanhe Era*"]. In Huang and Fu, eds. *Zhongguo fangzhi xuejia yanjiu*.

Luo Hongzeng 羅宏曾. *Wei Jin Nanbei chao wenhua shi* 魏晉南北朝文化史 [*Cultural History of Wei, Jin, and the Northern-Southern Dynasties*]. Chengdu: Sichuan renmin chubanshe, 1989.

Ma Dezhen 馬德真. "Ruhe yuedu *Sanguo zhi* Pei zhu" 如何閱讀三國志裴注 ["How to Read Pei Songzhi's *Commentary to the Records of the Three States*"]. In Miao Yue 繆鉞. *Sanguo zhi daodu* 三國志導讀 [*Readers Guide to the* Record of the Three States]. Chengdu: Ba-Shu chubanfa hang, 1988.

Ma Feibai 馬非百. *Qin ji shi* 秦集史 [*Collected Histories of Qin*]. Beijing: Zhonghua shuju, 1982.

Ma Zhijie 馬植杰. *Sanguo shi* 三國史 [*History of the Three States*]. Beijing: Renmin chubanshe, 1997.

Meng Mo 蒙默 et al. *Sichuan gudai shigao* 四川古代史稿 [*Draft History of Ancient Sichuan*]. Chengdu: Sichuan renmin chubanshe, 1989.

Meng Wentong 蒙文通. *Ba-Shu gushi lunshu* 巴蜀古史論述 [*Essays on the Ancient History of Ba and Shu*]. Chongqing: Sichuan renmin chubanshe, 1981.

Miao Yue 繆鉞. *Sanguo zhi daodu* 三國志導讀 [Reader's Guide to the Record of the Three States]. Chengdu: Ba-Shu chubanfa hang, 1988.

———. "Chen Shou Sanguo zhi pinglun" 陳壽三國志評論 ["A Critical Essay on Chen Shou's *Record of the Three States*"]. In Miao Yue 繆鉞. *Sanguo zhi daodu* 三國志導讀 [*Readers Guide to the* Record of the Three States]. Chengdu: Ba-Shu chubanfa hang, 1988.

———. "Chen Shou yu Sanguo zhi" 陳壽與三國志 ["Chen Shou and the *Records of the Three States*"]. In Wu and Yuan. *Zhongguo Shixue shilun ji* 中國史學史論集 [*Collected Essays on Chinese Historiography*]. Shanghai: Shanghai renmin chubanshe, 1980.

Mou Jun-sun 牟潤孫. *Lun Wei-Jin yilai zhi chongshang tanbian ji qi yingxiang* 論魏晉以來之崇尚談辯及其影響 [*On the Indulgence in 'Discourse and Polemics' By Scholars of the Wei-Chin Time and Its Influence in Subsequent Ages*]. Hong Kong: Chinese University of Hong Kong, 1966.

Nakabayashi Shiro 中林史朗 and Watanabe Yoshihiro 渡邊義浩, eds. *Sangokushi kenkyu yoran* 三國志研究要覽 [*Essential Research on The Record of the Three States*]. Tokyo: Jinbutsu Oraisha, 1996.

Pi Xirui 皮錫瑞. *Jingxue tonglun* 經學通論 [*Comprehensive Discourses on Canonical Studies*]. Beijing: Zhonghua shuju, 1954. Reprint, 1998.

———. *Jingxue lishi* 經學歷史 [*History of Canonical Studies*]. Taibei: Yiwen yinshuguan, 1966.

Qian Mu 錢穆. "Jingxue yu shixue" 經學與史學 ["Classical Studies and Historiography"]. In Du Weiyun 杜維運 and Huang Jinxing 黃進興, eds. *Zhongguo shixue shi lunwen xuanji* 中國史學論文選集 [*Selected Essays on Chinese Historiography*]. Taipei: Huashi chubanshe, 1977.

———. *Liang Han jingxue jingu wen pingyi* 兩漢經學今古文平議 [*Evaluation of the Old and New Text Classical Studies in the Han Dynasty*]. Taibei: Sanmin shuju, 1971.

———. "Luelun Wei, Jin, Nanbei chao xueshu wenhua yu dandshi mendi zhi guanxi" 略論魏晉南北朝學術文化與當時門第之關係 ["A Summary Essay on the Academic Culture of the Wei, Jin, and Northern-Southern Dynasties and Contemporary Master-Student Relationships"]. In *Xinya xuebao* 新亞學報. 5.2 (1959): 23–77.

"Sanguo manhua" 三國謾畫. Online source: http://www.shiji.cc/san/index.php. Accessed August 2005.

Sanguo yanyi 三國演義. N.p.: Jiangsu shaonian ertong chubanshe, 1994.

Song Zhimin 宋治民. *Shu wenhua yu Ba wenhua* 蜀文化與巴文化 [*Shu Culture and Ba Culture*]. Chengdu: Sichuan daxue chubanshe, 1998.

Sun Zhaohua 孫照華. "*Sanguo zhi* he Chen Shou de shizhi" 三國志和陳壽的史識 ["*The Records of the Three States* and Chen Shou's Historical Consciousness"]. In *Shixue yanjiu* 史學研究 (1997): 28–32.

Tan Qixiang 譚其驤 et al. *Zhongguo lishi dituji* 中國歷史地圖集 [*The Historical Atlas of China*]. Shanghai: Ditu chubanshe, 1982.

Taniguchi Fusao 谷口房男. *Kayōkoku shi jinmei sakuin* 華陽國志人名索引 [*Index to Persons in the* Records of the States South of Mount Hua]. N.p: Tosho kankokai, 1981.

Tang Changru 唐長孺. *Wei, Jin, Nanbei chao shi luncong* 魏晉南北朝史論叢 [*Collected Essays on Wei, Jin, and Northern-Southern Dynasties History*]. Beijing: Sanlian shudian chubanshe, 1955.

———."Nan-bei xuefeng de chayi"南北學風的差異 ["Differences in Northern and Southern Scholarship"]. In *Wei, Jin, Nan-bei chao, Sui, Tang shi san lun* 魏晉南北朝隋唐史三論 [*Three Essays on Wei, Jin, Northern-Southern Dynasties, Sui, and Tang History*]. Wuhan: Wuhan daxue chubanshe, 1992.

———. "Sixiang xueshu de bianhua: Wei, Jin, xuanxue de xingcheng ji qi fazhan" 思想學術的變化：魏晉玄學的形成及其發展 ["The Transformation of Thought and Scholarship: The Form and Development of Wei-Jin Mystery Learning"]. In *Wei, Jin, Nan-bei chao, Sui, Tang shi san lun* 魏晉南北朝隋唐史三論 [*Three Essays on Wei, Jin, Northern-Southern Dynasties, Sui, and Tang History*]. Wuhan: Wuhan daxue chubanshe, 1992.

———. *Wei, Jin, Nan-bei chao, Sui, Tang shi san lun* 魏晉南北朝隋唐史三論 [*Three Essays on Wei, Jin, Northern-Southern Dynasties, Sui, and Tang History*]. Wuhan: Wuhan daxue chubanshe, 1992.

Tang Yan 唐晏. *Liang Han Sanguo xuean* 兩漢三國學案 [*Intellectual Trends in the Two Han Dynasties and the Three States*]. Taibei: Shijie shuju, 1962.

Tong Enzheng 童恩正. *Gudai de Ba-Shu* 古代的巴蜀 [*Ancient Ba-Shu*]. Chongqing: Chongqing chubanshe, 1998.

Wan Shengnan 萬繩楠. *Wei, Jin, Nanbei chao wenhua shi* 魏晉南北朝文化史 [*A Cultural History of the Wei, Jin, and Northern-Southern Dynasties*]. Anhui: Huangshan shushe, 1989.

Wang Fuzhi 王夫之. "Sanguo" 三國 ["The Three States"]. In *Du Tongjian lun* 讀通鑑論 [*Essays on Reading the* Comprehensive Mirror]. Shanghai: Shangwu, n.d.

Wang Hua 王化. "Qiao Zhou mu" 譙周墓 ["The Grave of Qiao Zhou"]. In Wang Zhihou 王只厚 ed. *Mingren mingsheng* 名人名勝 [*Famous People and Events*]. Chengdu: Sichuan cishu chubanshe, 1990.

Wang Xiaoyi 王曉毅. *Wang Bi pingzhuan* 王弼評傳 [*Critical Biography of Wang Bi*]. Nanjing: Nanjing daxue chubanshe, 1996.

Wang Yunwu 王雲五 and Fu Weiping 傅緯平, eds. *Zhongguo jingxue shi* 中國經學史 [*A History of Chinese Canonical Studies*]. Taipei: Shangwu yinshu guan, 1972.

Wu Ze 吳澤 and Yuan Yingguang 袁英光 , eds. *Zhongguo shixueshi lun ji* 中國史學史論集 [*Essays in the History of Chinese Historiography*]. Vol. 1. Shanghai: Renmin chubanshe, 1980.

Xie Xianghao 謝祥皓 and Liu Zongxian 劉宗賢. *Zhongguo ruexue* 中國儒學 [*Chinese Classicism*]. Chengdu: Sichuan renmin chubanshe, 1998.

Xu Caian 徐才安. *Sichuan gudai shihua* 四川古代史話 [*Historical Talks on Ancient Sichuan*]. Chongqing: Chongqing chubanshe, 1992.

Xu Fuguan 徐復觀. *Liang Han sixiang shi* 兩漢思想史 [*Intellectual History of the Two Han Dynasties*]. 1975. Reprint. Taibei: Xuesheng shuju, 1992.

Xu Gongchi 徐公持, ed. *Wei Jin wenxueshi* 魏晉文學史 [*History of Wei and Jin Literature*]. Beijing: Renmin wenxue chubanshe, 1999.

Xu Heping 徐鶴屏. "Shixi Shu-Han dui shaoshu minzu de zhengce" 試析蜀漢對少數民族的政策 ["An Analysis of Shu-Han's Governmental Policies Toward Ethnic Minorities"]. In *Zhongnan minzu xueyuan xuebao: Zhexue shehui kexue ban* 中南民族學院學報：哲學科學版 (1988): 4, 34–38.

Xu Jijun 徐吉軍. *Zhongguo sangzang shi* 中國喪葬史 [*History of Chinese Mourning and Burial*]. Nanchang: Jiangxi gaoxiao chubanshe, 1998.

Xu Yiping 徐希平, ed. *Gaoshang de tianlu—xiang, cha, yao, jiu* 高尚的天祿香茶藥酒 [*The Highest Blessings from Heaven: Inscense, Tea, Medicines, and Alcohol*]. Chengdu: Sichuan renmin chubanshe, 1997.

Xu Zhaoren 徐兆仁. *Sanguo taolüe* 三國韜略 [*Summary of Three States Military Affairs*]. Beijing: Zhongguo renmin daxue chubanshe, 1995.

Xu Zhongshu 徐中舒. *Lun Ba-Shu wenhua* 論巴蜀文化 [*Essays on Ba-Shu Culture*]. Chongqing: Sichuan renmin chubanshe, 1982.

Yan Gengwang 嚴耕望. "Handai junxian xuexiao zhidu" 漢代郡縣學校制度 ["Organization of Commandery and District Academies in the Han Dynasty"]. In *Dalu zazhi* 大陸雜誌 vol. 6, no. 10 (1953): 6, 14, 22.

Yang Puwei 洋卜為. "Rushen cu yitong—tantan Qiao Zhou de quanjiang" 辱身促一統—談談譙周的勸降 ["Cursing the Body and Urging Unification: Speaking of Qiao Zhou's Recommendation to Surrender"]. In Yang Puwei, ed., *Sanguo shi sanji* 三國史散記: *Random Notes of Three Kingdoms History*. Nanchong: Sanguo shi shuyuan, 2000.

———. "Kouwen Qiao Zhou" 叩問譙周 ["Inquiries on Qiao Zhou"]. In *Sanguo zhi shuyuan yuankan* 三國志書院院刊 (2000): 47.

Yang Chen 陽晨. *Sanguo huiyao* 三國會要 [*Collected Essentials of the Three States*]. Reprint. Taipei: Shijie shuju, 1960.

Yang Shuda 楊樹達. *Handai hunsang lisu dao* 漢代婚喪禮俗考 [*Examination of Han Period Marriage and Funerary Ceremonies and Customs*]. Shanghai: Shanghai yiwen chubanshe, 1988.

Yang Yaokun 陽耀坤, "Yanjiu *Sanguo zhi* cankao shu jianjie" 研讀三國志參考書簡介 [*A Basic Introduction to Research Aids for the* Records of the Three States]. In Miao Yue 繆鉞. *Sanguo zhi daodu* 三國志導讀 [*Reader's Guide to the* Record of the Three States]. Chengdu: Ba-Shu chubanfa hang, 1988.

———. *Wei, Jin, Nanbei chao shi lungao* 魏晉南北朝史論稿 [*A Draft History of the Wei, Jin, and Northern-Southern Dynasties*]. Chengdu: Chengdu chubanshe, 1993.

Yang Yaokun and Wu Yechun 伍野春. *Chen Shou Pei Songzhi pingzhuan* 陳壽裴松之評傳 [*Critical Biographies of Chen Shou and Pei Songzhi*]. Nanjing: Nanjing daxue chubanshe, 1998.

Yi Lang 一郎. "Qiao Zhou nianpu" 譙周年譜 ["Chronology of Qiao Zhou"]. In *Sanguo zhi shuyuan yuankan* 三國志書院院刊 (2000): 44–46.

Yin Yungong 尹韻公. "Sanguo shidai yu xinwen xinxi chuanbo" 三國時代與新聞信息傳播 ["The Three States Period and the Transmission of News"]. In *Zhongguo wenhua yanjiu* 中國文化研究 no. 15 (1997): 30–37.

Yoshikawa Tadao 吉川忠夫. "Shuku ni okeru shin'i no gaku no dentō" 蜀における讖緯の學の傳統 ["The Tradition on the Study of the Books on Prophesy (ch'en-wei) in the Shu Region"]. In Yasui Kōzan 安居香山, ed. *Shin'i shisō no sōgōteki kenkyū* 讖緯思想の綜合的研究 [*Collected Studies on Prophetic Thought*]. Tokyo: Kokusho Kankōkai, 1984.

Yu Qiding. *Xian Qin Liang Han rujia jiaoyu* 先秦兩漢儒家教育 [*Pre-Qin–Han Classicist Education*]. Ji'nan: Qi-Lu shushe, 1987.

Yu Yingshi 余英時. *Shi yu Zhongguo wenhua* 士與中國文化 [*The Cultured Gentleman and Chinese Culture*]. Shanghai: Shanghai renmin chubanshe, 1987.

Yue Shi 樂史. *Taiping huanyu ji* 太平寰宇記 [*Records of the World of Great Peace*]. Preface dated 1803. Reprint, Taipei: Wenhai chubanshe, 1963.

Zhang Dake 張大可. *Sanguo shi yanjiu* 三國史研究 [*Studies on Three States History*]. Lanzhou: Gansu renmin chubanshe, 1988.

Zhang Keli 張可禮. *San Cao nianpu* 三曹年譜 [*Chronological Biography of the Three Caos*]. Ji'nan: Qi Lu shushe, 1983.

Zhang Shunhui 張舜徽, Cui Shuting 崔曙庭, and Wang Ruiming 王瑞明, eds. *Sanguo zhi cidian* 三國志辭典 [*A Dictionary to the* Records of the Three States]. Ji'nan: Shandong jiaoyu chubanshe, 1992.

Zhang Xinke 張新科 and Yu Zhanghua 俞樟華. "Yan Zhitui bian *Shiji*" 顏之推辨史記 ["Yan Zhitui's Discourse on the *Grand Scribe's Records*"]. In *Shiji yanjiu shilue* 史記研究史略. Xi'an: San Qin chubanshe, 1990.

Zhang Zhigao 張至皋. "Sichuan diming cheng youlai he kequ yanbian" 四川的名稱由來和x區演變 ["On the Origins and Evolution of the Name 'Sichuan'"]. In *Shehui kexue yanjiu* 社會科學研究, 5 (1979): 35–36.

Zhao Guohua 趙國華. "Sanguo shiqi de Wu Shu guanxi" 三國時期吳蜀關係 ["Wu Shu Relations in the Three States Period"]. *Wei Jin Nanbei chao Sui Tang shi* 魏晉南北朝隋唐史 [*Wei, Jin, Northern and Southern Dynasties, Sui, and Tang History*] (1997.3): 5–10. First published in *Huazhong shifan daxue xuebao: zheshe ban* (Wuhan) 華中師範大學學報：哲社版〔武漢〕(1997.1): 113–119.

Zhao Yi 趙毅. "Lun Shiji yu Huayang guozhi de guanxi" 論史記與華陽國志的關係 ["Essay on the Relationship between *The Grand Scribe's Records* and the *Records of the States South of Mount Hua*"]. In Jia Daquan 賈大泉 ed. *Sichuan lishi yanjiu wenji* 四川歷史研究文集 [*Collected Studies on Sichuan History*]. Chengdu: Sichuan sheng shehuikexuue yuan chubanshe, 1987.

Zhong Zhaopeng 鐘肇鵬. "Yan Zun" 嚴遵. In Jia Shunxian 賈順先 and Dai Dalu 戴大祿, eds. *Sichuan sixiang jia* 四川思想家 [*Sichuan Thinkers*]. Chengdu: Ba-Shu chubanshe, 1987.

———. *Chenwei lunlüe* 讖緯論略 [Summary Essays on Prophetic-Apocryphia]. Shenyang: Liaoning jiaoyu chubanshe, 1991.

Zhou Yiliang 周一良. "Cao shi Sima shi zhi douzheng" 曹氏司馬氏之鬥爭 ["The Conflict Between the Cao and Sima Clans"]. In *Wei Jin Nanbeichao shi zaji* 魏晉南北朝史雜記 [*Miscellaneous Notes on the History of the Wei, Jin, and Northern and Southern Dynasties*]. Beijing: Zhonghua shuju, 1985.

———. "Wei Jin Nanbei chao shixue yu wangchao shandai" 魏晉南北朝史學與王朝禪代 ["Wei, Jin, and Northern-Southern Dynasties Historiography and the Abdication of Dynasties"]. In *Beijing daxue xuebao* 北京大學學報. No. 2 (1987).

Zhu Dawei 朱大渭, "Du Sanguo zhi di jige fangfa wenti" 讀三國志的幾個方法問題 ["Several Methods for Reading the *Records of the Three States*"]. In Miao Yue 繆鉞. *Sanguo zhi daodu* 三國志導讀 [*Reader's Guide to the* Record of the Three States]. Chengdu: Ba-Shu chubanfa hang, 1988.

———. *Liuchao shi lun* 六朝史論 [*Essays on Six Dynasties History*]. Beijing: Zhonghua shuju, 1998.

Zhu Dawei 朱大渭 and Liang Mancang 梁滿倉. *Wuhou chunqiu* 武侯春秋 [*The Annals of the Martial Marquis*]. Beijing: Tuanjie chubanshe, 1998.

Zhu Dongrun 朱東潤. *Shiji kaosuo* 史記考索 [*Investigations on* The Grand Scribe's Records]. Shanghai: Huadong shifan daxue chubanshe, 1996.

Zhu Xiuxia 祝秀俠. "Lun Hanjian Qiao Zhou" 論漢奸譙周 ["Essay on the Traitor Qiao Zhou"]. In *Sanguo renwu xinlun* 三國人物新論 [*New Essays on Three States Personages*]. Shanghai: Guoji wenhua fuwushe, 1945. Reprinted under the title "Lun Qiao Zhou" 論譙周 ["Essay on Qiao Zhou"]. Taipei: Yiwen shuju, 1987.

Zhu Xizu 朱希祖. "Shu wang benji kao" 蜀王本紀考 ["Investigations on the *Basic Annals of the Kings of Shu*"]. In *Shuowen yuekan* 說文月刊, 3.7 (1942), 117.

WORKS IN WESTERN LANGUAGES

Bagley, Robert, ed. *Ancient Sichuan: Treasures from a Lost Civilization*. Seattle: Seattle Art Museum, 2001.

Balazs, Etienne. "Political Philosophy and Social Crisis at the End of the Han Dynasty." In Etienne Balazs. *Chinese Civilization and Bureaucracy: Variations on a Theme*. H. M. Wright, trans. New Haven: Yale University Press, 1964.

———. "Nihilistic Revolt or Mystical Escapism: Currents of Thought in China During the Third Century." In Balazs, *Chinese Civilization and Bureaucracy*.

Berkowitz, Alan J. *Patterns of Disengagement: The Practice and Portrayal of Reclusion in Early Medieval China*. Stanford: Stanford University Press, 2000.

Bielenstein, Hans H. "Wang Mang, the Restoration of the Han Dynasty, and Later Han." In Twitchett and Loewe, *The Cambridge History of China*, 223–290.

———. *The Bureaucracy of Han Times*. Cambridge: Cambridge University Press, 1980.

———. "The Restoration of the Han Dynasty" In *Bulletin of the Museum of Far Eastern Antiquities*, 26 (1954): 1–209; 31 (1959): 1–287; 39 (1967): 1–198; 51 (1979): 1–300.

———."Han Portents and Prognostications." In *Bulletin of the Museum of Far Eastern Antiquities* 56 (1984): 97–112.

Biot, Édouard. *Essai sur L'Histoire de L'Instruction Publique en Chine*. Paris: Benjamin Duprat, Libraire, 1845. Reprint. Taipei: Chung-wen, 1969.

Birrel, Anne. *Chinese Mythology*. Baltimore: Johns Hopkins University Press, 1993.

Bol, Peter. *"This Culture of Ours": Intellectual Transitions in T'ang and Sung China*. Stanford: Stanford University Press, 1992.

Brewitt-Taylor, C. H. *Romance of the Three Kingdoms*, 2 vols. Shanghai, 1925; Reprint, Rutland,Vermont: C. E. Tuttle, 1959.

Ch'ü T'ung-tsu. *Han Social Structure*. Edited by Jack L. Dull. Seattle: University of Washington Press, 1972.

Chan. Alan K. L. "The Essential Meaning of the Way and Virtue: Yan Zun and 'Laozi Learning' in Early Han China. *Monumenta Serica*, 46 (1998).

Chang, K. C., ed. *Food in Chinese Culture*. New Haven: Yale University Press, 1977.

Chavannes, Edouard, trans. *Les Mémoires historiques de Se-ma Tsien*. 6 vols. 1895–1905. Reprint (with supplement). Paris: Adrien Maisonneuve, 1967–1969.

Cheng, Te-k'un. *Archaeological Studies in Szechwan*. Cambridge: Faculty of Oriental Studies at the University Press, 1957.

Chittick, Andrew B. "Pride of Place: The Advent of Local History in Early Medieval China." Ph.D. dissertation, University of Michigan, 1997.

———. "Dynastic Legitimacy during the Eastern Chin: Hsi Tso-chih and the Problem of Huan Wen." *Asia Major*. Third series. 11.1 (1998).

———. "The Life and Legacy of Liu Biao: Governor, Warlord, and Imperial Pretender in Late Han China." *Journal of Asian History* 37/2 (2003): 155–186.

———. "The Development of Local Writing in Early Medieval China." *Early Medieval China* 9 (2003): 38–40.

Chōhachi, Itano. "The t'u-ch'en 圖讖 Prophetic Books and the Establishment of Confucianism." *Memoirs of the Research Department of the Toyo Bunko* 34 (1976): 47–111; 36 (1978): 85–107.

Crump, J. I., trans. *Chan-kuo Ts'e*. Revised edition. Ann Arbor: Center for Chinese Studies, University of Michigan, 1996.

Csikszentmihalyi, Mark, and Michael Nylan. "Constructing Lineages and Inventing Traditions through Exemplary Figures in Early China." In *T'oung Pao* 89 (2003): 87–97.

Cutter, Robert Joe. "Cao Zhi (192–232) and His Poetry." Ph.D. dissertation, University of Washington, 1983.

———. "Poetry from 200 B.C.E. to 600 C.E." In *Columbia History of Chinese Literature* . Ed. Victor Mair. New York: Columbia University Press, 2001, 248–273.

Cutter, Robert Joe, and William G. Crowell. *Empresses and Consorts: Selections from Chen Shou's* Records of the Three States *with Pei Songzhi's Commentary*. Honolulu: University of Hawai'i Press, 1999.

Declercq, Dominik. *Writing Against the State*. Leiden: Brill, 1998.

de Crespigny, Rafe. *Generals of the South*. Canberra: Faculty of Asian Studies, Australian National University, 1990.

———. trans. *The Last of the Han, Being the Chronicle of the Years 181–220 A.D. as Recorded in Chapters 58–68 of the* Tzu-chih t'ung-chien *of Ssu-ma Kuang*. Centre of Oriental Studies Monograph 9. Canberra: Australian National University, 1969.

———. "The Three Kingdoms and Western Jin: A History of China in the Third Century A.D." In *East Asian History* v. 1 (June 1991) and no. 2 (December 1991).

———. *The Records of the Three Kingdoms*. Occasional Paper 9. Canberra: Center of Oriental Studies. Australian National University, 1970.

———. trans. *Emperor Huan and Emperor Ling: being the Chronicle of Later Han for the years 157 to 189 A.D. as recorded in Chapters 54 to 59 of the* Zizhi tongjian *of Sima Guang*. Canberra: Faculty of Asian Studies, Australian National University, 1989.

———. *To Establish Peace*. Canberra: Faculty of Asian Studies, Australian National University, 1996.

DeBlasi, Anthony. *Reform in the Balance: The Defense of Literary Culture in Mid-Tang China*. Albany: State University of New York Press, 2002.

de Groot, J. J. M. "On Chinese Divination by Dissecting Written Characters." *T'oung Pao* 1 (1890): 239–247.

DeWoskin, Kenneth J., trans. *Doctors, Diviners, and Magicians of Ancient China: Biographies of* Fang-shih. New York: Columbia University Press, 1983.

Dien, Albert E., ed. *State and Society in Early Medieval China*. Stanford: Stanford University Press, 1990.

Dubs, Homer H., trans. *The History of the Former Han Dynasty*. 3 vols. Baltimore: Waverly Press, 1938–1955.

Dull, Jack. "A Historical Introduction to the Apocrypha (ch'an-wei) Texts of the Han Dynasty." Ph.D. dissertation, University of Washington, 1966.

Durrant, Stephen. "Ssu-ma Ch'ien's Conception of Tso chuan." *Journal of the American Oriental Society* 112.2 (1992): 295–301.

Eberhard, Wolfram. "The Political Function of Astronomy and Astronomers in Han China." In *Chinese Thought and Institutions*, ed. John K. Fairbank, 33–70. Chicago: University of Chicago Press, 1957.

Eberhard, Wolfram, and R. Müller. "Contibutions to the Astronomy of the San-Kuo Period." In *Monumenta Serica*, v. 2 (1936–1937).

Ebrey, Patricia. *The Aristocratic Families of Early Imperial China*. Cambridge: Cambridge University Press, 1978.

Eno, Robert. "Towards a History of Confucian Classical Studies." In *Early China* 17 (1992): 195–214.

Fang, Achilles, trans. *The Chronicle of the Three Kingdoms (220–265): Chapters 69–78 from the* Tzu chih t'ung chien *of Ssu-ma Kuang (1019–1086)*. Edited by Glen W. Baxter. 2 vols. Cambridge: Harvard University Press, 1965.

Farmer, J. Michael. "Art, Education, and Power: Illustrations in the Stone Chamber of Wen Weng." In *T'oung Pao* LXXXVI (2000): 100–135.

———. "What's in a Name? On the Appellative 'Shu' in Early Medieval Chinese Historiography." In *Journal of the American Oriental Society*, 121.1 (2001): 44–59.

———. "The World of the Mind in Early Medieval Sichuan." Ph.D. dissertation, University of Wisconsin–Madison, 2001.

———. "Qiao Zhou and the Historiography of Early Medieval Sichuan." In *Early Medieval China* 7 (2001): 39–77.

———. "How I Came to Doubt Qing Scholarship: The Case of Yao Zhenzong and Qiao Zhou's *Records of the Later Han*." In *Monumenta Serica* 51 (2003): 237–251.

Faurot, Jeannette L. *Ancient Chengdu*. San Francisco: Chinese Material Center, 1992.

Feng Yu-lan. *A History of Chinese Philosophy*. 2 vols. Derk Bodde, trans. Princeton: Princeton University Press, 1953.

Frankel, Hans. "Fifteen Poems by Ts'ao Chih: An Attempt at a New Approach." In *Journal of the American Oriental Society*, 84 (1964): 1–14.

Galer, Scott W. "The Foundation of Text Critical *Shiji* Commentary: Xu Guang and the *Shiji yinyi*." Ph.D. dissertation, University of Wisconsin–Madison, 2003.

Gardner, Daniel K. "Confucian Commentary and Chinese Intellectual History." In *Journal of Asian Studies*, 57.2 (May, 1998): 397–422.

Gong Kechang. *Studies on the Han Fu*. David R. Knechtges et al., trans. New Haven: American Oriental Society, 1997.

Goodman, Howard L. *Ts'ao P'i Transcendent: The Political Culture of Dynasty-Founding in China at the End of the Han*. Seattle: Scripta Serica, 1998.

Henderson, John. *Scripture, Canon, and Commentary: A Comparison of Confucian and Western Exegesis*. Princeton: Princeton University Press, 1991.

Hendrichke, Barbara. "Early Daoist Movements." In *Daoism Handbook*. Ed. Livia Kohn. Leiden: Brill, 2000.

Henricks, Robert. *Philosophy and Argumentation in Third-Century China: The Essays of Hsi K'ang*. Princeton: Princeton University Press, 1983.

Henry, Eric. "Chu-ko Liang in the Eyes of His Contemporaries." *Harvard Journal of Asiatic Studies* 52.2 (1992): 589–612.

Hervouet, Yves. *Le Chaptitre 117 du Che-ki (Biographie de Sseu-ma Siang-jou); traduction avec notes*. Paris: Presses Universitaires de France, 1972.

———. *Un poète de cour sous les Han: Sseu-ma Siang-jou*. Paris: Presses Universitaires de France. 1964.

Ho, Peng Yoke. *The Astronomical Chapters of the* Chin Shu. Paris: Mouton, 1966.

Ho Ping-ti. *The Cradle of the East*. Chicago: University of Chicago Press, 1975.

Holcombe, Charles. *In the Shadow of the Han*. Honolulu: University of Hawai'i Press, 1994.

Holzman, Donald. "The Place of the Seven Sages of the Bamboo Grove in Chinese History." *Kansai Asiatic Society Occasional Papers* 3. Kyoto, 1955.

———. "Les Sept Sages de la Forêt des Bambous et la société de leur temps." *T'oung Pao* 44 (1956): 317–346.

———. *Poetry and Politics: The Life and Works of Juan Chi*. Cambridge: Cambridge University Press, 1976.

———. "Protest in Third-Century China: Ruan Ji and Ji Kang Against the Sima Usurpers." In *En suivant la Voie royale: Mélanges en hommages à Léon Vandermeersch*. Ed. Jacques Gernet and Marc Kalinowski. Paris: École française d' Extrême Orient, 1997, 345–359.

Hou, Sharon S. J. "Wang Bao." In *Indiana Companion*, 1:871–872.

Hsia, C. T. "The Romance of the Three Kingdoms." In *The Classic Chinese Novel*. Ed., C. T. Hsia. New York: Columbia University Press, 1968.

Hsiao, Kung-chuan. *A History of Chinese Political Thought*. F. W. Mote, trans. Princeton: Princeton University Press, 1979.

Hsu, C. Y. "The Activities and Influences of Fang-shih." In *Asian Culture* 19.2 (1991): 59–86.

Huang Tzu-ch'ing and Chao Yün-ts'ung, trans. "The Preparations of Ferments and Wine." In *Harvard Journal of Asiatic Studies* 9 (1945): 24–44.

Hucker, Charles O. *A Dictionary of Official Titles in Imperial China*. Stanford: Stanford University Press, 1985.

Hulsewé, A. F. P. "Watching the Vapors, An Ancient Chinese Technique of Prognostication." *Nachrichten der Deutschen Gesellschaft für Natur—under Völkerkunde Ostasiens, Hamburg* 125 (1979): 210–221.

Jablonski, Witold. "Wen Wong." *Rocznik Orientalistyczny* 21 (1957): 135–140.

Jia Sixie 賈思勰. "The Preparation of Ferments and Wines." Translated by Huang Tzu-ch'ing and Chao Yün-ts'ung. *HJAS* 9 (1945–1947): 24–44.

Karlgren, Bernhard, trans. "The Book of Documents." *Bulletin of the Museum of Far Eastern Antiquities* 22 (1950): 1–81.

———. trans. *The Book of Odes*. Stockholm: Museum of Far Eastern Antiquities, 1974.

———. "Glosses on the *Book of Documents*." *Bulletin of the Museum of Far Eastern Antiquities* 20 (1948): 39–315.

Keightly, David N., ed. *The Origins of Chinese Civilization*. Berkeley: University of California Press, 1983.

Kern, Martin. "Ritual, Text, and the Formation of the Canon." In *T'oung Pao* 87 (2001): 43–91.

Killigrew, John. "Zhuge Liang and the Northern Campaign of 228–234." *Early Medieval China*, 5 (1999): 55–91.

Kleeman, Terry F. *Great Perfection: Religion and Ethnicity in a Chinese Millennial Kingdom*. Honolulu: University of Hawai'i Press, 1998.

Knechtges, David R. *The Han Rhapsody: A Study of the Fu of Yang Hsiung (53 B.C.–A.D. 18)*. Cambridge: Cambridge University Press, 1976.

———. "The Liu Hsin/Yang Hsiung Correspondence on the *Fang Yen*." *Monumenta Serica*, v. 33 (1977–78): 309–325.

———. *The Han shu Biography of Yang Xiong (53 B.C.–A.D. 18)*. Tempe: Center for Asian Studies, Arizona State University, 1981.

———. trans. *Wen xuan, or Selections of Refined Literature*. Volume 1, *Rhapsodies on Metropolises and Capitals*. Princeton: Princeton University Press, 1982.

———. trans. *Wen xuan, or Selections of Refined Literature*. Volume 2, *Rhapsodies on Sacrifices, Hunting, Travel, Sightseeing, Palaces and Halls, Rivers and Seas*. Princeton: Princeton University Press, 1987.

———. trans. *Wen xuan, or Selections of Refined Literature*. Volume 3, *Rhapsodies on Natural Phenomena, Birds and Animals, Aspirations and Feelings, Sorrowful Laments, Literature, Music, and Passions*. Princeton: Princeton University Press. 1996.

Kohn, Livia, ed. *Daoism Handbook*. Leiden: Brill, 2000.

Kramers, R. P. *K'ung Tzu Chia Yü: The School Sayings of Confucius*. Leiden: Brill, 1950.

Kroll, Paul W. "Portraits of Ts'ao Ts'ao: Literary Studies on the Man and the Myth." Ph.D. diss., University of Michigan, 1976.

Laing, Ellen Johnston. "Neo-Taoism and the 'Seven Sages of the Bamboo Grove' in Chinese Painting." *Artibus Asiae* 37 (1974): 5–54.

Leban, Carl. "Managing Heaven's Mandate: Coded Communications in the Accession of Ts'ao P'ei, A.D. 220." In Roy and Tsien, *Ancient China*, 315–41.

———. "Ts'ao Ts'ao and the Rise of Wei: the Early Years." Ph.D. dissertation. Columbia, 1971.

Le Blanc, Charles, and Susan Blader, eds. *Chinese Ideas About Nature and Society*. Hong Kong: Hong Kong University Press, 1987.

Legge, James, trans. *The Chinese Classics*. 5 vols. 1861–1872. Reprint. Hong Kong: Hong Kong University Press, 1960.

———. trans. *The Li Ki*. 2 vols. In F. Max Müller, ed. *Sacred Books of the East*. London: Oxford University Press, 1885.

———. *The Four Books* . Reprint. Taipei: Huangjia tushu, 1984.

Levy, Howard S. "Yellow Turban Religion and Rebellion at the End of the Han." In *JAOS* 4 (1956): 214–227.

Lewis, Mark Edward. *Writing and Authority in Early China*. Albany: State University of New York Press, 1999.

Lippiello, Tiziana. *Auspicious Omens and Miracles in Ancient China: Han, Three Kingdoms, and Six Dynasties*. Sankt Augustin: Monumenta Serica Institute, 2001.

Lo, Andrew. "San-kuo yen-i" In Nienhauser et al., eds. *Indiana Companion*, 668–671.

Lu Zongli. *Heaven's Mandate and Man's Destiny in Early Medieval China: The Role of Prophecy in Politics*. Ph.D. dissertation. University of Wisconsin–Madison, 1995.

———. *Power of the Words: Chen Prophesy in Chinese Politics* A.D *265–618*. Bern: Peter Lang, 2003.

Lynn, Richard John. *The Classic of Changes: A New Translation of the* I Ching *as Interpreted by Wang Bi*. New York: Columbia University Press, 1994.

Makeham, John. *Name and Actuality in Early Chinese Thought*. Albany: State University of New York Press, 1994.

———. "He Yan, *Xuanxue* and the Editorship of the *Lunyu jijie*." In *Early Medieval China*, 5 (1999): 1–35.

———, trans., *Balanced Discourses*. New Haven: Yale University Press, 2002.

Mansvelt Beck, B. J. "The Fall of Han." In Twitchett and Loewe, *The Cambridge History of China*, 317–376.

———. *The Treatises of Later Han: Their Author, Sources, Contents and Place in Chinese Historiography*. Leiden: Brill, 1990.

Mao Han-kuang. "The Evolution in the Nature of the Medieval Genteel Families." In *State and Society in Early Medieval Chna*. Albert Dien, ed., 73–109.

Mark, Lindy Li. "Orthography, Riddles, Divination, and Word Magic: An Exploration in Folklore and Culture." In *Legend, Lore and Religion in China*. Sarah Allan and Alvin P. Cohen, eds., 43–69. San Francisco: Chinese Materials Center, 1979.

Mather, Richard B., trans. *Shih-shuo Hsin-yü: A New Account of Tales of the World*. Minneapolis: University of Minnesota Press, 1976.

———. "Some Examples of 'Pure Conversation' in the Shih-shuo hsin-yü." *Transactions of the International Conference of Orientalists in Japan* 9 (1964): 58–70.

———. "The Controversy over Conformity and Naturalness During the Six Dynasties." *History of Religions* 9.2–3 (1969–1970): 160–180.

Miao, Ronald. *Early Medieval Chinese Poetry: The Life and Poetry of Wang Chung-hsüan (*A.D. *177–217)*. Wiesbaden: Steiner, 1982.

Michaud, Paul . "The Yellow Turbans." In *Monumenta Serica* 17 (1958): 47–127.

Needham, Joseph, and Wang Ling, eds. *Science and Civilisation in China, Vol. 3: Mathematics and the Sciences of the Heavens and the Earth*. Cambridge: Cambridge University Press, 1959.

Ngo, Van Xuyet. *Divination Magie et Politique Dans la Chine Ancienne*. Paris: Presses Universitaires de France, 1976.

Nienhauser, William H., Jr. "An Interpretation of the Literary and Historical Aspects of *Hsi-ching tsa-chi*" *(Miscellanies of the Western Capital)*. Ph.D. dissertation. Indiana University, 1972.

——— et al., eds. *The Indiana Companion to Traditional Chinese Literature*. Revised edition. Taipei: Southern Materials Center, 1986.

———. ed. *The Grand Scribe's Records*. vols. 1, 7. Bloomington: Indiana University Press, 1994.

———. "The Role of Han Dynasty Texts in the Development of Chinese Fiction." *Asian Culture Quarterly*, vol. 13, no. 4 (1985).

Nylan, Michael. *The Canon of Supreme Mystery by Yang Hsiung*. Albany: State University of New York Press, 1993.

———. "The Chin Wen/Ku Wen Controversy in Han Times." In *T'oung Pao* LXXX (1994).

———. "Han Confucianism." In *Imagining Boundaries: Changing Confucian Doctrines, Texts, and Hermeneutics*. Eds. Kai-wing Chow, On-cho Ng, and John B. Henderson. Albany: State University of New York Press, 1999, 17–56.

———. "The Legacies of the Chengdu Plain" In Robert Bagley, ed. *Ancient Sichuan: Treasures from a Lost Civilization*. Seattle: Seattle Art Museum, 2001.

———. *The Five "Confucian" Classics*. New Haven: Yale University Press, 2001.

Nylan, Michael, and Nathan Sivin. "The First Neo-Confucian: An Introduction to Yang Hsiung's 'Canon of Supreme Mystery' (T'ai hsuan ching, c. 4 B.C.). In Le Blanc, Charles and Susan Blader, eds. *Chinese Ideas About Nature and Society*. Hong Kong: Hong Kong University Press, 1987.

O'Hara, Albert. *The Position of Woman in Early China According the the* Lieh Nü Chuan. Taipei: Mei Ya Publications, 1971.

Pas, Julian F. *Historical Dictionary of Taoism*. Lanham, Maryland: Scarecrow Press, 1998.

Plaks, Andrew H. *The Masterworks of the Ming Novel*. Princeton: Princeton University Press, 1987.

Robinet, Isabelle. *Taoism: Growth of a Religion*. Trans., Phyllis Brooks. Stanford: Stanford University Press, 1997.

Rogers, Michael, trans. *The Chronicle of Fu Chien: A Case of Exemplar History*. Chinese Dynastic Histories Translations no. 10. Berkeley: University of California Press, 1968.

Romance of the Three Kingdoms. Adapted by Zhang Qirong and translated by Wu Jingyu. Singapore: Asiapac, 1995.

Rowley, H. H. *Prophecy and Religion in Ancient China and Israel*. New York: Harper and Brothers, 1956.

Roy, David T., and Tsuen-hsuin Tsien, eds. *Ancient China: Studies in Early Civilization*. Hong Kong: The Chinese University Press, 1978.

Sage, Stephen. *Ancient Sichuan and the Unification of China*. Albany: State University of New York Press, 1992.

Saso, Michael. "What Is the Ho-t'u?" *History of Religions* 17:1 (August 1977): 399–416.

Schaberg, David. *A Patterned Past: Form and Thought in Early Chinese Historiography*. Cambridge: Harvard University Asia Center, 2001.

Schafer, Edward H. "The Early History of Lead Pigments and Cosmetics in China." *T'oung Pao* 44 (1956).

———. *The Golden Peaches of Samarkand: A Study of T'ang Exotics*. Berkeley: University of California Press, 1963.

———. *The Vermilion Bird: T'ang Images of the South*. Berkeley: University of California Press, 1967.

———. "Hunting Parks and Animal Enclosures in Ancient China." In *Journal of the Economic and Social History of the Orient* 11 (1968): 318–343.

———. "Tang." In K. C. Chang, ed. *Food in Chinese Culture*. New Haven: Yale University Press, 1977.

Schwartz, Benjamin I. *The World of Thought in Ancient China*. Cambridge: Belknap Press, Harvard University Press, 1985

Serruys, Paul L-M. *The Chinese Dialects of Han Time According to Fang Yen*. Berkeley: University of California Press, 1959.

Shih, Vincent Yu-chung, trans. *The Literary Mind and the Carving of Dragons*. New York: Columbia University Press, 1959.

Shryock, John K. *The Origin and Development of the State Cult of Confucius*. 1932. Reprint. New York: Paragon, 1966.

Smith, Kidder. "Sima Tan and the Invention of Daoism, 'Legalism,' et cetera." In *Journal of Asian Studies* 62, no. 1 (Feb, 2003): 129–125.

Steele, John. *The I-Li or Book of Etiquette and Ceremonial*. London: Probsthain, 1917. Reprint. Taipei: Ch'eng-wen Publishing, 1966.

Stuart, G. A. *Chinese Materia Medica, The Vegetable Kingdom*. Reprint. Taipei: Southern Materials Center, 1987.

Sun, E-tu Zen, and John De Francis, eds. *Chinese Social History*. American Council of Learned Societies, Studies in Chinese and Related Civilizations, no. 7. Reprint. New York: Octagon Books, 1966.

Swann, Nancy Lee. *Food and Money in Ancient China*. Princeton: Princeton University Press, 1950.

T'ang Yung-t'ung. "Wang Pi's New Interpretation of the I Ching and Lun Yü." Translated by Walter Liebenthal. In *Harvard Journal of Asiatic Studies* 10 (1947): 124–161.

Teng Ssu-yü, trans. *Family Instructions for the Yen Clan*. Leiden: Brill, 1968.

"Three Kingdoms." Online source: http://china-on-site.com/pages/comic/comiccatalog2.php. Accessed August 2005.

Tillman, Hoyt. "Historic Analogies and Evaluative Judgments: Zhuge Liang as Portrayed in Chen Shou's Chronicle of the Three Kingdoms and Pei Songzhi's Commentary." In *Oriens Extremus*. Vol. 43 (2002 [2004]): 60–70.

———. "Textual Liberties and Restraints in Rewriting China's Histories: The Case of Ssu-ma Kuang's Re-Construction of Chu-ko Liang's Story." In The *New and the Multiple: Sung Senses of the Past*. Ed. Thomas H. C. Lee. Hong Kong: The Chinese University Press, 2004.

———. "Some Historical and Philosophical Sources of the *Sanguo yanyi*: Sima Guang and Chen Liang on Zhuge Liang." In *Three Kingdoms and Chinese Culture*. Eds.,

Kimberly Besio and Constantine Tung. Albany: State University of New York Press, 2006.

Tjan, Tjoe Som. *Po Hu T'ung: The Comprehensive Discussions in the White Tiger Hall, Introduction: A Contribution to the History of Classical Studies in the Han Period.* Leyden: Brill, 1949.

Tsien, Tsuen-hsuin. "A Study of the Book Knife in Han China (206 B.C.–220 A.D.)" In *Chinese Culture* 12.1 (1971): 87–101.

Tung Tso-pin. *Chronological Tables of Chinese History*. Hong Kong: Hong Kong University Press, 1960.

Twitchett, Denis. "Problems of Chinese Biography." In Wright and Twitchett, *Confucian Personalities*, 24–39.

———. "Chinese Biographical Writing." In *Historians of China and Japan*. Eds. W. G. Beasley and E. G. Pulleyblank. London: Oxford University Press, 1961, 95–114.

Van Ess, Hans. "The Old Text/New Text Controversy: Has the 20th Century Got It Wrong?" In *T'oung Pao* 80 (1994).

———. "The Apocryphal Texts of the Han Dynasty and the Old Text/New Text Controversy." *T'oung Pao* 85 (1999).

Vervoorn, Aat. "Zhuang Zun: A Daoist Philosopher of the Late First Century B.C." *Monumenta Serica* 38 (1988–1989): 69–94.

———. *Men of the Cliffs and Caves: The Development of the Chinese Eremitic Tradition to the End of the Han Dynasty*. Hong Kong: Chinese University Press, 1990.

Wagner, Rudolph G. *The Craft of a Chinese Commentator: Wang Bi on the* Laozi. Albany: State University of New York Press, 2000.

———. *Language, Ontology, and Political Philosophy in China: Wang Bi's Scholarly Exploration of the Dark (Xuanxue)*. Albany: State University of New York Press, 2003.

———. *A Chinese Reading of the* Daodejing: *Wang Bi's Commentary on the* Laozi *With Critical Text and Translation*. Albany: State University of New York Press, 2003.

Waley, Arthur. *The Book of Songs*. New York: Grove Press, 1996.

Watson, Burton, trans. *Courtier and Commoner in Ancient China: Selections from the* History of the Former Han *by Pan Ku*. New York: Columbia University Press, 1974.

———. trans. *Records of the Grand Historian*. 2 vols. New York: Columbia University Press, 1961.

———. trans. *Records of the Grand Historian*. Revised edition. 3 vols. New York: Columbia University Press, 1993.

———. trans. *The Tso chuan: Selections from China's Oldest Narrative History*. New York: Columbia University Press, 1989.

Wilhelm, Hellmut. *Heaven, Earth, and Man in the Book of Changes*. Seattle: University of Washington Press, 1977.

Wilhelm, Richard, trans. *The I Ching or Book of Changes*. Translated into English by Cary F. Wright, Arthur and Denis Twitchett, eds. *Confucian Personalities*. Stanford: Stanford University Press, 1962.

Yang Lien-sheng. "Great Families of Eastern Han." In *Chinese Social History*. Sun and De Francis, eds., 103–134.

Yang, Winston. "The Literary Transformation of Historical Figures in the *San-kuo chih yen-i:* A Study of the Use of the *San-kuo chih* as a Source of the *San-kuo chih yen-i*." In *Critical Essays on Chinese Fiction*. Eds. Winston L. Y. Yang and Curtis P. Adkins. Hong Kong: Chinese University Press, 1980.

Yi Jingshan. "Chairman Mao Liked the Chinese Comic 'Romance of the Three Kingdoms.'" Online source: http://eng.cartoonwin.com/articles/articles004.html. Accessed August 2005.

Yoshikawa Tadao. "Scholarship in Ching-chou at the End of the Later Han Dynasty." In *Acta Asiatica* 60 (1991): 1–24.

Yu Yingshi. "Individualism and the Neo-Taoist Movement in Wei-Chin China." In *Individualism and Holism: Studies in Confucian and Taoist Values*. Donald J. Munro, ed. Ann Arbor: Center for Chinese Studies, The University of Michigan, 1985.

———"Han" In Chang, ed. *Food in Chinese Culture*.

Index